Envisioning Dance on Film and Video

Envisioning Dance on Film and Video

Judy Mitoma, editor

Elizabeth Zimmer, text editor

Dale Ann Stieber, DVD editor

Nelli Heinonen, associate editor

Norah Zuñiga Shaw, assistant editor

Routledge *New York and London*

Published in 2002 by
Routledge
711 Third Avenue,
New York, NY 10017
www.routledge-ny.com

Published in Great Britain by
Routledge
2 Park Square, Milton Park,
Abingdon, Oxon OX14 4RN
www.routledge.co.uk

Routledge is an imprint of the Taylor & Francis Group.

The Pew Charitable Trusts is gratefully acknowledged for their support in the preparation of *Envisioning Dance on Film and Video*.

10 9 8 7 6 5 4 3 2 1

Cataloging-in-Publication Data is available from the Library of Congress.

ISBN 978-0-415-94170-9 (hbk)
ISBN 978-0-415-94171-6 (pbk)

CONTENTS

Corresponding DVD excerpts are in bold type

FOREWORD

Judy Mitoma

This book marks the conclusion of a three-part project that has spanned a fulfilling six-year period. In 1996 the fledgling UCLA Center for Intercultural Performance (CIP) began the UCLA National Dance/Media Project, an ambitious initiative made possible by a multi-year grant from The Pew Charitable Trusts. Under the supportive guidance of Marian Godfrey and Cora Mirikitani, UCLA joined a second program, the National Initiative to Preserve America's Dance, lovingly called NIPAD. First housed at the Kennedy Center, Washington, D.C., and now at Dance USA, NIPAD is administered by the dedicated and able hands of Andrea E. Snyder. Together the UCLA National Dance/Media Project and NIPAD are called SAVE AS: Dance.

The mission of the UCLA National Dance/Media Project is to increase the capacity of the field to effectively record dance. We worked with a wide array of

From left to right: Evann Siebens, Lisa Gross, Judy Mitoma, and Ellen Bromberg during the 1998 Pew Fellowship Program in Los Angeles. Photo by: John Bishop.

Pew Leadership Group at work 1998.
Photo by: John Bishop.

dance and media professionals to identify, develop, and support outstanding work in film and video. We began by assessing and evaluating activity in dance/media across the country, inviting a distinguished group of dance and media artists, educators, producers, and directors to serve as a Leadership Group. Each year from 1997 to 2000, some forty individuals gave generously of their time to attend lively three-day gatherings. Members of the group shared information and engaged in thoughtful debate on the long-term needs of the field. One outcome of this process was the recommendation that we publish a book on dance/media.

Intensive ten-week Pew Fellowship Programs, held from 1998 through 2000, were designed to develop the craft and understanding of dance film/video. Of the 200 applicants from across the country, we were able to invite 24 Fellows, a mix of directors, choreographers, documentary filmmakers, educators, cinematographers, and animators. They all reported isolated working conditions, limited resources, and little professional recognition; yet, despite these obstacles, they were able to develop viable creative strategies. While a few of the Fellows had attended film school, there is no place in the United States specifically designed to train in the filming of dance, and they longed for an opportunity to work with others. Interestingly, almost all had worked or are still working as dancers or choreographers.

Each year eight individuals would spend the winter quarter on the UCLA campus, working from morning until night in lively seminars, workshops with distinguished visiting faculty, and laboratory experimentation in the studio. Over the course of the quarter we screened a wide range of work the group considered "best practices" in dance film/video. The Fellowship Program was designed for both independent and team projects. With the assistance of John Bishop in developing the curriculum, a distinguished group of directors, editors, and producers were invited as guest faculty. They included Merrill Brockway, Matthew Diamond, Girish Bhargava, Rhoda Grauer, and Bob Lockyer. We are grateful to directors Matthew Diamond and Margaret Selby for inviting us on the set to observe their crews in action as they recorded dance on large-scale, multicamera live-switch projects. The Fellows savored the time spent implementing their own independent workshop projects, which they designed, filmed, and edited. They generously supported one another at the camera, in lighting, at the editing bay, and on the dance floor. Several of these activities took place on the streets, mountains, and beaches of Los Angeles.

The Fellows were quick to form a learning community, and within ten weeks they covered many of the aesthetic, technical, and administrative issues that comprise this collaborative endeavor. The relationship between Fellows and the Leadership Group was critical to the success of the program. The Fellows attended the three-day meetings, adding new insights in the ensuing interchange. Moreover, they represent our future. Many of the veterans and the younger generation have gone on to work together professionally. At the end of each residency, Fellows were invited to apply to NIPAD for funds to support their next project. Most of these have been completed, adding to the body of work. Fellows who began as strangers continue to support one another well beyond their time in the program.

Envisioning Dance on Film and Video, with its accompanying DVD, is our way of sharing these conversations, presentations, and lessons learned. You will hear from many Fellows and Leadership Group members in these essays and video excerpts. The UCLA National Dance/Media Project and this volume were funded by The Pew Charitable Trusts. Although we claim full responsibility for the contents of this book, we wish to acknowledge the contribution of the Trust to every aspect of the effort.

The program would not have been possible without the support of the UCLA Department of World Arts and Cultures and the School of Arts and Architecture. Lilian Wu and Carol Endo Bowen assisted in the launch of the project. John Bishop helped structure the curriculum and facilitated the laboratory sessions for the Fellows. Today he continues to guide the Dance Video program at WAC. Rhoda Grauer introduced me to the larger world of dance film/video and was critical to the conception and design of the Leadership Group. My admiration for her continues as she has gone on to make films in Indonesia.

The program depended on a talented and dedicated student and staff work force. First Sue Fan and later Marcia Argolo saw us through complicated operations and supported everyone involved with kindness and concern. Jo Parks, who now resides in England, and Ming Ng, who now spends much time in China, provided masterful frontline support as we interacted with the large cast of characters and their idiosyncratic needs. Mark Eby and Huy Phun set up editing bays and supervised and lugged equipment, services much appreciated by the Fellows. Countless others provided help on the complex details of this project, including Etsu Garfias, Kateri Hyung, Yayoi Robinson, and Mercedes Ryden.

The publication process could not have succeeded without the focused support of Nelli Heinonen, now working in Finland. Her patient and tireless efforts provided the day-to-day discipline required to keep the project on track. Dale Ann Stieber painstakingly secured rights to the video clips on the DVD, a formidable task demanding attention to technical and legal details. In her steady and focused way, Karen Washburn took time from her studies to work on the bibliography. Norah Zuñiga Shaw stepped in during the final phase of manuscript preparation and photo editing, taking great care as we completed the work.

Finally, from across the country, Elizabeth Zimmer has applied her skilled and enthusiastic hand to all stages of manuscript preparation. Her gift as an editor, her good humor, and her indomitable spirit have made this journey a pleasure. Undertaking this enormous task, we pooled our talents, worked enthusiastically as a team, and learned a great deal in the process. Without the intelligent and creative insight of the Fellows, Leadership Group, and our UCLA team, this publication and DVD would not have come together. It has been a privilege to work with each and every one.

Judy Mitoma
UCLA Center for Intercultural Performance
Los Angeles
2002

UCLA National Dance/Media Fellows
Ellen Bromberg, Mark Eby, Lisa Gross, Johannes Holub, Sharon Kinney, Laura Margulies, Bridget Murnane, Evann Siebens, Charles Dennis, Victoria Marks, Marlene Millar, Diana Sherwood, Morleigh Steinberg, Philip Szporer, Carmella Vassor, Andy Abrahams Wilson, Valida Hadzimuratovic-Carroll, Pooh Kaye, Eva Lee, Linda Lewett, Judy Lieff, Carol Lyn McDowell, Mitchell Rose, and Charles Steiner.

UCLA National Dance/Media Leadership Group
Ken Brecher, Bonnie Brooks, Sharon Dahl, Matthew Diamond, Rhoda Grauer, Barbara Horgan, Pualani Kanaka'ole Kanahele, Jackie Kain, Alan M. Kriegsman, Sali Ann Kriegsman, Leslie Hansen Kopp, Bob Lockyer, Madeleine Nichols, Bonnie Oda Homsey, Eiko Otake, Deirdre Towers, Jac Venza, and Suzanne Weil.

Contributing their counsel and expertise to our process have been Howell Begle, John Bishop, Peter Bogdanoff, David Gere, Marina Goldovskaya, Robert Rosen, David Roussève, Peter Sellars, Christopher Waterman, and Robert Winter. Our collaborators at The Pew Charitable Trusts included Marian Godfrey, Cora Mirikitani, and Jacqueline M. Flaherty, and at NIPAD Andrea E. Snyder, and Gregory Ruffer.

WORDS FROM THE TEXT EDITOR

Editing a book about dance on film and video was not, I must confess, the way I thought I'd spend the better part of two years of the prime of my life. I've always been in the phalanx of the dance world that believes dance suffers mightily in the transfer from three dimensions to two. I was actively hostile to the notion of trying to can the live experience.

I'm a member of the last American generation that came to literacy and live theater before we encountered television and home-stereo sound—the last generation to privilege live performance over recorded, exactly replicable art. Editing *Envisioning Dance on Film and Video* seemed, at first, like collaborating with the enemy, helping to shift even more attention and resources to a second-hand rendition of a medium I loved for its immediacy.

Elizabeth Zimmer in front of the *Village Voice*, New York City, 2001. Photo by Charles Steiner.

To be sure, for years I have been part of the natural audience for dance film. I began my intimate involvement with dancing, my period of compulsive studying and obsessive performance viewing, while living far from the New York dance world, in Vermont and on both coasts of Canada. Viewing films (in the decades before the widespread availability of home video) was a major part of my dance education. Later, the demands of my newspaper job found me screening videos to get a sense of artists whose work was on its way into my realm.

Then I was invited to contribute an essay to a magazine specializing in high-end home theater installations, and I spent weeks looking at dance on film. I watched a clutch of Busby Berkeley and Fred Astaire movies, some wonderful products of the Merce Cunningham operation, and Matthew Diamond's *Dancemaker.* I also listened to beleaguered choreographers who had begun to realize how essential good video documentation was to every aspect of their professional lives. When Judy Mitoma proposed the notion of this book, designed to include film and video clips on an accompanying DVD, I found the opportunity hard to resist.

We are living, for better or worse, in a world where unmediated cultural experiences are increasingly rare, and where most people encounter dance on television before they ever see it on a stage. Plays have a natural second life on screen and in the video store; visual arts have been successfully catalogued on video and streamed to computers; and the widespread availability of excellent classical recordings, while improving access to serious music for millions of listeners, increasingly threatens the phenomenon of the symphony orchestra.

Meanwhile, a new generation of film directors—men and women raised with television and home video and MTV—are beginning to realize the potential of dance on film. Michael Bay, who directed the 2001 blockbuster *Pearl Harbor*, told the *New York Times* about a college course he took on film musicals. "It's strange," he said, "but when filmmakers are forced to solve the problems you need to solve to shoot dance, they really find themselves using the film medium to its fullest."

His remark drives home the necessity for a publication like this one, which might tempt young film artists to collaborate with dancers, and encourage choreographers to seek out gifted cinematographers. Relatively few dance companies have access to prime-time-quality recordings of their work, which has deprived them of access to an audience already reluctant, or unable, to leave home and visit a theater. The only way to reach these people will be through recordings, either on broadcast television or in storable forms. Numerous studies have demonstrated that, far from discouraging people from visiting the theater, good dance videos inspire them to save their pennies and make the trip.

If our lives in dance are to coexist with cameras and screens, we might as well—in the immortal words of *Whole Earth Catalogue* editor Stewart Brand—get good at it. This volume contains essays by professionals in every aspect of the dance film collaboration: choreographers, directors, cinematographers, film and video editors, producers, programmers, critics, archivists, librarians, scholars, historians, and experimental animators. Many of these people have spent more than 30 years getting good at it. Some are the pioneers in the field, with unparalleled access, knowledge, and memory of how things were and how they are now. Most of the material derives from and pertains to the English-speaking world, primarily in the United States, but we include a personal essay from Argentina, a critical essay on a choreographer working in Germany, and discussions of films about Japanese and Indian classical and popular forms.

I arrive at the end of this process with a new understanding of the challenges facing artists as they transform dance works for the screen, and a new appreciation for the willingness of dance artists to grapple with these challenges in print. Much of my work involved editing the writing of people who edit for a living: edit film, edit steps, edit reams of material into manageable formats. I learned a great deal from them and from their words, and I'm pleased to share their work with readers. My deep gratitude goes to Nelli Heinonen, whose obsessive care with manuscripts flying around the world in various electronic formats made the whole project possible.

Elizabeth Zimmer
New York
January 2002

GUIDE TO THE DVD

Dale Ann Stieber

Virtually everyone working in dance today uses electronic media technology in some way. Despite the rich developments of the past 100 years, surprisingly little has been published about the historic, aesthetic, and technical concerns of dance, film, and video. This book and its companion DVD (provided in a sleeve inside the back cover of the book) together offer readers and viewers access to a stirring history of human creativity and invention.

The unprecedented companion DVD provides examples that bring the commentary to life. It is essential to a full appreciation of the text and has value as an independent reference. Forty titles totaling two hours of excerpted works are drawn from the films and videos discussed in the book. Titles selected for inclusion represent a broad range of creative activity in the field.

Interactive features enhance both the text and the DVD. In each essay, the companion video excerpts are identified, numbered, and highlighted with a DVD box illustrated with the icon DVD. The DVD features a corresponding table of contents so that a reader can quickly locate and view the video excerpt. In addition, it provides key production credits and information on where and how to see the full work. Readers can approach the publication from two perspectives: they can choose to read an essay independently, then later go to the DVD to view the related video; or they may view video excerpts of interest, then go to the book to read the text.

TIMELINE

A Century of Dance and Media

Virginia Brooks

Notes: Bold type indicates landmark dance films/videos. Regular type indicates advances in film/video technology.

1880s Etienne-Jules Marey (France) and Eadweard James Muybridge (Great Britain) begin experimenting with sequential photographs to study animal motion.

1887 H. W. Goodwin invents celluloid film.

1894 Louis Lumière patents the cinematograph (a machine that combined the functions of camera and projector).

1894 Thomas A. Edison films Ruth Dennis (later known as Ruth St. Denis) doing a skirt dance outdoors.

1895 December 28—first film projected to a paying public at the Grand Café on the Boulevard des Capucines, Paris.

1896 The first exhibition of Edison's projecting version of a Kinetoscope, called the Vitascope, shows the Leigh sisters doing their umbrella dance, New York City.

1899 First magnetic recording of sound

1902 Peter Elfeldt first records the Royal Danish Ballet performing the choreography of August Bournonville.

1903 Georges Méliès, in *The Magic Lantern,* uses 12 corps dancers and a soloist.

Edwin Porter's *The Great Train Robbery* is the longest film made to date (12 minutes); it contains a sequence of square dancing and a man clog-dancing while other troopers shoot at the ground near his feet.

1905 The first regular cinema is established in Pittsburgh, Pennsylvania.

1906 Louis Lumière films Loie Fuller in her *Fire Dance.*

1907 August Musger invents slow motion.

Lumière develops a process for color photography using a three-color screen.

1912 London has 400 movie houses; each day around 5 million people in the United States go to the cinema.

1914 Vernon and Irene Castle star in *The Whirl of Life*.

Edward S. Curtis directs *In the Land of the Head-Hunters*, a love story filmed among the Kwakiutl of British Columbia, which suggests a dawning interest in an indigenous point of view.

1916 Denishawn Dancers appear in D.W. Griffith's epic *Intolerance* (see chapter 8). DVD 5

Anna Pavlova acts in *The Dumb Girl of Portici*.

1919 Hans Vogt (with Massolle and Engl) experiments on a new sound film system.

1919 Charles Chaplin parodies Nijinsky's *Afternoon of a Faun* in *Sunnyside*.

1922 Robert Flaherty directs *Nanook of the North*, which portrays intimate details of Inuit life.

1924 Fernand Léger makes "Le Ballet Mécanique," his landmark avant-garde film in which he experiments with camera-created motion and rhythm.

Anna Pavlova is filmed dancing her solos including *The Dying Swan*, on the set of Douglas Fairbanks's *The Thief of Bagdad*.

René Clair makes *Entr'acte*, a Dadaist film, to be shown during the intermission of the ballet *Relâche* (Theatre Closed) by Picabia.

1927 *The Jazz Singer*, with Al Jolson, becomes the first "talkie."

John L. Baird demonstrates the first video system.

1928 Diaghilev uses film projections in Léonide Massine's ballet *Ode*.

Sergei M. Eisenstein makes a rapid montage of three soldiers dancing in three different styles in his film *October*.

1928 First scheduled television broadcasts by WGY, Schenectady, N.Y.

First color motion pictures exhibited by George Eastman in Rochester, N.Y.

1929 All-dancing, all-singing revue films begin to appear.

Rouben Mamoulian directs *Applause*, which contains very fluid, rhythmic motion by the standards of early sound film.

Mary Wigman's *Hexentanz* is filmed in Germany c. 1929 (see chapter 21) DVD 15, DVD 16

1929 Kodak introduces 16mm color movie film.

1930 Busby Berkeley is brought to Hollywood to make a film version of the Ziegfeld show *Whoopee* (see chapter 11).

1931 May 26: Maria Gambarelli is the first dancer to go before a television camera in America.

1932 A spectator films Olga Spessivtzeva in a rehearsal of *Giselle*, Act 1, from a box in a London theater.

1933 Farnsworth transmits first electronic TV picture Bell.

1933 Busby Berkeley directs his first "backstage" musicals (*Gold Diggers of 1933, Footlight Parade*, and *42nd Street*), in which the dance movement is created by the camera and the editing.

Fred Astaire makes his first film, *Dancing Lady,* with Joan Crawford. His fabled partnership with Ginger Rogers begins. They make nine films in the next seven years: *Flying Down to Rio* (1933), *The Gay Divorcee* (1934), *Top Hat* (1935) *Swingtime, Follow the Fleet* (1936), *Shall We Dance* (1937), *Carefree* (1938), and *The Story of Vernon and Irene Castle* (1939). They made one more film together in 1949, *The Barkleys of Broadway.*

1934 **_The Merry Widow,_ one of several operetta films choreographed by Albertina Rasch, is directed by Ernst Lubitsch using an unusual mobile camera floating above the waltzing dancers.**

Roy Del Ruth directs *Kid Millions,* in which the Nicholas Brothers appear.

Shirley Temple makes her screen debut, "Baby Take a Bow," in *Stand Up and Cheer,* directed by Hamilton McFadden.

Air for the G String is filmed with Doris Humphrey and her ensemble (see chapters 8, 10). DVD 6

1935 **Max Reinhardt directs *A Midsummer Night's Dream,* containing a ballet choreographed by Bronislava Nijinska.**

Shirley Temple and Bill "Bojangles" Robinson dance together in two films: *The Little Colonel* and *The Littlest Rebel.*

Kinetic Molpai choreographed by Ted Shawn is filmed at Jacob's Pillow, Mass. (see chapter 9). DVD 7

1936 **Agnes de Mille choreographs dances for Irving Thalberg's *Romeo and Juliet.***

1937 **J. Benoit-Lévy directs *La Mort du Cygne,* starring Yvette Chauvivre and Mia Slavenska, the first feature film with the ballet world as its subject matter. (It will be remade in the U. S. in 1947 as *The Unfinished Dance,* with Margaret O'Brien and Cyd Charisse.)**

1938 **During a visit to the Netherlands East Indies, Rolf de Maré and Claire Holt film the traditional dances of Bali performed by I Mario and dancers of Peliatan, Tabanan and Ubud, and the traditional funeral dances of the Torajas of the Makale region, Celebes (Borneo) villages of Kondongan and Kalembe.**

1939 Cinerama is introduced at the 1939 New York World's Fair. It is improved in 1952 with a three-lens system and resolved into the single-lens 70mm process.

The artistic use of color begins and becomes the rule in Hollywood by the 1950s.

National Film Board of Canada established.

1940 **Walt Disney's *Fantasia,* directed by Ben Sharpsteen, contains music by Bach, Tchaikovsky, Dukas, Stravinsky, Beethoven, Mussorgsky, and Schubert, choreographed with animation.**

1941 **CBS presents *The Country Dance Society,* the first group to have a weekly show on Sundays.**

1942 **_For Me and My Gal_ marks the screen debut of Gene Kelly, co-starring with Judy Garland. Busby Berkeley directs the dramatic sections. Bobby Connolly is the choreographer.**

1943 **_Lamentation,_ choreographed and performed by Martha Graham, is directed on 16mm film by Mr. and Mrs. Simon Moselsio, preceded by a brief on-screen discussion of modern dance with critic John Martin.**

1945 **Kitty Doner and Pauline Koner begin a dance series on CBS called *Choreotones.***

Valerie Bettis becomes staff choreographer for the *Paul Whiteman Show*, choreographing a 15-minute ballet each week.

***A Study in Choreography for Camera*, a film directed by Maya Deren, creates new film space for dancer Talley Beatty (see chapter 3) DVD 1.**

1948 Michael Powell and Emeric Pressburger direct *The Red Shoes*, with Moira Shearer, Léonide Massine, Robert Helpmann, and Ludmilla Tcherina.

1949 Stanley Donen and Gene Kelly co-direct *On the Town*; Kelly also choreographs and stars with Frank Sinatra, Jules Munshin, Vera-Ellen, Betty Garrett, and Ann Miller. This is a remake of the 1944 Broadway musical inspired by the ballet *Fancy Free*, choreographed by Jerome Robbins.

***Through the Crystal Ball*, the first half-hour, all-dance show on TV, airs five episodes over a couple of months, including *Cinderella*, choreographed by George Balanchine with Herbert Bliss and Tanaquil LeClerq, and *The Wild West*, choreographed by Todd Bolender with LeClerq and Patricia McBride.**

CBS presents Ballet Theater in *Les Sylphides*.

1950 Nora Kaye and Igor Youskevitch perform *Giselle*, the first full-length ballet presented on television by CBS.

1951 *An American in Paris*, written by Alan Jay Lerner and directed by Vincente Minnelli, wins an Academy Award. The 17-minute title ballet is choreographed by Gene Kelly and danced by him and Leslie Caron.

***Showboat*, directed by George Sidney with choreography by Robert Altman, stars Marge and Gower Champion. The third screen version of the Edna Ferber novel, it is nominated for an Academy Award for the cinematography of Charles Rosher.**

***Trance and Dance in Bali* is produced by Gregory Bateson and Margaret Mead from Material filmed by Bateson and Jane Belo in Pagoetan Village in 1937–39, written and narrated by Mead.**

1952 Gene Kelly and Stanley Donen direct and choreograph *Singin' in the Rain* (see chapter 12).

***Limelight*, directed by Charles Chaplin, has dance sequences performed by Melissa Hayden and André Eglevsky.**

***Omnibus* begins and continues on CBS for nine and a half years, including such dance programming as Agnes de Mille's *Rodeo*, Eugene Loring's *Billy the Kid*, and Gene Kelly in *Dancing Is a Man's Game* (see chapter 1).**

1953 Most U.S. movie theaters are adapted for CinemaScope film projection. JVC begins research into video recording.

1954 The zoom (variable focal length) lens, first used in the USA, is introduced on the Bolex camera.

Peak of the pre-videotape era: CBS produces 70 hours of live programming a week, all kine-recorded on almost 1 million feet of film stock.

1954 *Seven Brides for Seven Brothers*, one of the first dance films in wide-screen format, is directed by Stanley Donen with choreography by Michael Kidd and Matt Mattox.

Ed Sullivan begins presenting his "really big" show, which continues until 1971 and includes such dance programming as the first American television appearance of the Sadlers Wells Ballet with Margot Fonteyn and Michael Somes, the Royal Danish Ballet

in *Napoli*, the London Festival Ballet, Ruth Page's Chicago Opera Ballet, Roland Petit's Ballet de Paris, and the Moiseyev Dancers. In 1960, Jerome Robbins Ballet USA was granted two days of camera rehearsal and presented on videotape in a two-program format.

Mid-1950s Color is introduced on television; becomes popular by 1966.

1956 **NBC broadcasts the Sadlers Wells Ballet in *Sleeping Beauty*, choreographed by Frederick Ashton after Petipa, to an audience estimated at 30 million viewers.**

Dance Films Association, Inc. (DFA), first nonprofit service organization for dance and film, is founded by Susan Braun after her futile search for films on her favorite dancer, Isadora Duncan. DFA promotes excellence in dance films and video and public awareness through festivals, screenings, publications, grants, and workshops (www.dancefilmsassn.org).

1956 Ampex sells the first practical videotape recorder, developed by Charles Ginsburg and Ray Dolby, with four heads and a transverse scanner using 2″ tape running at 14,400 rpm.

1957 ***A Dancer's World*, directed by Peter Glushanok with Martha Graham, is produced by Nathan Kroll for Pittsburgh's WGED-TV, an alternative venue to commercial television.**

***Invitation to the Dance*, an all-dance film in three sections directed by Gene Kelly in 1952, is released. The first two parts, based on classical ballet, starring Igor Youskevitch, Claire Sombert, Tamara Toumanova, Diana Adams, and Claude Bessy, are less successful than the final section, in which Kelly dances in a live action/animation version of *Sinbad the Sailor*.**

1958 **CBS presents Balanchine's *Nutcracker*, with the choreographer as Drosselmeier, on Christmas night, broadcast live, with director Ralph Nelson employing a single crane-mounted camera.**

Marcus Blechman directs Helen Tamiris in a film of her *Negro Spirituals*.

Peter Glushanok directs *Appalachian Spring* with Martha Graham for Pittsburgh Public Television.

1958–59 **Shirley Clarke, a Martha Graham-trained dancer, makes *Bridges-go-round*, in which the bridges of New York dance through the film techniques of pixillation and optical printing.**

1959 **Ludovic Kennedy directs *The Sleeping Ballerina*, a profile of Olga Spessivtzeva's life as a dancer and her time in a sanitarium.**

1960 **Boston's WGBH, a public television station, begins the series "A Time to Dance," hosted by Martha Myers and produced by Jac Venza (see chapter 6).**

1961 ***West Side Story*, directed by Jerome Robbins and Robert Wise and choreographed by Robbins with dancers Rita Moreno, Eliot Feld, and Russ Tamblyn, wins an Academy Award.**

1962 Worldwide, 951 videotape recorders are in use.

1963 Sony markets first home videotape recorder—an open-reel, 1/2" helical scan deck, for $995.

1964 ***Viva Las Vegas*, directed by George Sidney, stars Elvis Presley and Ann-Margret in a "rock" musical with editing to the hard beat of the music.**

1965 Sony introduces first monochrome 1/2" Video Rover portapak—used almost immediately by New York video artist Nam June Paik.

1966 The "Dance USA" series produced by Jac Venza for WNET/New York includes the program *Dance: Four Pioneers*, directed by Charles Dubin, on the work of Martha Graham, Doris Humphrey, Charles Weidman, and Hanya Holm (see chapter 6).

***L'Adolescence*, directed by Vladimir Forgency, features Lubov Egorova teaching in Paris.**

***Romeo and Juliet*, directed by Paul Czinner using his multi-film-camera technique, stars Margot Fonteyn and Rudolf Nureyev.**

Tamara Toumanova appears in Alfred Hitchcock's *Torn Curtain*.

Hilary Harris directs *Nine Variations on a Dance Theme* (see chapter 3). DVD 2

1967 Sony markets its DV2400, the world's first portapak VTR, leading to an explosion in do-it-yourself television and revolutionizing the medium.

1968 *Pas de deux*, choreographed by Ludmilla Chiriaeff, is directed by Norman McLaren, employing extraordinary lighting and optical printing. Dancers are Margaret Mercier and Vincent Warren (see chapter 30). DVD 26

1969 Sydney Pollack's *They Shoot Horses, Don't They*, a film about a six-day dance marathon in the 1930s, includes an amazing performance by Gig Young.

***Sweet Charity*, directed and choreographed by Bob Fosse, is saved by the performances of Chita Rivera, Shirley McLaine, Paula Kelly, and Sammy Davis Jr.**

1969 Sony introduces the first videocassettes—3/4" U-matic, 1 hour (available in the US in 1971) and allows other manufacturers to sell machines that play the cassettes, establishing a world standard.

1970 An estimated 231 million television sets are in use worldwide.

1970 Nicholas Roeg makes the film *Walkabout*, which includes an aborigine dance performed by David Gumpilil.

1971 Artist Doris Chase makes *Circles I*, the first of her many dance films.

The first Dance on Camera Festival is sponsored by Dance Films Association (DFA).

1972 "Ballet for All" series directed by Nicholas Ferguson is made in the U.K. and broadcast on BBC.

Bob Fosse choreographs and directs *Cabaret*, winning an Academy Award for best director.

1973 The film *American Ballet Theatre: A Close-up in Time*, directed by Jerome Schnur, includes discussion of the history and repertory of the company as well as excerpts from *Swan Lake*, *Les Sylphides*, *Rodeo*, and *The River*, and the complete *Pillar of Fire*.

1974 Alvin Ailey introduces *Alvin Ailey: Memories and Visions*, directed for PBS by Stan Lathan, which includes excerpts from *Cry*, *The Lark Ascending*, and *Revelations*.

The first of three anthologies, *That's Entertainment*, is produced by MGM, directed by Gene Kelly et al.

In the television series "Camera Three," Merrill Brockway directs a program on Merce Cunningham, *A Video Event with M.C.*, combining four screens showing the same dance event from varying angles (see chapter 37).

1975 **Videographer Charles Atlas and Merce Cunningham collaborate on *Westbeth*.**

David Hahn directs *In a Rehearsal Room*, which includes choreography by William Carter to the music of Pachelbel performed by Cynthia Gregory and Ivan Nagy.

Dennis Diamond starts archiving dance performances on video at Dance Theater Workshop (see chapter 20).

1975 Sony offers the Betamax, the first popular home VCR, in November in the US. The console sells for $2295 and one-hour 1/2" tape cassettes for $15.95. Sony seeks to create a standardized format (as it had with U-matic in 1969) by getting seven other companies to produce machines to play Beta cassettes.

1976 **The landmark "Dance in America" series, funded in 1975, begins its first year of broadcast with programs on the Robert Joffrey Company, Twyla Tharp, Martha Graham, the Pennsylvania Ballet, and American Ballet Theatre. Over the next 20-odd years, the original directors and producers—Emile Ardolino, Merrill Brockway, and Judy Kinberg—are joined in this endeavor by other directors, including Jerome Schnur, Charles Dubin, Kirk Browning, Edward Villella, Twyla Tharp, Thomas Grimm, Don Mischer, Brian Large, Margaret Selby, Michael Smuin, and Matthew Diamond (see chapter 1).**

1976 In October, JVC introduces VHS (Video Home System) to the marketplace, offering a VHS VCR for $885. Sony sells a Betamax VCR deck for $1300 and advertises that "you can tape something off one channel while watching another and build your own library of favorite shows." MCA/Universal and Disney file a lawsuit, finally won by Sony in 1984.

1977 **Herbert Ross directs *The Turning Point*, a feature fiction film set in the dance world. It features Anne Bancroft and Shirley McLaine in non-dancing roles, and Leslie Browne, Mikhail Baryshnikov, and a host of other stars performing.**

Twyla Tharp and Don Mischer explore the possibilities of dance on the small screen in *Making Television Dance*.

John Badham directs *Saturday Night Fever*, with John Travolta.

American Ballet Theatre's *Nutcracker*, choreographed by Mikhail Baryshnikov and directed by Tony Charmoli (who used a handheld minicam camera to walk into the dance action) airs on NBC.

1978 ***Dune Dance*, produced and directed by ex-Cunningham dancer Carolyn Brown, is based on improvisation; the dancers, led by Sara Rudner, play in the sand with such rhythmic precision that traditional ballet music was added for a winningly comic affect.**

Milos Forman directs the film version of the stage success *Hair*, with choreography by Twyla Tharp.

Meredith Monk's *Quarry*, a meditation on a child's dreams about World War II, is performed by her group The House, directed by Amram Nowak. This is one of the few films produced by the Jerome Robbins Archive of the Dance Collection that have been cleared for release; another is *Torse*, a collaboration between Merce Cunningham and Charles Atlas that uses two synchronous films projected simultaneously on adjacent screens. The continuity between the two is produced by chance.

1979 Sony introduces Beta scan, which allows "visible picture" while fast-forwarding.

1979 **"The Magic of Dance" series, directed by Patricia Foy in the U. K., is narrated by Margot Fonteyn (broadcast in the U. S. in 1985).**

All That Jazz, directed and choreographed by Bob Fosse, wins an Academy Award for editing.

16 Millimeter Earrings by Meredith Monk (see chapter 15). DVD 11

Deep Hearts, directed by Robert Gardner, looks at a competition called *gerewol,* in which young male dancers compete in a contest of beauty, grace, and manliness in a nomadic tribe in the Niger Republic of Africa (see chapter 51). DVD 40

No Maps on My Taps, directed by George T. Nierenberg, explores tap dancing with historical footage from the 1930s and portraits of three master hoofers, with a finale at Harlem's Smalls Paradise (Spain, *Dance on Camera* 1998) (see chapter 13). DVD 8

1980 Sony introduces first consumer camcorder.

1980 "Dance in America"'s *Two Duets* is unusual in that the first part—Jerome Robbins rehearsing *Other Dances,* followed by a performance of the piece by Baryshnikov and Makarova—originated on film; the second part, *Calcium Light Night* choreographed by Peter Martins, was taped in a studio. The contrast between the softer quality of film and the harder tone of video dictated the production choices.

Alan Parker's *Fame,* with choreography by Louis Falco, tells the stories of the High School of Performing Arts in New York City and becomes the basis for a TV series.

1981 The long-running series "Eye on Dance," hosted by Celia Ipiotis, begins in New York, first on cable and later on broadcast television.

The first collaboration between Spanish feature film director Carlos Saura and flamenco dancer Antonio Gades results in *Blood Wedding,* based on the Lorca play. In 1984 they produce *Carmen,* and finally, in 1986, *El Amor Brujo.*

MTV begins 24/7 broadcasting of visualizations of popular music. Some of these clips include dance. Michael Jackson is the first big success in this venue with *Beat It,* in 1982, directed by Bob Giraldi. In 1983, the best seller is its long form version, *Thriller,* directed by John Landis (see chapter 2).

Merrill Brockway and CBS Cable partner to produce programs such as George Balanchine's *Robert Schumann's "Davidsbundlertanze,"* Twyla Tharp's *Confessions of a Cornermaker,* and May O'Donnell's *Dance Energies.*

ABC Arts's *A Portrait of Giselle* is directed by Muriel Balash and hosted by Anton Dolin.

1982 A film without words, *Le Bal,* directed by Ettore Scola, weaves dancing into the history of a small Paris ballroom from 1936 to 1983.

Ellis Island, an award-winning short film directed by Meredith Monk and Bob Rosen, and choreographed and composed by Monk, is filmed on location in New York City.

Charles Atlas directs *Channels/Inserts* for the Merce Cunningham Dance Company (see chapter 5). DVD 3

1983 *He Makes Me Feel Like Dancin',* Emile Ardolino's film about Jacques d'Amboise and his National Dance Institute, wins an Academy Award for best documentary feature (and an Emmy in 1984).

Merrill Brockway directs a two-part documentary on George Balanchine for WNET.

Flashdance, directed by Adrian Lyne and choreographed by Jeffrey Hornaday, stars Jennifer Beal as a Pittsburgh welder, working as an exotic dancer at night, who finally decides to audition for the Pittsburgh Ballet (with the help of film stand-in dancer Marine Jahan).

1983 Sony introduces Beta HiFi—VCR with FM-quality sound.

1984 **_Backstage at the Kirov_ is directed by Derek Hart, who employs a camera mounted on a Steadicam to allow a cameraman to follow "swans" as they enter the stage, giving viewers the dancers' view.**

1985 Sony introduces the 8mm format. The VHS group counters with compact VHS known as VHS-C, but it only records for 20 minutes.

1985 **_A Chorus Line_, Richard Attenborough's film, demonstrates the problems encountered in trying to "open out" a production originally designed for the stage.**

Dance Black America (1983), a documentary of a festival held at the Brooklyn Academy of Music directed by Chris Hegedus and D. A. Pennebaker, includes a variety of styles and personalities from the African American dance community. Telecast on Great Performances, PBS Channel 13, New York on Jan. 27, 1985.

Madonna's music video _Material Girl_ reenacts Marilyn Monroe's "Diamonds Are a Girl's Best Friend" sequence from _Gentlemen Prefer Blondes_ (1955) (see chapter 2).

"Alive From Off Center" (later ALIVE TV), a pioneering arts television series, debuts on American public television. The 12-season experimental series brings together dancers, choreographers, visual artists, film and video makers, public television, and cable and foreign broadcasters (www.pbs.org/ktca/alive/alive.html) (see chapters 7, 44).

1986 **Elliot Caplan directs _Points in Space_ for the Merce Cunningham Dance Company (see chapter 5). DVD 4**

1987 **_Dirty Dancing_, directed by Emile Ardolino, stars Patrick Swayze and Jennifer Grey as unlikely dance partners at a Borscht Belt resort.**

Husk by Eiko and Koma (see chapter 14). DVD 9

1988 **Meredith Monk directs and choreographs the feature-length _Book of Days_ (see chapter 15) DVD 10**

Circles—Cycles Kathak Dance, directed and produced by Robert Gottlieb, explores Kathak, the classical dance of Northern India (see chapter 47). DVD 38

1988 Super VHS format is introduced, equaling 8mm in picture quality but not in sound.

1989 **The feature film _Tap_, directed by Nick Castle, stars Gregory Hines, Savion Glover, and Sammy Davis, Jr. It contains a challenge dance among tap-dance greats including Sandman Sims, Bunny Briggs, Jimmy Slyde, Harold Nicholas, and others.**

1989 Sony introduces the Hi8 video format.

1990 **_Dead Dreams of Monochrome Men_, choreographed by Lloyd Newson/DV8, is reworked perceptively for the screen by director David Hinton.**

Madonna's music video _Vogue_ (see chapter 2).

In the televised version of _Le Dortoir_, choreographed by Danielle Tardif, Gilles Maheu, and Carbone 14 Dance Company, the inmates of a dormitory discover sex and love, God and death (see chapter 30). DVD 28

New England Dances, directed and produced by John Bishop, is a documentary on the revival of traditional music and dance in Maine and Massachusetts (see chapter 46). DVD 37

1991 In *Roseland*, choreographed by Wim Vandekeybus and directed by Walter Verdin, dancers in a fascinating old building take chances and move in a very fluid way.

Elliot Caplan directs *Cage/Cunningham*, a documentary about the remarkable partnership of Merce Cunningham and John Cage (see chapter 5).

1992 A 35mm, wide-screen camera version of a stage work, *Beach Birds for Camera*, choreographed by Merce Cunningham and directed by Elliot Caplan, begins in black and white and moves seamlessly to color, preserving the integrity of the original while adding the clarity of Caplan's vision (see chapter 5).

Peter Greenaway's visually arresting film *Rosas*, choreographed by Anne Teresa de Keersmaeker, is a woman's solo filmed in the magnificent empty foyer of the Ghent Opera in contrast black and white, with 35mm resolution and depth of field.

The Dance Heritage Coalition is founded to provide the public access to dance materials, to continue documentation of dance employing both traditional methods and developing technologies, to preserve existing documentation, and to provide education regarding methods, standards, and practice for access, documentation, and preservation (www.danceheritage.org).

The ongoing "Dance For The Camera" series is launched by the Arts Council of England (ACE) and BBC by Bob Lockyer and Rodney Wilson. Original dance films are made collaboratively by teams of choreographers and directors for television (see chapter 28).

1993 The National Initiative to Preserve America's Dance (NIPAD) is launched with a grant from the Pew Charitable Trusts. Through its grantmaking and communication activities, NIPAD's mission is to foster America's dance legacy by supporting dance documentation and preservation as an integral and ongoing part of the creation, transmission, and performance of dance.

Le P'tit Bal, choreographed and directed by Philippe Decouflé and performed by him and Pascale Houbin, is a gem of a film about emotions portrayed through controlled movement (see chapter 28). DVD 24

Risible Chick, choreographed by Leslie Lindsay and directed by Nick de Pencier (see chapter 30). DVD 31

Dancing, an eight-episode documentary series, developed and produced by Rhoda Grauer, includes dance traditions of 18 different cultures (see chapter 27). DVD 20

1994 *Achterland*, choreographed and directed by Anne Teresa de Keersmaeker and performed by her company Rosas, is a film of astonishing contrasts and dynamics, neatly captured by the camera and the editing.

Outside In is supported by the Arts Council of England's "Dance for the Camera" series. Choreographed by Victoria Marks for six differently abled dancers from London's CandoCo, the film, directed by Margaret Williams, is a stream of seamless movement filled with visual surprises (see chapters 38, 39). DVD 34

Mothers and Daughters by Victoria Marks and Margaret Williams (see chapters 38, 39). DVD 35

Touched, another "Dance for the Camera" film, is choreographed by Wendy Houstoun and directed by David Hinton. The sense of people in a bar, interacting in a claustrophobic, choreographed manner, is both captured and created by the camera (see chapter 28). DVD 22

1995 Sony offers the first "affordable," consumer-oriented digital video camcorders, with a direct line to non-linear editing systems and lossless multigenerational editing; independent production seems to be on the horizon.

1995 Frederick Wiseman's _Ballet_, a documentary, compresses ten weeks of rehearsal and touring with American Ballet Theatre into 170 minutes of cinema verité, concentrating on the institution rather than on its individual participants.

Donald McKayle, Carolyn Adams, and Julie Strandberg create the _Rainbow Etude_, based on McKayle's masterwork _Rainbow 'Round My Shoulder_, as part of the Etude Project of the American Dance Legacy Institute (see chapter 23, 24). DVD 19

the village trilogy, choreographed, directed, and produced by Laura Taler (see chapter 30). DVD 30

Falling Down Stairs, produced by Rhombus Media, intimately chronicles a collaboration between Mark Morris and Yo-Yo Ma (see chapter 30). DVD 29

Boy, choreographed by Rosemary Lee and directed by Peter Anderson, is commissioned by the BBC and the Arts Council of England as part of the "Dance for the Camera" series (see chapter 28). DVD 21

Hands, also commissioned by the "Dance for the Camera" series, choreographed and performed by Jonathan Burrows, is a movement exploration using only the hands (see chapter 28). DVD 23

The George Balanchine Foundation Video Archives is initiated (see chapter 22). DVD 17 DVD 18

1996 Mats Ek's _Carmen_, directed by Gunilla Wallin, is an imaginative treatment of unusual choreography.

Enter Achilles, choreographed by Lloyd Newson and directed by Clara van Gool, is a strong narrative, mixing reality and fantasy. The dance movement and natural gesture are enhanced by interaction with the camera and editing (see chapter 29). DVD 25

In _CRWDSPCR_, directed by Elliot Caplan, Merce Cunningham choreographs using the computer program LifeForms (see chapter 5).

Lodela, choreographed by José Navas and directed by Philippe Baylaucq, is an arresting duet inspired by _The Tibetan Book of the Dead_ (see chapter 30). DVD 27

1997 _Bella Figura_, choreographed by Jiri Kylian and directed by Hans Hulscher, is the culmination of a long and fruitful collaboration beginning with the stage films of Kylian's early works _Sinfonietta_, _Symphony of Psalms_, and _Soldiers' Mass_. With totally unobtrusive camera work and editing. the choreographic design and the dynamics of the performance are always preserved.

1998 Matthew Diamond's Oscar-nominated documentary _Dancemaker_ follows Paul Taylor and his dance company from rehearsal to a tour through India and a New York season threatened by a strike (see chapter 35, 36). DVD 33

The first UCLA National Dance/Media Fellowship Program is launched by the UCLA Center for Intercultural Performance. Over three years (1998–2000), the program admits accomplished professionals and UCLA graduate students from the field of dance/media to develop sophisticated, practical models for dance documentation that can be disseminated to and duplicated by other individuals and institutions.

1999 *A Midsummer Night's Dream*, choreography by George Balanchine, performed by the Pacific Northwest Ballet, directed by Ross MacGibbon, filmed for High Definition TV.

Dennis Diamond, one of the original video archivists in New York, begins offering Quicktime video clips of dance companies for the Internet (see chapter 20).

Bill T. Jones collaborates with Paul Kaiser and Shelley Eshkar on *Ghostcatching*, an innovative virtual dance created using motion capture technology (see chapters 17, 18). DVD 13

Sistersister (Argentina), choreographed by Susana Szperling and directed by Silvina Szperling (see chapter 32). DVD 32

2000 In *Billy Elliot*, directed by Stephen Daldry with choreography by Peter Darling, a working-class boy in a northern British town decides he wants to dance instead of taking boxing lessons, and he finds a dance teacher who thinks he should audition for the Royal Ballet. Years later, his father and brother come to London to watch him in a performance of Matthew Bourne's *Swan Lake*.

"Nursed in Pele," directed by Mark Eby, is an excerpt of the documentary video *World Festival of Sacred Music, the Americas, Los Angeles 1999* (see chapter 49). DVD 39

Kammer/Kammer by William Forsythe (see chapter 16). DVD 12

2001 *Returning Home*, directed by Andy Wilson (see chapter 43). DVD 36

SELECTED BIBLIOGRAPHY

Grun, Bernard (based on Werner Stein's Kulturfahplan) *The Timetables of History*. New York: Simon & Schuster, 1982.

Jordan, Stephanie and Dave Allen, eds. *Parallel Lines: Media Representations of Dance.* London: John Libbey, 1993.

Katz, Ephraim. *The Film Encyclopedia*. New York: G. P. Putnam's Sons, 1979.

Limbacher, James L. *Four Aspects of Film*. New York: Brussel & Brussel, 1968.

Parker, David, and Esther Siegel. *Guide to Dance in Film.* Detroit, Michigan: Gale Research, 1978.

Rose, Brian G. *Television and the Performing Arts*. Westport, Conn.: Greenwood, 1986.

Roud, Richard, ed., *Cinema: A Critical Dictionary. Vol. I.* New York: Viking, 1980. (Particularly the article by Arlene Croce, "Dance on Film".)

Spain, Louise, ed. *Dance on Camera: A Guide to Dance Film and Video.* Lanham, Md.: Scarecrow, 1998.

The catalogues of Dance on Camera from the IMZ, Vienna, 1991–2000.

INTRODUCTION

Judy Mitoma

The invention of film and video technology has had a profound impact on dance: on access to it, and on the creation, understanding, and appreciation of it. For the first time, we could see dance across boundaries of race, class, and geography, a dissemination process critical to the development of the field. Dance did not (and still does not) have a practical notation system; consequently, recording on film and video provided the first practical means of documentation. Dancers use cameras as research tools, to study technique, to review and analyze choreography, and to build performance skills. The ethnologist, who previously relied on written and photographic accounts, is able to capture moving images of dance in cultural contexts, providing a valuable tool for research. Film and video have spawned entirely new forms of dance, created when director and choreographer go beyond the constraints of the body and find new ways to capture human motion. Whether a documentation tool, a study aid, or a creative medium, the recorded moving image has forever changed the way we perceive and experience dance.

Early film pioneers were quick to recognize that dance was an ideal subject for demonstrating the magic of their new invention. Thomas Edison captured the exotic, the seductive, the "enchanting" vitality of "dancing girls," including Miss Ruth Dennis. In late Victorian times, film allowed audiences to witness dance at a socially safe distance, from the seat of a movie theater. As early filmmakers chose their subject matter, they shaped the public's definition of dance, forming attitudes about the form and its performers for many decades to come.

The introduction of new technologies at the turn of the century had a polarizing effect on the dance profession. Many believed they threatened a fundamental value of dance—direct interpersonal encounters. Isadora Duncan, for example, did not allow anyone to film her dancing (a person hiding behind a tree recorded the only known footage of her). During this time, dancers were at the mercy of filmmakers who were interested in technology rather than dance itself. Few dancers had the luxury of using cameras, and even fewer knew anything about editing and other post-production possibilities. Furthermore, in these early years the expense of recording a concert was formidable.

The 1960s ushered in a generation of dancers eager to take control of the camera so they might design and produce video documents of their own. Creating dance for the camera is a natural extension of the dance artist's skills—sensitivity to visual form, motion, space, time, and light, as well as a passion to communicate.

Faced with the high cost of touring and restaging dance, it is logical for dancers to look to technology as a means of participating in global exchange.

Today, with the advent of digital technology, we witness myriad approaches. Increasingly, dancers work to capture the essential features of their work through creative use of the camera, editing, sound, and even special effects. Recent advances in home equipment make it possible to create more complex renderings of dance. Most recently, we have seen individuals making dance specifically for the camera. Choreographed at the editing bay, these works do not exist as a separate entity. It is exciting to see film and video used as part of performance, enlivening theatrical concepts of stage design. Projections and closed circuit cameras are becoming a choreographer's answer to stage sets. With increased accessibility and availability of equipment and decreasing production costs, dancers are investing much creative capital in recording technology.

Now considered a principal tool of the trade, cinematic documents are found in the personal collection of every dancer, on the shelves of every dance department, as samples for promotion or grant-making, in archives, and in the catalogues of international distributors. However incomplete and uneven these efforts may be, they make up a chronicle of dance history that will remain for future generations.

This volume introduces the reader to an extraordinary group of individuals whose work sets the standard for the field. Their first-person reflections give us a glimpse of the rewards as well as the untold complications they face in their search for choreographic, cinematic, and technical solutions. Telling these stories requires more than mere words; therefore, many authors have graciously given us permission to excerpt their work for inclusion in the companion DVD. The contents of the disc do more than illustrate the essays; they are subjects of study themselves, to be viewed frequently and in detail. The use of camera and editing techniques, locations, light, and the aesthetics of framing can be studied in these clips. Deirdre Towers has contributed a filmography that points the reader to other outstanding works in the field.

Essays in this volume are clustered around general themes and need not be read in sequence. Rich fields of activity embracing a spectrum of roles are made personal by the accounts of 55 dedicated professionals. Directors give insight into how they define goals for their projects and design work plans, considering such things as the wishes of choreographers, camera angles, and dancers moving across space and through light. We hear from cinematographers, responsible for the technical control of equipment, on their quest to capture moving images with care and artistry. Outstanding choreographers explain how they recast their stage work for an entirely new medium. The editor, a behind-the-scenes player, comments on the painstaking process of translating visual material into seamless sequences. Producers map obstacle courses and the personal challenge of putting funds and creative teams together. We include the voices of documentary filmmakers who combine careful research with cultural sensitivity as they present the dances of other cultures. The archivist, the keeper of the record, discusses the importance safeguarding work for future generations.

While the goal of most dance film and video is to render invisible the complex process of production, this book attempts to make these efforts transparent. Each writer in this volume has developed his or her own approach. Their highly diverse opinions indicate that there is no single standard, formula, or solution to the question of how best to record dance. They have written to encourage a new generation of dancers, filmmakers, and researchers. Just as they have developed their proficiency by learning from those who have come before them, they generously share their experience with those who, we hope, will follow.

Part I

Setting the Record

CHAPTER 1

Dance as Television: A Continuing Challenge

Jac Venza

At the middle of the twentieth century, American dance was flourishing as never before, while television began to invade every aspect of public consciousness. Why, I wondered, didn't this most visual performance art form and this new, seductive visual medium produce a love-at-first-sight relationship? Here are some of my recollections of the story over the past 50 years, as seen from the center of this troubled marriage.

CHICAGO

By the time I was eight, I knew I would be an artist, but I don't remember where I got this idea. By twelve I had decided on a career as a theater designer, inspired by a red-haired actress sent to teach in the Chicago Park district by Roosevelt's Depression-era Federal Arts Project. At seventeen, I discovered ballet with the very artistic Lewin Sisters. The grim wartime atmosphere of Chicago in the mid-1940s disappeared when the Ballets Russes rolled into the opera house. Presenting the recently imported, exotic classic ballets of Serge Diaghilev, the young Ballet Theatre company added to those classics the American audacity and youthful choreographic vision of Agnes de Mille and Jerome Robbins. After performances, the Lewin Sisters and I waited at the stage door to get a closer look at the glamor of Alexandra Danilova and Alicia Alonso and the out-of-tights hunkiness of Andre Eglevsky and John Kriza. Waiting outside the opera house, I wondered how I could ever become a part of the dance world. I knew it would certainly not be as a dancer, because by now I was a design student at the Goodman Theater School—and I had seen myself in tights.

I could not know that the opportunity to develop a creative involvement with the world of dance would come from a place neither the dancers nor I had ever heard of: television.

NEW YORK: CBS

With the end of the war in 1945, the potential to be drafted passed, allowing me to move to New York and complete the studies necessary to become a professional union theater designer. By 1949, the radio networks began a continuing schedule of live television broadcasts. The day I received my union card, I was

Set design by Jac Venza for CBS's 1962 *Lamp Unto My Feet* production of Alvin Ailey's *Revelations*. Photo by J. Peter Happel.

hired to design sets by the pioneer CBS television staff. Everyone was young and inexperienced. We learned our craft in action. It was necessary to work fast and be creative, bold, and decisive to survive the weekly schedules of early television. The style of my pre-television commercial artwork suited the look of the new experiments with television variety shows.

At CBS, I had my first encounters with the era's dancers and choreographers. Being in New York allowed me to expand my fascination with dance beyond ballet. I had access to Broadway and the scattered modern dance concerts. However, with only a week of rehearsal and a day in the studio, live television was not an atmosphere to nurture the creation of dances with the depth of contemporary works by the era's ballet and modern choreographers. Agnes de Mille, Jerry Robbins, and Hanya Holm had created on Broadway a new American popular dance vocabulary that rivaled the popularity of prewar tap dancing. Revues like *Your Show of Shows* and the *Ed Sullivan Show* created a kind of television vaudeville that allowed for short excerpts of concert dance. However, if an excerpt from a classic ballet was to be aired, they preferred the boys in jeans and boots instead of the revealing shock of tights.

On various television shows, the budding choreographer Bob Fosse created popular jazz numbers for his wife Marianne Niles and himself. Once a year, a live holiday fairytale ballet special would be presented, such as the Royal Ballet's version of Ashton's *Cinderella* or the young New York City Ballet in Balanchine's *Nutcracker*.

The networks gave American audiences the kind of dance entertainment that could be watched by the entire family. Chorus dancers looked and behaved like the cheerleaders a college football game. Sometimes support dancers would be cast to boost the sex appeal of the star. The racial segregation that was still strictly enforced in much of America was reflected in the ways dance numbers were staged. White performers and artists of color were not permitted to touch each other. Black girls danced with Sammy Davis Jr., black boys danced with Lena Horne. A white and wholesome chorus backed up Patti Page, white and sexy dancers hovered around Dean Martin, and Jackie Gleason each week introduced a new Rockette-like spectacle with the June Taylor Dancers.

Although the remarkable new television technology could bring live dancers into the living room, it was produced in a studio environment that was a setback from the evolving advances of the postwar concert dance scene. The cameras needed so much light, all from above, that side modeling of dancers was impossible. To prevent the wobbling of camera lenses, the very heavy mobile camera bases required stable, poured-concrete floors. A long day on these floors was disastrous for the feet and backs of dancers accustomed to the spring of wooden studio and stage floors. The limited size of the early television tube was disappointing to an audience used to watching wide-screen MGM movie musicals.

The only way to record early-1950s television dance was with a kinescope, a simple device that produced a 16mm film recording off the black-and-white tube. Although the image was primitive, it enabled the new network to expand its national audience size by flying kinescopes to markets not yet reachable by antenna or cable. Since talent contracts required full payment for reuse of these kinescopes, they were seldom rebroadcast, and the protection of those archives dwindled. By the mid-1950s more and more television series were produced on 35mm film in Hollywood studios experienced with global redistribution of their film products. Comedies, action westerns, and police shows dominated most of these series, with no viable place for dance.

Despite all the limitations, a few choreographers seemed to thrive in this frenzied creative environment. Peter Gennaro's works led to a career on Broadway, and John Butler, who had danced with Martha Graham, found inventive ways to cast soloists from the Martha Graham Dance Company or American Ballet Theatre in popular revues like the Kate Smith show. In fact, Butler financed his first concert works with his lucrative and steady television work. He introduced me to some of the new generation of choreographer-dancers like Alvin Ailey, Geoffrey Holder, and Glen Tetley, who counted on television or Broadway to support a few annual concerts at the 92nd Street YMHA.

Assigned to design a live Christmas special, I bonded instantly with Butler and his dancers over a pathetic pizza Christmas dinner rushed between the last camera dress rehearsal and air. John had smuggled some of his less cheerleader-like concert dancers into the program, heavily disguised as reindeer. But it would be another ten years before these concert artists would find a nurturing home on television, with the creation of a fourth, noncommercial network. The experimental pioneer phase of this process was called the National Education Network (NET). Eventually it was subsidized by Congress and renamed the Public Broadcasting Service (PBS).

In the late 1950s I began to see the possibilities of a concert dance sensibility at CBS in a few areas where the size of the audience was less important than fulfilling the local license requirement for educational and religious programs. Despite budget limitations, the educational half-hour series "Camera Three" consistently presented the fine arts, including small concert dances by such choreographers as Paul Taylor, John Butler, and Merce Cunningham. Several times a season, the religious series *Lamp Unto My Feet* did dance "specials" on religious themes, like Alvin Ailey's *Revelations* or a new dance work based on biblical themes. All these series were scheduled early Sunday morning—the least desirable time slots for commercial sales—which became defiantly known as the "cultural ghetto."

My first television award was from *Dance Magazine*. Surprisingly, it was for the innovative use of dance on *Adventure*, a live Sunday afternoon hour-long series collaboration between CBS and New York's Museum of Natural History. As associate producer, my job was to think of how to visualize artistically the natural history and science stories of leading scientists, which would be juxtaposed with live interviews with Mike Wallace and Charles Collingwood. We called upon the seasoned television experience of John Butler to illustrate with a shadow play the tragedy of the Inca king and the loss of his gold treasure to the Spaniards. How genetic formulas control our inherited physical traits was demonstrated as a zany square dance.

Samuel Barber was commissioned to create a ballet score for a variety of ethnic instruments that he chose from the museum's anthropology collection. The dance was choreographed by Butler and danced by Glen Tetley, Mary Hinkson, and Yuriko of the Graham company. Since dances were so often featured in the various *Adventure* anthropological films of world cultures, it would have been absurd for the same series to object to this multicultural trio of modern dancers partnering one another.

It became clear to us on the creative team of *Adventure* that television was a perfect medium for big subjects, intellectually or artistically, but only where audience ratings did not dominate scheduling. It was a lesson that would be learned by the Ford Foundation and the creators of *Omnibus*, the most successful arts series ever created for a commercial network.

Omnibus, a weekly show with a new kind of erudite host, Alistair Cook, appeared just as the last variety showcases for dance, like the *Bell Telephone Hour* and *Ed Sullivan*, were disappearing from television in favor of more popular Hollywood action films and situation comedies. *Omnibus* began with an unqualified stance toward presenting the fine arts in ways unlike the current concert and theater performances of music and dance. It was out to draw new audiences to the arts, without watering down the level of the works presented. The series began with two great evangelical "talkers," Leonard Bernstein on Beethoven and Agnes de Mille presenting her abbreviated history of dance. They talked straight to the camera, intimately introducing audiences to how a great American conductor/composer and dancer/choreographer think and work. The best musicians and dancers of the day performed to illustrate their ideas. The critical acclaim for the programs proved undeniably that television could be a great communication medium for bringing world-class artists and ideas right into every American home, free of charge. The problem was that by network standards, too few American homes watched, even though the Ford Foundation and Aluminium of Canada continued to sponsor the series.

Throughout its run, *Omnibus* continued to showcase dance in important programs like Gene Kelly's lively essay *Dancing Is a Man's Game* and American masterworks like Agnes de Mille's ballet *Fall River Legend* and José Limón's *The Moor's Pavane.*

Once *Omnibus* had proved its point about the suitability of television as a great new cultural medium, the Ford Foundation began to look for another media platform whose broadcast standards would not be compromised by the size of ratings. The foundation began to support educational television projects being produced by new noncommercial stations that began to appear around the country, usually launched by the philanthropic support of local universities and arts organizations. Ford's seed support was given to a new organization, based in New York, called National Educational Television (NET). Ford's financing would be used to encourage more ambitious educational projects and to support a national distribution center for these programs in Ann Arbor, Michigan. Since these stations were not linked like a network, the NET Ann Arbor Center would archive the tape masters and produce duplicate tapes for distribution by mail. If forty stations were currently signed up, ten tape masters would be shipped to stations to be broadcast for a week in any way that suited their market, and then rotated on to the next station on the routing list.

In 1959, an invitation to WGBH in Boston by Greg Harney, a former CBS lighting designer, introduced me to this NET program initiative. I was impressed to find this small, noncommercial local station supported by all the celebrated educational and art institutions in the area, including the Boston Museum and Symphony and Brandeis, Boston, and Harvard universities. WGBH was looking for an experienced producer for an educational, nine-part, half-hour dance series. Martha Myers, a teacher from Williamstown, had proposed a much-needed project that would introduce people to dance through video. Myers hosted the programs, laying out basic dance themes that would be illustrated by performance demonstrations. A pilot had already been produced with Myers's students. I was tempted to take on the project if we could attract major ballet and modern dancers to provide the dances that would best demonstrate Myers's themes.

Although the budget was only around $10,000 per program, I was optimistic about getting the best artists, because it would be the first time most of them would be asked to record their concert works on camera. The response to the idea of the series by the dance community was remarkable. Each week, a new group of dancers headed to the studio in Boston. Choreographic theme programs presented the works of Antony Tudor, Alwin Nikolais, Herbert Ross, John Butler, and José Limón. Performance style was discussed and performed by Tudor, Nora Kaye, Hugh Laing, Jacques d'Amboise, Melissa Hayden, Maria Tallchief, Andre Eglevsky, Alexandra Danilova, and Frederic Franklin. Ethnic dance included the work of the Jimenez-Vargas Spanish Dancers, Geoffrey Holder, and Carmen de Lavallade. The studio facilities were primitive compared with network standards of the day, but we learned many valuable lessons that still apply today. The most important lesson for me was to put every effort possible into attracting the best dancers and choreographers for each program, because even if the production style became outdated, the historic record of important artists would become more valuable over time. Although these programs were recorded on tape, they were distributed widely by the University of Indiana to the educational community as film kinescopes, long before any form of tape equipment was available in schools or dance studios.

WGBH had new tape-recording machines that allowed us to record the dance sequences out of program order, taping the most difficult dances first when the dancers were still fresh. We learned to put the lights on ahead to heat up the studio, while the dancers were doing their warm-up exercises. Dancing a long day was more acceptable in the WGBH studio because it had been an old roller skating rink and still had a wonderful wooden floor. We found that to enhance a dancer's elevation, the camera lens should be lower than the heavy camera pedestals of the time allowed. However, if the lens was lower, then the studio grid and lights needed to be higher—much higher than our roller skating rink permitted. In the *Swan Lake* pas de deux, Eglevsky lifted Maria Tallchief dangerously near the ceiling electric fixtures. It was the first time we had to discourage dancers from leaping too high.

I had been able to arrange a three-month leave of absence from CBS to produce *A Time to Dance*. On my return, I was more conscious than ever of how few opportunities there were on the horizon to do network programs focused on any of the fine arts.

In 1964, Don Kellerman, a CBS colleague, happened to mention that he was leaving his job to join a new NET-Ford Foundation initiative being staffed in New York to create prime-time programs not intended for academic use. When I described my Boston dance series experience at WGBH, Don immediately offered me an executive producer role in the new cultural affairs division that he was to head. Although the Ford grant did not specify arts programs, from the very first days all of us NET cultural producers focused on the wealth of music, theater, and dance subjects never seen on the three commercial networks.

However, before we could start creating performance programs, we had to negotiate special new television guidelines for contracts with performers and music unions. NET was not hooked up for simultaneous transmission, and each station wanted multiple uses that best suited its own community and wanted to be able to broadcast shows at appropriate times for those different uses. It would be over a year before the new contractual arrangements were finalized.

Hearing that my old friend John Butler had successfully set his most successful work, a dance version of Carl Orff's *Carmina Burana*, on the vital new Netherlands Dance Theater, I set off to find an old Dutch castle setting where we might produce the work completely on location. Fearlessly—relying on Butler, the venturesome director Karl Genus's knowledge of shooting dance, and the stagecraft resources of the dance company—we prepared six different interior and exterior dance floors, rented from and installed by a local wedding tent company. The videotape trucks were hired from London and were outfitted primarily for exterior sporting events. Considering the elaborateness of the program concept and the number of ways it could have been a disaster, the program was a huge success. So even before we had resolved our working arrangements with the American unions, my future in noncommercial television was linked again with dance.

Since this era's black-and-white videotape cameras still required a great amount of extra light, it was not possible to tape dance in theater performances with a paying audience. Therefore, all the early dance programs either were commissioned especially for camera or were composed of repertory dances adapted for studio production. Each program was a collaboration between the television producer and director and the choreographer or artistic director of a dance company.

An ambitious collaborative commission with Lincoln Center was based on an idea of the composer William Schuman, the first head of Lincoln Center. To dramatize the unique creative voice of each artist, a story from a short play by Frank Gilroy was given to Anna Sokolow to create a ballet and to Mark Bucci to compose a short opera. This 90-minute program won the coveted Prix d'Italia before I had even heard of this international competition. The second Lincoln

Center commission, from Agnes de Mille, proved too complex for NET's limited funds. John Butler's *Ballet of the Five Senses* was a successful showcase for his concert dance company, with a different dance for each of the senses, to very different original scores.

Around this time, NET broadcast *A Dancer's World*, Nathan Kroll's first film collaboration with Martha Graham, in which she speaks but never dances. Fortunately, Kroll was able to lure Graham, by now past her prime, to record her in-studio performance of *Appalachian Spring* and other works.

A Lincoln Center initiative to create a permanent modern dance company at the center offered an opportunity to create a definitive portrait of José Limón by juxtaposing archive films of his early years with a studio revival of *The Moor's Pavane* that reunited his original cast. The program closed with his most recent work, *Missa Brevis*, an evocation of wartime to music by Zoltan Kodaly. This program remains the last and most expansive video portrait created with Limón's collaboration. Working with him instilled a sense of urgency for us to record America's pioneers of dance.

The possibilities of setting the highest artistic goals for all our NET programs were more than I had ever dreamed would be possible on prime-time national television. The optimistic climate for dance was enhanced by the fact that NET's chief of programming, William Kobin, was a committed dance fan.

In 1964, NET initiated a survey of the contemporary state of American arts. I was assigned six half-hours for a series called *USA Dance*. The series included a documentary of the blossoming of the modern dance movement at Bennington College in the 1930s, with revivals of early dances by Doris Humphrey. Three other programs of modern dance included Anna Sokolow's *Rooms*, Glen Tetley's *Loves*, a new dance in progress, and *Three Faces of Jazz*, which presented three newly commissioned modern dances, by Grover Dale, John Butler, and Donald McKayle, to jazz accompaniment. Four Balanchine excerpts danced by Suzanne Farrell, Arthur Mitchell, Edward Villella, Melissa Hayden, and Jacques d'Amboise represented New York City Ballet. Robert Joffrey presented his own troupe dancing ballet excerpts by himself, Anna Sokolow, and Gerald Arpino. (See sidebar, "USA Dance.")

Around this time, the Rockefeller Foundation initiated experimental video workshops in San Francisco, Boston, and New York, offering up-to-date technology for artists attracted to the new medium. So as not to inhibit innovation, these videos were not committed for broadcast. Under Susan Dowling's leadership at WGBH-Boston and later under David Loxton at WNET in New York, many of the new choreographers created works for the labs. One notable New York program was Twyla Tharp's *Making Television Dance*, which allowed Tharp to explore a wide variety of video avenues initiated by the lab.

An NET summer series of live broadcasts from summer festivals offered an opportunity to share the unique atmosphere of Jacob's Pillow with a national audience. The ailing but indomitable elderly founder, Ted Shawn, left his hospital bed to host the programs.

Black culture was now celebrated on New York's weekly *Soul* series, produced and hosted by Ellis Haizlip. Haizlip was an ideal producer for a big studio production of the repertory works of the Alvin Ailey American Dance Theatre, America's most important black modern dance company. With Alvin Ailey as host, the program included Judith Jamison, in her prime, dancing *Cry* and a definitive first color recording of *Revelations*.

While NET was demonstrating the ways a noncommercial television service could provide America with a much needed alternative, the United States Congress was deliberating the Carnegie report on a federally funded network that would be called PBS—the Public Broadcasting Service.

Several years before the launch of PBS, I was asked to head NET's first drama department, where we created *NET Playhouse*, America's first noncommercial drama series. Once PBS assumed the responsibility for the national service, the Ford Foundation's new initiatives were no longer necessary and most of its staff was disbanded. The New York public television station, renamed WNET, absorbed the NET library, and I was invited to move my complete drama unit to the local Channel Thirteen/WNET and PBS.

Luckily, my new boss, Robert Kotlowitz, was also a great lover of dance, and he asked me to follow through on a National Endowment for the Arts–funded proposal for a program celebrating American Ballet Theatre's twenty-fifth anniversary. Though the endowment grant was far from the budget needed for such an enormous project, it was that opportunity the Lewin Sisters and I had dreamed about outside the Chicago stage door almost 20 years before. The program, to be directed by Jerome Schnur, was designed to demonstrate ABT's wide range of ballet styles. The plan was overly ambitious and would require a different production strategy. Although a ballerina can dance full out on point for a two-hour performance, we would be spending a week of long studio taping days on camera, expecting "full-out" performance from morning until night.

ABT's repertoire of modern ballets included a full performance of Antony Tudor's *Pillar of Fire* and the first half of Agnes de Mille's *Rodeo*, each introduced by the choreographer. Excerpts from Fokine's *Les Sylphides*, Petipa's *Black Swan Pas de Deux,* and Lander's *Études* presented the classic roots of the company. Also included was an excerpt from Alvin Ailey's first ballet on point, *The River*, danced to a new Duke Ellington score. Although the production innovations initiated for this program sound simplistic, they created a caring atmosphere for the dancers and choreographers that had a long-range impact on how the dance world would view collaborations with television:

- A Los Angeles film studio was hired that had been converted to video but had a wooden floor rather than the usual concrete floor.
- A separate, warmer adjoining studio without cameras was hired for dancers' classes and warm-up.
- Since the video cameras needed a cool studio, the lights in the performance area were turned on in advance to warm it for the dancers.
- Adjustments of choreography for camera were planned and rehearsed prior to the costly full facility studio time with the dancers in costume and makeup.
- Special diet-minded catering was provided all week for the dancers.
- Taping sequences were planned with the ballet master, who knew the particular needs of each dancer.
- All music was prerecorded to facilitate editing separate takes of the same dance sequence.

This was the first big American-company ballet program on PBS, and its impact was important on two fronts. First, it inspired the National Endowment for the Arts to consider funding a series of such programs that could bring America's largest and most accomplished dance companies to a potentially new national dance audience, free of charge.

The second initiative by Lincoln Center, again with Ford Foundation money, was to test whether the new light-sensitive cameras developed for outdoor sporting events could allow live broadcast from their theaters with a paying audience in attendance. These successful experiments led to the ongoing *Live From Lincoln Center* series.

DANCE IN AMERICA

When the NEA announced its request for proposals for their television dance series, I hired Emile Ardolino to collaborate with me on our WNET application. He had been a long-time partner of Gardner Compton, who had shot most of the record dance films for Genevieve Oswald's growing dance collection at the Library of the Performing Arts at Lincoln Center. If the project were funded, Merrill Brockway agreed to join Ardolino, leaving his CBS Sunday morning arts series *Camera Three*. Brockway would act as the chief producer and director for the series.

Having won the NEA funding, *Dance In America* was launched in 1976 as part of the new PBS series *Great Performances*, funded by the Exxon Corporation. Joining Ardolino and Brockway was Judy Kinberg, a CBS associate of Merrill's from *Camera Three*.

Over the next 26 seasons, the major part of the series's 87 programs would be produced and directed by these dedicated pioneers of dance on video. While the series has always included co-productions and acquisitions from other sources, Brockway, Ardolino, and Kinberg have been responsible for introducing and recording this era's most important American choreographers and companies for prime-time television.

Dance In America was the first commitment by a broadcaster to support a fine arts dance series for network primetime. Finally, all my years of fascination and involvement with television and dance would serve my role as executive producer. Emile Ardolino brought his unique library experience in recording and editing a wide range of choreographers. Merrill Brockway and Judy Kinberg brought their seasoned experience in television. The final key team member was the skilled editor Girish Bhargava.

This series was conceived as a showcase for the work of such divergent dance geniuses as Balanchine, Graham, Taylor, Cunningham, and Tharp. We knew we needed a production scheme that would allow a greater voice in the whole procedure by these uncompromising talents and their dancers. We agreed on some decisions up front:

- An hour was the ideal program length; exceptions were story-driven classics like *Swan Lake*.
- The form of each program would vary and would be determined with the choreographer or artistic director of the company.
- To attract audiences new to dance, documentary or historical material would introduce or link the dances.
- Each program could include ballet excerpts, but at least one complete work should be represented.
- New dances would be commissioned for the camera when the choreographer was truly interested in this initiative.
- Four or five days of rehearsal in a ballet studio would precede a five-day week of taping for studio productions, with a low-resolution camera to help determine what choreographic changes would be necessary. This would allow dancers to rehearse any reorientation of these performance changes for each specific camera setup.

- A special sprung wooden floor would be built in small enough modules to be shipped and set up in any desirable studio.
- A new floor design with an appropriate surface would be created for each ballet to accommodate the higher crane camera's views.
- A new AGMA/AFTRA public television pay rate would be negotiated with the dancers and television unions, consistent with the company status of each artist who was a contracted member of a dance company.
- Rather than cut the number of dancers or musicians for big, costly ballets, we could seek co-production partnerships. Sometimes, instead of cash, partners would offer attractive studio or editing facilities, resulting in many co-productions of American dancers under the excellent direction of Thomas Grimm at Arhus Denmark.
- When the physical size of a work like *Sleeping Beauty* was too costly for transfer to a studio, or a once-in-a-lifetime dance event was too important to miss, mobile video cameras would be brought to the theater. By this time, color recording in the theater was possible because the newest video cameras required only minor adjustments in lighting.
- It became imperative to make documentaries like *Trailblazers of Modern Dance* and Agnes de Mille's *Agnes, the Indomitable de Mille* while these aging pioneer voices of twentieth-century dance were still alive.

As the series expanded, other producers and directors, like Don Mischer, Rhoda Grauer, Catherine Tatge, and Matthew Diamond, collaborated with the WNET team. Under her PBS leadership, Suzanne Weil created *Alive from Off Center*, which commissioned new choreography for camera, at the St. Paul station. The significant impact of dance in world society, religion, and history was the sweeping subject of the nine-part WNET series *DANCING*, conceived and produced globally by Rhoda Grauer.

Jac Venza, Executive Producer for *Dance In America*, accepting the 1979 Emmy Award for Choreography by Balanchine, Part IV, "Outstanding classical program in the Performing Arts," with series producers Emile Ardolina (left), Judy Kinberg (right), and Merrill Brockway (behind). Photographer unknown.

The *Dance In America* library grew as an important historic record of twentieth-century dance. Also growing was our awareness of how vulnerable were the 2-inch master tapes of our earliest programs. In the late 1980s, Judy Kinberg conceived the *Dance In America* Preservation Project, the initial phases of which were completed in the mid-1990s. It was funded first with a grant from Belle and Murray Nathan in 1991, followed by a grant from the National Endowment for the Humanities in 1993. The *DIA* Preservation Project was the first tape restoration project funded by the NEH; prior to this grant, they had no precedent for tape preservation. The project is ongoing as *DIA* vigilantly remasters its tapes, restoring and transferring them to a new digital tape format. For the coming digital age, a variety of delivery platforms is being conceived that will finally interconnect these special dance video masterworks to that special future dance audience already interactively communicating globally. We all look forward to a future when this library, originally conceived for broadcast, is finally available to dance lovers everywhere—who will not have to wait at the stage door to get a close look at their beloved dancers.

CHAPTER 2

Music Video as Short Form Dance Film

Larry Billman

The battle to capture and harness dance began the moment the motion picture camera was invented. Early filmmakers believed that to create moving pictures, they had to photograph moving objects. Rushing locomotives, racing horses, and hundreds of dancers soon became the contents of the early short, silent films.

When sound was introduced, the movie musical was born. Filmmakers aimed their cameras at dance as if it were on a proscenium stage, with the audience at the vantage point of "the best seats in the house." The popular line dancers of the day kicked, tapped, twirled, and cavorted within a camera frame that was distant and passive. Movies were trapped within a huge picture frame, with dancers often moving out of that frame to disappear into the void.

But it was the camera that had to dance. With input from choreographers, filmmakers soon began experimenting with the "one-eyed monster," moving in closer to the dancers, using a variety of shots and angles. The camera panned and the lens focused into close-ups of the dancers' faces, giving them a fleshly impact. The camera went overhead, circled the dancers, and even went under their tap-dancing feet. A sense of motion and immediacy was included in commercial film dance.

The very nature of dance on film has long been a topic for discussion. Critic Arlene Croce wrote in her book *Afterimages*:

> Dance in film is a subject that has taken on a semblance of controversy owing to the insistence of some writers that a conflict between dance and film exists . . . [People] dancing in the movies are demonstrating one kind of human activity the camera can capture as well as any other. Movies can also invent dances that cannot be done anywhere except on film . . . Most successful screen dances lie somewhere between total cinematic illusion and passive recording . . . A cleanly photographed dance can be pretentious and boring; a complex cinematic extravaganza can be utterly devoid of kinetic charm.[1]

Over the decades, innovators such as Busby Berkeley, Fred Astaire and Hermes Pan, Robert Alton, Gene Kelly, and Stanley Donen experimented until the dance musical was created—a movie that itself danced and pulsated, swooped and panned. Berkeley never focused on "The Dance"; rather, his camera danced. He used quick edits, multiple angles and shots, and special effects to create his "dancing wallpaper," as Jack Cole would later call Berkeley's film musical visions.

Fred Astaire and Hermes Pan were determined to focus on the dance. "Either the camera will dance or I will," remarked Astaire. Keeping Astaire and his partners in full-frame at all times and having the camera follow them afforded Astaire seamless long takes that allowed the viewer to realize the physicality and immediacy of the dance.

Robert Alton's camera collaborations panned and dipped, preceded and followed the dancers in some of the most graceful movement sequences yet captured on film. His "Atchison, Topeka and the Santa Fe" number from *The Harvey Girls* (MGM, 1948) contains only a few dance steps, but the entire sequence itself pulses and sways with movement.

Most choreographers of the Hollywood films of the 1930s and 1940s had little input as to how their work would be photographed and edited. With Gene Kelly's star status allowing him major input into the dance contents of his films, he was single-minded about his goal. "When I came to Hollywood, it was as an actor-dancer, certainly not as a choreographer. But soon after my first picture I realized that no director in Hollywood was seriously interested in developing the cinematic possibilities of the dance. No one cared about finding new techniques or improving the old ones. I decided that that would be my work."[2]

From his arrival in film with *For Me and My Gal* (1942), Kelly studied the effect of filmed dance and realized that speed, distance and the dancer's environment were all altered by the camera. While a close-up gave strength to actors, it weakened the power of the dancer. "I did *Cover Girl* (1944) . . . and that's when I began to see that you could make dances for cinema that weren't just photographed stage dancing. That was my big insight into Hollywood, and Hollywood's big insight into me."[3] Kelly often remarked, "Photographing dance is trying to take a three-dimensional activity and putting it into a two-dimensional frame."

As the movie musical reached its height in the 1950s, the genre itself became obsolete. This American art form went into mothballs as audiences flocked to rock-'em-sock-'em high-tech adventure yarns for their escapist spectacles. After the dance-dry decades of the 1960s and 1970s, the 1980s were suddenly filled with dance on commercial film, for three reasons: to elicit the nostalgia of the early rock 'n' roll innocence, to showcase the new forms of social dance, and to facilitate the greatest opportunity for dance makers to create on film since the invention of the camera: the music video.

Brief musical shorts featuring recording artists began with "Soundies" in the 1940s. These films were created to be part of the movie-house experience of the time, which included a cartoon, newsreel, short subject, and feature film. The form started out as static, passive camera recordings of vocal and instrumental artists, with dance as backdrop. Such future dance innovators as Gower Champion (before he paired with Marge), Gene Nelson, Katherine Dunham, and Luigi were captured on film in this form. Soundies eventually became more innovative, as directors and choreographers were allowed to participate in the creative process with such fusions of film and dance as *Jammin' the Blues*, a 1946 Warner Brothers short in which dancers Archie Savage and Marie Bryant move in silhouette, appear in multiple images and at abstract angles, and are artfully integrated into the whole.

In the 1950s, Scopitone (a form of a visual jukebox) was invented; for 25 cents, patrons could see their favorites perform. Into the 1960s, pop vocalists sang their hits, with dancers included to wiggle the go-go social dance vocabulary of the time in the background. The camera shots that featured dance were voyeuristic peeks at the jiggling pelvises and posteriors of bikini-clad young girls.

With the new technology of video, the form took a giant step. In the mid-1970s, choreographer Earl Barton produced a series of single-song pieces and tried to sell them to television, but the networks were reluctant to air all-music programs. Without the once popular musical variety TV shows of the previous decades, exposure for the recording artists had diminished, and the commercial need for the music video was born.

MTV, a new television network, premiered August 1, 1981, and popularized this new short film/music and dance form. With a limited budget, the struggling network asked record companies for free promotional music videos for their "all-music television"—and the rest is history. At first produced in limited quantity to spur record sales, music videos soon became an industry. Not only did they give exposure to artists and help sell records, but the videos themselves became commercial successes. They were sold in video stores, shown widely on other television networks worldwide, and given awards for excellence. The careers of many budding feature film directors and choreographers started in music videos. In previous decades, the evolution of stage dance had influenced dance on film. Now, the ever-changing social dance vocabularies used in music video are producing the greatest impact on filmed dance since the innovations of Busby Berkeley and Fred Astaire.

Purists lift their noses or roll their eyes at the mention of dance in this short film form, where the vocabulary has almost always been social dance. In very few instances, ballet, modern, or jazz dance have been used. These are pop works, created for the 15-minutes-of-fame culture. The choreography is learned by millions of young people, who can perform the extensive routines from memory. The archival treasure that music video will be for future historians is immeasurable. If only the music video had existed when the world danced the turkey trot or the Charleston!

Before the creation of MTV, musicians and filmmakers were experimenting with another all-music film form. Dance had not yet been invited into the mix. In "Birth of an MTV Nation,"[4] Jack Holzman, Senior Vice President of Warner Communications, recalled:

> I'd been involved with music videos—"clips," we were calling them then—a long time. When we came out with the Doors album in 1968, we made a video of them doing 'Break On Through.' Did it with our own in-house camera, and maybe it cost $1,000. We sent it around to the afternoon dance shows, and it helped get a great deal of attention . . . Years pass, and I see a video called 'Rio,' made by Michael Nesmith, formerly of the Monkees, and it was a whole different order of magnitude from anything I'd seen. He understood that music was just not about audio, but had a visual component which could carry further the meaning of the song.

In the same *Vogue* article, Michael Nesmith recalled: "I was living in Carmel and making videos, mostly for Europe. If you get a song on TV stations over there, it's almost assured to be a hit. 'Rio' was the first. It wasn't me singing in front of the camera, but a series of disparate images that proceed from the spirit of the song."

Queen's "Bohemian Rhapsody" (1975) integrated multiple images of band members in what was dubbed a "music clip." David Bowie created "clips" such as "Fashion" and "Ashes to Ashes." "Twilight Zone" (Golden Earring, 1982), directed by Dick Maas, included full production numbers and used a top cinematographer—the first video to do so.

Various critics and historians credit Busby Berkeley with creating the format of the music video. Berkeley's ever-unfolding kaleidoscopic patterns and complete montage/scenarios certainly had a commercial advantage. By the time the lengthy musical sequence was over and the song had been repeated endlessly, viewers knew the song by heart. But Berkeley's intent was never to exploit the song; it was to visualize the music in a dance between the camera and his marching and posing performers—most often scantily clad young women. Because Berkeley was a dance director and not a choreographer, his vision was never about dance. It was about dancing images.

Other critics have credited Walt Disney's *Fantasia* (1940) as "the first unintentional long-form music video." The artists at the Disney Studios were encouraged to visualize the music in this groundbreaking film. This was all music without words, tone poems that set free the imagination of the animators. The integration of film techniques, choreography (some by George Balanchine), and dance would never be the same. Critic Walter Terry wrote, "In *Fantasia*, Walt Disney has assembled the richest qualities of his choreography: humans, animals, and flowers dance in ballets which poke fun at dancing and ballets which exalt it." Mary Jane Hungerford went so far as to call *Fantasia* "cinedance" in *Dance Magazine*, as the constantly moving images created a film that danced, rather than a film with dance.[5]

Walt Disney continued to create films that can be classified as precursors to music video. *Saludos Amigos* and *The Three Caballeros* combined live Latin American dancers with animated whirling flowers, exploding fireworks, and bursting stars, with Carmelita Maracci contributing portions of the choreography. In *Make Mine Music* (1946), a compilation film that visualized popular music, Tatiana Riabouchinska and David Lichine were surrounded in their dance by fanciful animated images. In the same film, "All the Cats Join In" is one of the most exuberant swing dance/animation/film marriages of all time.

The filmic style of music videos was certainly influenced by director Richard Lester in the Beatles' film debut, *A Hard Day's Night* (1964). Because the Beatles themselves did not dance (the listeners were supposed to do that), the film does not contain a single dance step, yet the movement and energy of the musical sequences never stop, achieved by a variety of moving shots and quick edits. The staging was done by the camera and in the editing room. Later called montage editing, it "attacks the viewer with quick, choppy images from different angles," said Don Cox in *Dance Magazine*. Choreographer Jeffrey Hornaday later described "montage editing" to Cox as being "used to minimize the 'flatness' from the two-dimensional plane of the camera."

In the beginning, dance in music video was used sparingly behind and around basically non-dancing stars. The acceptance of enriched, integrated dance in the new form began with the historic collaboration among choreographer Michael Peters, director Bob Giraldi, and the unique song-and-dance talents of Michael Jackson on the video "Beat It" (1983). "Beat It" also changed the face of the basically white artist exposure on MTV as Michael Jackson began to dominate the music industry. In 1983, Jackson, Peters, and director John Landis would then expand the form to a 13-1/2-minute-long mini-film of song, dance, effects, and creativity with "Thriller." "The dance helps in telling the story," said choreographer Peters. "It's energetic. It makes them (the viewer) feel that they want to dance. Someone will look and say, 'God, I wish I could do that.' I want people to do that."[6]

Kevin Metheny, program director at MTV, agreed: "Dancing suddenly appeared cooler to a broader segment. Michael Jackson just helped speed that up." Metheny admitted that of the 30 or so video clips MTV scans each week, those with dance invariably stand out.

Because of their fame, both Michael Jackson and his sister Janet Jackson spent most of their non-performance time in the safety of their home, watching videos of movie musicals. There, they were inspired by Astaire, Kelly, the Nicholas Brothers, and the choreographic work of Michael Kidd and others. When the Jacksons began making music videos to promote their music, the movie musical was their inspiration and matrix. Others soon followed and were able to add the latest technical advances to the mix. Not since James Brown, Chubby Checker, and Elvis Presley wove dance and movement into their performances in the 1960s did the pop music world have so many charismatic vocalists who could dance.

For Madonna's "Material Girl," Kenny Ortega reimagined Jack Cole's staging of Marilyn Monroe's quintessential "Diamonds Are a Girl's Best Friend" sequence from *Gentlemen Prefer Blondes* (1955). Paula Abdul's "Cold Hearted" was inspired by Bob Fosse's erotic airline commercial in *All that Jazz* (1979), and her dance with an animated wolf stemmed from her childhood memories of Gene Kelly and Jerry the Mouse in *Anchors Aweigh* (1945). Janet Jackson's "Alright" was an homage to Michael Kidd's opening sequence from *Guys and Dolls* (1955), with Kidd himself asked to co-create it. To further enhance its classic movie musical luster, Jackson's video included appearances by the Nicholas Brothers and Cyd Charisse. Lionel Ritchie's "Dancing on the Ceiling" sprang from Fred Astaire's and Stanley Donen's collaborative wall-and-ceiling dance in *Royal Wedding* (1951). And for Michael Jackson's "Smooth Criminal," Vincent Paterson found inspiration and guidance in many sources.

From the originally direct approach of using dance and the camera to reflect the song, choreographers and directors began to explore more abstract ways in which to illustrate the music. Toni Basil pioneered in the form with the feature film *Head* (1968) and with videos for her own recording career. The careers of pop singer-dancers Paula Abdul (who also choreographed), Madonna, Janet Jackson, M.C. Hammer, and Prince were enhanced by MTV exposure in such groundbreaking musical numbers as "Knocked Out," "Vogue," "What Have You Done for Me Lately?," "U Can't Touch This," and "When Doves Cry." Many non-dancing singers soon realized the power of dance and enlisted choreographers to co-create some of their best work: Lionel Ritchie's "All Night Long" (choreographed by Susan Scanlan), Billy Joel's "Uptown Girl" (Michael Peters), and Stevie Nicks's "Stand Back" (Jeffrey Hornaday).

Dance was now used lavishly, giving exposure and challenges to choreographers and employment to new generations of dancers. It also offered carte blanche for experimentation from the dancemakers. Basil remarked in 1988, "When I got involved with commercial films it was impossible to choreograph for the medium. Directors would constantly make us choreograph for a proscenium and then try to put it on film or video. All the film technique I'd been learning on my own was virtually useless until video became popular ten years later."[7]

Music videos were complete scenarios within themselves. They didn't come out of anything, nor did they have to segue into anything else. The Soundies and Scopitone films had been quite primitive, with the numbers focusing on the singers or instrumentalists in a one-set performance location. Usually filmed in the old proscenium setting with few cameras, angles, or technical effects, dance was used as a back-up, simplistically illustrating the lyrics or theme of the song. But with the new technical advances in film on a music video, the sky was the limit—or rather, the imagination of the creative team and the budget were. Choreographers collaborated conceptually with the directors and the stars to create individual musical numbers with imaginative visuals. The staging, direction, and editing of music videos forced directors and choreographers to reexamine how dance itself was to be used in film. They became one of the major innovations of the decade. "It's an incredible tool that anybody can use," said Michael Peters. He continued, "You can expand and really collaborate with an artist. It's so new and so experimental that there are no parameters on it. Nobody's saying, 'This is the form.' It's really open-ended."[8]

During the height of the dance-driven videos, these were not cheaply filmed musical numbers. They were full-blown expensive production numbers approaching the scale of the MGM golden years in terms of creativity and budget. As film director Martin Scorsese—who eagerly accepted the challenge of directing the music video—stated, "The American musical is an art form." Retrospectives are already being created to illustrate the prolific and inventive work of choreographers in these videos during the 1980s and 1990s, with awards being bestowed annually by MTV, even as the Academy of Motion Picture Arts and Sciences continues to ignore the input of choreography in feature films.

Several dance-driven videos even made *TV Guide*'s list of "The 100 Greatest Music Videos Ever Made."[9] #1, "Thriller," directed by John Landis, received the comment. "This is the only horror flick in which the dead get a dance sequence. And dance wonderfully, since Michael Jackson is among them." Of #2, Madonna's "Vogue," it was noted, "With the dancers' ethnic hues and a body-as-art motif, 'Vogue' envisions affluence as a state of mind. Above all, it celebrates aspects of gay culture."

The controversy about music video techniques of filming dance continues. Choreographers have impassioned feelings about working in the medium. Lynne Taylor-Corbett remarked:

> With Tharp and Cunningham, the balance of the dance outweighs the balance of the music. It's a different medium. Video for TV has to be more palatable and more cosmetic. You're trying to reach a mass audience. If you're turning on MTV, you're turning it on to see what pops up. If you turn on Twyla Tharp, you're turning it on to see what Tharp has created.[10]

In music videos, dance is not captured by the camera. The film itself dances and leaps, twirls and pops. Similar to what Busby Berkeley did, music video filming takes dance as one of the moving components and then morphs and uses it. Rather than completing the physicality of dance, the movement is enhanced or created by special effects: slow motion, multiple images, computer-generated graphics. The energy of the dance helps create excitement with extended arms, turns, contracting hips or torsos, flying hair, or passing silhouettes. In the split-second edits, the movements do not complete themselves but instead become part of the movement of the film.

Whereas "dance-ins" had been previously used in films to perform for non-dancing stars, now dance-ins with specific dance skills (turns, acrobatics, gymnastics, leaps, etc.) are used as an integral part of the choreography. With the new quick-cut montage editing, dancers are hired to perform fantastic stunts that, when melded into the editing process, make it appear as if superhuman people were performing the dancing, pushing the human body beyond its limits. Paula Abdul's music videos feature extraordinary single stunts by young male dancers who could complete nearly uncountable pirouettes or staggering gymnastic feats. Often, one solo dance routine would be performed by dozens of people in bits and pieces of expertly edited cuts. Filmmakers in the 1920s dazzled audiences by offering dance acts of mind-boggling tricks and skills, one following the other. Music video choreographers and filmmakers now presented those thrills shot by shot.

Choreographers needed to learn about and use as their tools the ever-increasing film techniques. On *Dance in America*'s "Everybody Dance Now," a 1991 segment of PBS's *Great Performances*, the choreography, filming, and editing techniques for music videos were discussed and illustrated in depth, featuring the leading choreographers of the medium at the time. In the program, Martin Scorsese discussed directing Michael Jackson's "Bad," choreographed by Michael Peters:

> The dance steps themselves were worked out to combine with the camera movement so that the camera itself is dancing and the dolly grips were as important as some of the dancers. I wanted to make something classical the way the great choreographers moved in the late forties, early fifties and the films that I saw growing up . . . Some of the dance music videos disturb me because it's really lots of quick cuts and flashes and I don't really see the dance . . . But we are clashing two forms. Maybe the video itself is the dance. You know, the piece of film itself and the impression that it gives to the mind when you're flashing by on those channels . . . maybe it speaks another language to a younger generation. Who knows?[11]

Rosie Perez (who was choreographing TV's *In Living Color* at the time) stated her personal opinions: "Videos to me are like a fantasy, like a dream. And when you dream, you dream so rapidly, so fast, so therefore the movement has to be the same thing. It like has to hit you and go, hit you and go, hit you and go."

Vincent Paterson remarked: "There is a power in using dance in a very quick-cut, chopped up, edited version. Dance is not always used in that format, but it can be used merely for energy or excitement, as much as a visual or costume change or lighting design." Michael Peters encapsulated it: "Music videos are indicative of what we are, the way our culture has gone—instant gratification, how fast, you know, I mean, my attention span is this short so you better do it really fast because otherwise I'm gonna hit that remote button and change the channel!"

In a similar discussion in *Dance Magazine* (October 1984), Susan Scanlan said, "It's just butchering the dance. To butcher the choreography to four counts, four counts, four counts—that's posing. I'll go to see a dance video now and you don't know whether the guy knew three steps or what." Lynn Taylor-Corbett agreed: "Anything conceptual is just lost."

At the height of those dance-filled music videos of the 1980s, the dance films of the same period were being compared to music videos. "Watching *Flashdance* is pretty much like looking at MTV for 96 minutes. Virtually plotless, exceedingly thin on characterization and sociologically laughable, it at least lives up to its title by offering an anthology of extraordinarily flashy dance numbers . . . This may be the first main line commercial film to incorporate trendy break dancing into its proceedings, and aspects of disco, Aerobicize and even Kabuki new wave are provocatively on view—the closest feature film equivalent to music promo videos" wrote *Variety* (4/15/83).

"In the alternative-rock-ruled early 1990s, dancing was not a requirement. Who wants to sweat in flannel?" wrote author Christopher John Farley in "All the Right Moves." "Now, with teen pop topping the charts, good choreographers are in demand. Three in particular have emerged as major movers and hip shakers," wrote Farley in an article about choreographers Tina Landon, Darrin Henson, and Fatima Robinson. "Watch a day of MTV, and you won't see much that compares favorably with the abstract poetics of Merce Cunningham or the rich ethnic synthesis of Garth Fagan." The three emerging leaders in music video dance were all self-taught, with Henson admitting he "never actually trained anywhere . . . I used to watch music videos on TV and imitate what I saw," and Robinson saying "The clubs are my classroom."[12] Popular culture spawned popular culture.

The music videos of the late 1990s and early 2000s enlist the popular dance vocabularies of the time: hip-hop, salsa, break dancing, martial arts, and the "cane-carrying black-fraternity step show routines." Pounding feet into the floor and jabbing at the air with taut arm movements, punctuating with bent knees and thrusting hips, the softness of the girl singers of previous decades has turned sexually aggressive. Led by Madonna (and the first time she grabbed her crotch), it was fueled by Janet Jackson, transformed from a soft-fleshed, innocent girl to a buffed and buxom woman. Some of the other leading female pop singers of 2001 (Britney Spears, Christina Aguilera, Jennifer Lopez) are "playfully carnal," provocatively dressed vixens—dancing women in control.

The return of the boy bands to the music charts once again gave young people dancing men as icons. 'N Sync, 98°, and the Backstreet Boys heightened their white-bread personas by doing street dances à la "Sweet Boys in the Hood." In the music videos of all these groups, the line dance is back in full force. "Most clips follow the format Michael Jackson perfected in his epic 1983 video 'Thriller': a single dancer out front, with a phalanx of dancers in the rear echoing his steps."[13] There are no variations of patterns, but rather rows and rows of thrusting dancers performing the same choreography. The arm gestures do not illustrate the lyrics, and the dance does not drive or move the story line but instead adds relentless movement. Tony Award-winning choreographer Susan Stroman commented, "In music videos, it's about the energy . . . and the sound of the instrumentation. The lyrics and plot points are not as important . . . anything that exposes youngsters to dancing is, on balance, a good thing." Instances of inventive dance—such as Alanis Morissette's "So Pure," a montage of period movement choreographed by former Tharp dancer Kevin O'Day, and Daniel Ezralow's organic contributions to Andrea Bocelli's "O Mare E Tu"—manage to get produced.

The music video choreographers of the new millennium, such as Landon, Henson, Robinson, Wade Robson, Jamal and Rosero, and S.T.O.R.M., are looking at the concepts and camera work of Busby Berkeley, Stanley Donen, Robert Alton, Jack Cole, Bob Fosse, Michael Kidd, and other commercial film/dance masters of the past to enrich their music video work. Although the vocabulary is not considered "classic" by dance purists, these latest street or club dance moves create instant megabyte time capsules of how the young express their physicality. In Dan Cox's prophetic 1984 *Dance Magazine* piece, Twyla Tharp said, "It is clear to me that the future of dance is in cassettes, not in live performance. It may not be in the next five years, or the next ten, but ultimately that's what it's all about. People have got to make this little box work in relation to dance." The music video dance makers are incorporating filmic techniques, technical advances, and creative team collaboration on an unprecedented level in capturing dance on film.

NOTES

1. Croce, Arlene. *Afterimages* (New York: Knopf, 1997).
2. "September Calendar. The Museum of Modern Art Presents a Gene Kelly Dance Film Festival," *Dance Magazine* (September 1962).
3. Fuller, Graham. "Gene Kelly," *Interview* (May,1994).
4. Anson, Robert Sam. "Birth of an MTV Nation." *Vogue* (November 2000).
5. Hungerford, Mary Jane. "Must Screen Dances Be Incidental?" *Dance Magazine* (June 1947).
6. Cox, Dan. "Video Fever!," *Dance Magazine* (October 1984); hereafter cited as Cox.
7. Grubb, Kevin, "Basil Blasts Off," *Dance Magazine* (March 1988).
8. Cox, 1984.
9. Tannenbaum, Rob. "100 Greatest Music Videos Ever Made," *TV Guide* (December 4, 1999).
10. Cox, 1984.
11. *Everybody Dance Now*, "Great Performances: Dance in America," PBS (1991).
12. Farley, Christopher John. "All the Right Moves," *Time* (September 11, 2000).
13. Farley, 2000.

CHAPTER 3

The Kinesthetics of Avant-Garde Dance Film: Deren and Harris

Amy Greenfield

Maya Deren's *A Study in Choreography for Camera* (1945) and Hilary Harris's *Nine Variations on A Dance Theme* (1966) redefined the possibilities for the creative transformation of dance into avant-garde film.[1] Both films center on the solo modern dancer. Both are shot in black and white. Both transform modern dance into cinema through specific techniques that reveal the structural essence of modern dance in a way possible only on the screen. Both films use continuity of dance motion to overcome fragmentation of the body in time and space, asserting a transcendent sense of the wholeness of the human individual. And both use dance to reveal principles of cinematic motion.

Harris openly acknowledged his debt to Deren's *A Study* in making *Nine Variations*. His dance theme—the 50-second dance phrase that Bettie de Jong performs—recalls many of Talley Beatty's movements in *A Study,* such as the contraction, the spiral of the pelvis around the center of the body, and the leg extension. These connections allowed Harris to draw upon the cinematic aspects of Deren's films. Yet, for all of their links to each other, each film is a unique personal vision of creative filmdance.

DVD 1

A Study in Choreography for Camera (1945) 2 min 12 sec
Full work

Production Note: "In *A Study in Choreography for Camera*, the movement of the dancer creates a geography in the film, that never was. With a turn of the foot he makes neighbors of distant places."—Maya Deren, *Film Culture* (no. 39, 1965)

DVD 2

Nine Variations on a Dance Theme (1966) 12 min 58 sec
Excerpt 3 min 49 sec

Production Note: "The sensation of our own movement and the perception of movement in the world around us are very primal experiences from early infancy. It is in this world of movement (the kinesthetic experience) that film and dance make their most exciting and unique contributions."—Hilary Harris, *Dance Perspectives* (no. 30, Summer 1967).

A STUDY IN CHOREOGRAPHY FOR CAMERA DVD 1

Maya Deren, with the help of her collaborator and first husband, the cinematographer Alexander Hammid, is considered the founder of the avant-garde film movement. Film scholars, historians, and critics who regard Deren as an avant-garde icon too often deny the fact that dance was central to her work. Through Deren, American dance became central to the history of American avant-garde film. Choreographer-anthropologist Katherine Dunham was a major influence on Deren throughout her career. Talley Beatty, dancer and collaborator on *A Study*, was a Dunham company member when Deren was the troupe's business manager.

A Study in Choreography for Camera is only three minutes long and highly condensed. A brief description of it follows:

> A male dancer in black tights, his chest bare, twists slowly among birch trees, as the camera passes him like an invisible traveler, and "finds" him again and again. He inexplicably, impossibly moves to another and yet another tree, until he's seen against the sky. Surveying

Hilary Harris on camera while Amy Greenfield directs Janet Eilber on location shooting Greenfield's filmdance feature, *Antigone/Rites of Passion*, in the late 1980s in the Berkshire Mountains. Sean McElroy assists Harris and Jay Rabinowitz looks on. Photo by Robert A. Haller.

the distant horizon, he raises his arms and a leg. As he lowers the leg, in midstream the film CUTS so that as his leg continues down, we see that he has been magically transported into a room. He is alone. He recoils in a series of serpentine contractions framed by the geometry of a fireplace. With an arch of his torso and open arms he moves, exploring. Each step places him in a different room until the film CUTS. Suddenly the dancer moves at full speed away from the camera, revealing him in a gigantic sculpture gallery. From the rear of the gallery he turns and runs as if propelled diagonally toward us. CUT to a CLOSE-UP of his face in front of a four-headed circular Buddha statue. As he turns slowly and then faster and faster, he seems a moving version of the Buddha, until the film CUTS. Beatty rises out of a room into the sky, leaping into mid space, arcing again and again across the sky, his legs and arms wide open in silhouette, suspended, until he slowly sinks and finally lands lightly, his legs spread in second position plié.

In *A Study,* each dance motion is designed for a specific location and for one or more specific (though invisible) cinematic manipulations of that motion. The manipulations create an impossible contradiction between what was actually performed and what is perceived on film—without denying the nature of the real motion. The film is constructed (edited) so that a movement continues across a cut smoothly, but the space "jumps" to another location, thereby asserting the "magical" power of motion over discontinuities of space and time.

Deren has written on the specific techniques she used to make her filmdance. Here is a detailed analysis of the techniques and shooting process of the first scene in the birch forest. She had her cinematographer pan the camera from right to left, passing Beatty as he slowly spiraled against a distant tree. Then she directed both Beatty and the cinematographer to stop. Beatty would reposition himself at another tree to the left and closer to the camera, and begin his spiraling again as if no gap in time had transpired, twisting his torso in the opposite direction. The camera would again pan left, and again find and pass him. This precise procedure would be repeated, with Beatty closer and more erect each time. The idea was to cut these shots together so that the edit points were invisible, making it seem as if there were no break in time or space, thereby creating the illusion of Beatty being either cloned or magically transported from place to place in the forest without interrupting his own flow of motion.

Amy Greenfield with Hilary Harris on location at Ruggles Mine in New Hampshire during the late 1980s shooting of Greenfield's filmdance feature, *Antigone/Rites of Passion*. Photo by Robert A. Haller.

A film sequence like this had never been seen before, but the technique used—stopping the camera and then moving the subject, so that the subject pops up "instantaneously" in another place—was originated by magician-turned-filmmaker George Méliès at the turn of the twentieth century. Méliès's subjects were usually dancers from the Folies Bergères, and Deren carried on his tradition by melding cinema-as-magic with dance. Deren combined the "trick" film with Buster Keaton's innovation of cutting on exact movement continuity so that his comic character "walks" across time and space. (Keaton was a major inspiration for artists when Deren made *A Study*.) *A Study* demonstrates that the development of creative filmdance is not an isolated phenomenon but culls aspects of the history of cinema, uses them uniquely, and so carves out its own history.

Because Beatty moves with such slow, continuous control in the first scene, later in the film, when he spins against the Buddha sculpture, we think he controls his own speed, very slow, then continually faster and faster. Actually, he was spinning at a constant speed. Deren was smoothly hand-cranking the camera motor from 64 to 8 frames per second. Thus, the camera created the illusion that Beatty speeds up. If Beatty himself really had changed his speed, his face wouldn't stay (as it does) in a constant, exact relationship to both statue and film frame. Through precise cinematic manipulation of dance motion, we see controlled visual composition within the frame while experiencing a dynamic of motion.

The film climaxes with Beatty's leap, which was really Deren's "leap." It was filmed in slow motion, backward, and each section of the movement's arc was filmed as a separate fragment. The fragments were then edited so that they overlap. The entire combination of cinematic manipulations created a leap that is impossibly long (30 seconds) and free of the laws of gravity.

NINE VARIATIONS ON A DANCE THEME DVD 2

Although Hilary Harris was indebted to Deren's *A Study*, his working process in making *Nine Variations* was vastly different from hers. Perhaps the difference in their cinematic approaches is the difference between the 1940s and the 1960s. Harris was part of the close-knit New York experimental and documentary film community of the 1960s, but on the edge of it. His work was considered too accessible for the strict avant-gardists, though Deren herself awarded him one of her Independent Film Foundation awards. Later, his documentary *Seaward the Great Ships* won an Academy Award. No matter what genre he worked in, Harris searched for the communication of film kinesthetics in movement—from ships to abstract shapes to modern dance. *Nine Variations*, a very formal film with roots in the 1950s, uses formal modern dance; but in the freedom of his process in making it, Harris was very much a part of 1960s personal filmmaking.

In Harris's 12-minute, black-and-white, 16mm short, Bettie de Jong lies on her side in the middle of a large, sunny loft, with a wall of windows behind her. She starts to move, circling her arm in an act of discovery of space. She contracts, spirals up to her knees, continues to turn until she stands and lifts her arms and left leg to second position extension, pauses, lowers her leg and arms. Turning, spiraling in plié, she returns to floor and the same position in which she started. No one movement is separate, and the whole phrase is structured as a constant-speed loop.

Throughout the execution of the phrase, the camera circles around de Jong as smoothly as she herself moves. This astounding circling camera is both a development of the panning camera in the first scene of *A Study in Choreography for Camera* and a daring innovation that annihilates all reference to front, back, right, and left. We see that the phrase has been designed to be the center of an omnidirectional concept of screen dance space.

Each time the same phrase is repeated, the camera integrates new screen dance dynamics into the already discovered ones. For instance, in the second variation, Harris again circles the camera, closer and at a lower angle, in a way that makes it impossible to tell which is turning, the camera or de Jong. The result is that we experience the sensation of turning. At times, it seems that de Jong and the room itself circle with and against each other. We see and experience a new sense of dance kinesthetic—a relative kinesthetic—which increases throughout the film.

In the fourth variation, the camera travels not around but very close to her body. The camera flows with and against her movement, so that though the body is seen in close-up, it isn't arbitrarily cut off by the film frame; the camera and dancer continually move through the frame. Thus, the screen becomes a dynamic field, and the viewer can pinpoint details of movement without losing a sense of where the dancer has come from and is going.

The fifth variation combines this flowing camera (when de Jong's movement is flowing) with a contrasting series of percussive overlapping cuts (when she contracts percussively). The overlapping cuts are another aspect of *Nine Variations* derived from *A Study*. But Deren only overlaps three shots of Beatty contracting (after he arrives for the first time in the interior location). In *Nine Variations,* these cuts operate as beats: specific repeated rhythms that Harris develops increasingly throughout the rest of the film.

In the seventh, while maintaining the close-up flow, Harris tilts the camera off the upright axis, turning with de Jong as she rolls onto her back. We see the floor upside down, as she hangs in space, looking "down," with her back against the upper part of the frame. In this one move, Harris shows us that screen dance space not only has no front, back, right, or left, but also no stationary up or down. Here we experience screen dance space as vertigo.

In the eighth variation, we fully experience Harris's own sensation of making love to the dancer with the camera. The camera, in extreme close-up, seems to be inside her. Outer body and inner sensation are conflated. The edits cut fast and directly from hand to foot to knee, to a lock of hair, creating a "cinematic body" of moving fragments that relate to an unseen whole: a new kind of body existing only in cinema.

In the first eight variations, no matter how close-up or fast-cutting, each variation follows the dance phrase literally from beginning to end. In the ninth variation, Harris breaks time continuity. Time moves backward and forward. He makes a new phrase through editing, which seems to both exist within the dancer's memory and presage the future (evoking Deren's psychodramas, especially the last sequence of *At Land*).

The entire variation uses every camera move in the film, creating a free kinesthetic flow of filmdance that erupts into sheer ecstasy. Harris here extends Deren's concept of overlapping cuts to symphonic proportions, a musical climax communicating human transcendence through dance, turning the mortal, finite body into an organism of infinite possibility.

The most personal shots in the film are the final ones: de Jong's face as she looks with longing toward the floor, as if it were her lover to whom she is returning, until her cheek comes to rest gently on the floor, and the camera comes with her to its final rest. At the end of *Nine Variations*, we feel the same sense of completion and calm as in *A Study*. We come away from both films with a transcendent sense that a single human has come through a complex journey in which the fragmentation of cinema techniques transforms the body and the continuity of movement. Both end with the single human in harmony with self and world.

CONTRASTS

In *A Study*, each movement—and sometimes a fragment of a movement—was filmed one way, in separate shots, according to a preconceived plan, then edited together to make a purely choreographic continuity. In *Nine Variations*, by contrast, one set phrase was actually performed in real time, in one place, continuously, from beginning to end. Harris filmed that phrase over and over, never repeating his camera moves. The dance phrase is the material around which the intense cinematic convolutions center, like an obsessive lover, circling, entering into, breaking up, reconstructing, and transforming the real phrase.

Before making *A Study*, Deren carefully scripted the action in relation to camera. The filming process realized her preconceived shots. She wrote that it didn't matter which of the three camera people on the film shot what. But Harris's reason for making *Nine Variations* was his desire to discover for himself, behind the camera, over a period of a year, the "kinesthetic sense" of cinema in relation to formal dance. Harris wrote that even the last time de Jong and he met, he was still discovering new ways of filming the single 50-second dance theme. Instead of making a magical sleight-of-hand film, his process allowed Harris to structure the film so that the viewer would experience the camera and cutting process and come to a deep experience of dance kinesthetics in a new cinematic way.

Although there were experimental filmdances before it, *A Study in Choreography for Camera* was the first experimental filmdance to be written about, in *Dance Magazine* and in the *New York Times*. It was a milestone. Deren hoped it would stimulate many such films. Would experimental and art film dance have developed without Deren's making *A Study*? Yes. Would the films have looked different? I think so. Important contemporaries of Harris's, such as Shirley Clarke and Ed Emshwiller, were certainly affected by Deren's central role as catalyst. Even aspects of Michael Powell's formidable original dance sequences in *The Red Shoes* were influenced by *A Study*.

Harris's *Nine Variations* has had an impact on Hollywood's filming of dance. John (*Saturday Night Fever*) Badham, a great admirer of *Nine Variations*, had dancer Janet Eilber work off of *Nine Variations* for the dance dream sequence in *Whose Life Is It Anyway*. Moreover, in the circling smooth perfection of the first several variations, Harris's camera work for *Nine Variations* is a precursor to the steadicam, perhaps even influencing such films as *Flashdance*.

The influence of both filmmakers and of both films on my own highly experimental film and video dance work since the 1970s has been pivotal. Seeing Deren's work and reading her writings on the transformations of dance as cinema in *Film Culture* were the catalysts that pushed me from a more conventional career as a dancer/choreographer into making experimental film/video/dance. Her writing influenced me as much as the films. For instance, although her own use of the camera was actually quite traditional, Deren wrote of the incalculable and uncategorizable kinds of movements possible with the handheld camera in direct relationship to the body. This became the hallmark of my use of the camera.

The person who most helped me realize this camera technique was Hilary Harris. As Harris openly acknowledged his debt to Deren in *A Study*, I openly acknowledge my debt to him. Hilary was my mentor in film structuring. He then served as cinematographer for two of my films, *Element* and *Tides*, and principal cinematographer (with Pat Saunders and Judy Irola) for my *Videotape for a Woman and a Man* and my feature filmdance, *Antigone/Rites Of Passion*.[2]

In many ways, my early work was the opposite of *Nine Variations*—perhaps a postmodern rebellion from its formal classicism. Yet the goal of establishing a kinesthetic identification between a symbiotic camera and dancer—making love through the camera with the movement, as Harris put it—was one of our common goals. Even while applying his discoveries, Hilary rejoiced in and aided my own discoveries. I had the extraordinary opportunity to direct my own mentor (ironically, such was the relationship between Deren and Alexander Hammid).

Hilary started a film, *Body Song*, in which he paid me the compliment of applying my vision of the nude dancer in nature performing basic movements to his own vision and aesthetic. Hilary died late in 1999. He never finished *Body Song*. Perhaps someday I'll finish the raw footage and edit it "for" him.

Are *A Study* and *Nine Variations* important for young experimental filmdance makers now? Yes, though I doubt most have seen the films. Deren and Harris worked with primitive equipment compared with today's computers, and yet the films still have much to teach all of us about using mind and imagination and passion and the strictness of learned skill truly to dance with our new technology.

NOTES

1. *A Study in Choreography for Camera* can be rented on video as part of Deren's work, from Mystic Fire/Winstar TV and Video. On film it is available from the Filmmaker's Cooperative in New York.
2. *Nine Variations on a Dance Theme* is available on film only, from the Filmmaker's Cooperative.

CHAPTER 4

The Master and the Movies: Barbara Horgan on George Balanchine's Work with Television and Film

Robert Greskovic

Barbara Horgan, 2001. Photo by Charles Steiner.

Barbara Horgan, an aspiring actress and student at Columbia College in New York City, began working for the New York City Ballet in 1953. She became George Balanchine's personal assistant, working closely alongside the ballet master until his death in 1983. He bequeathed a number of his ballets to Horgan, who headed the Balanchine Trust (which oversees the dissemination of Balanchine's choreography around the world) from 1983 through 2000. She is now a trustee and general director.

George Balanchine, born Georgi Balanchivadze of Georgian ancestry in St. Petersburg, Russia, in 1904, spent his early years as a dancer—and eventually as a choreographer—in western Europe, notably under the watchful eye of the fabled impresario Serge Diaghilev. Upon Diaghilev's death in 1929, and after a brief period making his way around Europe, Balanchine (as he was theatrically rechristened by Diaghilev), at the behest of American scion Lincoln Kirstein, emigrated to the U.S. in 1933. Upon arriving, Balanchine expressed his pleasure at being able to live and work in the land that produced such remarkable performers and beauties as the movie star Ginger Rogers.

Though he remained committed to championing ballet in America (where, up to his arrival, it had been cursory at best), Balanchine was always fascinated by motion pictures. In particular, he had an abiding interest in film. During two separate sojourns working in the Hollywood film industry, in 1937 and 1939, he found much to learn, much to admire, and much to inspire him toward envisioning his view of lyric and fantastical theater for the screen. During this post-Depression era, so-called escapist entertainment flourished in the U.S., led to a great degree by movie musicals starring Rogers and her incomparable partner, Fred Astaire. (Balanchine called Astaire America's finest dancer.) Even while live theater as opera-house spectacle remained Balanchine's primary interest and focus, the moving picture medium continued to fascinate him—and to frustrate him.

In 1948, Balanchine and Kirstein established the New York City Ballet, soon adding Jerome Robbins as the company's other main ballet master. In 1953, to assist with the company's administrative duties, the troupe hired Barbara Horgan. Notable chapters in Balanchine's involvement with film and television

New York City Ballet production of the movie version of *A Midsummer Night's Dream* with Barbara Horgan, George Balanchine, Gordon Boelzner, and Paul Mejia relaxing on the set; choreography by George Balanchine (1964). Photo by Martha Swope. Courtesy of Time Pix.

occurred during Horgan's tenure with NYCB. These include several programs filmed in Montreal, as kinescopes, for the Canadian Broadcasting Corporation (CBC) from the mid-1950s through the 1970s; a 15-ballet project filmed in Berlin in 1973 (disastrously, as far as Balanchine was concerned); and a 1967 feature-film production of Balanchine's 1962 two-act ballet, *A Midsummer Night's Dream*. Additionally, and probably most notably, during the late 1970s the Public Broadcasting Service's *Dance in America* series produced several programs of Balanchine's ballets on which the choreographer worked personally, and to his ultimate satisfaction. Balanchine also collaborated with director Merrill Brockway, who had been involved with *Dance in America* before he moved to the short-lived enterprise known as CBS Cable, where the two men worked on filming one of Balanchine's last works, *Robert Schumann's 'Davidsbündlertänze'* (1980).

To put on the record a sense of Balanchine's work with moving images of his dances and to air her views on the use of visual media to continue Balanchine's legacy, Horgan spoke about this aspect of his career. The bracketed portions elaborate and/or explain certain aspects of her commentary. —Robert Greskovic

BH: [Balanchine] had a great respect for movies. He often discussed his background in Hollywood, with regard to the principal photographer that he worked with, Greg Toland. He claimed that Greg Toland taught him everything with regard to the use of the camera. He was very specific about creating for the camera.

[When Balanchine first went to Hollywood in 1937 at the behest of Samuel Goldwyn, Greg Toland was a camera operator for Goldwyn. Besides filming *The*

Goldwyn Follies (released in 1938) with Balanchine's choreography, Toland also shot such films as *Palmy Days* (1932) and *Roman Scandals* (1933), both starring Eddie Cantor. His photography for *Citizen Kane* in 1941 won him an Oscar.]

RG: It's remarkable how confident Mr. B. seemed when he was showing his ideas to Samuel Goldwyn. Can we assume Balanchine was a really quick study, and learned everything, immediately, from Toland?

BH: He considered himself a professional. Part of his job was to learn about it.

RG: Balanchine specifically told a somewhat confused Goldwyn to think "montage." Is this something that he got from his study with Toland, or do you think that, coming from the French avant-garde scene, the world around Diaghilev, he acquired any film sensitivity there? Or was it mostly an American thing?

BH: I think Balanchine was very eclectic. Between leaving Russia and arriving in America, he's in Europe for 10 years—London, Copenhagen, all over the place—and he's making a living. He's a young man; he's part of that period. And once he leaves Russia, he's exposed to a great many areas of artistic expression, museums, and so forth. In film, there was a great deal happening in Europe between 1924 and 1934, and then he comes to America and he sees more. He had this incredible facility to absorb, and learn, and remember. The problem with learning is what you remember, and geniuses (at least the one or two that I've met) have this capacity to "call up," if you will. He had a great respect for what film could do, and was very aware of what it *couldn't* do. Especially with dance. Because he knew, unlike other choreographers I worked with, how to translate from the proscenium to celluloid. He knew the difference between proscenium and three dimensions and flat. But he respected film, as a medium, more than television. With film, you had dimension.

RG: They each had their own integrity?

BH: Exactly. What he enjoyed in Hollywood was being given the opportunity by Goldwyn to create [dance] for the film. He wasn't asked to reproduce *Apollo* or *The Prodigal Son*. He was told to make a ballet for Vera Zorina. Here was an opportunity to fashion a new creation.

[The result was the now famous "Water Nymph Ballet" which featured a de Chirico-like horse, and a beauteous woman-cum-water nymph rising, bone dry, from a waterlily-covered reflecting pool, which got recycled for the ballet of hippos in Disney's 1940 *Fantasia.*]

RG: There are pictures of Balanchine toying with little figurines for the animators of *Fantasia.* Did he express any interest in animation?

BH: He wanted to do cinematic tricks. Chroma-key, etc. By that time, he had already gotten very interested, because of *Star Wars.*

RG: He admired it?

BH: Not necessarily the film but the technology. He called me on a Saturday in the summer and said, "Let's go to the movies." I almost fainted.

RG: Because that was unusual.

BH: *Very*! He'd read all about *Star Wars*, and it was to him what movies should be. Because they could do something that you can't do onstage, and that's always a treat. In fact, based on that, he began to promote *The Nutcracker*, for which he had done, with [the composer] Nicholas Nabokov, a film scenario. It wasn't the *Nutcracker* you see onstage, but "The Nutcracker and the Mouse King, " the fairytale that you read and see in E. T. A. Hoffmann. He and Nabokov had made a film script for it, which Balanchine finally wasn't happy with. However, he talked about it, and he went to one or two producers about the possibility of making a film, using the new technology. He kept saying, "Like *Star Wars.*" He said, "The world needs a fairytale." What could be done with film technology that you couldn't do on the stage? That's the way he addressed film.

RG: Speaking of popular culture, did Balanchine ever talk about watching television as television?

BH: Oh, he loved all that stuff. He'd call you in the middle of dinner, and he'd say, "Turn to Channel 7." And it would be *Charlie's Angels*. And *Wonder Woman*. He also liked *Barnaby Jones*.

RG: Do you think he responded to the performers?

BH: He liked the conciseness of it. They told the whole story in either half an hour or an hour, period. It was entertaining; it was simple. He *loved* the girls, I mean, especially *Charlie's Angels*. He loved Hollywood when he was there; he liked those tall blond girls, and he really enjoyed Hollywood. He always spoke about his days there with great love and affection.

RG: Before Balanchine worked on *Dance in America*, he did TV specials in the '50s and portions of dances on *Ed Sullivan*, and *Kate Smith*, etc. Did he find any of that an agreeable experience, or was it all more or less disappointing?

BH: It was disappointing, but he didn't expect anything from it, because he knew the conditions were so bad. He did it for various reasons. He did *The Ed Sullivan Show* as a favor to Maria [Tallchief], or Andre [Eglevsky], or Eddy Villella. But his participation in *The Bell Telephone Hour* in the '60s was income for the company and exposure. I don't remember if he was in charge of directing.

RG: What about his specific complaints regarding the limitations of television? Was it essentially that it's flat, or that he's out of control, to the point where he might say, "My dancers don't look beautiful?"

BH: I think it was because of the flat image. Then you were also confined with regard to how people enter and exit. You didn't see a proscenium; dancers suddenly disappeared off the screen. He had to rearrange entrances and exits. Also, there were constraints in regard to how the diagonals looked. There are a lot of diagonals in Balanchine's ballets. And diagonals didn't look like anything, because you couldn't get far enough away from them. And then there was the shortening of the body, and the whole issue of where the camera should be positioned. He always argued with directors about where he wanted *his* camera. He did one *Live from Lincoln Center* telecast [1978], and he never did it again. He kept fighting about the way they shot *Coppélia*. He fought every inch of the way. Balanchine wanted to be able to see the stage clearly; he thought the lights should be adjusted. The TV people would say, "Oh, you can't do that; nothing can be changed." He didn't like the camera placement; he sometimes wanted the camera at the back of the orchestra in order to show all the action.

The *Live from Lincoln Center* telecasts were still in the throes of development, and the only way that it could be sold to the constituents, meaning the Opera, the Philharmonic, etc., was if nothing would be changed, and the filming wouldn't be in the way.

Balanchine remained very particular about how he wanted the camera moved—to make the dancers look less squatty, let's say. Television didn't have the sophisticated lenses that movies had, even in the '30s. This is what he learned from Greg Toland: 35mm has a range that is very different from the box cameras that were used in early television. There was no choice about what lens you were going to use.

RG: Were the CBC filmings, in the late '60s, more pleasant experiences?

BH: Yes, because the CBC came to us, and it was done live in Montreal. They had really good facilities. It was a large studio; the orchestra was *there*. And the setup—you had a whole week to work, almost 10 days, which allowed [Balanchine] to restage for the camera. He seemed to love the director very much; he liked the cameramen and the huge studio.

RG: Were ballets for the CBC programs his choices, or the director's?

BH: I think it was collaborative. I remember the producer was very musical, very articulate and very knowledgeable.

RG: Around that same time, in '67 to be precise, there was a project to film Balanchine's *A Midsummer Night's Dream*. How did that come about?

BH: A man named Richard Davis, a movie producer, was married to a dancer Balanchine had known in Russia. Balanchine proposed that Davis produce *A Midsummer Night's Dream*. Davis made a deal and he put up the money. Unfortunately, we ended up at a studio which was quite small.

It was decided to keep the original Karinska costumes [Karinska was the company's primary costume designer at the time], but the sets were by another very good designer. *But*, in order to film it within the budget and number of days allotted, there had to be an overnight turnover, meaning the set had to be changed for the next day. And we were only allowed a certain number of days for each scene. Alas, the first scene turned out to be [dark and nearly] black, because of the lighting. So, when we saw the rushes, it was too late. We should have refilmed it. The sets were fascinating, real foliage, etc. It was a real forest; it was fabulous! But the lighting! We lost the first scene; you can't see it. The rest of it was rather good. In fact, I think the whole thing turned out to be really quite wonderful. But the public had absolutely no interest in seeing it in a movie house! They opened it in a movie theater. Big-budget movies spend so much money on the production, and then they spend an equal amount on the promotion! But that didn't happen in this case. So *Dream* died a studio death. Then they sold the television rights to ABC. ABC aired it, but since the film was done in Panavision, TV cut off the edges, so people just "appear."

But Balanchine was very satisfied with the film. Once it got out of the darkness, it looked like a movie of that time.

RG: He was especially put off by a 1973 project to film 15 of his ballets in Berlin. What was that experience like?

BH: He was bitterly disappointed. He was seduced into thinking that because [film producer] Reiner Moritz wanted to do these ballets, he would finally have his wish: his ballets on film.

RG: And the repertory for *that* series was his choice?

BH: It was a combination of Moritz and Balanchine. What Moritz didn't *tell* Balanchine, until after the deal was consummated, was that he wouldn't be allowed to direct. We all made the assumption that Balanchine would be directing, in the same way that he had worked with director Dan Erickson on *A Midsummer Night's Dream*, or with Jac Venza: that it would be a collaborative effort. And, all of a sudden Moritz arranged for his directors to come to New York to look at the repertory.

Balanchine said, "Who *are* these people?" And Moritz said, "My directors." Balanchine said, "But *I'm* going to direct." And Moritz said, "No, you're not." Now here are the ironies: (1) We were gullible to not ask this question to begin with; there's no one else to blame but us! (2) Balanchine felt he'd made a commitment. It was a lot of employment for the company, and at that point, he said, "We have to go ahead with it, and we'll make do." (3) Then we go, and there are two different directors in two different studios—actually three directors, two studios. And it became patently clear after two and a half weeks that the directors were getting *really* behind schedule. And guess who had to be used?

Balanchine went back and forth to each studio. We had 12-hour, 14-hour days. And he rearranged things. And after all that, Moritz refused to allow him to edit. And the films were edited *so badly* by their directors, that Moritz never was able to sell them, and went bankrupt. The material was lost. Forever. Now, on one hand, I'm thrilled. But, people—archivists—say all the time, "Oh, if we could only get the outtakes!"

When Balanchine died, Judy Kinberg and Merrill Brockway [who were working on a two-part television documentary about Balanchine's career] found outtakes of *Serenade*, and pasted them together, and of course it looks *marvelous.* But the Berlin experience soured Balanchine on certain individuals. Not the *media.* He respected the media. Individuals failed him.

So even before Merrill got to *Dance In America*, Jac Venza called and asked to make an appointment with Lincoln [Kirstein], and Lincoln took me. And Emile [Ardolino] was there. Lincoln, of course, didn't have much patience with television. So he wasn't just rude, he was impossible! And we stormed out! Next thing you know, I have a letter hand-delivered from Merrill Brockway. He was very clever; he had composed a letter that essentially said that he was the new boy on the block; that he was preparing a series to be called *Dance in America* and that it would be an unconscionable title without Balanchine's participation; perhaps Balanchine would consider meeting with him at his convenience at any time, at any place. The two of them went for lunch. And Mr. B. loved him! Because Merrill talked to him through music, and Mr. B. got curious. He talked to him as a musician. Music was really key to the whole thing.

RG: Balanchine collaborated on four of these *Dance in America* shows called "Choreography by Balanchine." Was he happy with the results?

BH: Yes. I think the one he ended up liking best of all was the work done by Merrill Brockway for CBS Cable's *Davidsbündlertänze.* He always said the ballet looked its best in that program. He even said to Merrill, "I made this for you."

RG: Meaning, when he choreographed the ballet, he immediately saw how good it would be for television.

BH: Yes.

["The Balanchine Library" series began its release in 1995: By early 2001 there were 12 tapes: four releases, with slight emendations, of the "Choreography by Balanchine" series for *Dance in America*; three cassettes in *The Balanchine Essays* series, explicating Balanchine's teaching methods and theories; one tape originally made for CBS Cable; one documentary focusing on Balanchine's ballerinas; a repackaging of Warner Home Video's 1994 release of *George Balanchine's 'The Nutcracker,'* and a two-part program of excerpts from a New York City Ballet performance 10 years after Balanchine's death. Further essays in the technical series are awaiting release. All these current releases are different from the series of "Interpreters' Archive" tapes documenting the efforts of individuals who worked directly with Balanchine on specific ballets and roles over the years. (See the section of this volume by Nancy Reynolds, chapter 22.)]

RG: Let's talk about the Balanchine Library.

BH: Bob [Robert] Hurwitz, a great admirer of Balanchine's, spearheaded this venture through Nonesuch, with enthusiastic help from his boss, Bob Krasnow, a dance fan and Time Warner executive. Both men simultaneously had the idea of putting the Balanchine repertory on video. Meanwhile,

Thirteen/WNET had earlier looked into the possibility. Thirteen got money from the National Endowment for the Arts to do a feasibility study. It took them 10 years to get to the point where they were prepared to negotiate the media rights to their programs, to firm up deals with all of the [parties involved]. *Very* complicated. And Bob Hurwitz was in a position, thanks to the interest of Bob Krasnow, to offer them a deal. It was actually Paul Epstein, a member of the Balanchine Trust and its attorney, who suggested to Hurwitz that he [do] the Balanchine Library. All these things take an extraordinary amount of time. I had already started with [Merrill Ashley and Suki Schorer] on the Balanchine essay videos [examining the teaching and technical aspects of Balanchine's work]. And Bob Hurwitz, much to his credit, wanted to (and did) buy the distribution rights. He actually licensed the whole series, even though I hadn't finished it, and he cut a deal for the first five, and an option for the rest. But he also bought the distribution rights for other *Dance in America* shows.

RG: What are the plans for future offerings?

BH: I want to see what happens, to see how these products will or will not be utilized, vis-à-vis copyright, monetary conditions, control. I am under the impression that at some point, someone within the framework of the Internet community, the digital community, may come up with a really interesting formula, with regard to education and allowing individuals to look at a product that will encompass a lot of Balanchine—at the ballets, the teaching, the technique, the music, the score, the whole kit 'n' caboodle. And I feel very strongly that at some point this technology and all the materials for the technology will be available, and something really good will happen to it.

The Balanchine Trust has the copyright for the choreography, not the programs. I don't expect riches. Don't misunderstand me. I see all of this happening, with regard to free access, and maybe there will be some kind of [user fee] like A.S.C.A.P.'s. I do not see this as a money machine. I *do* see it as excellent material for education, and education in dance. If young people want to get college credits for taking a dance course, or a literature course, or whatever you take as a minor, they should do all of this. It could be on disk. The *Encyclopaedia Britannica* is on disk!

RG: Are there future plans for retrieving things from the past—say, to release *A Midsummer Night's Dream* on cassette?

BH: Nobody seems to have the master. Nobody seems to know where it is. *If* it's in the vault somewhere, it may have disintegrated. This is one of the great problems with a lot of films and videos. If they haven't been taken care of, and transferred, they're gone!

At one point, we made an effort to find the outtakes of the Moritz films. They had such wonderful casts. We're so interested in seeing them. But, you know, if we *could* find them, I don't think anybody would want them. There is, now, an interest in the CBC films, and [the video distributor Kultur] is trying to put a deal together with the CBC to digitize them and restore them. These were kinescopes, mind you, so they were *really* fragile.

If somebody came to me and said, "We'd like to an interactive Balanchine program"—yeah! I've had this fantasy, since I first looked at CD-ROM. I thought, "Gee, wouldn't it be wonderful to do the definitive *Concerto Barocco*, where you would have the ballet, and you would be able to isolate the soloists. Then you could punch up the score, then read about Baroque, then a history of Bach and a history of Balanchine. Then you could isolate a step in "2nd Movement," let's say, and you'd have a little bit of the Balanchine essays. You'd call it all *up*.

CHAPTER 5

Merce Cunningham's Choreography for the Camera

David Vaughan

In a statement written by Merce Cunningham in 1994, entitled "Four Events That Have Led to Large Discoveries," he describes the major phases of his career as a choreographer:[1] his collaboration with the composer John Cage, which led to the disassociation of dance and music that is a key element of Cunningham's dance aesthetic; his use of chance operations as part of his choreographic process; his work with video and film; and his exploration of computer technology.

It is the third of these "Events" that concerns us here. Cunningham's work with video and film began in the 1970s. (So Cunningham says in the statement quoted above, but in 1961 he had choreographed a short *Suite de danses* for Canadian television.) In 1972, he choreographed a dance called *TV Rerun*, for which the décor, credited to Jasper Johns, consisted of one or more persons on stage photographing the performance with a still, movie, or television camera (on occasion, Cunningham himself was a camera operator).

At various times, works from the Cunningham company repertory had been filmed or televised, though never under Cunningham's own supervision. For example, *Variations V*, a large-scale mixed media work with film sequences by Stan VanDerBeek and television images distorted by Nam June Paik, first performed in New York in the summer of 1965, was filmed under the Swedish director Arne Arnbom in the studios of Norddeutscher Rundfunk in Hamburg in the following year. In the fall of 1968, Cunningham was invited by KQED in San Francisco to create an extended work for television, *Assemblage*, in collaboration with a filmmaker, Richard Moore, to be shot on location in Ghirardelli Square in that city.

However, the final product in these and other cases was controlled by another hand than his own, and Cunningham was dissatisfied with it. Like Fred Astaire when he first went to Hollywood in the early 1930s, Cunningham decided he had better learn something about camera techniques if he wanted to control the way his dances looked on the screen. In 1970, Charles Atlas had come to work for the Cunningham Dance Company as a stage manager; he was also a budding filmmaker. On tour with the company in Berkeley, California,

Merce Cunningham (at left) directs a high-angle shot for *Coast Zone*, 1983. In front of cameras: Helen Barrow and Joseph Lennon. Photo by Terry Stevenson. Courtesy of the Cunningham Dance Foundation.

DVD 3
Channels/Inserts (1982) 32 min Excerpt 2 min 48 sec

Production Note: Cunningham and Atlas divided the studio into sixteen possible areas for dancing and used chance methods based on the I Ching to determine the order in which the spaces would be used, the number of dancers to be seen and events that would occur in each space.

DVD 4
Points in Space (1986) 55 min Excerpt 2 min 57 sec

Production Note: Interviews as well as scenes from rehearsals in New York and London take the viewer through the complexities and exhilaration of bringing new dance to television.

and in Paris, he made a film of Cunningham's dance *Walkaround Time*. This seemed more satisfactory to Cunningham than earlier efforts, and he saw that a collaboration with Atlas would be possible.

Cunningham has said that he never owned even a still camera when he was growing up; at this point, he bought a video camera with which he could experiment in his studio. "I had to learn how to switch it on and off; that was my level."[2] What struck him immediately was that the camera views space in a different way from the spectator in the theater. In the theater, the space narrows in perspective from the proscenium opening to the rear; in television, the space widens out from the small aperture of the camera. He saw that it was not possible to make the television screen look like the stage; working with the camera would require a radical revision of spatial structure.

The first project he worked on with Atlas was *A Video Event*, a two-part program for CBS's *Camera Three*, early in 1974. This was directed by Merrill Brockway, but Cunningham and Atlas took an active part in planning the various sequences with him in Cunningham's own studio before moving uptown to the CBS studios. Their first original work for video was *Westbeth*, later in 1974, named for the building where Cunningham had the studio where the piece was shot. In the statement quoted above, Cunningham wrote:

> Camera space presented a challenge. It has clear limits, but it also gives opportunities of working with dance that are not available on the stage. The camera takes a fixed view, but it can be moved. There is the possibility of cutting to a second camera which can change the size of the dancer, which, to my eye, also affects the time, the rhythm of the movement. It can also show dance in a way not always possible on the stage: that is, the use of detail which in the broader context of theatre does not appear.[3]

Westbeth was inevitably rather primitive, but in its six sections Cunningham and Atlas tried to investigate some of the possibilities suggested above, showing the dancers in close-up or in deep focus, or filmed with multiple cameras, or in segments joined together in the editing process.

There followed a series of video- or filmdances, each of which explored a different aspect of the medium; taken together, they in effect constituted a grammar of choreography for the camera. Thus, *Blue Studio: Five Segments* (1975), commissioned by the WNET/TV Lab, was a solo work for Cunningham himself that experimented with the Chroma-key process; in the final section, five Merce Cunninghams danced at once. Cunningham and Atlas worked again with Merrill Brockway in 1976 on "Event for Television," a program in the *Dance in America* series for WNET. In addition to excerpts from the Cunningham repertory (as in his live "Event" performances), this included a short original segment called *Video Triangle.*

For the next eight years, Cunningham and Atlas were able to complete a film or video project every other year. In November and December 1977, they made a longer original video piece, shot in the Westbeth studio, called *Fractions I.* This work for eight dancers played with the idea of fragmenting images among a number of screens. Action taking place simultaneously in different areas of the studio was seen both on the main screen and on monitors set up within the range of the main camera. In what was to become a regular practice, *Fractions* was adapted for the stage in the following year—reversing the usual procedure, in which stage works are adapted for television. Cunningham and Atlas had in fact done this with *Squaregame Video* in 1976. The dance *Squaregame*, first performed earlier that year, had been conceived with video adaptation in mind, so that little restructuring was necessary. In 1977, Atlas also made a film version of *Torse* (1976) to be shown on a double screen, one showing the whole stage and the other closer details. (In 1978, Atlas also filmed *Exchange*, which remains unedited.)

Their videodances dealt principally with movement within the frame, rather than movement of the frame—that is, they had mostly used a stationary camera and very little editing. Now they moved into film with *Locale* (1979), in which they began to investigate the possibilities of a moving camera—not only in front of but around and among the dancers. The use of the Steadicam has become commonplace in feature movies; in *Locale,* Atlas used it to film virtually continuous takes in the first section of the piece, and Cunningham choreographed his movements as precisely as those of the dancers. (Atlas put together a short documentary, *Roamin' I*, about the making of *Locale.*)

DVD 3 *Channels/Inserts* (1981) was also a filmdance, in which Atlas attempted to give the illusion of simultaneous action in different parts of the Westbeth studio not only by the time-honored method of cross-cutting, but also by the use of traveling mattes in which one image seems to disintegrate, revealing another

Merce Cunningham (left) with Elliot Caplan, filmmaker, during the filming of *Points in Space*, 1986. Photo by Robert Hill for BBC. Courtesy of Cunningham Dance Foundation.

one behind. For *Coast Zone* (1983), the company moved out of Westbeth to a larger location, the Synod House of St. John the Divine, so that Atlas could introduce crane shots. The film also used the technique of deep focus. All three films were adapted for the stage.

Coast Zone was the last project Atlas worked on with Cunningham; he was succeeded as filmmaker-in-residence by Elliot Caplan, who had worked as his assistant. Caplan's first collaboration with Cunningham was a short video-dance, *Deli Commedia* (1983–85), a kind of homage to silent film comedies made with simple technical means and using students rather than members of the dance company. Caplan also made two instructional tapes, *Cunningham Dance Technique: Elementary Level* (1985) and *Intermediate Level* (1987), with Cunningham's own commentary, as well as the cinematic portrait *Cage/Cunningham*, on which he worked for several years before its eventual release in 1991.

DVD 4

Their first major work together was *Points in Space*, commissioned by BBC Television and shot in its studios in London, England, in May 1986. The title came from a favorite quotation of Cunningham's, Albert Einstein's statement "There are no fixed points in space," which seemed to him to express his perception of the nature of the space in video, offering multiple points of view rather than a single one. *Points in Space* was adapted for the stage, with more changes than usual (Cunningham's own role was omitted, and the order of the sections was rearranged).

The other projects that Caplan worked on with Cunningham were all, in one way or another, adaptations of existing dances. When they were offered the possibility in 1988 of making a video at the Sundance Institute in Provo, Utah, at short notice, they decided to make a version of *Changing Steps* (1973) because this dance consisted of a number of solos, duets, trios, quartets, and quintets that could be performed in any order, in any space, and in any combination. They were shot in various locations, indoor and outdoor, and intercut with rehearsal footage, some of it taped in Westbeth at the time of the dance's creation by Cunningham himself. In effect, therefore, the video moves not only in space but in time as well.

Beach Birds (one of the first dances Cunningham made with the use of LifeForms computer software) was first performed in the summer of 1991. At the end of that year, he and Atlas made a 35mm wide-screen film version, *Beach Birds for Camera*, shot in color in the historic Kaufman Astoria Studios in Queens, New York, and in black and white in a studio in New York City. Again, Cunningham considerably reworked the dance for the film version, adding three dancers and shortening the length slightly.

David Vaughan, 2001. Photo by Charles Steiner.

Caplan's last film for the Cunningham Dance Foundation was *CRWDSPCR*, a documentary on the making of the dance of that title in 1993 (the film was not completed until 1996). However, in 1996 he created a multi-screen installation using material from *Beach Birds for Camera*. This led to a collaboration with Cunningham on a live dance, *Installations*, first given in May of that year, in which the décor was a video installation by Caplan consisting of still images of the dancers projected onto screens either standing on the stage or suspended above it.

Atlas returned to work with Cunningham in 1999, when he was commissioned to make a documentary, *Merce Cunningham: A Lifetime in Dance*. For this Cunningham choreographed a number of dances that were eventually used as a separate short filmdance, *Mélange*, often appended to the longer film. (Some of the material found its way into the dance Cunningham was working on at the time, *Interscape*.) Cunningham himself continues to be fascinated by the camera: he has a camcorder with which he records the world around him and his dancers at work and at play.

NOTES

1. Merce Cunningham: "Four Events That Have Led to Large Discoveries (19 September 1994)," first published in David Vaughan, *Merce Cunningham/Fifty Years* (New York: Aperture, 1997), 276.
2. Quoted in *The Dancer and the Dance: Merce Cunningham in conversation with Jacqueline Lesschaeve;* (New York and London: Marion Boyars, 1991), 190.
3. Op.cit., 276.

CHAPTER 6

Program Lists of Dance in America, A Time to Dance, *and* Arts USA

Jac Venza

For more than thirty years, public television services in New York and across America have taken the lead in recording classical and contemporary dance and sharing it with a wide public. The following pages chronicle several dance series, many of them made under the supervision of Jac Venza, that have been broadcast widely; Venza's essay (chapter 1) details some of the high points in the process of conceiving, making, and airing these programs.

DANCE IN AMERICA

Programs Shot in a Studio without an Audience	**Orig. Air Date**	**Choreographer(s)**	**Producer(s)**	**Director(s)**	**Copyright**
City Center Joffrey Ballet	1976	Gerald Arpino, Léonide Massine, Kurt Jooss & Robert Joffrey	Emile Ardolino	Jerome Schnur	Thirteen/ WNET
Sue's Leg/ Remembering the Thirties	1976	Twyla Tharp	Merrill Brockway	Merrill Brockway	Thirteen/ WNET
Martha Graham Dance Company	1976	Martha Graham	Emile Ardolino	Merrill Brockway	Thirteen/ WNET
Pennsylvania Ballet	1976	Hans van Manen, George Balanchine, Benjamin Harkarvy & Charles Czarny	Emile Ardolino	Merrill Brockway	Thirteen/ WNET
American Ballet Theatre	1976	Eugene Loring & Sir Frederick Ashton	Emile Ardolino	Merrill Brockway	Thirteen/ WNET
Merce Cunningham Dance Company: An Event for Television	1977	Merce Cunningham	Emile Ardolino	Merrill Brockway	Thirteen/ WNET

Programs Shot in a Studio without an Audience	Orig. Air Date	Choreographer(s)	Producer(s)	Director(s)	Copyright
Dance Theatre of Harlem	1977	Louis Johnson, George Balanchine, Lester Horton, Arthur Mitchell & Geoffrey Holder	Emile Ardolino	Merrill Brockway	Thirteen/ WNET
Pilobolus Dance Theatre	1977	Pilobolus	Emile Ardolino & Judy Kinberg	Merrill Brockway	Thirteen/ WNET
Choreography by Balanchine – Part I with the New York City Ballet	1977	George Balanchine	Emile Ardolino	Merrill Brockway	Thirteen/ WNET
Choreography by Balanchine—Part II with the New York City Ballet	1977	George Balanchine	Emile Ardolino	Merrill Brockway	Thirteen/ WNET
Paul Taylor Dance Company	1978	Paul Taylor	Emile Ardolino	Charles S. Dubin	Thirteen/ WNET
San Francisco Ballet: Romeo and Juliet	1978	Michael Smuin	Emile Ardolino & Judy Kinberg	Merrill Brockway	Thirteen/ WNET
Choreography by Balanchine—Part III with the New York City Ballet	1978	George Balanchine	Emile Ardolino & Judy Kinberg	Merrill Brockway	Thirteen/ WNET
Choreography by Balanchine—Part IV with the New York City Ballet	1979	George Balanchine	Merrill Brockway & Judy Kinberg	Emile Ardolino	Thirteen/ WNET
The Feld Ballet	1979	Eliot Feld	Judy Kinberg	Emile Ardolino	Thirteen/ WNET
Martha Graham Dance Company: Clytemnestra	1979	Martha Graham	Emile Ardolino & Judy Kinberg	Merrill Brockway	Thirteen/ WNET
Divine Drumbeats: Katherine Dunham and Her People	1980	Katherine Dunham	Merrill Brockway & Catherine Tatge	Merrill Brockway	Thirteen/ WNET
Nureyev and The Joffrey Ballet: In Tribute to Nijinsky	1981	Michel Fokine & Vaslav Nijinsky	Emile Ardolino & Judy Kinberg	Emile Ardolino	Thirteen/ WNET
L'Enfant et Les Sortilèges (The Spellbound Child) with the New York City Ballet	1981	George Balanchine	Emile Ardolino & Judy Kinberg	Emile Ardolino	Thirteen/ WNET
Bournonville Dances	1982	Auguste Bournonville	Judy Kinberg & Edward Villella	Edward Villella	Thirteen/ WNET
The Green Table with The Joffrey Ballet	1982	Kurt Jooss	Judy Kinberg	Emile Ardolino	Thirteen/ WNET

Programs Shot in a Studio without an Audience	Orig. Air Date	Choreographer(s)	Producer(s)	Director(s)	Copyright
The Catherine Wheel	1983	Twyla Tharp	Alan Yentob & Rhoda Grauer	Twyla Tharp	The Catherine Wheel Inc.
The Magic Flute with the New York City Ballet	1983	Peter Martins	Judy Kinberg	Merrill Brockway	Thirteen/WNET
San Francisco Ballet: A Song for Dead Warriors	1984	Michael Smuin	Judy Kinberg	Merrill Brockway	Thirteen/WNET
A Choreographer's Notebook: Stravinsky Piano Ballets by Peter Martins	1984	Peter Martins	Judy Kinberg	Merrill Brockway	Thirteen/WNET
Baryshnikov by Tharp with American Ballet Theatre	1984	Twyla Tharp	Don Mischer & Rhoda Grauer	Don Mischer & Twyla Tharp	A Don Mischer Production Inc.
An Evening of Dance & Conversation with Martha Graham	1984	Martha Graham	Thomas Grimm	Thomas Grimm	Martha Graham Dance Company
The Taylor Co.: Recent Dances	1985	Paul Taylor	Pierre Morin	Pierre Morin	Societe Radio-Canada
Alvin Ailey American Dance Theater: Three by Three	1985	Alvin Ailey, Bill T. Jones & Donald MacKayle	Catherine Tatge & Ellis B. Haizlip	Patricia Birch	Tatge Production Inc. & Ellis B. Haizlip Co.
Dance Theatre of Harlem in A Streetcar Named Desire	1986	Valerie Bettis, Frederic Franklin & Geoffrey Holder	Judy Kinberg & Thomas Grimm	Thomas Grimm	Thirteen/WNET
Mark Morris	1986	Mark Morris	Judy Kinberg & Thomas Grimm	Thomas Grimm	Thirteen/WNET
David Gordon's Made in USA	1987	David Gordon	Rhoda Grauer	Don Mischer	Don Mischer Productions
Paul Taylor: Roses and Last Look	1988	Paul Taylor	Judy Kinberg & Thomas Grimm	Thomas Grimm	Thirteen/WNET
Balanchine & Cunningham: An Evening at American Ballet Theatre	1988	Merce Cunningham & George Balanchine	Judy Kinberg & Thomas Grimm	Thomas Grimm	Thirteen/WNET
Baryshnikov Dances Balanchine	1989	George Balanchine	Judy Kinberg & Thomas Grimm	Thomas Grimm	Thirteen/WNET

Programs Shot in a Studio without an Audience	Orig. Air Date	Choreographer(s)	Producer(s)	Director(s)	Copyright
A Night at the Joffrey	1989	Sir Frederick Ashton, William Forsythe & Gerald Arpino	Judy Kinberg & Thomas Grimm	Judy Kinberg & Thomas Grimm	Thirteen/ WNET
The Search for Nijinsky's "Rite of Spring"	1990	Vaslav Nijinsky, reconstructed by Millicent Hudson	Judy Kinberg & Thomas Grimm	Judy Kinberg & Thomas Grimm	Thirteen/ WNET
American Indian Dance Theater: Finding the Circle	1990	Various	Catherine Tatge	Merrill Brockway	Thirteen/ WNET
A Tudor Evening with the American Ballet Theatre	1990	Antony Tudor	Judy Kinberg & Thomas Grimm	Judy Kinberg & Thomas Grimm	Thirteen/ WNET
Balanchine in America	1990	George Balanchine	Judy Kinberg & Thomas Grimm	Judy Kinberg & Thomas Grimm	Thirteen/ WNET
Alvin Ailey American Dance Theater: Steps Ahead	1991	Alvin Ailey	Margaret Selby & Thomas Grimm	Thomas Grimm	Danmarks Radio & RM Arts
Ballerinas: Dances by Peter Martins with the New York City Ballet	1991	Peter Martins	Judy Kinberg & Thomas Grimm	Judy Kinberg & Thomas Grimm	Thirteen/ WNET
Paul Taylor's Speaking In Tongues	1991	Paul Taylor	Judy Kinberg	Matthew Diamond	Thirteen/ WNET
In Motion With Michael Moschen	1991	Michael Moschen & Janis Brenner	Skip Blumberg	Skip Blumberg	In Motion Production Inc.
Lar Lubovitch Dance Co. & Momix: Pictures on the Edge	1992	Lar Lubovitch & Moses Pendleton	Niv Fichman & Barbara Willis Sweete	Barbara Willis Sweete & Bernard Herbert	Rhombus
Three Dances by Martha Graham	1992	Martha Graham	Fiona Morris	Peter Mumford	Danmarks Radio
American Indian Dance Theater: Dances for the New Generations	1993	Traditional American Indian Dance	Barbara Schwei and Hanay Geiogamah	Phil Lucas & Hanay Geiogamah	A Production of Barbara Schwei and Hanay Geiogamah in Association with Phil Lucas Productions and Thirteen/ WNET

Programs Shot in a Studio without an Audience	Orig. Air Date	Choreographer(s)	Producer(s)	Director(s)	Copyright
Garth Fagan's Griot New York	1995	Garth Fagan	Margaret Selby	Matthew Diamond	Thirteen/ WNET
Two by Dove	1995	Ulysses Dove	Margaret Selby	David Hinton	Thirteen/ WNET
Twyla Tharp: Oppositions	1996	Twyla Tharp	Fiona Morris	Derek Bailey	Low Flying Pictures
The Wrecker's Ball, Three Dances by Paul Taylor	1996	Paul Taylor	Judy Kinberg	Matthew Diamond	Thirteen/ WNET
A Hymn for Alvin Ailey	1999	Various	Orlando Bagwell	Orlando Bagwell	ROJA Productions
Holo Mai Pele	2001	Created by Pualani Kanaka'ole-Kanahele and Nalani Kanaka'ole. Additional Choreography by Kekuhi Kanahele-Frias and Huihui Kanahele-Mossman	Dominique Lasseur & Catherine Tatge	Catherine Tatge	International Cultural Programming & Pacific Islanders in Communi-cations

Programs Shot in a Theater with an Audience	Orig. Air Date	Choreographer(s)	Producer(s)	Director(s)	Copyright
Two Duets: Choreography by Jerome Robbins and Peter Martins	1980	Jerome Robbins & Peter Martins	Emile Ardolino & Judy Kinberg	Emile Ardolino & Kirk Browning	Thirteen/ WNET
The American Dance Festival: Pilobolus	1980	R. Barnett, Lee Harris, Moses Pendleton, Jonathan Wolken & Allison Chase	Sidney J. Palmer	Emile Ardolino	South Carolina Educational Television
The Tempest: Live with the San Francisco Ballet	1981	Michael Smuin	Emile Ardolino & Judy Kinberg	Emile Ardolino	Thirteen/ WNET
Paul Taylor: Three Modern Classics	1982	Paul Taylor	Emile Ardolino & Judy Kinberg	Emile Ardolino	Thirteen/ WNET
Paul Taylor: Two Landmark Dances	1982	Paul Taylor	Emile Ardolino & Judy Kinberg	Emile Ardolino	Thirteen/ WNET
Balanchine Celebrates Stravinsky	1983	George Balanchine	Barbara Horgan	Emile Ardolino	New York City Ballet
American Ballet Theatre: Don Quixote	1984	Mikhail Baryshnikov after Marius Petipa & Alexander Gorky	Scott Robin	Brian Large	NVC Video Corporation

Programs Shot in a Theater with an Audience	Orig. Air Date	Choreographer(s)	Producer(s)	Director(s)	Copyright
American Ballet Theatre at the Met	1985	Michel Fokine, Kenneth MacMillan & Natalia Makarova after Marius Petipa	Michael Bronson	Brian Large	NVC Video Corporation
San Francisco Ballet in Cinderella	1985	Lew Christensen & Michael Smuin	Judy Kinberg	Emile Ardolino & Michael Smuin	Thirteen/ WNET
Choreography by Jerome Robbins with the New York City Ballet	1986	Jerome Robbins	Judy Kinberg	Emile Ardolino	Thirteen/ WNET
In Memory Of . . . : A Ballet by Jerome Robbins	1987	Jerome Robbins	Judy Kinberg	Emile Ardolino	Thirteen/ WNET
Gregory Hines: Tap Dance in America	1989	Tad Tadlock	Don Mischer & Rhoda Grauer	Don Mischer	Don Mischer Prod.
La Sylphide with the Pennsylvania/Milwaukee Ballet	1989	August Bournonville	Judy Kinberg	Merrill Brockway	Thirteen/ WNET
The Hard Nut with the Mark Morris Dance Group	1992	Mark Morris	Judy Kinberg	Matthew Diamond	Thirteen/ WNET
Balanchine Celebration, Part I with the New York City Ballet	1993	George Balanchine	Judy Kinberg	Matthew Diamond	Thirteen/ WNET
Balanchine Celebration, Part II with the New York City Ballet	1993	George Balanchine	Judy Kinberg	Matthew Diamond	Thirteen/ WNET
Billboards with The Joffrey Ballet	1994	Laura Dean, Charles Moulton, Margo Sappington & Peter Pucci	Richard Somerset-Ward	Derek Bailey	NVC Arts
Variety and Virtuosity: American Ballet Theatre Now	1998	Marius Petipa, Antony Tudor, James Kudelka, Nacho Duato, Sir Kenneth MacMillan and Clark Tippet	Judy Kinberg	Judy Kinberg & Thomas Grimm	Thirteen/ WNET
American Ballet Theatre in Le Corsaire	1999	Choreography by Konstantin Sergeyev, after Marius Petipa. Staged by: Anna Marie Holmes	Judy Kinberg	Matthew Diamond	Thirteen/ WNET

Documentaries	Orig. Air Date	Choreographer(s)	Producer(s)	Director(s)	Copyright
Trailblazers of Modern Dance	1977	Sir Frederick Ashton, Ted Shawn, Ruth St. Denis, Doris Humphrey & Isadora Duncan	Merrill Brockway & Judy Kinberg	Emile Ardolino	Thirteen/ WNET
Beyond the Mainstream	1980	Steve Paxton, Trisha Brown, Yvonne Rainier David Gordon, Kei Takei & Laura Dean	Merrill Brockway & Carl Charlson	Merrill Brockway	Thirteen/ WNET
Balanchine, Parts I & II	1984	George Balanchine	Judy Kinberg	Merrill Brockway	Thirteen/ WNET
Agnes, the Indomitable De Mille	1987	Agnes De Mille	Judy Kinberg	Merrill Brockway	Thirteen/ WNET
Bob Fosse: Steam Heat	1990	Bob Fosse	Judy Kinberg	Judy Kinberg	Thirteen/ WNET
Dancing for Mr. B.: Six Balanchine Ballerinas	1990	George Balanchine	Anne Belle	Anne Belle	Seahorse Films Inc.
Everybody Dance Now	1991	Various	Margaret Selby	Margaret Selby	Thirteen/ WNET
Bill T. Jones/Arnie Zane & Company	1992	Bill T. Jones	Mischa Scorer	Mischa Scorer	Antelope West for BBC Television
Accent on the Offbeat	1995	Peter Martins	Susan Froemke & Peter Gelb	Ballet Sequences: Peter Martins	Sony Classical Film & Video, A Division of Sony Music Entertain-ment, Inc.
A Renaissance Revisited	1996	Various	Judy Kinberg	Judy Kinberg	Thirteen/ WNET
Suzanne Farrell: Elusive Muse	1997	Various	Anne Belle	Anne Belle and Deborah Dickson	Seahorse Films, Inc.
Busby Berkeley: Going Through the Roof	1998	Busby Berkeley	Margaret Smilow	David Thompson	Alternate Cur-rent, Turner Entertainment Company, NHK
Free to Dance	2001	Various	Madison Davis Lacy & Adam Zucker	Madison Davis Lacy & Adam Zucker	American Dance Festival

A TIME TO DANCE

Jac Venza

A Time To Dance, begun in 1960, is a series of nine television programs produced by Jac Venza, directed by Greg Harney, and moderated by Martha Myers for National Educational Television and Radio Center, a non-profit corporation which provides a coast to coast network of educational television stations. The films are kinescopes made from the original television presentations.

"A TIME TO DANCE": Martha Myers, assistant professor of dance at Smith College, introduces the series with paintings, sculpture, and film sequences illustrating the origins and development of dance. Three major forms of dance—ethnic, ballet, and modern—are performed by the Ximenez-Vargas Ballet Español in flamenco and other Spanish dances; Melissa Hayden and Jacques d'Amboise in a pas de deux; and Daniel Nagrin, choreographer, in an original work, *Strange Hero*.

"CLASSICAL BALLET": The historical background of classical ballet is explained and basic positions and steps demonstrated. Maria Tallchief and Andre Eglevsky perform pas de deux from *Swan Lake* and *Sylvia*.

"INVENTION IN DANCE": Martha Myers and Alwin Nikolais discuss the choreographer's need to experiment with new forms. Ruth St. Denis performs her solo *Radha*, and a student of Isadora Duncan performs in Duncan's style. Nikolais presents the Henry Street Playhouse Dance Company in works illustrating his own innovations in modern dance.

"A CHOREOGRAPHER AT WORK": John Butler discusses various elements of concern to the choreographer. Excerpts from Butler's works are presented, as well as his concert dance, *Three Promenades to the Lord*.

"THE LANGUAGE OF DANCE": Modern dance choreographer José Limón explains the language of dance, showing how emotions are revealed through natural gestures, and how these gestures are transformed into dance movements. Featured is the television premiere of Limón's *There Is a Time*. The score, written especially for the dance, is Norman Dello Joio's *Meditations on Ecclesiastes*.

"GREAT PERFORMANCES IN DANCE": Walter Terry and Martha Myers discuss the relation between choreographer and performer. Matters of style and interpretation are illustrated by Alexandra Danilova and Frederic Franklin. After their performance of the waltz from *Le Beau Danube*, Edith Jerrell and Thomas Andrew do the same waltz to show how individual interpretations can alter the effect of the choreography. Rare film clips of Anna Pavlova, Irene and Vernon Castle, and Argentinita are included.

"MODERN BALLET": Anthony Tudor describes the changes in ballet by contrasting passages from classical and modern ballets, and shows how new conceptions of theme and characterization brought about innovations in the structures of dance works. Nora Kaye and Hugh Laing perform excerpts from *Undertow*, *Lilac Garden*, *Romeo and Juliet*, *Dim Lustre*, and *Pillar of Fire*.

"ETHNIC DANCE": Geoffrey Holder and Carmen de Lavallade explore the significance of ethnic dance in its native settings. They show how folk dances can be adapted for theatrical productions and illustrate their ideas with performances of West Indian dances. Included are excerpts from *Bele*, *Yanvaliou*, and *Banda*.

"DANCE: A REFLECTION OF OUR TIMES": Choreographer Herbert Ross considers the use of dance as social commentary. John Kriza and Ruth Ann Koesun, of American Ballet Theatre, are featured in a pas de deux from Ross's *Paen*. They are joined by a group to perform *Caprichos*, a savage attack on human foibles and cruelty, based on Goya's commentaries to his *Caprichos* etchings.

ARTS USA

By Jac Venza

ARTS USA: "THE ROBERT JOFFREY BALLET" (1965): Excerpts from five ballets in the repertory of this young American company, now the Joffrey Ballet Chicago. Robert Joffrey created a seven-minute condensation of a ballet class especially for this program. Works by Anna Sokolow and Gerald Arpino are also included.

ARTS USA: "ECHOES OF JAZZ" (1965): The development of jazz dancing from the traditional shuffle and sand dances through the "cool" performances of the 1960s. Grover Dale choreographed and performed a work to a 1950s composition by Ellington; Donald MacKayle used a blues work from New Orleans; John Butler worked to a 1960s Kenton score. The performers included Paula Kelly, Carmen de Lavallade, Mary Hinkson, Ross Parkes, and Dudley Williams

ARTS USA: "FOUR PIONEERS" (1965): America's major dance figures worked, taught and performed at the Bennington School of the Dance in the 1930s and 1940s. In photographs and films, and in contemporary performances of their work, Martha Graham, Doris Humphrey, Charles Weidman, and Hanya Holm evoke those years. Statements from each provide the commentary.

USA DANCE: "NEW YORK CITY BALLET" (1966): Four pas de deux from ballets choreographed by George Balanchine. The choreographer also introduces each of the works and discusses his working methods and basic beliefs about dance as a means of expression. Sequences are from *Meditation*, *Tarantella*, *Agon,* and the *Tschaikovsky Pas de Deux.* Jacques d'Amboise, Melissa Hayden, Arthur Mitchell, Patricia McBride, and Suzanne Farrell are the performers.

USA DANCE: "IN SEARCH OF LOVERS" (1966): This program traces the creation of a new dance work entitled *Lovers* from the moment choreographer Glen Tetley first meets with his performers until the completion of the work. The dancers are Carmen de Lavallade, Scott Douglas, Mary Hinkson, and Tetley. Music is by Ned Rorem.

USA DANCE: "ANNA SOKOLOW'S *ROOMS*": A selection of dances from Sokolow's work exploring themes of life, hope, death, love, and despair in contemporary city life. Created in 1954, it is one of the first serious dance works to use a jazz score. Kenyon Hopkins is the composer.

CHAPTER 7

Dance Program List of Alive TV, aka Alive from Off Center

Alyce Dissette

In 1984, the National Endowment for the Arts launched a major funding initiative targeted as the avant-garde's foray into public television's prime time, recognizing that individual programs made by artists gain only sporadic access unless they can be formatted into a series with a specific profile. The resulting series that took shape, *Alive From Off Center* broadcast from 1985–1996 on PBS, was about moving out of television studios and theaters and making the collaborative art of video and filmmaking available to a new generation of artistic voices. This national summer television series was made possible by the aggressive vision of several individuals: the NEA Film and Television Program Director, Brian O'Doherty, the NEA Dance Program Director, Nigel Redden; the PBS National Programming Staff at that time Suzanne Weil and Katherine Wyler; and ALIVE's first Executive Producer, Melinda Ward. The PBS base of operations selected by the NEA was KTCA/Minneapolis-St. Paul, working for the initial season in collaboration with the Walker Art Center.

Executive Producers: Melinda Ward (seasons 1–3), John Schott (seasons 4–6), Alyce Dissette (seasons 7–9), Neil Sieling (seasons 10–12)

Funders: AT&T Foundation, Corporation for Public Broadcasting, Ford Foundation, Jerome Foundation, John D. and Catherine T. MacArthur Foundation, National Endowment for the Arts, Northwest Area Foundation, Rockefeller Foundation

A production of ALIVE TV and Twin Cities Public Television (KTCA/St.Paul-Minneapolis)

SUMMARY OF DANCE PROGRAMS 1985–1996

Season 1, 1985

Season 1 only: a production of KTCA/St. Paul-Minneapolis and the Walker Art Center
Host: Susan Stamberg
Short Video Artworks
Ringside, by Michael Schwartz, dancer Elizabeth Streb
Sharkey's Day, by Laurie Anderson
Sankai Juku, Japanese Butoh dance group
Video Dance
Maasai: Pages from the Book of Rain, by Gary Hurst
Parafango, by video artist Charles Atlas, choreographed by Karole Armitage and composer David Linton

Summer Dances
Window Dance (from *George's House,* choreographed by Dan Wagoner)
Coney Island, an excerpt from *From an Island Summer* by Karole Armitage and Charles Atlas, directed by David Atwood
Dance in Front of the Church (from *Secret of the Waterfall* by Douglas Dunn and Charles Atlas)
City Hall Plaza (from *District One* by Rudy Perez)
Street Dances (from *You Little Wild Heart* by Marta Renzi)

Season 2, 1986

Host: Susan Stamberg
Animation, Dance and Comedy
Luminare by John Sanborn and Dean Winkler
Jump by Charles Atlas with choreography by Philippe Decouflé and music by the Residents
These Are the Rules by Doug Hall
The Sounds of Defiance by Teddy Dibble
Fire, Light, Sticks/Rotary Action
Fire, Light, Sticks by Michael Moschen, directed by Skip Blumberg, music by David Van Tieghem, produced in association with the Brooklyn Academy of Music
Rotary Action by choreographers Bill T. Jones and Arnie Zane, directed by Geoff Dunlop
Video Theater and Dance
Visual Shuffle
Fractured Variations, directed by John Sanborn and Mary Perillo, music by Bill Buchen and Scott Johnson, choreographed by Charles Moulton
Rude Raid, produced for French Television, directed by Mark Caro, choreographed by Régine Chopinot
Three Choreographers
Accumulation with Talking plus Water Motor, directed by Jonathan Demme, choreographed by Trisha Brown
Nine-Person Precision Ball Passing, directed by Skip Blumberg, choreographed by Charles Moulton
Caught, directed by Roberto Romano, choreographed by David Parsons, music by Robert Fripp
Choreography by David Gordon
Dorothy and Eileen, directed by Ed Steinberg
Close-up, directed by Steinberg, features Gordon and Valda Setterfield
Panel, played by Gordon himself

Season 3, 1987

Host: Laurie Anderson
As Seen on TV
Bill Irwin as actor, dancer and clown, directed by Charles Atlas, choreography by William Whitener and Diane Martel
Metabolism/Geography
By Molissa Fenley and video artists John Sanborn and Mary Perillo
Metabolism, music by David Van Tieghem
Geography, soundtrack by James Newton

Five Dances on Video
Airdance and *Landings,* by Elizabeth Streb
Hail the New Puritan, Michael Clark and company, directed by Charles Atlas
Daytime Moon, choreographed by Min Tanaka, directed by Sandy Smolan, soundtrack by Libby Larson
Ellis Island
By Meredith Monk and Bob Rosen
Calabash/Sticks/Aquamirabilis
Women of the Calabash, directed by Skip Blumberg
Aquamirabilis, choreographed by Dee McCandless, music by Gene Menger

Season 4, 1988

Hosts: Ann Magnuson, William Wegman

Alter Image

Love Me Gangster, written by Malcolm Bennett and Aidan Hughes

Rory McLeod

Dustbin Dance, music by Pookie Snackenberger, choreographed by Micha Bergese

Laurie Booth in Camera

The Shivering Man, by Angela Conway and Michael Clark

Men Die Sooner/Endance

Men Die Sooner by Tom Cayler, directed by Niles Siegel

Endance, choreographed by Timothy Buckley, directed by John Sanborn, music by "Blue" Gene Tyranny

The World Within Us/Commitment

The World Within Us, by Terry Flaxton, narrated by Jonathan Pryce, starring Llewellyn Rees

Commitment: Two Portraits, by Blondell Cummings

Nun, an excerpt from the stage performance *The Art of War,* a collaboration between Cummings and writer Jessica Hagedorn

The Kitchen Presents

Three experimental videos coproduced by The Kitchen, Ex Nihilo and *Alive from Off Center*:

Godard, by French director Robert Cahen and the American composer John Zorn

The Fourth Dimension, by Zbigniew Rybczynski

Sotto Voce, by French director Jean-Louis Le Tacon and New York choreographer/dancer Stephen Petronio

Two Dance Companies from Canada

Jericho, performed by Montreal Danse, choreographed by Daniel Levelle

Tell, by Montreal Danse, choreographed by Paul-Andre Fortier

Human Sex Duo No. 1 choreographed by Edouard Lock

Exhibition, directed by Bernar Hebert, choreographed by Daniele Desnoyers

Dancing Hands

Finger Tapping, by Harold Nicholas

Ballet Hand Isolations, by Robert LaFosse

Joe and Blanche, by Blondell Cummings and Keith Terry

Hip Hop Hands, by Steve "Wiggles" Clemente and Gilbert "Shalimar" Kennedy

Cassie's Dream, an interpretation by Wendy Perron of a text by Sophie Healy

X-Ray, by Wendy Perron and Lisa Bush

Prevailing Conditions (Handshake Sequence), by Ellen Fisher

Between Two Hands, by Sally Hess

Body Music for Hands, by Keith Terry

Season 5, 1989

Dance/Video Collaborations

Untitled, directed by John Sanborn and Mary Perillo

Arms, directed by Isabelle Hayeur for Agent Orange, featuring choreographer Susan Marshall and dancer Arthur Armijo

Relatives, directed by Julie Dash, choreographed by Ishmael Houston-Jones

Codex

Codex, directed and choreographed by Philippe Decouflé

Mountain View

Mountain View, directed by John Sayles and choreographed by Marta Renzi. Principal cast Jane Alexander, Jace Alexander, Marta Renzi & Dancers

Multicultural Dance

Shaman's Journey, by Raoul Trujillo, directed by Susan Rynard for Agent Orange

DanceBrazil, led by Jelon Vieira, directed by Bernar Hebert, produced by Agent Orange

Undertow, directed by James Byrne, featuring dancers Eiko and Koma, music by Ushio Torikai

Book of Days DVD 10

Book of Days, by director, composer, and choreographer Meredith Monk, co-production by Ken Stutz Company and The House Foundation

From San Francisco: Dancing on the Edge

Shorebirds Atlantic, by Rinde Eckert and Margaret Jenkins

29 Effeminate Gestures, by Joe Goode

The Black Dress, by Ellen Bromberg

Season 6, 1990

The Lyon Opera Ballet's *Cinderella*

Cendrillon (Cinderella), by Maguy Marin, performed by the Lyon Opera Ballet, music by Sergei Prokofiev, directed by Mans Reutersward

Kumu Hula: Keepers of a Culture

Kumu Hula: Keepers of a Culture, by Robert Mugge and Victoria Holt Takamine

House of Tres/It Doesn't Wait

House of Tres, directed by Diane Martel and Jeff Preiss

It Doesn't Wait, choreographed by Doug Elkins and directed by Mark Obenhaus

Dance of Darkness

Dance of Darkness, by Edin and Ethel Velez

The Myth of Modern Dance

By Douglas Dunn, directed by Charles Atlas

Video Dance

Mass, choreographed by Elizabeth Streb and video artist Mary Lucier, music by Earl Howard

La Chambre, by French Company L'Esquisse, choreographed by Joelle Bouvier and Régis Obadia

Tango Tango, choreographed by Lila Greene and directed by Francois Girard

---

Season 7, 1991

Praise House

Praise House, by the performing ensemble Urban Bush Women, directed by Julie Dash

Dinizulu & Contenders

Dinizulu, by Dinizulu and His African Dancers, Drummers and Singers. produced, directed and edited by Skip Blumberg

Contenders, by choreographer Susan Marshall, directed by Mark Obenhaus, music by Pauline Oliveros

Roseland

The Weight of a Hand, The Bearers of Bad News, and *What the Body Does Not Remember,* by Wim Vandekeybus

Dances In Exile & Loose The Thread

Dances In Exile, by Ruby Shang, directed by Howard Silver, texts by David Henry Hwang, narrated by B. D. Wong

Loose the Thread, choreographed by Brenda Way for ODC/San Francisco, produced by Wendy Blair Slick and San Francisco's KQED-TV

The Dormitory (Le Dortoir) DVD 28

The Dormitory (*Le Dortoir*), directed by François Girard, choreographed by Gilles Maheu, and performed by the Montreal-based dance theater group Carbon 14 (Carbon Quatorze)

Used Alive 1985–1989

Used Alive 1985–1989 is a special compilation drawn from past *Alive* programs and assembled as a collage of art and life in the 1980s. Includes Laurie Anderson, Eric Bogosian, Spalding Gray, Meredith Monk, David Gordon, William Wegman, Ann Magnuson, Peter Fischli, David Weiss, Bill T. Jones, Blondell Cummings, Tom Cayler, and Micha Bergese.

Season 8, 1992

Punch & Judy Get Divorced

Featuring music from the now-classic Warner Brothers cartoons by Carl Stalling, scored by Greg Ford and Hal Willner, written and staged by David Gordon, directed by Mark Pellington and David Gordon

MTV: The Reagan Years

An *Alive TV* co-production with MTV music television, directed by Pam Thomas in collaboration with MTV and *Alive*

American Flash Cards

Thanksgiving Prayer, by writer William S. Burroughs and filmmaker Gus Van Sant

Gotham, a montage of footage from new and vintage Hollywood B-movies, music by John Zorn, filmed by Henry Hills

Pull Your Head to the Moon, by David Rousseve and Ayoka Chenzira (See chapter 44)

Too Darn Hot, directed by Adelle Lutz and Sandy McLeod

Sharp Rocks, by visual artist Hachivi Edgar Heap of Birds

Reckin' Shop: Live From Brooklyn

Directed by Diane Martel

Not-For-Saturday-Morning Animations

Creature Comforts, directed by Nick Park

Wake Up Call, directed and choreographed by Pooh Kaye

Photocopy Cha Cha, directed by Chel White

Balance, by Christoff and Wolfgang Lauenstein

Picnic, by animator Paul Vester

Season 11, 1995

Touched/Red Book

Touched, directed by David Hinton DVD **22**

Red Book, by Janie Geiser

Season 12, 1996

Still/Here, Written and choreographed by Bill T. Jones

Part II
Looking Back

CHAPTER 8

From Méliès to Streaming Video: A Century of Moving Dance Images

Virginia Brooks

DVD 5
Intolerance (1916) 177 min
Excerpt 1 min 48 sec

DVD 6
Air for the G String (1934)
6 min
Excerpt 2 min 35 sec

People have always danced, and static representations of movement abound, from the earliest cave drawings to Edgar Degas's paintings of racehorses. The desire to reproduce experiences of actual movement gave rise to Chinese mirrors, zoetropes, praxinoscopes,[1] mechanical slides in magic lanterns, Eadweard Muybridge's series of still camera shots of a horse in motion (made to settle a gentleman's bet about whether a horse ever had all four feet off the ground at one time), and finally, in the late 1800s, the early experiments with motion picture cameras.[2] After a century of cinema, that simple movement captured on celluloid has evolved into fantastic manipulation of digital data, producing a new reality limited only by a director's imagination and needs. The first audiences, engaged by the simple production values of film fragments, could hardly have conceived of our present-day motion pictures, videotapes, digital videodiscs, broadcast television, and computer displays.

What were those early moving pictures like? The Lumière brothers recorded single events happening in front of a stationary camera—workers leaving their factory, a baby eating breakfast, a train coming into the station (and frightening female viewers as the realistic engine, belching smoke, approached them). And there were films of dance, successful in recording the movement because the camera did only its basic job. It was fixed in one place, just like a member of the audience, while the dancer performed in the small area prescribed by the stationary camera and its single focal-length lens. The experience of the dance—life-sized human bodies, performing simple choreography just once—changed into a small, flat duplicate of the event, whose light patterns might be projected for viewing anywhere, anytime. In this manner, Thomas Edison recorded Miss Jesse Cameron, child champion sword dancer, and made films of Anabelle in her serpentine dance, and of Princess Rajah, dancing while balancing a chair in her teeth. In 1894, Edison recorded two minutes of Ruth Dennis performing a skirt dance. Lit only by the sun, the film showed her doing high kicks, outdoors at the side of a building. Once again, only the dancer moved: the camera, and therefore the background, were still.

A review of the first exhibition—on April 23, 1896—of Edison's projecting version of a Kinetoscope called the Vitascope[3] mentions "the Leigh sisters in their umbrella dance. The effect was the same as if the girls were there on the stage; all of their smiles and kicks and bows were seen." Edison filmed very simple dances, almost mechanical and repetitious, suitable for the loop format of the nickelodeon, where, to the public's amazement, the picture moved and could be viewed over and over again.

In the early 1900s, court photographer Peter Elfeldt used a single fixed camera to film dancers from the Royal Danish Ballet performing the choreography of August Bournonville. The resulting images are satisfactory if rather self-conscious records, and they remain useful 100 years later.[4]

During the same period that Edison, Elfeldt, and Paul Theiman and F. Reinhardt (with the ballerina Yekaterina Geltzer in Moscow) were recording live performances, Georges Méliès and Emile Cohl in France were beginning to use film techniques to make inanimate objects dance and to animate still figures. They were creating choreography that existed only on the screen. (Méliès also used real dancers in his 1903 fantasy *The Magic Lantern*.) These filmmakers were the predecessors of such creative directors as Fernand Léger, Busby Berkeley, Maya Deren, Ed Emshwiller, Shirley Clarke, Norman McLaren, and Hillary Harris, who recorded movement of many sorts to realize their extraordinary filmic visions.

By 1909, Ruth Dennis had left the family farm in New Jersey and had transformed herself into Miss Ruth St. Denis, a concert dancer well-known and well-produced in Europe and then in the United States. With her husband, Ted Shawn, she established the Denishawn School of Dance in California in 1915; D. W. Griffith used dancers from this school in the Babylonian segment of his film *Intolerance* (1916). Griffith used a new technique in this film, mounting a camera on an elevator, which in turn rode on a railroad car. One shot opened on a small central group of dancers and then slowly moved up and back to reveal the entire enormous and fabulous multilevel set: stairs covered with dancers and extras by the hundreds. That camera movement also changed the aesthetic quality and the kinetic impact of the dance movement. **DVD 5**

Such techniques, newly invented and available to filmmakers, began to dominate. Elizabeth Kendall describes the relationship as it evolved during that period:

> Both film and dance in America were built on their creators' deep sense of rhythmic continuity . . . movies evolved a modern, fluid, movement-conscious, and peculiarly American language. It included dancing. Dance scenes could control rhythm and pace and allude to emblematic modern states of mind . . . The usefulness of dance in silent movies guaranteed it a place in the nation's consciousness but took away its identity. Movies made dance a presence, a mood, instead of a choreographic art with rules . . . movie directors with a brilliant feel for motion . . . used dance to their own ends.[5]

Hollywood dancers performed uncredited choreography. It was important that fragments of dance, surviving the final cut, add to the overall production values, but the choreography was not important in its own right. Directors chose elements of the movement to create dance as they envisioned it to be appropriate for the screen.

The introduction of sound film in the late 1920s enabled filmed dance to be synchronized with music, restoring that vital component. At first, the innovation of sound recording restrained the mobility of the camera, and when dance sequences were shot, the camera reverted to the stationary perspective it had in the earliest days of film. An early sound-for-film experiment resulted in the simple but sublime record of Doris Humphrey's *Air for the G String* in 1934. **DVD 6**

As sound film technique became more refined, the effect of camera and editing activities on choreographic form became more evident.

The speed with which the technical complexity of filming evolved, and the subsequent economic pressures of labor and materials imposed on filmmakers, undercut the experimentation that might have resulted in an orderly development of the craft of filming dance. For the most part, the conventions already established for narrative filming prevailed, and the art of choreography, with its very different requirements, was not considered. Dance itself rarely surfaced as subject matter for feature-length films. It might serve as an interlude, more or less directly related to the plot and choreographed for the camera. Such interludes seldom bore any resemblance to works originally meant for proscenium presentation. Sometimes, as in the camera-created extravaganzas of Busby Berkeley, they would be impossible to reproduce on the stage. Often the effect of the proscenium stage was simulated for the beginning of a dance number in an effort to integrate it into the plot as a whole, and then the dance would continue in film space with no break in continuity.

On the other hand, ballet performances occasionally were merely inserted into narrative films. The plot came to a halt in *Florian*[6] while Irina Baranova danced material from *Coppélia*. In *I Was an Adventuress*,[7] the story was already over when Vera Zorina performed excerpts from *Swan Lake*, reconceived for the screen by George Balanchine.

The first full-length feature film with ballet as its subject was *La Mort du cygne* (directed by J. Benoit-Levy, 1938) with Yvette Chauvivré and Mia Slavenska. Ten years later came *The Red Shoes* (directed by M. Powell and E. Pressburger, 1948), with Moira Shearer, Robert Helpmann, and Léonide Massine. Both films intercut dance sequences with shots of the audience or of other actors (except during the title ballet of the latter film) in order to continue the action of the plot. Very successful at the box office, these were films *about* dance, not films *of* dance. The way they juxtapose performance shots and reaction shots does not correspond to the actual viewing of live performance in a theater. Members of a dance theater audience may look away from the stage if distracted, if the choreography is uninteresting, or if the dancing is second-rate, but their intention upon entering the theater is usually to watch the show. The movie theater audience kept their eyes on the screen to follow a story taking place in film time, not a performance taking place in real time.

Would a film audience stay attentive to a dance performance in real time? Writing in *Dancing Times* in 1927, just before sound was common and perfectly synchronized with the film, British dance critic Edwin Evans commented that dance on the screen in real time was too slow for the new film audience. He thought that film had its own demands and aesthetics based on rapidity of action:

> Someday perhaps we may have an audience capable of feasting its eyes upon beauty, beautiful movement, beautiful grouping, beautiful scenery . . . The audience will have to learn to appreciate beauty of movement before it will be prepared to dispense with its anecdotal pretext . . . the first screen ballets will be story ballets . . . crowded with incident as no ballet has ever been . . . when we have got thus far . . . the producers will begin to strive after something better which on the screen has proved so elusive. Even then, I do not think they will ever neutralize that element of rapid action. They will compromise with it. They will continue to make concessions to it whilst profiting by such sense of beauty as they may by then have succeeded in nursing to life. The way of the screen is compromise. But, of course, every transfer of an art to another medium demands compromise.[8]

Directors certainly did compromise, more and less successfully, from the musical comedies of Ernst Lubitsch, such as *Love Parade* and *The Merry Widow*, choreographed by Albertina Rasch in the late 1920s and early 1930s, through the big Hollywood musicals by directors Stanley Donen, Vincente Minnelli, and Rouben Mamoulian and dancer-choreographers Robert Alton, Eugene Loring, Michael Kidd, and Gene Kelly in the late 1940s and early 1950s.

Evans predicted correctly. For many years, dancing was subordinated to plot, even though the dance may have been the more interesting element. Frequently the dance on view was composed of visual fragments, such as parts of the body and close-ups of the costumes. There were, of course, instances in which dance was successfully included in feature-length films, used to advance plots and develop characters. *Singin' in the Rain* (1952), directed by Gene Kelly and Stanley Donen,[9] *Seven Brides for Seven Brothers* (1954), directed by Stanley Donen and choreographed by Michael Kidd, *Oklahoma!* (1955), directed by Fred Zinneman and choreographed by Agnes de Mille, and *West Side Story* (1961), directed by Jerome Robbins and Robert Wise all contain examples of special imagination in staging the dance sequences and integrating them into the pictures as components of equal importance with other elements of the production.

The most consistently successful efforts by far at faithfully presenting choreography were those of Fred Astaire. Working with many different directors and several choreographers, after his third film he assumed control over the recording of his dances. He insisted on relatively long takes that included the full figures of the dancers, interspersing edits (cuts) with camera movements as transitions to reduce the amount of visual disruption, providing film technique nearly as seamless as his dancing.[10] The cinematic rhythm introduced by camera movement and by editing[11] complemented the inherent rhythm of Astaire's choreography and performance.

Full-length ballet films and television programs began to appear in the 1950s and 1960s. *Giselle,* performed by members of Ballet Theatre (now American Ballet Theatre) and televised on NBC in 1950, is preserved on kinescope, documenting not only the performances of Nora Kaye and Igor Youskevitch but also the inadequacy of their performing space, dominated at center bottom by a prompt box. Feature-length films of complete ballets—including *The Sleeping Beauty, Romeo and Juliet, Cinderella,* and *Swan Lake*—were produced in Great Britain and the Soviet Union; in 1966, Balanchine's *Midsummer Night's Dream,* filmed in wide-screen aspect ratio, was the first American entry into feature-length ballet film presentation. The Hollywood musicals evolved with the change in musical tastes, and George Sidney's *Viva Las Vegas* (1964) was very successful at the box office, with Elvis Presley and an editing rhythm driven by the beat of rock and roll.

Notable short films from this period include Peter Glushanok's *Dancer's World* (1957) and *Appalachian Spring* (1959) and Alexander Hammid's *Night Journey* (1961), all with Martha Graham. Two exceptional films in the experimental genre were *Nine Variations on a Dance Theme* (1967), directed by Hilary DVD 2
Harris with the dancer Bettie de Jong, and Norman McLaren's tour de force of optical printing, *Pas de deux* (1968). DVD 26

In her 1965 *Dance Magazine* article and later in a report for the National Endowment for the Arts, Allegra Fuller Snyder classified films of dance into three groups: simple recordings of choreography; documentary films of performance; and "choreocinema," a term coined by John Martin, in which the choreographer and the cinematographer join efforts to produce a new artistic entity.[12]

Record notation films are at one end of the continuum. Produced with simple methods of filming, these motion pictures may be used for movement analysis in industry or medicine, for anthropological study of dance as ritual, or as records to supplement written notation for restaging and study purposes. Although these films may not be visually interesting in their own right, they are valuable tools, for they permit careful analysis and preserve one of the means by which a work may be reconstructed or restaged with accuracy.

At the other end of the continuum are the creative interactions between film technique and dance: cinedance, choreocinema, or videodance. The purpose here is to allow filmmakers or video artists to express themselves in films or tapes that use dance as raw material. These films may emphasize pure abstract moving patterns on the screen; they may show movements, combinations, and relationships that could not be seen in the real world; or they may present the dance as the filmmaker (who may also be the choreographer) creates it. They are, in fact, works of a primarily filmic nature.

Between these endpoints lie the documentary films, or translation films, which attempt to preserve the feeling of the performance. The purpose of these films is to present the dance as it was choreographed for live performance, maintaining and enhancing as far as possible the values intended by the choreographer, as expressed by the dancers, and as experienced by the audience in the theater. The choreographer's art and the dancers' performance are being portrayed and presented. The dance is on the screen instead of on the stage.

Allegra Fuller Snyder proposed that the documentary type of film was the most significant, since it was interesting to the general public and conveyed, as it should, the live performance values. She also pointed out that the documentary film could be used for restaging, whereas the notation or record film was rarely suitable for viewing by the general public. Helen Tamiris[13] suggested that, in fact, both kinds of film were equally important material to study—not just for reviving work, but for scholarship as well. Films of notation (and written notation systems, now incorporating computer-generated dance figures) are necessary to remount the actual steps of a dance—*necessary, but not sufficient.* If the restagers and the audiences of tomorrow are to be provided with the full essence of what the dance was and the full measure of the choreographic intention, that essence could be conveyed best in a documentary, or translation film.

The rules for making record films are defined by the need to see, as clearly as possible, all the steps, and all the dancers, all the entrances and exits, and to hear how the music or other sound interacts with the choreography. Such rules may be enumerated readily.

By contrast, there are no rules for choreocinema or videodance, other than those that govern film and video technique. The choreographer may play the dominant role if the the work is to be choreographed for the camera; the filmmaker will make the final choices if the dance is to be constructed through film techniques. These are aesthetic decisions, not subject to preconceived rules of right or wrong.

The ideals for documenting performance, however, are much more complex and depend on the interaction of many variables. As Snyder noted in 1965, most filmmakers do not consider documenting performance a job for film people; they would prefer to work on more creative cinedance. Most choreographers would prefer to work on the dances themselves and find it difficult to make the time and raise the additional money to make documentaries. A very small community of film and video directors, many of them with previous training in dance themselves or with experience in making record films, has worked on specific techniques for filming performance as a translation, although there has been a proliferation of video archiving of dance across the world.

And why does it matter, this difficult—some would say impossible—translation task? It became important to me when there were no live performances available where I lived. I yearned for some film, or even tiny, black-and-white 1950s television, substitute! Indeed, there are many people who cannot attend live performances of dance, and they deserve a chance to see performances on a screen that truly convey what the dances look and feel like in the theater.

In the 1970s and 1980s, several important factors emerged to propel forward the development of dance films choreographed for the proscenium and made for the camera. There was an enormous increase in public interest in dance and dancers, and a corresponding increase in government and corporate funding to support the endeavor. Feature films presented dance both in fiction—*The Turning Point, Hair, Flashdance,* and *Dirty Dancing*[14]—and in documentaries about companies and dancers, including *ABT—A Closeup in Time, I Am a Dancer* (Nureyev), and *Alicia Alonso.*[15] Interesting short format films such as *Westbeth, In a Rehearsal Room,* and *Dune Dance*[16] appeared. In 1983, Emile Ardolino's film about Jacques d'Amboise, *He Makes Me Feel Like Dancin',* won both an Emmy and an Academy Award.

At the same time, the insatiable appetite of the small screen (and producers' recognition of the dance boom) resulted in regular series of television programs devoted to dance companies and their repertories. In 1976, the extraordinary *Dance in America* was born, a series made with collaboration between the choreographers, the directors and knowledgeable producers (see chapters 1, 6, and 37).

Dance choreographed for the camera became regular television fare as producers of popular music realized the benefits of a moving visual accompaniment to promote their songs. In 1981, music videos, often made by directors skilled in producing effective advertising commercials, began to feed 24-hour television channels. The music was the driving force but the collaboration meant that dance on the small screen was watched by an enthusiastic new audience.

Videotape recorders now made it possible to view all the films that had been languishing undistributed and even created a market for new films and video programs. Huge new video stores and catalogs for rental and sale from distributors added big sections devoted to dance programs.

There were still problems, however. At a trivial but frustrating level, different video formats made it difficult to see tapes from other countries. More important (and a continuing difficulty) was the fact that many of the principles needed to achieve good translations from stage to screen were often violated.[17]

Tight money and a scarcity of good new material caused a plateau in the 1990s. The number of programs being made worldwide continued to increase, but the percentage of the increase was not as great as in the previous two decades. There were some bright spots: Elliot Caplan scored with two award-winning films, *Cage/Cunningham* (1991), a documentary about this enduring partnership, and *Beach Birds for Camera* (1992), a remarkable translation of the Cunningham stage work. Matthew Diamond began a very auspicious collaboration with Paul Taylor, resulting in two programs for *Dance in America, Speaking in Tongues* and *The Wrecker's Ball,* as well as the feature-length documentary film *Dancemaker,* which had a successful theatrical release (see chapter 35). Carlos **DVD 33**
Saura followed his 1980s trilogy made with Antonio Gades with three more flamenco films in the 1990s.[18]

There were more festivals promoting dance on the screen.[19] There has also been foundation funding for efforts to preserve dance and to support programs to explore methods of documentation.[20]

As we enter the second century in the history of moving images, we must continue to explore means to film dance in a way that makes it accessible for the enormous audience that could be engaged. People are waiting in their homes all over the world, in front of television sets receiving high-definition broadcasts live from satellites, in front of flat home entertainment screens hooked up to digital video players, and even in front of their computer screens calling up streaming video—all with the freedom of choice to watch whatever they find pleasing. If dance is to continue in its many forms, both in live performance and on these many screens, we have a responsibility to produce programs that this vast congregation will value because both the performances and their presentations are worth seeing.

NOTES

1. Olive Cook, *Movement in Two Dimensions* (London: Hutchinson, 1963), 13–14, 127–129.

2. George C. Pratt, *Spellbound in Darkness* (Greenwich, Connecticut: New York Graphics Society, 1973), 1–54; hereafter cited as Pratt.

3. *New York Dramatic Mirror*, vol. 35, no. 905 (May 2, 1896) 19 (as cited in Pratt, 16).

4. These films can be seen at the Dance Division of the New York Public Library and Museum of the Performing Arts, Lincoln Center.

5. Elizabeth Kendall, *Where She Danced* (Berkeley and Los Angeles: University of California Press, 1984), 134–136; first publication (New York: Alfred A. Knopf, 1979).

6. Directed by E. Marin, 1940; choreographed by Ernest and Maria Matray.

7. Directed by G. Ratoff, 1940.

8. Edwin Evans, "Screen-ballet," *Dancing Times* (December 1927) 330, 332.

9. See Beth Genné's article in this volume.

10. Arlene Croce, *The Fred Astaire and Ginger Rogers Book* (New York: Outerbridge and Lazard, 1972); John Mueller, *Astaire Dancing: The Musical Films* (New York: Alfred A. Knopf, 1985).

11. The affective tone, or momentum almost regardless of the subject matter; see Raymond Spottiswoode, *A Grammar of Film* (Berkeley: University of California Press, 1962); Julian Hochberg and Virginia Brooks, *The Perception of Motion Pictures in Cognitive Ecology*, 2nd ed., M. P. Friedman and E. C. Carterette, eds. (San Diego, CA: Academic Press, 1996). This chapter is revised and rewritten from the first edition of *The Handbook of Perception*, 1978, 205–292.

12. Allegra Fuller Snyder, "Three Kinds of Dance Films: A Welcome Clarification," *Dance Magazine*, vol. 39, September 1965, pp. 34–39; "The Relationship of Film to Dance: A Report and Analysis of Problems, Needs, Possibilities and Potentials in this Area" (unpublished report for NEA Dance Program Office, Washington, D.C., March–June 1968).

13. Helen Tamiris, "Film and/or notation," *Dance Observer*, October 1959, 117–118.

14. *The Turning Point* (1977) directed by Herbert Ross; *Hair* (1979) directed by Milos Forman; *Flashdance* (1983) directed by Adrian Lyne; *Dirty Dancing* (1987) directed by Emile Ardolino.

15. *American Ballet Theatre—A Closeup in Time* (1973) directed by Jerome Schnur; *I Am a Dancer* (1973) directed by Pierre Jourdan; *Alicia Alonso* (1976) directed by Victor Casaus.

16. *Westbeth* (1975) directed by Charles Atlas with Merce Cunningham; *In a Rehearsal Room* (1975) directed by David Hahn, choreography by William Carter; *Dune Dance* (1980) directed by Carolyn Brown.

17. For some discussion of conditions for translation see Virginia Brooks, "Why Dance Films Do Not Look Right," *Studies in Visual Communication*, vol. 10, no. 2 (Spring 1984), 44–67; "Apollo in Translation," *New Dance Review* (January–March 1991), 7–10.

18. Carlos Saura with Antonio Gades: *Blood Wedding* (1981); *Carmen* (1984); *El Amor Brujo* (1986); *Ay, Carmela* (1990) with Alberto Portillo; and two documentaries, *Sevillanas* (1991) and *Flamenco* (1994).

19. The longest continuously running festival devoted to dance programs, "Dance on Camera," produced by Dance Films Association, Inc. New York City, since 1971, has been joined by "Dance Screen," IMZ, Vienna,; "Berner Tanztage," Bern, Switzerland; "Dance on Screen, The Place," London; "Dancing for Camera Festival," American Dance Festival, Durham, NC; "Festival International de Video Danza de Buenos Aires," Argentina; "Il choreografo elettronico Napolidanza," Naples, Italy; "Mostra Video Dansa," Barcelona, Spain; "Moving Pictures Festival," Toronto, Ontario, Canada; "Springdance Cinema," Utrecht, The Netherlands; and "Grand Prix Carina Ari," Paris, among others!

20. The Pew Charitable Trusts funded NIPAD (the National Initiative to Preserve America's Dance) in 1993, followed in 1997 by funding for a new partnership, SAVE AS: DANCE , which added the UCLA National Dance/ Media Project to the NIPAD efforts.

CHAPTER 9

Ted Shawn's Moving Images

Norton Owen

The ephemeral nature of dance has been a challenge to its creators for centuries, and so it is not surprising that preservation would have been a concern as modern dance began to develop in the early 1900s. The pioneering dancer-choreographer Ted Shawn (1891–1972) was as aware as anyone that his creative efforts were totally dependent upon the live bodies that executed his choreography. His frustration at losing his painstakingly trained men dancers in the 1930s is evident in this letter to a friend: "It is as if you had painted a picture and the blue or the crimson had decided to walk off and go somewhere else."[1]

DVD 7
Kinetic Molpai 1935, 22 min
Excerpt 2 min 4 sec

Production note: "Shot on silent film using a hand-cranked camera, *Kinetic Molpai* was transferred to video 50 years later, at which time some speed corrections were made and a new soundtrack was added."—N.O.

One of Shawn's strategies to stabilize his choreographic "colors" was to fix his dances on film, an undertaking that had its roots in his very earliest dance experiences. When Shawn was only 21 years old and working as a stenographer in the Los Angeles Water Department while teaching dance by night, he submitted a number of motion picture scenarios to the local movie studios. The Thomas A. Edison Company accepted one of his ideas, and the result was *Dances of the Ages* (1913), a silent film featuring Shawn and his partner, Norma Gould. Walter Terry described the film:

> In a handful of brief scenes Ted and Norma ranged from primitive man through classical Greek and courtly French to the current ballroom hits. Their students served as a corps. By today's standards it is pretty silly, but it was a film landmark in its day. Movie producers were not interested in dancing per se, but dance movements provided the camera with special challenges. In *Dances of the Ages*, for example, bearded and learned ballet masters were gathered along the sides of a huge refectory table and, as they deplored the dances of the day, history unrolled before them while dancers, in miniature, performed on the table top.[2]

After Shawn teamed up with Ruth St. Denis the following year and formed Denishawn, there were more opportunities to collaborate with the nascent film industry. Shawn appeared on screen as a faun with Gloria Swanson in a Cecil B. De Mille picture entitled *Don't Change Your Husband* (1919), and Denishawn dancers were part of the spectacular Babylonian scene in D. W. Griffith's *Intolerance* (1916). In addition, many screen stars of the day studied at Denishawn, including Lillian and Dorothy Gish, Mabel Normand, Myrna Loy, and notably, Louise Brooks, who had begun her career in the Denishawn

DVD 5

Ted Shawn (right) overseeing a film session with his company of men dancers at Jacob's Pillow, Calif., 1935. Photographer unknown.

Company. In 1924, several Denishawn works were filmed in Santa Barbara, California, including Shawn in *The Death of Adonis*, Doris Humphrey in *Valse Caprice*, and the full Denishawn Company in *Cuadro Flamenco*. Other Shawn dances were filmed in exotic locations during the company's 1925–26 tour of the Orient, including *Cosmic Dance of Siva* at a Mahabalipuram temple in India and *Choeur Dansé* in Singapore.

There is an intriguing reference to a 1922 Shawn film experiment in *Musical America*, although the film (or films) may be lost. Talkies were still a thing of the future at that time, which helps explain the momentous nature of the article's opening sentence: "The prediction . . . that films would ultimately be set to music, instead of music to the films, has already been fulfilled."[3] The article goes on to describe a new series of films at the Rivoli, Rialto and Criterion theaters in New York. Known as "music-films" and directed by J. F. Leventhal, these color films were choreographed by Shawn. Leventhal is quoted with the following description of the format: "The music-films have been prepared in such a way that the film sets its own artistic interpretation. The conductor, Mr. [Louis] Horst, is seen on the screen conducting the dance. The conductor in the theater orchestra follows the baton on the screen, and thus synchronizes picture and orchestra."[4] The only film mentioned by name, *Burmese Dance*, doesn't appear in any known film list, and other titles in the series are not specified. The featured dancers reportedly included Martha Graham and Charles Weidman.

After the breakup of Denishawn in the early 1930s, Shawn began documenting the activities of his revolutionary new all-male company at Jacob's Pillow. This included an ambitious plan to preserve the entire repertory of Ted Shawn's Men Dancers on film. Using a hand-cranked camera, he recorded more than 60 dances during the 1930s on 16mm black-and-white silent film. A 1938 program insert publicizes this effort:

> Friends have repeatedly asked us if we have recorded our dances on moving picture film. We are equipped now with a moving picture camera which takes 16mm film, and with electric light in the studio, using super-sensitive film, we can make very creditable records of our dances. The accidents of previous years, and the other possibilities that are ever present which might suddenly terminate the work of the group, have forcibly reminded us that if the group stops dancing the dances themselves are lost. There is much talk these days of a Museum of the Dance, and the founding of a library of films of great dancers. If and when such an organization is formed, a complete record of the dances of Shawn and His Men Dancers would be a valuable contribution to the literature of the dance.

Ted Shawn in a pose from his *Death of Adonis* as it was recorded on silent film in Santa Barbara, California, in 1924. Photographer unknown.

DVD 7

The flier goes on to suggest that a $5 contribution would make it possible to film one short dance, while $25 would support "a whole ballet."

All of the films Shawn made during the 1930s may still be seen today in their original format. Films of the most prominent works, including *Kinetic Molpai*, *Olympiad*, and *Labor Symphony*, were transferred to videotape during the 1980s and synchronized with new soundtracks recorded by Shawn's composer-pianist, Jess Meeker. These restorations were made possible by several grants from the now-discontinued Dance/Film/Video Program of the National Endowment for the Arts, and are available for viewing at Jacob's Pillow, the Library of Congress, and the New York Public Library Dance Collection.

The existence of so much film material of Shawn's activities is a testament to his strong feelings about recording dance on film, expressed in a 1938 lecture at Peabody College:

> It has always been a vital necessity that the finest and best in the dance should be preserved for future students and audiences but, until very lately, the only thing that could be preserved were relics and photographs. But now we have the colored sound-film and, for the first time in the world's history, we have a medium by which we can preserve the greatest technical and choreographic achievements of the greatest artists in the dance. Experiments in this field have been conducted for some time through the medium of the sixteen-millimeter film but, though this has immediate practical use in teaching or as an aid to memory, the size of the film and the lack of sound accompaniment makes the system inadequate and apt to give a false impression to people who have not seen the dance in actual performance. At present, in fact, the small film is really little more than a system of dance notation.[5]

The fact that Shawn invested the time and money in making these films would seem to indicate his commitment to preservation, but he also exhibited a startlingly casual attitude at times toward these priceless materials. A 1953 letter from Shawn to "Brother" St. Denis (the only sibling of Ruth St. Denis) reveals that many of the most valuable Denishawn and Men Dancers films were misplaced for 13 years. "I became aware that these films, partly Orient films and partly Men's Group films, were still missing, but there was not any one moment where the issue became urgent," Shawn wrote. Records do not indicate exactly where or when the films turned up, though the titles in question are now safely shelved with the rest of Shawn's collection.

After Shawn's company was dissolved in 1940, he took on the role of impresario, a shift that was reflected in the Pillow's documentation efforts. In 1941, Dwight Godwin made a color film of Ruth St. Denis in *Radha*, revived at Jacob's Pillow some 35 years after the premiere that launched St. Denis's career. Godwin also filmed Alicia Markova outdoors in several solos that year. Dancer-educator Steffi Nossen made color films of various Pillow activities during the summers of 1941 and 1942, capturing such artists as Asadata Dafora, Anna Duncan, and La Argentinita. It was at this time that Shawn began encouraging the practice of filming at the Pillow during performances, rather than organizing special sessions in natural light.

Wartime shortages temporarily stalled the effort to record live performances, but in 1945 filming resumed in earnest. At this time, Shawn allowed Baltimore dance educator Carol Lynn to begin filming performances in the new Ted Shawn Theatre—at her own expense. Lynn was a former Denishawn student who had been involved with the Pillow since the mid-1930s, first supervising the women students and then becoming dean of the entire school. Among the dozens of companies and artists she captured with camera between 1945 and 1962 were the Royal Danish Ballet, Ballet Rambert, and National Ballet of Canada, all in their U.S. debuts; the rarely filmed Ram Gopal, Pearl Primus, and Carmelita Maracci; and the early companies of José Limón, Merce Cunningham, and Robert Joffrey.

The cooperative arrangement between Lynn and Shawn broke down in 1963, when she was offered $20,000 by the Lena Robbins Foundation for her

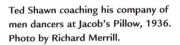

Ted Shawn coaching his company of men dancers at Jacob's Pillow, 1936. Photo by Richard Merrill.

entire collection of Jacob's Pillow films. Shawn was incensed by the offer, maintaining that the films were the joint property of Lynn and Jacob's Pillow, and he informed Lynn that he considered the proposed sale to be illegal. Lynn responded that she would gladly accept a much smaller payment from the Pillow, and a bargain was struck for $5,000. This included some 54,000 feet of film that was later copied in its entirety so that the New York Public Library Dance Collection and the Pillow could each have access to the films. Shawn made the official donation of this film archive to the New York Public Library in 1968 and stored the Pillow's copies in the new vault of the Lee National Bank. These copies have since been moved to the controlled environment of Blake's Barn on the Pillow grounds.

Fortunately, there is continuing interest in incorporating the Jacob's Pillow films in documentaries, using them for historic reconstructions and mining their riches in other ways. The George Balanchine Foundation and the New York Public Library Dance Collection have initiated efforts in recent years to transfer Carol Lynn's films of Balanchine ballets to videotape, synchronizing new soundtracks to the movement. The pas de deux from *Sylvia* and *The Firebird*, with Maria Tallchief and Michael Maule, and excerpts from *La Valse*, with Tanaquil LeClercq and Nicholas Magallanes, have now been successfully transferred by Ron Honsa and his company Moving Pictures, utilizing similar technology to that which he devised for adding sound to films of the Men Dancers.

At Jacob's Pillow, the 255 films made during Shawn's era are now supplemented by videotapes of virtually every program presented in the past 20 years. By maintaining the film archive that Shawn left behind, as well as continuing to document the Festival's ongoing activities, Jacob's Pillow is doing its part to achieve Shawn's dream to "organize and finance the recording and preserving of living great dancers and all dance film in existence."[6]

NOTES

1. Betty Poindexter. "Ted Shawn: His Personal Life, His Professional Career, and His Contributions to the Development of Dance in the United States of America from 1891 to 1963" (Ph.D. dissertation, Texas Woman's University, 1963), 271.

2. Walter Terry. *Ted Shawn, Father of American Dance* (New York: Dial, 1976), 18.

3. "Art of Interpretive Dance Brought to Audiences through Medium of Film," *Musical America* (July 22, 1922), 19.

4. "Art of Interpretive Dance Brought to Audiences through Medium of Film," *Musical America* (July 1922), 19.

5. Ted Shawn. *Dance We Must* (Pittsfield, Mass.: Eagle Printing & Binding, 1940), 142.

6. Ted Shawn. *Thirty-three Years of American Dance* (Pittsfield, Mass.: Eagle Printing & Binding, 1959), 33.

CHAPTER 10

Doris Humphrey's Air for the G String

Ernestine Stodelle

DVD 6
Air for the G String (1934)
6 min
Excerpt 2 min 35 sec

In 1934, without fanfare, an exquisitely choreographed quintet to Johann Sebastian Bach's "Air" from his *Third Orchestral Suite in D Major* was filmed at the Paramount Studios in Long Island City, New York. The choreographer of the work, an emerging modern dancer named Doris Humphrey, was then at the beginning of her career, and though *Air for the G String* had already been performed by her ensemble, Humphrey herself had not previously danced the leading role. At a later date, however, fate decreed otherwise. The unexpected departure from her group of Sylvia Manning, who had created the central role, made it necessary for Humphrey to take her place. As a result, the film has earned historical renown as the sole record of Doris Humphrey's personal appearance in a complete filming of one of her own works. Other existing films of Humphrey consist of excerpts of her dancing, with or without sound accompaniment.

Significantly adding to the quality of the film as a visual experience is its cathedral-like setting: Two massive columns evoke an impression of spiritual kinship between the smoothly flowing music and the worshipful radiance of the dancers, who appear to be participating in a ritual. Grouped together at the beginning, near the edge of the stage with their backs to the audience, their long golden scarves folded on the floor behind them, the dancers begin to move upstage, hands devoutly lifting as though in prayer. Four of the dancers wear magenta pink sheaths, in contrast to their leader, who wears turquoise-blue. As they move, their scarves unfold into five streaming lines of golden silk. Thus costumed (by Pauline Lawrence), the dancers seem to be the devoted acolytes of the regal central figure. There is not one staccato movement in *Air for the G String*. The relationship between the dancers suggests that of sisters participating in a deeply felt ceremony.

It was my good fortune to have been chosen to perform in this film, together with Cleo Atheneos, Dorothy Lathrop, Hyla Rubin, and Humphrey herself. The shooting of the very short piece took all day. For each of several takes, we danced the entire six-minute work full out, accompanied by a live orchestra playing offstage. Disciplined dancers that we were, and indoctrinated by the examples of our indefatigable directors, Doris Humphrey and Charles Weidman, we were not fazed by the task of performing the dance over and over

Doris Humphrey in *To the Dance,* 1937. Photo by Bois, Courtesy of Charles H. Woodford.

again at the request of the film director. The incredible stamina and patience of Doris, a seasoned performer, was the inspiring force behind our efforts to re-create a stage work for the screen.

Approximately 40 years later, I received an invitation to mount this beautiful composition on the New York-based José Limón Dance Company. The fact that José had been a member, like myself, of the Humphrey-Weidman company in the early years, and that we had danced together not only in their works but also in those we had created in the subsidiary ensemble called "The Little Group," gave the invitation special meaning. I felt that I was once again in the "family" of my youthful experiences, and I rejoiced in the pleasure of re-creating Doris's lovely, smooth-flowing work.

The Limón dancers, chosen by Ruth Currier, brought the stage version back through their live performances, as have other companies for which I have been invited to teach and direct *Air for the G String* in subsequent years. The work demands musical sensitivity, along with a unique awareness of spiritual interrelatedness on the part of the dancers who aspire to bring Humphrey's translation of Bach's "Air" into pure dance form. Re-creating *Air for the G String* has been a memorable experience.

CHAPTER 11

Optic Nerve: Busby Berkeley and the American Cinema

Elizabeth Zimmer

The consummate showman of his era, a self-trained choreographer who lifted the hearts of Americans during the Great Depression with extravagant displays of female pulchritude, Busby Berkeley created kaleidoscopic effects on stage and screen. Fifty years after the apex of his career, his work is beginning to be recognized as serious "cinema."

Berkeley's show-business heritage and early exposure to military life prepared him uniquely well for his extraordinary career on Broadway and in Hollywood. Born in 1895 in Los Angeles, he was the younger child of theatrical director Francis Enos and actress Gertrude Berkeley. When America entered World War I, he enlisted in the army, joining the artillery and requesting officer's training. Despite a reputation as a prankster, he was sent to France, commissioned a second lieutenant, put in command of a battery of 200 men, and assigned to teach them about howitzers—and to conduct military drills. "I worked out a trick drill for 1200 men," he said, which they could do "in silence, without any audible orders." He used these skills and talents in his subsequent creative work.

After his discharge, Berkeley went right into the theater, working in touring companies as actor, stage manager, and director. In 1929, he became, according to biographer Tony Thomas, "the first producer in the American theater to be responsible for directing a musical containing his own created and staged dances, and establishing a precedent for talented men like Jerome Robbins, Michael Kidd, and Gower Champion."[1]

Then, just as musicals seemed to be dying out on screen, Samuel Goldwyn invited Berkeley to Hollywood. He learned to choreograph for the one-eyed box that was the camera, sent away the additional camera crews traditionally used on big pictures, and announced that he would "plan every shot and edit in the camera." He made his biggest splash with his first major works, *Gold Diggers of 1933* and *42nd Street.*

Gold Diggers, one of Berkeley's greatest accomplishments, shows the faces and physiques of World War I heroes reduced to begging in the streets in the face of the Depression. It contains astonishing optical effects, including neon violins and swirling wired skirts. Its sequel, *Gold Diggers of 1935,* features 56 showgirls at 56 white baby grand pianos performing, in Berkeley's words, "a kind of military drill in waltz time"; the choreography for "Lullaby of Broadway" uses 100 dancers and a girl who tumbles to her death from a skyscraper. Berkeley's visual imagery, especially in films like *Dames*, anticipated "op art" and the work of M. C. Escher, which became hugely popular with 1960s "heads"—the same audience that rediscovered Berkeley and made him a cult figure.

A number of his great middle-period films, including *42nd Street*, set up a classic triangle: a girl, her bumptious sugar daddy, and the young, good-natured, often penniless guy who loves but can't support the girl—a situation with great resonance in 1933. It's the depths of the Depression, Roosevelt is just being elected, and "the show business" is one industry that can create something out of nothing. Despite modern accusations that his films exploit and depersonalize women, objectifying them as mosaics, aspics, flower petals, jigsaw puzzles, lozenges, and a variety of other startling things, in fact most of the women in his films are smart, competent, and spunky, and most of his heroes seem to like that in a mate. As Mickey Rooney announces early in 1940's *Strike Up the Band*, "I see women as just people!"

Nevertheless, Berkeley often did see them in the conventional workstations of women of the period—at ironing boards or vanity tables, in beds and bathtubs—and in conventional decorative roles. There was safety, apparently, in numbers; whereas a single woman might be perceived as a threat or need to be acknowledged as a person, dozens of women could be shaped into brilliant abstract patterns, which director Arthur Freed called Berkeley's "instinctive surrealism." In *Strike Up the Band*, an orchestra of fruit comes to life. In *Girl Crazy* (1943), he mobilized 100 dancers in a rodeo finale, and in *The Gang's All Here* (1943), with Carmen Miranda, he launched another fruit fantasia.

Berkeley made his reputation as a dance director "largely on nerve," without ever having studied dance, though his experience with military drills was clearly central to his unique aesthetic. What he did was essentially a bolder version of what many postmodern choreographers do: he hired accomplished performers and gave them instructions, letting them do what they were good at, telling them where to stand, when to go and when to stop. His real craft was in moving the camera, constructing shots visible only to that single eye, which he contrived to pull far enough away from the performers to enable the filming of extremely large areas—big enough to contain, say, dozens of pianos and hundreds of people in careful arrangements.

Berkeley developed marvelous special effects and made broad visual puns; the girls in *We're in the Money* wear huge quarters and perform maneuvers that prefigure the football stadium "wave." His movies had dancing babies—real ones—more than half a century before the trendy animated baby icon swept television and the Internet. He lifted the idea of dancing buildings from the Diaghilev ballet *Parade*. He was as much a visual artist as a film director, constructing surrealist collages of women and props and winding stairs, sending dye billowing through water and light through smoke. He often dramatized the abyss into which he was probably staring, but he found comfort and safety in communities, in dance bands and theater companies, colleges, and small towns, and his films manifest his understanding of the power of community to get things done.

The world of those films is primarily white: African Americans are seen in the stereotypical roles of maids and Pullman porters, and in the climactic numbers of a couple of films that draw on minstrel traditions. The 1939 *Babes in*

Arms (adapted from a Broadway show of the same name for which George Balanchine had been the original dance director) fascinates in the way it demonstrates the ability of a community—even a gang of kids—to solve a desperate problem. In doing this, it plunders many genres (opera, minstrelsy, vaudeville) and styles (Swedish cinema) and calls on Berkeley's secret weapon, the military drill. The minstrel number in this film is washed out by a hurricane—perhaps an unconscious commentary on the cultural changes ahead—and here, as so often, the solution to real social problems is to dance, and, of course, to march. Though the war in Europe is still "over there," rumblings of concern can be felt. "We've got no goose-step," they sing, "but we've got Suzy-Q step!"

In 1948, Berkeley directed *Take Me Out to the Ball Game*, starring Esther Williams, Frank Sinatra, Gene Kelly, and Jules Munshin. A big success, it was nevertheless his last directorial outing. He subsequently staged dances or musical numbers for seven more films, including two Esther Williams vehicles, *Million Dollar Mermaid* (1952) and *Easy to Love* (1953). The latter features 80 water skiers carrying big flags, a hundred girls in a pool shaped like Florida, and shots from helicopters with Williams on a trapeze hanging from a plane; critics called this his "crowning achievement." His final film credit was as second unit director producing whimsical circus sequences for the 1962 *Jumbo*, a Doris Day/Jimmy Durante picture with songs by Rodgers and Hart and a screenplay by Sidney Shelton. He told a reporter who interviewed him on the set, "I still shoot with only one camera, just as I did in 1930, and I still edit everything in the camera. I give the cutters only as much as I want, and all they have to do is put it together."

Berkeley spent his last years in Palm Desert, California, leaving to tour when his films were revived in the 1960s and to advise on the 1971 Broadway revival of *No, No, Nanette.* He died in 1976.

NOTE

1. Tony Thomas and Jim Terry, *The Busby Berkeley Book* (Greenwich, CT: New York Graphic Society, 1973) 23.

CHAPTER 12

Dancin' in the Rain: Gene Kelly's Musical Films

Beth Genné

Gene Kelly, drenched and euphoric, dancing down the street in the driving rain, swinging his umbrella and singing of his love for Debbie Reynolds—this sequence from *Singin' in the Rain* is one of the great moments in cinema.[1] Why does it so enthrall us? Heroes in love and singing about it are a dime a dozen in Hollywood musicals. The simple but catchy song Kelly sings and the brilliant dance that accompanies it are part of it—but not the whole story, for *Singin' in the Rain* is cinematic, a sound moving picture. The way those "pictures" of Kelly are composed, edited, and integrated with the music makes the difference. It provides a multi-sensory experience unique to sound cinema.

Gene Kelly in *Singin' in the Rain* © 1952. Photo courtesy of Turner Entertainment Co., an AOL TimeWarner Company. All rights reserved.

The image we see is artfully arranged. Lighting transforms the rain into shimmering ribbons of silver. Warmly lit orange-yellow shop windows rhythmically punctuate the space of the screen, and the puddles through which the dancer splashes glimmer with the reflected glow of street lamps. And this enchanted picture moves to music. As Kelly shoulders his umbrella and begins to walk down the street, the camera, supported by the gentle, repetitive pattern of the tune he hums and its atmospheric orchestral accompaniment, "strolls" in front of him. It takes us with him: sitting in our theater seats, we too dance. In the climactic center section, when Kelly uses his open umbrella as a sail and catapults from sidewalk to street, we dance above him as the camera takes us back and up, riding a wave of sound over the glistening pavement.

Sound and image enhance each other's impact. Kelly's rhythmic movements celebrate and interact not only with the pulse, shape, color, and texture of the music, but also with the movement of the camera that shapes the space within which he moves. The visual rhythm of the cuts responds to changes in key and orchestral color. Kelly's steps act as a percussion instrument, embroidering a rhythmically intricate filigree of sound to underline and enhance his gestures and the simple tune he sings.[2] It's music visualized—or moving images musicalized. The overall impact is perhaps closer to dance than to any other art form.

Between moving picture and dance, though, there's a crucial difference. The dancer controls and moves only his own body, not the space around him. The film director combines the skills of painter and choreographer. Supervising the various artists working under his command, he controls the image in its entirety—and its movement. He decides what sound we will hear when we see a certain image. When dialogue is added to this synthesis, it too is enhanced, and in turn enhances its companion media: the moving image, the music, and the dialogue work together as an organic whole.

Kelly directed *Singin' in the Rain* with his collaborator Stanley Donen, as well as choreographing it and dancing in it. He took what he learned from dance and applied it to the new medium of cinema. In the process, he transformed the film musical, as well as cinema in general. *Singin' in the Rain* is consistently ranked among the top ten films of all time. Kelly, working with Donen and in other films with director Vincente Minnelli,[3] fundamentally affected the way movies are made and the way we look at them. And he did it with a dancer's eye and from a dancer's perspective.

Eugene Curran Kelly was born in 1912 in Pittsburgh, the great steel city of the American Midwest, to a family of Irish immigrants. He spent much time on the streets, and the rough-and-tumble sports he learned there would profoundly affect his choreography. He also spent a lot of time at the movies. His heroes (and influences) were the great "physical" performers of silent films, those who could create a character through physical virtuosity, timing, and inventiveness—comics Charlie Chaplin and Buster Keaton, and swashbuckler Douglas Fairbanks. Along with sound films came the incomparable Fred Astaire. Kelly was also strongly influenced by two extraordinary African American tap dancers, "Dancing Dotson" and Frank Harrington, whom he saw and learned from in Pittsburgh.

Kelly also studied ballet in Chicago with Berenice Holmes, a pupil and partner of Adolph Bolm, and with Alexander Kotchetovsky. There he learned the Fokine tradition of the creation of character through dance, and an emphasis on powerful male dancing. From Holmes and Kotchetovsky, and by reading "every book I could get my hands on about ballet,"[4] he developed an interest in the Diaghilevian concept of the dance as a "synthesis of the arts." He studied flamenco with Angel Cansino. Folk forms—especially the scintillating footwork of Irish dancing from his own tradition—were important to him too. He fell in love with the modern dancers Martha Graham, Doris Humphrey, and Charles Weidman, active in New York when he arrived there in the 1930s.

But Kelly wanted to craft his own style, to create a new kind of American dance that would be more accessible to the general public than the work of Graham and her colleagues, and that would suit the music of the American composers—Jerome Kern, George Gershwin, Irving Berlin, Richard Rodgers—then writing for musical theater and films. A politically liberal and socially concerned thinker, he was determined to bring the joy of dance to the kind of people he'd grown up with, working people who lived far from theaters and opera houses and could not afford to enter them. They *could,* however, spend a dime on an evening at the movies. When Kelly's success on Broadway in Rodgers and Hart's *Pal Joey* prompted the offer of a Hollywood contract, he seized it. Movies would be a forum for what Kelly called his "dance for the common man."[5]

Kelly's work on the film musical *For Me and My Gal* and the film drama *Pilot No. 5* interested him increasingly in directing dance in cinema, which, he immediately grasped, was entirely different from stage dance. He longed for increasing control over how he was presented on screen.

As a performer who also wanted to direct, Kelly needed someone whose eye he could trust, who understood dance, who could help teach and demonstrate his choreography, and, most important, who understood that the eye of the camera saw dance in a special way. He called on Stanley Donen, a dancer from South Carolina who was 12 years younger than he and also fascinated with film. Kelly had first met Donen as a chorus boy in *Pal Joey*. When Donen came to Hollywood, Kelly invited him to work as his assistant on the film *Cover Girl*.[6] The two eventually co-directed *On the Town*, *Singin' in the Rain*, and *It's Always Fair Weather*. Donen also made brilliant dance films like *Funny Face* and *Seven Brides for Seven Brothers*.[7] Although personal differences estranged them in the 1950s, their initial working relationship was catalytic. Donen described it in 1958, after their last film together:

> Gene and I were young, and excited about working with each other . . . we never got to bed before 3 or 4 in the morning, and we'd get up again at 6 o'clock and go back to the studio . . . Nothing is more fun than finding someone who stimulates you and who can be stimulated by you . . . rather than just adding up two and two, it multiplies itself, and you find yourself doing much better things—you are both carried away on the crest of excitement . . . You can never be sure where to divide the credit.[8]

Kelly's and Donen's interests were revealed in the extraordinary "street dances" in *Cover Girl* (1944), which introduced the new "ordinary" American character that Kelly developed throughout his career and for whom he created his "dance for the common man." It suited his compact, muscled, laborer's body, so unlike Fred Astaire's slender, elegant physique. Astaire had modeled his casually elegant persona and mid-Atlantic accent on the café society audiences of New York and London who admired him. Kelly identified with working-class Americans forever scarred by the Depression, and his almost aggressively energetic style and manner can be, in part, traced to his formative years in the streets of Pittsburgh.

The most striking difference between Astaire's and Kelly's dances can be seen in the way they were filmed and performed. Astaire was a pioneer of film dance who insisted on full framing of the dancer's body at all times, no cutting away from the dance, and editing meticulously to the music. However, many of Astaire's dances of the 1930s were conceived with a stage format in mind: the dancers at a set distance from a camera placed in front of them in an "ideal" theater seat and moving, for the most part, to parallel the dancers' movements. The dance itself was often performed either on a stage or in a stage-like setting (a pavilion or nightclub floor). There were, however, important exceptions, and they were influences on the Kelly-Donen style. Astaire had experimented with uniquely cinematic dance devices, among them the slow-motion dream dance in *Carefree* (1938) and the multiple dancing shadows of the "Bojangles" sequence in *Swing Time* (1936). Even more important was Astaire's dance stroll along a wooded path with Joan Fontaine in *Damsel in Distress*—a precursor of a type of dance and way of filming that Kelly and Donen would adopt, expand, and make their own.

In *Cover Girl*, many subsequent films, and *Singin' in the Rain*, Kelly used a street—a long, expansive space that covered the length of two sound stages. The dance had to be recorded by a mobile camera that could photograph the performers from a multitude of angles, giving a specifically cinematic orientation that was no longer frontal, but planned to be filmed from many different angles, with the separately positioned shots then edited together.[9]

The moving camera served a dual purpose: it both recorded the dance gesture and enhanced it, along with the drama the dance played out. Camera angles, too, were integrated with the choreography, as was the way the dancer's body was positioned within the frame. The camera viewed Kelly from either side, from the back, and at oblique angles, turning and cutting to aim from all four points of the compass. In each case, the viewer got what Kelly felt was the optimal view of the dancer's gestures.

This was a new way of choreographing that took unique advantage of the cinematic medium. It used to the fullest Kelly's dancer's eye "in constructing a dance. . . I know there's a certain angle . . . that is the most advantageous angle. You can't always be turning and facing one way."[10] Most of Kelly's shots—whether from front or side—include the dancer's full figure, surrounded by enough space to include the complete dance gesture and allow the dancer to shape the space within which he is working, in height, to each side, and in depth. Like Astaire, Kelly insisted on never cutting away from the performer during the dance, which ruins the continuity and unity of the choreography.

Kelly understood that framing affects the impact of any dance. The audience must be able to perceive the full line of the dancer and its relation to the surrounding space. Choreographers understand this instinctively; Kelly, Minnelli, and Donen were among the few directors who did. In this, they followed in the footsteps of Astaire, who, as a dance film pioneer, insisted that his directors take into account the relation between the shape of the screen and the shape of the dancer—a relation far different from that of the dancer to the proscenium frame of the stage, where the dancer is a less dominant element in the space around him.

The aspect ratio for Kelly's films—the ratio of the width to the height of the frame— was the "Academy ratio" (1.33:1). This held for the bulk of Kelly's films, as it had for Astaire's before him. This standard screen size, not far removed from the "golden section" (roughly 1.6:1) was in many respects ideal for the dancer; it coordinated well with human proportions, and indeed emphasized them. Kelly's frame allowed him to dominate the space and gave him room to move in it and to shape it. In his last three films, Kelly had to adapt to the new and unwieldy aspect ratio of Cinemascope, ranging from 2.35:1 to 2.55:1, in which the dancer becomes lost in the sea of space that surrounds him, but he solved those problems.

The way the variously angled shots were edited together added yet another level of complexity to Kelly's and Donen's task. Astaire faced this less frequently because his frontal camera positioning, with its "neutral" documentary stance, allowed the dancers to perform the entire dance in one take, their movement the only major activity on screen. Astaire (like a dancer on a stage) and his directors had only to contend with the internal shape, flow, and momentum of the dance.[11]

Kelly and Donen also faced another problem. Instead of filming a dance in one long take, they had to film it in a series of short takes, to allow for a variety of camera setups. The performers had the formidable task of remembering and sustaining the flow and dynamism of the dance as a whole, even as they were constantly interrupted.

Editing together the shots in Kelly's dance sequences added a new and specifically cinematic "pulse" to the dance. Kelly and Donen, like Vincente Minnelli, insisted on meticulously linking the editing to the accompanying music. Cuts from one shot to another occur in relation to musical counts and interact with changes in tempo, orchestration, and song section, as well as with the dance gesture. Kelly's description of how he worked with editor Adrienne Fazan on the dances for *An American in Paris* makes this process clear:

> In the cutting stage of the picture, I had a steady day to day work relationship with Adrienne. The dance numbers were all shot to be cut on a certain beat. When you get a good cutter like Adrienne, you say "Now in the middle of that turn on the third beat of the bar, as I'm turning, cut to this other angle and it won't look like a cut."[12]

Kelly's final remark, "It won't look like a cut," demonstrates his concern with making the cuts unobtrusive to the audience, integrated with the flow of the dances.[13]

Determined to create specifically cinematic dance, Kelly and Donen also considered the two-dimensional nature of the medium and the absence of the empathic audience-performer relationship of a live performance. As Kelly explains:

> What you do miss in motion pictures is, mainly, the kinetic force. On the stage you can do certain things, but I found out very early when I came to Hollywood that a dance I could do on stage that would hold up for seven minutes would boil down to about two minutes on the screen. This is mainly due to the lack of physical or kinetic force. Also, the personality of the dancer is missing in pictures. You're with the audience in the theater. You look at them and you can embrace them and they can embrace you so to speak, or you can hate each other, but you get no direct response from the screen. It is so remote from the empathy of the live theater.[14]

Or again:

> The dance is a three-dimensional art form, while the motion picture is two- dimensional. I would compare dancing basically to sculpture and the motion picture to painting. So the difficulties we have in transferring a dance onto film are simply those of putting a three-dimensional art form into a two-dimensional panel . . . but until we get three-dimensional pictures—and I don't mean the kind with the goggles and the eye strain, but three-dimensional pictures—you will never get the kinesthetic . . . expression of the real dance form.[15]

In the *Singin' in the Rain* dance, the camera that strolls in front of Kelly at the opening and swings out over the street adds its own kinesthetic "punch" to his dances. His wish to compensate for the loss of the impact on the audience of a live body in real space may also account, in part, for aspects of the particularly athletic and forceful dance style he developed: the extraordinarily vigorous tap attack, the repeated acrobatic stunts, and the stress on open and expansive gestures of the arms and legs.

As a choreographer and dancer, Kelly aimed to use dance as a vehicle for the development of a character within the context of an overall film narrative. Astaire did this too (witness his brilliant drunk dance in *The Sky's the Limit*), but Astaire's basic intention was, first and foremost, to make a dance choreographically interesting and, above all, entertaining: "I just tried to knock them in the aisles every time,"[16] he said. String together an evening of Astaire dances, and they make sense as an extraordinary series of choreographically fascinating divertissements. Do that with Kelly's work, and his dances won't be nearly as effective, or as interesting as choreography out of context. They create their fullest impact embedded within the film narrative as an expression of character, and integrated with the camera work, set, and atmosphere that he, as a director, supervised. Divorced from the character he creates, the overall film, and the camera movement, the dances are fine enough, but drained of two-thirds of their meaning and impact.

The musical drama Kelly most often played out was the drama of American courtship—as with most musicals, from the perspective of a young American male. In this he followed in the footsteps of Astaire, whose marvelous courtship dances were self-contained dramas of seduction embodied in an expanded form of ballroom dance. Kelly could do that too, but he was especially brilliant at those moments of euphoria in which his character expresses the "high" that comes with falling in love. "S'Wonderful" and "Tra La La" in *An American in Paris* and his extraordinary dance on roller skates in *It's Always Fair Weather* are good examples. *Singin' in the Rain* is a culmination of this theme. It takes Kelly's street dances, his American persona, and movements and props with which every American can identify and combines them with the vernacular gestures of walking, skipping, and running brought to their highest choreographic level.

Kelly also danced with children in his films. Some of his most charming and exhilarating moments involve them: the "Olvera Street" sequence in *Anchors Aweigh*, the "Children's Games" sequence in *Living in a Big Way*, and the "I Got Rhythm" sequence in *An American in Paris*. In *Singin' in the Rain*, Kelly transforms children's games into great dance: splashing in the gutter, jumping up and down in puddles, dragging an umbrella along a fence and using it as a sail. And he incorporates that delicious added element of danger, the flouting of parental authority—authority that he highlights by ending his dance with a policeman whose withering stare puts an end to his antics. In *Singin' in the Rain*, as in all his films, Kelly returns us to childhood, bringing out the child in all of us by reconnecting us with the joy of dance.

NOTES

1. Parts of this article first appeared in my doctoral dissertation, "The Film Musicals of Vincente Minnelli and the Team of Gene Kelly and Stanley Donen" (University Microfilms, 1984), and in another form in my obituary for Kelly written for *Dancing Times* (April, 1996).

2. Kelly's taps in this sequence were dubbed by Carol Haney.

3. With Minnelli, *The Pirate*, *An American in Paris*. With Donen as assistant, *Cover Girl*, *Anchors Aweigh*, (dance sequences only). With Donen as co-director, *Take Me Out to the Ball Game* (credit is given to Busby Berkeley but he did not have much to do with the filming), *On the Town*, *Singin' in the Rain*, *It's Always Fair Weather*. Kelly alone, *Invitation to the Dance* and *Hello Dolly*. Like Astaire, Kelly had control of the filming of most of the dance sequences in which he appeared in any film, including those not listed above, like *Living in a Big Way* and *As Thousands Cheer*.

4. Kelly interviewed by Marilyn Hunt, Dance Collection Oral History Archive, New York Public Library for the Performing Arts at Lincoln Center, March 10–14, 1975.

5. Betsy Blair Kelly Reisz, Kelly's first wife, who was his close companion at the time (and herself involved in liberal causes) made this decision clear in an interview with the author, May 11, 1999, London, England. Kelly continued this activity in Hollywood, attempting to break down racial barriers by insisting on dancing with the Nicholas Brothers in *The Pirate*, and defending the members of the Hollywood Ten during the McCarthy era.

6. Author's interview with Betsy Blair Reisz, May 11, 1999.

7. Recently a revisionist view of Kelly's and Donen's work promoted by author Stanley Silverman, his biographer (*Dancing on the Ceiling*, New York: Knopf, 1996) has put forward the idea that Kelly was largely responsible only for the choreography whereas Donen controlled the camera work—and was, more or less, the "real" director of the film. However, several sources refute this view. Saul Chaplin, a musical director who worked closely with Kelly and Donen on several films including their first, *Cover Girl*, disputes this view, as does dancer and actor Betsy Blair Reisz, Kelly's first wife. Both view Kelly as the leader and guiding force of the pair (Saul Chaplin, *The Golden Age of Movie Musicals and Me*, University of Oklahoma Press, 1994, 58–59, and interview with the author, August, 1995, 58–59.) "In every case, Gene was the prime mover and Donen the eager and talented pupil." Blair Reisz, a close observer of the Kelly-Donen relationship during their Hollywood career, also sees Kelly as the more powerful creative force in their artistic relationship and asserts that Kelly was as active behind the camera as in front of it, and involved in the pre- and post-production phases of the film. She describes Kelly playing the role of artistic and intellectual mentor to the young and talented Donen (author's interview with Betsy Blair Kelly Reisz, May 11, 1999). Director Vincente Minnelli, who worked with

Kelly on three films, made it clear that Kelly was always involved in the decision-making when it came to conceptualizing and filming dance sequences (author's interview with Vincente Minnelli, July, 23 1980). Kelly himself describes Donen in numerous sources as his "assistant" in the early films but gives credit to Donen as a co-director in *On the Town*, *Singin' in the Rain*, and *It's Always Fair Weather*. Kelly also discusses at length his own participation in the pre- and post-production stages of the film, including the planning of the camera angles in several interviews. Perhaps most important, Donen's own early interviews, given closer to the time when the films were made, present them as true collaborators (see James Clark, "Interview with Stanley Donen, *Films and Filming*, July, 1958). In an interview with this author on April 31,1986, Donen said that until their estrangement "it was a good collaboration" (see next note). It seems reasonable to assume, then, that Kelly, 12 years older than Donen and with an established reputation in New York and Hollywood by 1944, could have been initially the dominant artistic personality in their relationship, but that the two became increasingly equal in their relationship to the point where, by *On the Town* (1949) and *Singin' in the Rain* (1951), they were truly co-directors. Another argument against Silverman's view is that since we know that Kelly's choreography was conceptualized and planned with the moving camera in mind, choreographing would necessarily involve planning camera activity. Donen has never disputed Kelly's role as the creator of his choreography. Therefore, Kelly must have been involved in the camera work. Janice La Pointe Crump has also presented the notion that credit should be given to Kelly's female dance assistants Jeanne Coyne Kelly and Carol Haney for their role in the film's development. Betsy Blair Reisz, a dancer herself who knew Coyne well, views Coyne's participation as that of a rehearsal assistant and says that while Haney may have had some creative input, the overall choreographic conception should be credited to Kelly. Haney also dubbed the sound of water-logged tapping in the "Singin' in the Rain" dance.

8. Stanley Donen interviewed by James Clark, *Films and Filming*, July 1958, 7. When I read this quote to Donen in 1986, he approved it as a pretty accurate description of their relationship (author's interview with Stanley Donen, April 31, 1986).

9. It should be noted here that Busby Berkeley did begin in his films of the 1930s to exploit the unique qualities of his medium. But in his musicals, a remarkably active camera is used to create interesting visual effects, and dancers and dancing are really secondary: his camera becomes the "star" of the sequence, orchestrating the bodies and body parts of dancers to manipulate and, ultimately, abstract objects.

10. Gene Kelly, "Dialogue On Film," *American Film*, February 1979, 40.

11. See Croce, *The Fred Astaire and Ginger Rogers Book*, 126–7, for a description of Astaire's single-take system. See also John Mueller, *Astaire Dancing: The Musical Films* (New York: Knopf, 1985) and Jerome Delamater, *Dance in the Hollywood Musical* (Ann Arbor: University of Michigan Press, 1981) It should be stressed here that Astaire's camera is not always completely static—it may move, paralleling the dancers' movements, to keep the dancers within the frame and, on occasion, takes on a life of its own. In Astaire's films, however, the dancer's movement always remains the major movement on the screen. When working with directors he trusted, most notably Vincente Minnelli in the 1940s, Astaire began to allow more latitude in the movement of the camera.

12. Kelly quoted in Donald Knox, *The Magic Factory: How MGM Made "An American in Paris"* (New York: Praeger, 1972), 170.

13. It should be noted here that Kelly and Donen always "cut in the camera," meaning that their shots and angles were carefully planned in detail in advance. Only what was necessary was actually photographed—never any alternate shots. This insured that even if the finished film were given to someone else to edit, they would be forced (for lack of alternatives) to cut it the way Kelly and Donen had planned (Gene Kelly interviewed by John Russell Taylor, London, England, 1980).

14. Kelly quoted in Knox, *The Magic Factory*, 47.

15. Albert Johnson, "The Tenth Muse in San Francisco" (transcription of a lecture by Gene Kelly), *Sight and Sound*, Summer 1956, 47.

16. Astaire speaking at the American Film Institute when accepting their lifetime achievement award.

CHAPTER 13

No Maps on My Taps: *An Appreciation*

Lynn Dally

"... I got no maps ... on my taps ... I takes the raps ..."

—Chuck Green

No Maps on My Taps, an hour-long documentary by filmmaker George T. Nierenberg, emerged in 1980 at the same time my West Coast colleagues and I were creating a new format for tap dancing—live, and in concert. On a mission to rediscover, reinvent, and revive the form, we aspired to be the Modern Jazz Quartet of tap, a small chamber ensemble of distinctive soloists, each with a singular voice and able to participate fully as instrumentalists in the totality of the music-making. We were creating a tap-dance company with live jazz music, in which the creative collaborations and ideas of the dancers and musicians intended to engage an audience for a whole evening's presentation of tap dancing—not as a novelty, not as a seven-minute vaudeville song and dance routine, and not for the sake of nostalgia, but as a lively indigenous dance art worthy of attention and begging for new exploration.

No Maps went straight to the heart of our passion for tap dancing. As Nierenberg was investigating the roots of tap in its living history via the artistry of Bunny Briggs, Chuck Green, and "Sandman" Sims, we and dancers like us across the country were searching for living artists who were willing to share their life experiences and their dancing expertise. We particularly sought the African American influences that nurtured rhythm tap, because it was our perception that the rhythmic thread was broken when tap dance fell into disuse in the 1950s. We believed that if we could reconnect with "rhythm," we might have a chance at taking tap into the future. Nierenberg made a great gift to tap dance when he chose to film the stories of these three artists, all well known and revered in the field, with care and simplicity. His directorial approach allows us a clear view of the dancing and honest response in the close-ups.

No Maps poses the question "Is tap dance a dying art?" and then proceeds to inspire the viewer with a strong and straightforward narrative that carries us into the lives of three veteran African American tap legends. These artists may represent the end of an era, but their dancing is captured on film in such a way that people like me learned a lot from it and were inspired to find our own

Above: Lynn Dally and Buster Brown congratulate Harold Nicholas on his performance with Lynn and the Jazz Tap Ensemble at the Joyce Theater, New York City, November 1999. Courtesy of Jazz Tap Ensemble. Photo by Gayle Hooks.

Left: Lynn Dally and Gregory Hines celebrate his new work *Groove* created for the Jazz Tap Ensemble in Los Angeles, 1999. Courtesy of Jazz Tap Ensemble. Photo by Vladin Elakovic.

DVD 8
No Maps on My Taps (1979) 58 min
Excerpt 2 min 40 sec

Production Note: "At the time of the filming in 1978 one of my main challenges was recording the sound of the taps. We placed eight microphones around the periphery of the stage and I directed Lionel Hampton to keep the sound level of the band down so as not to overpower the taps. During the performance we suddenly lost the connection to the tap mics for two of the numbers. I didn't want to stop the performance and destroy the spontaneity so at the sound mix my only option was to pull the sound of the taps from any of the open mics during the performance, which included the musician and audience mics."—*George T. Nierenberg*

voices and create our own stories. As the late, great John Bubbles (often referred to as the father of rhythm tap) questions Chuck Green in their familial cross-country phone conversation, "Chuck, are you creatin'? . . . are you creatin' steps? . . . listen, Chuck, tap dancin's still alive–it just needs more people to execute it, that's all . . . And get more jobs in better places." Nearly 25 years after the release of *No Maps*, America has experienced a genuine rebirth of creativity and interest in tap, and John Bubbles's questions have been answered by legions of tap dancers, male and female, young and old, amateur and pro. As the first tap dance documentary, *No Maps* played an important role in this renaissance by capturing history and giving voice to the pertinent question "Are you creatin'?"

To tell this story, Nierenberg's research led him to create a context—specifically, to produce and film a live concert at Smalls Paradise, a well-known Harlem club of an earlier era. The concert would bring together three legendary tap artists who knew each other from show business but were probably never on the same stage at the same time, and who represented three very different aesthetics in tap dancing but shared a chemistry, or at least a camaraderie, that enabled the story to flow. He hired Lionel Hampton, who, like many traveling bandleaders, had engaged tap dancers to perform with his orchestra on many

NIERENBERG'S SECOND TAP DANCE DOCUMENTARY

Nierenberg was inspired to capture more live tap dancing in his 30-minute documentary *About Tap* (1982). With an introduction by Gregory Hines shot on the back fire escape of Harlem's Apollo Theater, he presents Chuck Green again, this time joined by Jimmy Slyde and Steve Condos. In contrast to *No Maps*, this film features several complete dances as well as in-studio improvisations by all three men. Close-up interviews focus entirely on each artist's point of view about dancing—what inspires him, what interests him, and the ways in which he experiences the joys and intimacy of this supremely rhythmic, highly musical dance form.

occasions. Nierenberg also developed other appropriate locations for the shoot, including the street in front and the alley behind the world-famous Apollo Theater, a small outdoor stage in the park, and a classic second-floor dance studio with upright piano, wooden floor, and windows looking down on the street. He created an atmosphere that gave a sense of the importance of this gathering to the artists, to their live audience, and to viewers of the film. He revealed the intimacy of backstage preparations, heightened the electricity of performance itself, and gently nudged the "challenge" concept into the story, giving a deeper understanding of how this art form is transformed and passed on. His compassionate interest in each man's life story created a lyricism that gives beauty to their sometimes very harsh daily experiences. He created a comfortable, familiar situation for the artists, which opened the way for a full expression of the spontaneity and creativity that are intrinsic parts of the dancing itself.

Ah, the dancing! What a pleasure to see these veterans in all their wonderful individuality. The stage show's opening number—a classic "BS Chorus," an old tradition of time steps and flash where unison dancing is the mode—is the only time in the entire film that we see a "group" dance. We learn, as the film progresses, that this art deals with each person's own inventions on the rhythms. We see a 1933 clip of the young Bunny Briggs doing the classic time step and "trenches," and then real "rhythm" and vernacular at the club. This "rhythm" dancing is what John Bubbles refers to when he speaks of "creatin'," and the contrast between the accomplished kid and the mature artistry of Briggs is also the history of tap and some of its innovation from the 1930s to the 1950s and 1960s.

Chuck Green improvises a cappella at the studio and then dances "Caravan" with Lionel Hampton's orchestra in the show. "Caravan" and "Take the A Train" are two of Green's signature tunes. Viewing a master's improvisational approach to jazz standards such as these Ellington pieces is enlightening; we see clarity and sparseness, punctuated by select moments of high, rapid articulation—and this from a man who is very large and yet goes into the air with astonishing grace. He almost hovers when he isn't more grounded in his sliding steps. And, of course, we are entertained by "Sandman" Sims's specialty, the old rhythms with the captivating gritty sound. Though his rhythms are in a sense rawer than those of the others, he too weaves a fabric of continuity and driving rhythmic energy.

The film clips of Bill Robinson and John Bubbles are priceless. They give us a clear picture of the power and presence of each of these great stars, and they let us in on the evolution of tap dancing. Bill Robinson's style, vocabulary, and musical presentation were crystal-clear, tight packages of eight-bar phrasing performed primarily from the balls of the feet, giving lightness and effervescence, a symmetry of phrasing, and a knowing delight to his audiences. Bubbles experimented with "dropping" the heels and thus added new dimensions to the rhythmic possibilities of tap dancing. He was a showman and an innovator whose artistry opened up the second half of the century for tap and allowed this simple art of four metal plates on the bottoms of shoes to proceed musically along with the development of jazz from swing to bebop and beyond.

Toward the end of the film, Chuck Green describes how a "melody" came to him. This poignant moment references the challenges and difficulties faced by these artists as they did what they had to do—dance. The film succeeds in delivering the experience of great dancing that is so "in the moment" there is no residue, and hence, "no maps."

Part III

Screen Testing

CHAPTER 14

A Dancer behind the Lens

Eiko Otake

DVD 9
Husk (1987) 9 min 38 sec
Excerpt 3 min 55 sec

Koma and I had rarely been interested in looking at ourselves on video—until 1983, when we started producing our own "media dance." Through actual hands-on involvement, we each have developed taste and gained knowledge specific to the medium, while still holding on to our reservations about "preserving" dance. We make media work not to record, but to investigate.

When video recording first became widely available in the dance field, Koma and I were, at best, indifferent to the medium. Although various performing venues have recorded our performances for their archives, we rarely looked at them, and then only if we felt it might be useful to make notes for ourselves.

We do not care to see our performance footage; it depresses us. Recorded on video, our dance generally looks dull because it is so slow. In a theater, I believe, the slowness allows us to breathe the space and develop a particular relationship with the audience, but on video, it just looks slow. What happens on stage is only half of what happens in a theater: audiences complete the work by receiving and reacting to it, and that relationship is impossible to record on videotape. In addition, the stage lighting, which is an important part of our work, does not translate onto video. A camera cannot see what a human can see, and therefore, filming needs special considerations.

EARLY LEARNING

We collaborated with Celia Ipiotis and Jeff Bush of Arc Video on *Tentacle* (1983) and *Bone Dream* (1985). We also have worked closely with James Byrne on *Elegy* (1984) and *Undertow* (1988). Early on, we understood that in order to be effective, we needed to choreograph a dance specifically for the camera. Realizing that video is inherently flat while dance is three-dimensional, we looked for ways to make a composition that emphasized depth.

We also examined various editing methods and discovered that our movement becomes less convincing when we produce a skillful edit. Picking up interesting scenes and connecting them makes the dance feel more arbitrary. A "cut-and-paste" method is often intrusive and too contrived for our slow movement. Furthermore, a high-tech look seems to deprive the audience of the immediacy

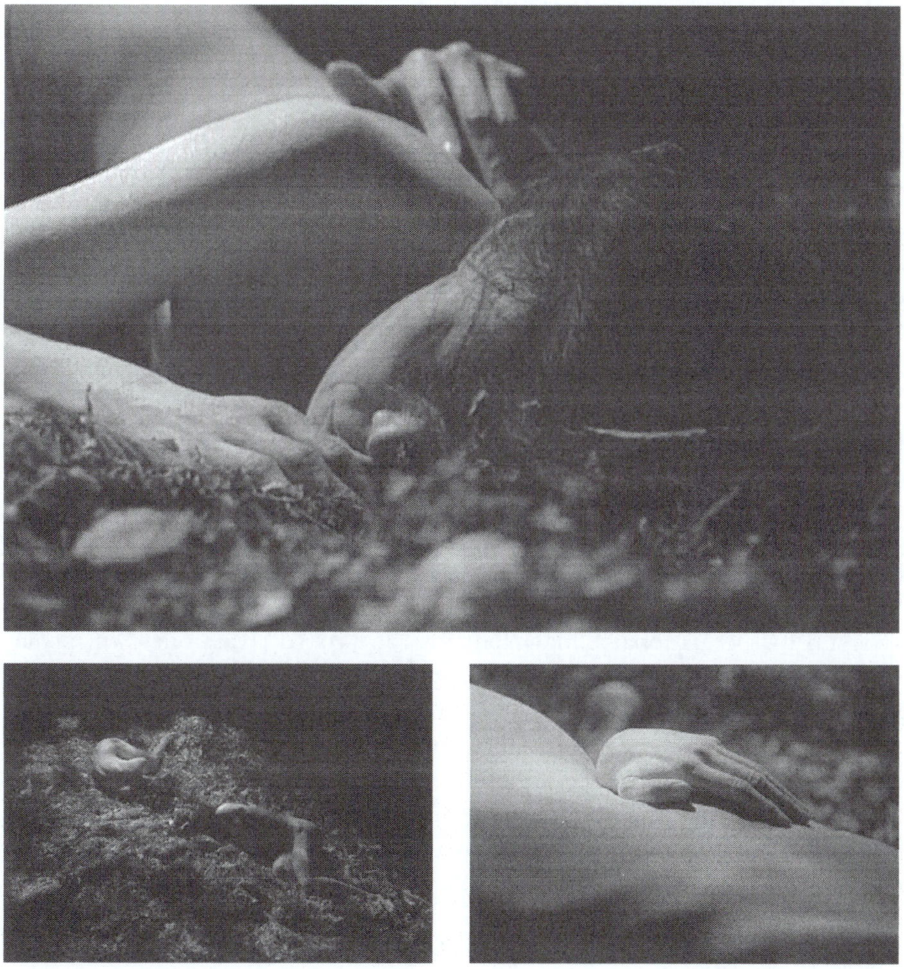

Eiko & Koma in *Breath*. Videotape Producer, Dance Division, The New York Public Library, Astor, Lenox and Tilden Foundations, 1999. Choreography by Eiko and Koma. Videography by Jerry Pantzer.

and the flow of the movement. A television viewer may be willing to give us less time than a member of the theater audience, but we hope to bring to video a sense of shared endurance similar to that in a theater, where the audience members are personally involved and, we hope, feel invested and rewarded. In order to achieve that, we searched for a way to employ an uninterrupted long take that is kinetically and visually satisfactory.

A composition integrating two mediums is a delicate balancing act. When the camera's movement and our movement do not relate, the result appears uninteresting. For example, when the camera moves too quickly, we as subjects become "tame" and lose our integrity. On the other hand, when Koma and I exhibit movement while the camera is too passive, viewers are left detached, and the choreography loses impact. To be effective, we had to feel each other and place ourselves "just right" in that particular square while the camera moved on us. In other words, the camera and our body movement should complement each other.

However, when "just right" is too tight, the relationship between camera and body can become overly intimate, like a very exclusive duet. Then a viewer loses her own entry point. Even though we realize that viewers' capacity to feel something profound is dictated by what they see in a frame, we do not want to control totally what a viewer would taste, nor spoon-feed calculated nuances to a wide range of spectators. There has to be breathing room for everyone. Better

In many parts of Asia, how people live their lives has radically changed in recent years. In Japan, for example, many customs that I remember from my childhood, such as all family members sleeping together in one room on a tatami mat, are no longer practiced. Nowadays, modern Japanese may likely live in a house complete with Western-style bathroom and bedroom. However, though they may physically live life not as differently from the West as they did in the past, I think people still carry their formed cultural viewpoint through generations. We, at least, do. I am not sure, though, if younger generations who have grown up in the modern way would actually feel and see the way we old-timers do. I feel more compelled, therefore, to speak from our viewpoint. —E. O.

yet, if what is in the frame can suggest what is outside of the frame and relate to it, viewers can sense that what they see is a part of a larger world. They may focus, but they are not bound.

The biggest argument we have had with videographers was about how low the camera should sit. For producing *Wallow* (a 1984 video adaptation from our stage work *Fur Seal*), we wanted the camera low, at the height from which seals see the world. Such an angle, we thought, would involve the audience in a sympathetic relationship with us, the performers as seals. However, the cameraman could not comply. It was physically difficult to shoot from such an angle. Westerners in general do not view the world from a low angle as we Asians do because they do not live, eat, or sleep on the floor; they sit high, and they die on a bed (see sidebar). Thus, it was often difficult for them to understand our insistence. The camera angle has been important for all our media works, because it is the viewpoint that frames the story. Later, this issue prompted us to operate the camera ourselves.

Husk DVD 8

In 1987, Koma and I received a Dance/Film/Video grant from the Dance Program of the National Endowment for the Arts to create our own media work. Considering our early experiences, we knew what we wanted: *Husk*, a ten-minute piece requiring no post-production. We wanted to express the intricate relationship between the camera and a body that speaks the primal myths: a body as a breathing landscape. We used an inexpensive camera for unrestricted exploration through playback, and to "choreograph" a piece. Then we rented broadcast quality equipment for the final shoot. This time, our ambition was not to hire a camera operator but for Koma to become one. In this way, we put our acquired knowledge to the test.

It took a while for each of us to get used to our new roles: Eiko as a solo performer and Koma as a cameraman, with both of us co-directing the process—a different kind of duet. We had technical problems to solve. We knew that a handheld camera almost always produces a slight jerk when used for a long shot. That was difficult even for Jeff, Celia, and James, who were used to handling the equipment. We had to find a way for Koma, a novice, to move a camera smoothly and imperceptibly. The other challenge was how to place the camera at an extremely low angle, so it would "crawl" on the floor. The lowest point of the tripod was still too high for that.

Our answer was using a tennis ball to replace the tripod. Koma had tried dollies, turntables, and laying the camera on many different-sized balls. He found that a tennis ball had the right height and the most reliable texture. He himself lay flat on the floor, something that was hard for other cameramen to do. With a bit of practice, the camera rotated, slid, panned, and moved ever so gently, but not mechanically.

In order for me to see how I was being seen, we placed monitors in different places outside of the camera frame during the recording. Thus, I could watch a monitor without facing the camera. When I saw that my face was not in a frame, I could even talk to Koma while he was videotaping. (I was probably yelling, while Koma was so concentrated on the camera that he could hardly breathe or talk.) So, instead of a video person directing or giving information, I, a dancer, was commenting and directing the camera's moves. This method gave us control of composition and timing so that we could record longer phrases. Because I did not have to rely on directions from anybody else, I could focus on keeping my movement spontaneous and nonchalant within a comfortable frame. We took three months to finish the piece. We mixed our own music, using the sounds of wind, insects, and a mountain stream. In a gentle wind that blew leaves and my hair, the costume, made out of leaves, revealed and concealed my bare skin.

Undertow

In 1988, the Walker Art Center commissioned another collaboration with James Byrne. With him, Koma and I wanted to do something we could not do by ourselves. The three of us reflected upon our previous collaboration on *Lament* and decided to find more unconventional camera positions that would contribute dramatically to the content of the work.

Heavy editing was necessary in *Lament* because of its lack of continuous takes. The piece required an expensive theater space; therefore, we could not constructively use a playback mechanism. This time, however, we budgeted for much experimental shooting. We shot and looked and then decided that the camera, with James on a ladder, should sway above us. We cut the side light sharply at knee height to create blackness from which Koma and I emerge and into which we sink back. We used the shortcoming of video—the fact that a camera cannot see what humans can see—to our advantage. The result was the unsettling *Undertow* (1988), in which the camera-eye and all the subjects sway. Because of the camera's floating motion, James had to hold it away from the ladder at times, which meant that he could no longer look into the viewfinder. The three of us relied on monitors to know each other's whereabouts. We composed and performed three uncut sections. Later, we connected them by simply fading in and out of darkness. Thus, the piece floated in both space and time as if coming from and going back to a void. The following year, *Undertow* was nationally aired on PBS as a segment of *Alive from Off Center*.

INSTALLATION: *BREATH*

In 1998, the video and film department of the Whitney Museum commissioned our four-week living installation, *Breath,* using video/film components. The curator, Matthew Yokobosky, suggested that Koma and I be physically on display during all hours that the museum was open. This was our first such attempt, and we were apprehensive about how the closed space would affect our psyches. We thought we would miss the sky and more expansive landscapes. We wanted to have a window to connect us to the outside, and we wanted the whole room moving and breathing, so we created an extensive organic environment in which numerous fans and lighting equipment were hidden from the spectators. Breezes both moved the set itself and changed the rays of light, as one sees the sunlight through tree branches in the woods. Along with the environment, we produced three hours of edited video that were incorporated into the installation. The images were all of our body parts. Shot with extreme back light, they looked like mountains and hills undulating sensually, both familiar and mythical. We found that, for the effects we needed, the cheapest home video equipment operated better with low light, because we were not looking for a realistic body image and we wanted to avoid details. I videotaped Koma; Koma videotaped me. Our recording camera was connected to a projector that showed huge images (which both of us could watch) onto the blackened back wall. Thus, we were seeing what we would be using in the installation. Each of us danced gently, seeing the shadow of our own landscape appear and disappear, as the other one zoomed in and panned.

I edited the footage for three simultaneously operating projectors. We constructed curved extensions at the corners of the gallery so that there were no straight lines or angles in the projection surface, and we painted all the walls black. The projectors were then aimed at different parts of the wall in different-sized images. By setting the projectors at their lowest level of brightness, intensity, and color, we succeeded in blurring video's characteristic borders. The three images sometimes merged into one and separated again. There was an elusive merging of landscape, body, cloud, and abstraction. Over time, we covered most of the walls with floating video images. However, only a portion of the audience realized that what they were seeing was a video because the images' deliberate vagueness became a part of the atmosphere. After all, in conventional use, when a video is off or when a video is projecting no image, there usually remains a monitor or a visible projected square. In our case, the occasional absence of video images created a black void that presented itself powerfully. The images became a mirage, and also a window to connect us visually to the landscape of the larger world. Because of the long hours, we took turns in the installation so one of us could see the exhibit from the audience's vantage point—Eiko seeing Koma dancing a duet with his or Eiko's body landscape as the video image shadowed or enveloped him, and vice versa. Often the room was so dark that people could see what was really happening only after their eyes adjusted. Only then did they realize that the videos were body parts meant both to mirror and to support our performers' bodies.

Documenting Breath

With funds from NIPAD (National Initiative to Preserve America's Dance), the Dance Division of the New York Public Library for the Performing Arts produced a video documentation of the Whitney installation. The producer, Madeleine Nichols, curator of the Dance Division, suggested Jerry Pantzer as our videographer, and we agreed. She encouraged us to think creatively for this archival document because the installation was quite different from other performances they had recorded. Jerry came to see the installation, loved it, and returned often, spending many hours in the gallery. The Dance Division supplied us with sophisticated equipment for recording: a Sony BVW 600 Betacam SP Videocamera, Chapman Super Peewee Dolly, and trucks. This machinery takes a long time to set up, but we had professional crews, which made this different from our previous productions. When at last the taping started, we had to go with our mutual instincts because shooting time was limited. The installation, unlike our stage work, did not have clear choreography: we were performing seven hours a day for four weeks. We wanted this video to be a crystallized impression of the installation.

All the original footage (more than four hours) was input to the AVID, and a timeline was prepared. We had been promised that we, as choreographers, would be involved with the editing. Even for Jerry, the use of the AVID Xpress was new, so François Bernadi, an editor, taught us how to handle some of the differences between analog and digital editing. In analog, many of the effects are instantaneous, while with the AVID, one has to render them, which takes time. But for accessing different points in a sequence, the AVID is very fast, making analog seem sluggish. When designing an effect, the AVID will give a 5-second demonstration without rendering, so it is a great tool for experimenting before composing an edit. Since the library purchased the AVID, we had no time constraint.

Jerry and I spent much time selecting footage and making marks on the AVID. This equipment is truly amazing and super-fast, like a word processor and more. We can cut, paste, merge, and print as we go along without ever rewinding a tape. The AVID can slow motion, reverse the footage, change color, and superimpose at our command. It was especially gratifying that we could see all our ideas and then make a decision without having to negotiate prices just to see the choices. I learned how to operate AVID alone so I could spend many hours composing and watching the selection.

Jerry worked hard to please me, but as we continued, I realized that his cinematic training was informing his choices. For me, this cinematic approach had too many phrases, each running for too short a time, to develop a kinetic drama. I saw that his masterful editing had its own flow. I liked it at first, but not at a subsequent viewing. The more I looked at his edit, the more clearly I felt it was not my editing. The body and environment were Eiko and Koma, but the time sense of the editing was not. I thought that in his beautiful edit, we became "beautifully shot" dancers, not the artists who were responsible for the concept. Koma and I conceived and executed the environment, inhabited it, and moved in it. Therefore, I thought, we could ask the viewers to trust us and to stay with us for a while. After some discussion with Jan Schmidt, production specialist of the Dance Division, Jerry and I decided to make two different versions: one for Eiko and Koma, and one for Jerry. At the library's public showing, we presented two different versions, and each of us spoke about the reasoning behind our aesthetic choices.

Titled *Breath* (1999), our version of this 15-minute video in many ways shows where we are now. We have held onto what we believe is essential: quiet breathing, kinetic communication, and an enduring relationship to the environment and time. However, we are no longer resistant to adventurous camera work, sophisticated tools, and elaborate editing, as long as we can decide how to use or ignore them. *Breath* crescendoes into a 7-minute uncut segment of our duet, scored but not choreographed tightly. This segment was the occasion of our biggest dispute. Although Jerry understood that Koma and I need an unconventional amount of time to involve a viewer with our bodies, he felt that the uncut phrase was much too long and not cinematic or theatrical. Nevertheless, Jerry agrees that this untreated section is a truthful rendering of what we do in performance. This collaboration gave us much to discover and reflect upon.

FILM AND VIDEO

Having created seven dance videos, we show them at public events as a part of our touring residency programs. We give videos away as souvenirs to workshop participants. While we appreciate the convenience of video format—easy to carry and affordable to produce—we recognize that on a screen we, as performers, have either to compete for viewers' attention or to be patient with their inattention. We have now transferred all our videos onto 16mm film, making them intentionally higher-contrast—with positive results. These films give us "black" that we never get in video. Films also open up other venues in which to present our work. They have been shown on gigantic screens in libraries, in prisons, and on college campuses. Koma and I dislike television monitors, probably because, in Japan, television was a rarity until we were in our teens. We therefore tend to regard television as an intruder in the life we had known before, the life with longer and darker nights that allowed us to dream. In comparison, film had long been an important artistic medium for both of us. Many cinematic works had provoked and profoundly affected us. People choose to go to see a film and choose what to see and with whom to see it. We want to make such works.

Therefore, Koma and I have been learning new technology, negotiating the process with our collaborators and creating works we feel comfortable with. Over the years, we have experimented with video and learned how to deal with it. We want to make work that we would want to see: a poetic merging of visual, sound, and kinetic composition that is neither dance documentation nor a television program. This is an inherently minor category, like poetry in the publishing industry, yet we all realize that poems are an essential part of our literary tradition. Minority forms have their place. Such independent media works may not be for broadcast, for home entertainment, or for booking and promotional use. Still, they can exist quietly, like books of poetry—if not for a mass market, at least for those who dare to open them.

CHAPTER 15

Wearing Three Hats: Process Notes from a Polymath

Meredith Monk

DVD **10**
Book of Days (1988) 75 min
Excerpt 2 min 53 sec

Production Note: "I originally drew preliminary storyboards for *Book of Days* but early on, I realized that I could conceptualize the film better by seeing more accurate drawings of what I had in mind. Yoshio Yabara, the art director of the film, rendered the images as we discussed how each scene would go. The storyboards became a kind of armature or skeleton of the work. Then I was free to fill or change things during the shoot."—M. M.

DVD **11**
16 Millimeter Earrings (1979) 4 min
Excerpt 2 min 11 sec

Production Note: "The silent black and white film that is included is the actual footage projected on a screen in front of a giant table in *16 Millimeter Earrings*. To the audience at that point in the piece, the table looked like a large white cube. After I removed the screen (which was made of plywood) the table was revealed. Later, a similar film sequence shot in color was projected on a large white dome, which I had placed over my head."—M. M.

Meredith Monk, 1988. Photo by Dominique Lasseur.

I've never made a dance film per se, but the fact that my films are for the most part nonverbal and nonlinear in structure naturally relates them to an art form that speaks without words. My deep interest has been to tackle the notion of cinematic syntax in a new way. In my early performance pieces, I combined disparate images into a montage within a live context. My question was: How could I as a soloist perform a disjunctive continuity that implied the flexibility and speed of film editing? It became a matter of razor-sharp transitions (like film cuts) and quick changes of focus, emotion, tension, and energy.

As a person who has attempted over the years to weave together music, images, and movement, I find film a perfect format for this integration of elements. As Eisenstein stated, "All art forms meet within the film frame." Film has always been a component of my work, both as an element in live performance and as a reality in itself, because of its fluidity of time and space and its power of scale and transformation. In live performance, to get from one space to another usually involves major set changes. Space in film (unless it is deliberately set up as abstract) can be refreshingly literal; against that, magical images can be counterpointed.

In film, you can also create a composite space by editing shots from different locations together to look like one place. DVD 10 In *Book of Days*, my feature-length film shot mostly in a medieval village in southern France, one scene took place in the cave dwelling of a "madwoman" who lived outside the village. When we originally storyboarded the scene, I thought it would be effective to shoot everything on location in the real cave as a medium-shot, in contrast to some of the extreme close-ups in other parts of the film. Back in New York after the French shoot, I realized that the cave scene lacked intimacy, so we built a facsimile of the cave wall in my downtown loft and shot matching close-ups of the action that we had filmed in France. We also shot additional footage in a tunnel in Central Park, to create the transition between the cave entrance and the cave itself.

Early on, I used film in my stage work as an element of resonance and scale. DVD 11 My first use of film within a live context was in *16 Millimeter Earrings* (1966), a 30-minute solo. A breakthrough piece for me, it incorporated vocal music (live and on tape—my first through-composed score), layers of sound (a sonic web of simultaneous loops), movement, objects, light, text, costumes, and three films projected on different surfaces within the stage space. While retaining its own integrity, each element as it combined with the others seemed to acquire an added luminosity and depth. What I had been intuitively glimpsing and hoping for came together: a complex interweaving of multiple elements adding up to a kind of poetry for the senses.

In *16 Millimeter Earrings*, I wanted to expand the experience of a live performance by working with the scale and physicality of film as a sculptural object. One of the main motifs of the piece was fire, manifest in a variety of materials: red crepe paper flames coming out of a giant table, and my hair dyed red, flaming up around my head. Finally, projected on a huge screen behind a room set up on stage was a film of a doll burning in a miniature replica of that room. After both the doll and the miniature room went up in flames, the film cut to an image of fire, and I rose out of a steamer trunk in the stage room to stand naked in front of the screen, my body masked and bathed in the flames. The scale of the film and its relation to the stage space made it possible to convey the power of effigy and death/rebirth with primal, visceral immediacy.

I also worked, in *16 Millimeter Earrings*, with portraiture. Early in the piece, a black-and-white film of my face in close-up going through a series of slow psychic transformations (really, ironic codes of emotion) was projected on a screen, which formed the front of a giant table. In the film I literally tore my hair (a red wig) out in anger, my real hair stood on end in fear, and painted tears came out of my eyes as I cried. Later on, the same film in color was projected on a large white dome that I held over my head like an animated mask. The image of my small body with a giant head and, at moments, my small live hand moving across my large filmed face contributed to the dream-like multidimensionality of the whole piece.

Time has been a major aspect of all my work—both historical time and the sense of time as a pliable medium that can be stretched, compressed, and formed into different cycles. Film easily provides this sense of plasticity. Cutting can create the implication of simultaneity and various time dimensions. Ironically, film by nature does not offer the literal physicality of a live situation, where simultaneous events can be presented and each audience member can choose what to look at and when to look at it. It is fundamentally a linear medium, with one image following another, except in a split or multiple screen format where visual choice is a possibility.

In *Ellis Island* (1980), a 30-minute short, and *Book of Days* (1988), a feature-length film, I worked on the juxtaposition of one historical period with another or others, each one delineated by gradations of black and white and color to create the different realities. *Ellis Island* was filmed on location at the legendary entry point in New York Harbor where, between 1890 and 1920, immigrants traveling steerage class to the United States were processed. I thought of Ellis Island as an archeological ghost poem. In 1980, the island was in ruins. Part of the process of making the film was uncovering shards of objects and memories of the people who had bravely passed through the place. Set against black-and-white images—inspired by photos of the period—were color images of contemporary tourists being led through the ruins. *Book of Days*, taking place mostly in

Toby Newman (left) and Pablo Vela in *Book of Days* (1988), a film by Meredith Monk. Photo by Dominique Lasseur.

fourteenth-century Europe, dealt with the constants and particularities of history. It viewed the Middle Ages through the eyes of contemporary media—for example, television interviews of the medieval characters—while the late twentieth century was seen through the visions of a young fourteenth-century girl.

In both films, I was director, composer, and choreographer, weaving the three means together into a unified composition. Wearing three hats creates a kind of built-in inner conversation (or argument, as the case may be). The special challenge of taking all three roles involves constantly keeping the larger whole in mind.

As a composer, I had to consider the primacy of the visual image as the first language of film, so I could not always develop the musical materials into long sustained forms. The rhythms of the images made their own demands. In *Book of Days*, I used some of the music as an overview field, an objective aural landscape outside of the reality of the images. Other music was more intimate. In some instances, the music created a kind of armature for the images to lie on; in others, the music became part of the action, identified the characters, or served as a language in itself. Since silence was the basis of the sound and there was almost no dialogue, the music became one set of tiles in the large mosaic of image, stillness, movement, character, and environment.

The "Plague" section of *Book of Days* is a montage dealing with the outbreak of the bubonic plague. Throughout the film we drew medieval parallels with contemporary life, sometimes expressed with humor and irony, sometimes with a more sober rendering of how human nature remains the same no matter the period. For the "Plague," I composed a metric whispered chant, which I used as the heartbeat of the section. Against that, images of the chaos, agony, and loss experienced by the inhabitants of the village are counterpointed, and intercut with a frenzied dance by a sinister Dance of Death figure and a map of the village filling up with what looked like seeping blood. Then there are images of a railing crowd silently yelling, in unison and in synch with the meter of the chant, as if ghost voices are coming through their mouths. The mob (as was true historically) is blaming the Jews in the town for their suffering. In "Plague," the violence and speed of the images, and the way they sometimes paralleled the rhythm of the music and sometimes jaggedly go against it, embody my strategy of suggesting the emotional power of the situation without spelling it out.

As choreographer of both *Ellis Island* and *Book of Days*, my interest was to incorporate movement sections in films that consist mainly of concrete, recognizable events and defined characters. The movement sections had to flow smoothly into the other scenes without destroying the integrity of the film. For example, in *Ellis Island* there is a scene of immigrants detained on the island, keeping their spirits up by dancing together gaily in an empty, desolate ballroom. I worked on very simple steps and patterns based on the social and folk dances of the period. I kept the camera still in a medium-long shot to create the boundaries of the room and emphasize the patterns of the dance. With that master shot as the base of the scene, I intercut close-ups of immigrants behind cage-like, wire mesh walls, saying good-bye to their loved ones, holding hands, or staring numbly into the camera. The contrast between the long shot of the lively dancing and the still, mute close-ups creates the tension of the actual situation: the very real possibility of the immigrants' forced return to their country of origin and the end of their dream.

In *Book of Days*, there is an idiosyncratic dance between the madwoman and the young girl in the madwoman's cave. By imitating the madwoman's move-

Book of Days (1988), a film by Meredith Monk. Photo by Dominique Lasseur.

ment, the young girl learns her visionary skills. Since I played the madwoman myself and Toby Newman, who played the young girl, was only 10 years old and untrained, I devised a movement game for us to play. My goal was always to move in a way that Toby didn't anticipate, and her goal was to follow me as quickly and closely as possible. The situation itself provided the humor and tenderness—as well as the fresh, authentic movement vocabulary—that I wanted for the scene.

Another movement section in *Book of Days* is the Dance of Death. I worked closely with Rob McBrien, who played Death, on movement so energized that it seemed to burn through his body. He chose to dance to one of my pieces, "Engine Steps," even though it would not be part of the final music track. We played a tape of the music, giving him a relentless underlying sound environment to work against as we filmed. We were trying for a trance-like intensity: the body danced by larger forces, the inexorable inevitability of death. Because, as director, I had already storyboarded the scene and for the most part had its overall structure and continuity in mind, I could work with Rob on short spurts of extreme kinetic energy, so that he could achieve a level of ecstatic transparency; I did not have to tire him out by shooting more footage than was necessary.

Whenever I make a film, I'm struck by the similarity between filmmaking and composing music. I've always believed that images themselves contain an inherent musicality, and that editing them together is like making music for the senses. My inspiration has been the great masters of the late silent film:

MOMENTS FROM A MOVIE

Because of our low budget on *Book of Days*, we had to keep to schedule no matter what the weather was. One day, it was pouring rain but we were scheduled to shoot the "Churchyard Entertainment" scene, a "show within a film" taking place on a platform in front of the old church. Based on accounts of early Christian church plays or masques, the scene consists of a series of absurd "acts" applauded or booed by a crowd standing in the courtyard. The acts culminate in the "grand finale"—a living painting inspired by the flat perspective and painted cosmologies of the Middle Ages. Starting from an empty frame with a man and woman kneeling in the middle, the picture is filled in little by little with creatures from different realms: angels, animals, Neptune, two-headed monsters, a king, troubadours, and finally, representing the seasons, autumn leaves, snow, grass growing from the bottom of the frame, and the sun.

Yoshio Yabara, our costume designer, had made brilliant, imaginative costumes from Tyvek, a cheap but sturdy paper. The performers' faces were painted shades of yellow, white, or blue (which created quite a stir in the restaurant of the local French hotel that catered our lunches). We also decided to make all the objects from cardboard and cover the platform with it, giving the whole "show" a droll, handmade ambiance. Even before we started to shoot, the rain was coming down. We had covered the floor of the platform with plastic; the performers in their thin paper costumes carried umbrellas and huddled under coats. When we couldn't wait any longer since the daylight was going, we shot the grand finale. The scene was very intricate, with many people to coordinate and a complicated cueing system. All the action took place within a static frame, so the rhythm of the entrances and the composition of the frame had to be just right. At the end of the scene, the camera pulled back to reveal the technicians throwing snow or holding the sun, adding one more layer of humor. We did one take, and something went wrong during the pullback. There were no cuts in the entire scene, so we had to do the whole thing again. By this time, the costumes, the stage, and the performers were soaked. We did the second take, which looked good.

Back in New York, examining the rushes carefully, we could see the "floor" of the platform disintegrating, the fingernails of one monster getting caught in the wet hair of the monster in front of him, the sun "melting," and the man and woman looking like two brave but miserably wet rats. But such is the magic of film that no one who has viewed that scene has ever told me that they noticed anything wrong at all!—M. M.

DVD 5 F. W. Murnau, Carl Dreyer, the D. W. Griffith of *Intolerance*, Sergei Eisenstein, and, of course, Buster Keaton. Each of these directors understood the metaphysical power of images and invented sophisticated structures of rhythmic complexity and freedom. They were not constrained by the specificity and particularity of text.

Since my work always treads the line between abstraction and figuration, my challenge in film has been to sustain a long, poetic, nonverbal form using only shards of narrative and, for the most part, nonpsychological action. In this way my films are closer to dance: they rely on gesture, music, the faces and bodies of the actors, and simple, clear situations to convey levels of content. Coming from both a music and a dance background, I have always trusted in a universal, nonverbal language that speaks directly and eloquently to the body and mind. The early silent films used images as a language that communicated to people all over the world. With the addition of sound, film became more a literary, storytelling medium. For me, breaking habitual expectations of a clear-cut narrative and making film that is not only musical and abstract but also reflective of the intricate nature of our world, has been a rich and exciting adventure. From using film as one component of a complex, live, multimedia performance work to making feature-length films that weave these elements together in the film frame, I continue to be captivated by the transformative power and magic of cinema.

Cut to dance of death figure in smoke

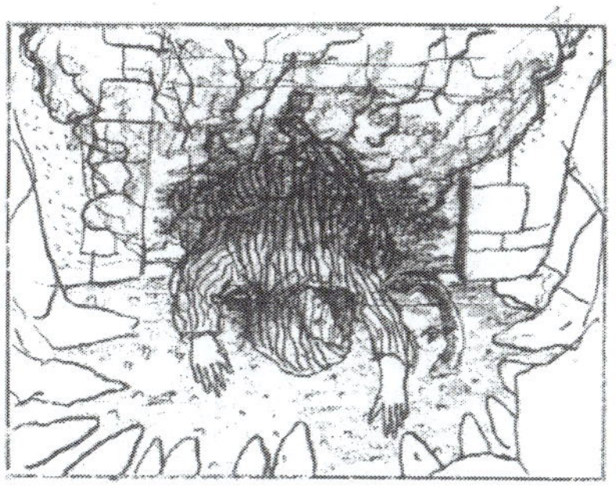

Cut to medium shot of dead madwoman and dead ferret, with people standing around them

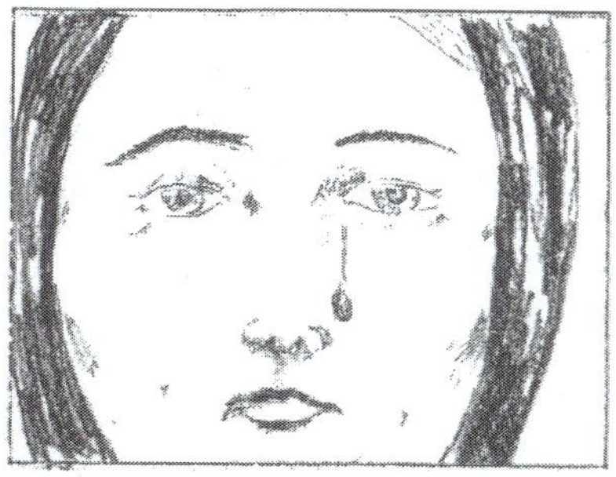

Cut to CU of girl with tear rolling down her face

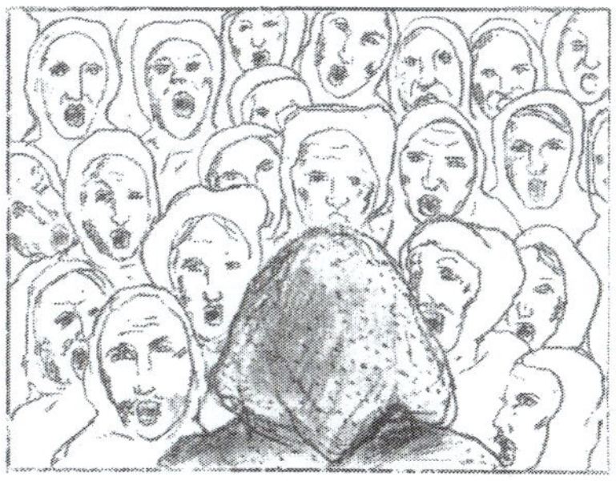

Cut to medium shot of mob confronting monk

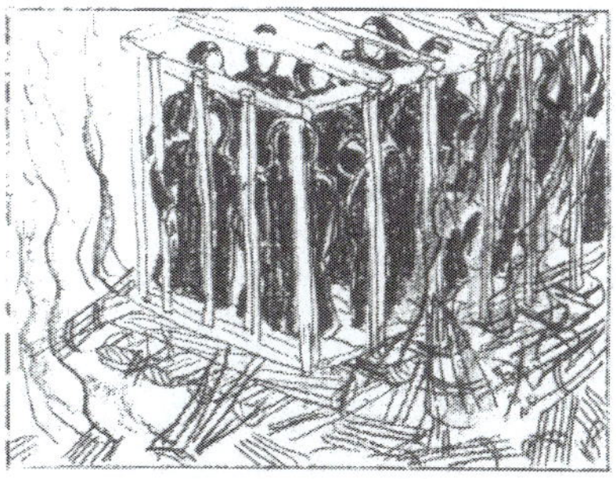

Cut to medium shot of Jews in a cage, with beginnings of a fire around them

Cut to long shot of marketplace, where more dead bodies with red X's are accumulating. Sound increasing in volume

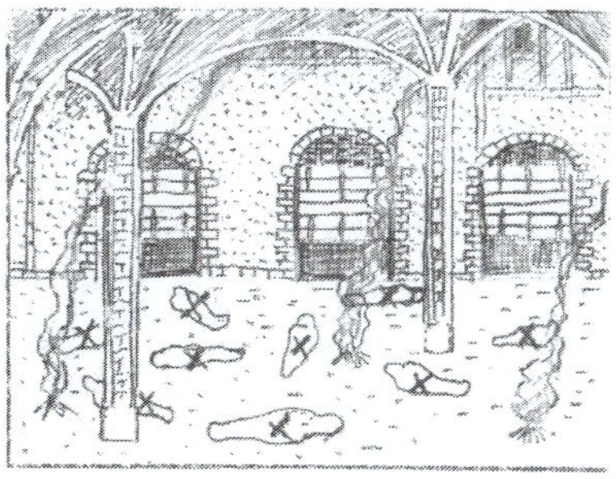

Cut to long shot of dead bodies with red X's on them

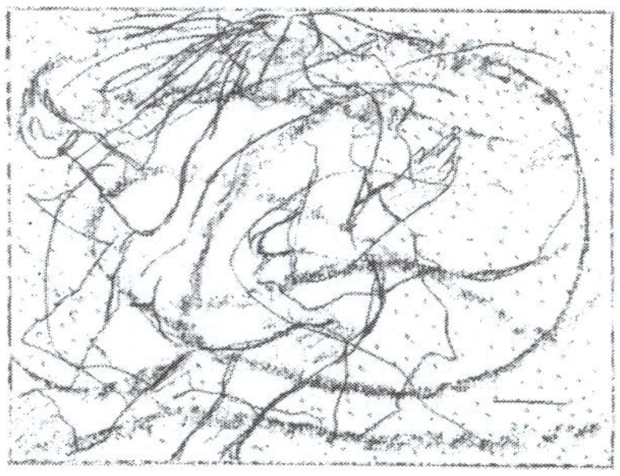

Cut to dance of death figure in smoke

Cut to shot of map with more red on it

Series of nine storyboards from *Book of Days*. "I originally drew preliminary storyboards for *Book of Days* but early on, I realized that I could conceptualize the film better by seeing more accurate drawings of what I had in mind. Yoshio Yabara, the art director of the film, rendered the images as we discussed how each scene would go. The storyboards became a kind of armature or skeleton of the work. Then I was free to fill out or change things during the shoot." —M. M. Storyboards by Yoshio Yabara

CHAPTER 16

Forsythe and Film: Habits of Seeing

Roslyn Sulcas

DVD 12
Kammer/Kammer (2000)
120 min
Excerpt 4 min 15 sec

Production Note: *Kammer/Kammer* premiered December 8, 2000. The excerpt is from the single camera PAL DV digital recording documenting the performance. The piece on stage used a "6 camera set up / 2 overheads / 3 fixed / 1 handheld / 2 Channel output on 6 plasma screens / 1 Barco Projector. The piece constitutes a line recording of a stage piece that is increasingly obscured from the public's view (until the stage becomes only a film set for a performance visible on screen)."—William Forsythe

William Forsythe, 2001. Photo by Judy Mitoma.

One of William Forsythe's most noticeable characteristics as a choreographer is his intense curiosity about other art forms. From the early works the American-born choreographer made for the Stuttgart Ballet through a freelance career in the early 1980s and the 40-odd ballets that he has made since becoming artistic director of the Frankfurt Ballet in 1984, his openness to stimulus from other fields has forged a distinctive theatrical style that abets his idiosyncratic and complex choreographic language. He extends the vocabulary of dance in a way that goes beyond the world of ballet even as it radically extends the possibilities of that form.

Forsythe grew up in Manhasset, Long Island, New York, where, he says, "like most American kids, film and TV were part of everyday life, part of my mental imagery."[1] In high school, he loved popular dance forms (rock 'n' roll, the Twist, the Mashed Potato) and choreographed several musical comedy productions for his classmates, but he only started formal dance classes at Jacksonville University in Florida when he began pursuing a liberal arts degree there. His majors were drama and humanities, but he was already particularly engaged with mathematics and art history, interests he took with him into a dance career when he left Jacksonville to join the Joffrey Ballet School in 1969. A short stint with the Joffrey Ballet preceded his entry into Stuttgart in 1973, just before the death of the company's director, John Cranko. He made his first work, *Urlicht*, for the annual young choreographers' Noverre Society performance in 1976.

Forsythe's keen sensitivity to the popular culture of his upbringing, his acute, ever-present intellectual curiosity, and his sense of the potential permeability of cultural forms have, from the first works made in Stuttgart, brought influences from many different disciplines to work. Film, architecture, mathematics, myth, linguistic theory, and philosophy have had the most consistent influence on his creative processes—not simply as visual or textual ingredients to be inserted into a dance work, but as paradigms or strategies for actually creating movement. I will look at the role of film in Forsythe's work because his use of this medium is perhaps the most consistent of all the cultural stimuli he has drawn upon during his choreographic career.

Forsythe's longstanding interest in the use of film techniques dates back to some of his earliest pieces for the Stuttgart Ballet, though most of these ballets retained a conventional neoclassical look and structure. "From very early on," he comments, "I created storyboards as a way of composing sequences of movement and thinking about the components of the dance." This sequential, "framed" way of thinking about movement was further developed in *Gänge*, a work made when he was guest choreographer for the Frankfurt Ballet in 1983. Although the ballet didn't use film as a visual element, it was "extremely film-oriented," according to Forsythe. "It took nine months to make, during which time I was reading Alain Robbe-Grillet and Roland Barthes's *Writing Degree Zero*, and trying to think cinematically. I worked with the dancers in terms of single frames, trying to reduce everything to its essential elements." The three-hour piece combines speech and dance in the enterprise of "dismantling the myth of ballet through ballet," breaking down its technical and theatrical components, then putting them back together in a context forever altered by the audience's new knowledge of its inner workings. "It was an attempt to stage a version of the kind of film that Robbe-Grillet was writing about," says Forsythe, "like Alain Resnais's *Providence*."

A year later, in 1984, Forsythe received an unexpected chance to work with cinematic techniques in their own medium, after being commissioned by the Vienna State Opera Ballet to participate in an Alban Berg evening. "The company was really terrible at that point," he explains, "and I tried to evade the project by suggesting that the music, *Three Orchestral Pieces,* was better suited to film than ballet. To my amazement, the director, Gerhard Brunner, said, 'OK, make a film.' He gave me the money allocated for the ballet, said that the orchestra had to be used, then gave us a free hand." Forsythe used painter Cara Perlman, photographer Gerard Benz, a musicologist—Marcus Spies—who was also a computer programmer, and two performers, Ron Thornhill and Alida Chase, while acting as cameraman and director, and he edited collectively with the group. His idea was "a narrative of moving pictures"—rather than choreography as such—composed of simple actions such as a hand gesture, Thornhill moving portraits by Perlman through the air, or Chase falling off a table. "We filmed it in the cellars of the Vienna Opera, and simultaneously photographed the sequences. The musicologist found that there were certain proportions Alban Berg was using in the structure of the music and programmed the timing of the appearance of the slides—how long they remained, when they faded or cut out. The principle of the film was degrees of motion on screen, moving towards more and more frames per second: from these static images, to the actual footage, to a last movement in which the slide sequences are refilmed and played fluidly."

This movement through different levels or layers of representations of reality (in this case performance, photography, film, film of photography) has been a consistent theme throughout Forsythe's work. He comments, apropos of his DVD 12 *Kammer/Kammer* (which premiered in Frankfurt in December 2000), "I actually worked on some of the exact things now that I was working on in *Berg Ab*: translating a live scene from a photograph to a set, then recreating the set on film, with the book containing the photograph itself as part of that set. I think that 17 years later, I was able to work this way without too much effort, because it has been such a constant subject; not films themselves, but film thinking."

This layering and framing is apparent in one of his most important early works for the Frankfurt Ballet, *The Interrogation of Robert Scott* (1986), based on improvisational techniques that Forsythe had been working on with the company. ("Robert Scott, trying to pin down the South Pole on a map, seemed to me a bit like a choreographer, a bit like a ballet dancer, trying to go someplace that actually doesn't need going to. . . . In ballet, your 'arrival' at a particular prescribed place is hard to determine.")[2] During a long series of solos in which the dancers focus on making detailed permutations of an extensive theme, their ballet-trained limbs mutating into hard-to-read configurations, a man's face, his expression neutral, is shown on a large television screen on one side of the stage. During most of the hour-long work, he calmly asks a repetitive series of questions ("Did you lose the beginning?" "Did it go in any particular order?" "Did I get where we were going?" "Was there a story?" "Was there a method of movement?" "Are there any documents?" "Any photo documents?"), quietly answering them himself ("yes," "no") after lengthy pauses. After a while, we realize that he is in fact being filmed live on stage, one of several people seated at a long table on the right, most of whom are wearing headphones and seem to be controlling the timing and order of events. This literal reframing of something taking place in front of us makes the man both less and more present. On screen, he is a talking head, a neutral analyst of the human psyche, a merciless interrogator of the exploratory process taking place on stage, a visual and aural counterpoint to the dance. On stage, he is small-scale and provisional, stripped of the authority and permanence accorded to him by the screen, just as the man Robert Scott is lost in the myth-making about "Robert Scott."

In the early 1990s, Forsythe used film in different ways in three successive full-length works: *Slingerland* (1990), *The Loss of Small Detail* (1991), and *As a Garden in This Setting* (1992). In all these ballets, the films were kept on a small scale, projected on television screens, backdrops, or even stool-tops; "a small window," as Forsythe describes the screen in *As a Garden*, on the exterior world. The films are of apparently arbitrary events: a piece of bread floating in a small lake, a spotted dog in the snow, blind people walking down a street, a bloody (perhaps tribal) ritual of some sort. Although all might be interpreted in the light of the atmosphere and content of the ballets, their primary function appears to be to add an extra textural and visual layer to the already complex stage context. *The Loss of Small Detail*, set in a pale gray-and-white universe, the

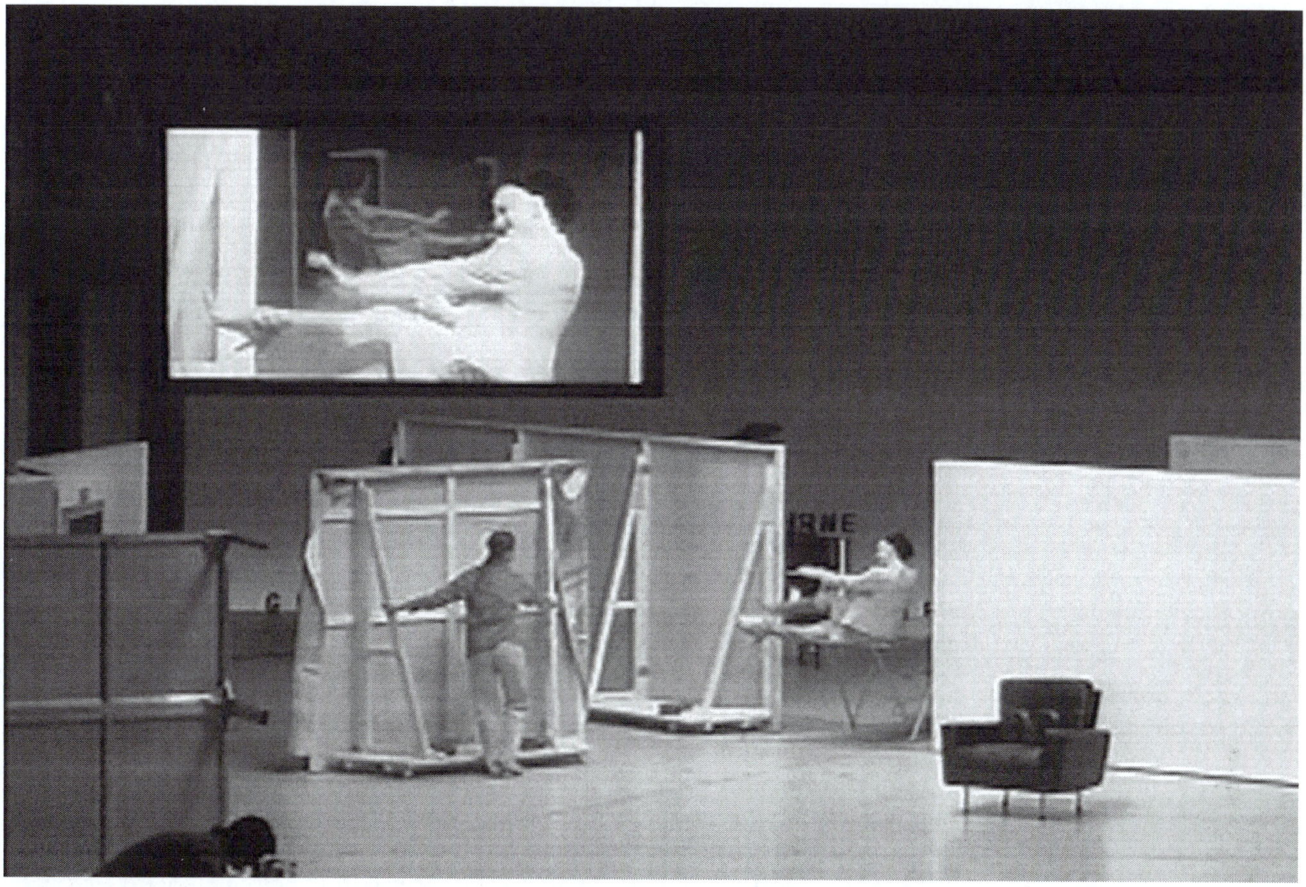

Still photograph from video documentary of Forsythe's multimedia stage work, *Kammer / Kammer* (2000), performed by the Frankfurt Ballet. Courtesy of William Forsythe. DVD 12

stage an enormous, empty white box, also employs cinematic techniques and themes in other ways. "*Loss* was conceived as a kind of film, but also as a description of an hypothetical projector," says Forsythe. "The whole piece was based on a grammatical tense, the future anterior, that you might describe as the state of a choreographer's projected imagination: 'this will already have happened.' While making a storyboard of the first version some years ago, I became aware that we live with the future anterior in order to act, to make. So the entire ballet is structured between texts, the actual events that happen, the films that you do see, the films that are spoken about that you don't see, the films or events that are close to what were described or hoped for, or not. It creates a kind of network of the reality of bringing these artworks to life—things that you thought were going to be there, that you thought were important or real, turn out to be literally yet another projection or illusion."

Forsythe also used the principles of film editing in structuring the choreography: "I like the idea in film that you can record several different versions of the same action, then choose the one you like, so in part two, I simply put more than one version of certain sequences onstage; the woman who narrates at the outset shows signs that say, 'Version A, version B,' and later talks about a film of a film, so that you have the idea that cinematic mechanisms are being revealed in different layers." Other spoken text also refers to a film: three women try to explain to us that we are "watching a film about contemporary characters" even as a naked spotted man, more evocative of the animals or decorated tribal figures already evoked in the piece, shuffles before them. At the end of the ballet, the banner of slowly scrolling text at the back of the stage remains fixed on "You are looking at a contemporary film"—a strange, dislocating injunction that seems to want to make us question what, indeed, we have just seen. For Forsythe, the importance of this dislocation seems to lie in the breaking down of boundaries between art forms. "It is a ballet," he says, "but there's a complex interweaving of texts, visual and spoken—and then later on you have a book, the program, to peruse and decide where the thing stops, or if it does stop."

This fascination with the mutability of forms is extended in a subsequent full-length work, the 1992 *Alie/na(c)tion*, in a much more specific way. Using the notion of a "cultural template"—"using other domains, like film, as points of departure and translating them into our own terms"[3]—Forsythe took several sequences from both Ridley Scott's *Alien* and James Cameron's *Aliens* and used them as "forms of organization" from which the dancers took choreographic cues. In Act I, a logic game turned nightmare, nine dancers scramble around, under, and over long wooden benches in complicated patterns, seemingly driven urgently by some unknown and unseen imperative. Two overhead television screens face them, emitting occasional noises and shrieks, while another dancer manipulates a complicated-looking and mysterious technological apparatus, and a seated man implacably counts out the passing time in seconds and minutes.

It is, in fact, the film extracts on the television screens that provide the dancers with organizational cues, not through copying the actors' movements but by "translating" the two-dimensional screen events into a physical reading. "We created an alphabet," says Forsythe, "built from specific gestures. When the dancers looked at the screen, they could choose one parameter—it could be a bodily part, or a color, or a geometric room shape—and work from that. Say you chose an arm, you might choose to spell *arm* with the given alphabet. But you also keep reading the screen, moving your body in the direction that the actor's arm was moving while spelling."

Nik Haffner, a dancer with the company, describes another technique, using color: "Red, say, will determine the movements in the room. If a red tablecloth appears in the left upper-hand corner of the picture, the dancer projects this onto the stage by lying down flat in the left upstage corner. She projects each point on the screen to a position on the stage as a kind of 'mapping,' retrieving all her movements, her pauses, her different places on the stage, as information from the color system. But of course, there are a lot of other possibilities. There are no fixed rules that cannot be broken."[4]

The dancers also had to be aware of the soundtrack, all reacting to specific lines in the same way, whatever else they were doing ("This might have actually happened about ten times," Forsythe comments drily), and take heed of the time counts, interrupting their improvisation to move to specific places at specific times. The effect is indeed alienating, and curiously upsetting: the dancers seem to inhabit an inaccessible and frightening world in which their movements are both ordinary (walking, running, jumping) and peculiarly complex, yet divorced from any context as they appear compelled to traverse the stage in odd and complicated sequences.

Forsythe used this technique again in a short piece called *Pivot House*, performed only a few times during a 1994 tour. This time, though, he used four television monitors playing very brief clips from different films, testing the dancers' ability to "translate" simultaneously. Haffner comments that "it was a kind of preparation for the next piece, *Eidos Telos*." While working on *Eidos*, Forsythe brought in a film editor to talk to the company about filmmaking techniques. "The edits that exist in cinema can actually work as scores for us," he explains, "and we now have methods for interpreting these films, extruding their organization into an organization on stage. It depends what the instructions are for the dancers in a particular scene, but screens can be read for duration or direction or specificity of movement; it's an interesting way to work because the movement gets organized by what the performers' eyes are attracted to, and this produces a very different quality to the dance."

In *Eidos*, the screens are again visible only to the dancers. One gives a running time count, a second shows brief film clips, and a third shows the letters "A" to "Z" in random order. (In a further refinement, the letters may be turned, twisted, or toppled, providing further directional possibilities for the dancers.) In the first part of the ballet, there are also clocks on stage that have letters rather than numbers, providing cues for working off the given movement alphabet. "The movement is never performed in its 'original' version," says Haffner: "The issue is rather to find a system for the movement catalogue we worked out, in order to edit or cut it at any time, to use filmmaker's jargon. Thus, at these moments the dancer himself determines on stage the sequence in which he compiles the material and also the way in which he reshapes it. Of course, the dancers are not obligated to work through everything that is offered; the mass of information could never be coped with. It's very seldom that Forsythe comes to us after a performance and says 'Great dancing.' But he often comes and says 'Good decisions.' That is really a totally different concept of choreography."

In all his ballets, Forsythe shows a preoccupation with multiple points of view. As well as frequently offering different elements simultaneously (film, dance, sound, speech, props) in the full-length theatrical works, even his straight dance pieces almost always—at some point—offer competing aspects for the audience to choose between momentarily. It might appear that it is not just the filmmaker's ability to cut and edit that Forsythe envies, but also the possibility of switching perspective and location at will. In the recent full-length works *Endless House* (1999) and *Kammer/Kammer*, Forsythe's proclivity for forcing the audience to choose between competing visual attractions is made into a structural device that deliberately aspires to these cinematic facilities. The genesis of *Endless House*, he says, was a documentary about the photographer Steven Meisel: "They were doing a shoot for Italian *Vogue*, and it had all these guys moving the sets around, moving the walls around, and using these big lights. I thought, that's it—I even had the light, which I'd been keeping for years, knowing that I'd use it one day."

DVD 12

Endless House, which was conceived for the cavernous Bockenheimer Depot, a theatrical space newly available to the Frankfurt Ballet, entirely undoes the frontal concept of the proscenium stage by occupying an extensive rectangle of space that the audience surrounds. Chairs are angled toward the stage, and mobile screens partition the performance spaces so that no one place allows full vision; audience members are encouraged to move around freely, as if at an exhibition of performance art. Like a director yoking together a succession of disparate successive scenes, Forsythe nonetheless shapes the work into a coherent theatrical experience, drawing us into different segments by opening and closing up the space, by skillfully deploying light, and by alternately assembling and disseminating ensemble dances and scenes. At other points, he makes several disparate smaller groups (a lyrical pas de deux, a tangled quartet, a man manipulating a woman's body) visually available all at once (rather like the multiple screens in *Time Code*, a 1999 film by Mike Figgis, who has also made a documentary about Forsythe.)[5]

DVD 12 The panoramic visual mobility achieved in *Endless House* is given its literal rendering in *Kammer/Kammer*, in which part of the stage action is presented as a film within a proscenium setting that uses similar mobile walls to form modular "rooms" ("It's like *Endless House,* but the audience have nice seats," Forsythe quips). The work is based on two texts—"Essay on My Life as Catherine Deneuve" by Anne Carson, and "Outline of My Lover" by Douglas Martin—each of which is narrated as an autobiographical account of inaccessible and lost love, in a patchwork of dramatic scenes that keeps the dance literally behind walls, often visible only on the large screens that hang over the stage and the audience. The filmed sections are extensive and live, their composition and timing determined at each performance by Philip Bussman, who designed the editing, and by Forsythe, who designed the shots. "Initially I knew that I wanted to use film," says Forsythe, "but as I was working on the piece, it became clear to me that it was going to be a live filming, a sort of hybrid. I wanted to bring film into the theatrical medium, like a fabulous magnifying glass. The piece is partly about intimacy, and film allows you to go up close, to get that thing that people miss in the theater. I also like the look of dancing on film."

Although it has several achingly beautiful dance passages, *Kammer/Kammer* is really more like a play that is filmed than a dance piece; it constitutes an almost full circle for Forsythe from using film as movement strategy to incorporating it as a direct means of representation. This new direction—if that is indeed what it proves to be—is, however, consistent with the curiosity about "ways of seeing" that has informed his career. "What you can do in this kind of—let's call it filmed theater," he says, "is create metaphors through withholding and absence. Film creates a new kind of curtain, a screen that falls in the path of vision. All the time, you're trying to figure out, where is the camera, where am I looking right now? You can hear the dancers in the next room, even glimpse them occasionally, and see exactly what they are doing on screen. But even though you might be satisfied with the image, something tells you, 'They should be here with me.' Is that a habit of seeing? What I like is that it creates a kind of desirous hunger, and it causes you to think, what is this, and why am I affected so?"

NOTES

1. All quotations by William Forsythe are drawn from the author's personal, unpublished interviews with the choreographer unless otherwise stated.
2. Roslyn Sulcas, "Kinetic Isometrics," *Dance International*, Summer 1995. This quotation was amended slightly by Forsythe, in personal correspondence, June 2001; hereafter cited as Sulcas, 1995.
3. Sulcas, 1995.
4. Nik Haffner, "Forsythe and the Media, a Report," sent to the author, June 2000.
5. *Just Dancing Around,* made for Channel 4, UK.

CHAPTER 17

Dancing and Cameras

Bill T. Jones

One of my first experiences of dance was watching the June Taylor Dancers on the *Jackie Gleason Show*. And yes, there was the brilliantly innovative choreography of Busby Berkeley in the old movies we watched every afternoon, until my mother made us turn the television set off just before dinner. But an even stronger impression was made by the way people danced around us all the time. Being migrant workers—a colony of itinerant African American fieldworkers seasonally migrating along the eastern seaboard—we were forced into a cultural enclosure that was hardly self-sufficient, though resourceful and vital in its social expressions. This enclosure imbued all social expressions—of which dance was a favorite—with a certain intensity, boldness, and daring. At various times, there was a jukebox in the workers' common room. Later, there was a short period when we even had a jukebox in our living room!

DVD 13
Ghostcatching (1999) 7 min 3 sec
Excerpt 2 min 34 sec

Production Note: "In these excerpts from *Ghostcatching*, fragments of Bill T. Jones's motion capture dancing have been resequenced and applied to a kinematic model rendered in a style of gesture drawing."—Paul Kaiser

In 1971, I met Arnie Zane at the State University of New York at Binghamton. Around this time I became besotted with dance, and infected Arnie as well. We were eager to experience it in any form. We were also intrigued by the "poetic cinema" of the late 1960s and 1970s. We studied at SUNY Binghamton with Ken Jacobs and Larry Gottheim, both of whom were avant-garde filmmakers, decidedly anti-narrative. Jacobs taught classes with an "analytical film projector," designed to demythologize the glamour of Hollywood movies by deconstructing their seductive effects through a frame-by-frame analysis. This process, like the photos of Eadweard Muybridge, encouraged us to approach movement in a cinematic fashion—that is, as a series of still pictures that could be joined, cut, spliced, and manipulated. We held technology in high regard, but in some suspicion. We were trying to re-create, on a human scale and in a homespun fashion, the illusions we witnessed in cinema. We were constantly using repetition, deconstructing sequences, and sometimes executing them backwards. In our early duets, one might see the two of us grappling, and then, at a later point, witness this partnering broken down into two solos, as if the duet were an object that could be taken apart.

That same year, 1971, saw the founding of the Experimental Television Center (ETC) in Binghamton. This was the brainchild of Ralph Hockings, a forward-thinking photography teacher at SUNY Binghamton. The Experimental

Television Center brought into our lives the Abe Colorizer, an image-processing device that was the precursor of many of the special effects we take for granted today. Also newly available was the CD Portapack, the first portable video recording machine. A gentle rivalry had sprung up between the Experimental Television Center and the progressive Cinema Department at the university. Ken Jacobs felt that film was life itself—that since it was the result of the passing of light through a filament, something natural, it was alive. It was magic: still pictures that moved! Video, on the other hand—the bombardment of electrons on a screen—resulted in a colder image that owed nothing to the natural beauty of light. Jacobs felt at that time that video could not be poetic. Arnie and I were poised, breathless with wonder and excitement, between these points of view. We were Romantics, preferring photography and films for their warmth and their reference to painting and other time-honored artistic practices rooted in handicraft.

Video was obliged to define itself as something other than "television," the great evil. However, artist Nam June Paik had made a convincing argument for the new medium when, in the late 1960s, as the first Portapaks became available, he said, "Paper is dead—except for toilet paper." The first cameras were clumsy and fragile, with batteries so big and heavy that they required a shopping trolley to be moved around. However, we were convinced that the future belonged to this electronic medium, capable of capturing motion and life, of creating and manipulating images that transcended the natural world.

In the summer of 1971, we took a job through a government employment program, helping to install the ETC. One of the perks of the job was that we were allowed to use the Portapaks and the various primitive special-effects devices available. We made a number of crude tapes reflecting what we'd seen in the avant-garde cinema: Andy Warhol and Hollis Frampton, Stan Brakhage, Michael Snow, Tony Conrad. All these people were important to us.

In my *Women in Art*, a very loose documentary of sorts, I interviewed various female friends, asking them what they thought about art. I included street scenes, and domestic sequences such as Arnie at his most androgynous in a bubble bath.

For Arnie's *The Devil's Gonna Get You*, he taped me in a sunlit room wearing a polka-dot dress and floral hat from a local thrift shop. With the neoclassical cupola of City Hall framed in the window behind me, I lounged and posed to a recording of the music of Bessie Smith. All these tapes were left with ETC when we abruptly departed at the end of the summer for Amsterdam. Some of them were erased.

In 1974, we returned to Binghamton to found the American Dance Asylum with Lois Welk and Jill Becker. We reestablished our relationship with the Experimental Television Center. Film, with its large, luminescent image, remained a seductive option, but it was prohibitively expensive. As choreographers, we found in video an affordable way to capture the ephemeral process of rehearsal and to document performances. The availability of the Portapak and a small community of video artists interested in our work exerted a strong influence on our thinking at the Dance Asylum.

One of the most successful videos either of us ever made is Arnie's *First Portrait Drawing*, created in collaboration with video artist Dena Crane. This work is a curious combination of photos and video footage. The photos are of a solo Arnie had danced against projected images of himself wearing an antique white sleeping gown, with the City Hall cupola in the background. These were edited into video footage of him moving in a dream-like, ritualized fashion, in and out of the loft-like upper floor of our home in Binghamton, to a vintage recording of Enrico Caruso singing "La donna è mobile."

We had our first experience with video in performance working with two video artists, Per Bode and Meryl Blackman. This collaboration connected our choreographic explorations to the quickly evolving world of the new technology. We saw its potential as a means of expanding the sense of space and time in live performance, as well as introducing an electronic counterpoint to the highly personal, weighted, non-virtuosic movement that Arnie, Lois Welk, Jill Becker, and I were creating.

With Meryl and Per, we did a site-specific performance at the ETC, utilizing cameras, monitors, and special-effects equipment in a work that explored real time and spatial relationships juxtaposed against electronic time delay, looping of imagery, and multiple points of view. We felt, as some audience members did, that combining electronic technology (subject to technical breakdowns) with our quirky dance movement was not a happy marriage. People felt torn about where to look and how to watch, so they never really relaxed into the experience. At the time—1977-78—Arnie and I decided in some frustration that video and dance did not work together.

The next time we used video with any confidence was in Section 3 of our 1983 collaboration with video media artist Gretchen Bender, *Freedom of Information*. Gretchen had said on more than one occasion, "Our insides are now outside." What she meant was that what had once been our deepest longings and fears were now the stuff of advertising and mass communication. This became the unacknowledged creed of much of our work throughout the 1980s and, in some ways, continues for me today.

For Section 3 of *Freedom of Information*, Gretchen Bender, using early digital animation techniques, created a film, a virtual landscape of dancing geometric forms that provided a lively counterpoint to Arnie's angular, hyperkinetic choreography. Gretchen also contributed to the evening a dense slide montage, a barrage of images that underlined our culture's preoccupation with visual glut and its obsession with the disjunction of space and time. The composer, David Cunningham, picked up on this theme, creating his score by constantly interrupting an old dance instruction record with loud electronic blasts and strange oral non-sequiturs that paralleled the projections. Arnie and I, through a relentless outpouring of dance phrases—sharp, violent, and energetic—joined Gretchen and David Cunningham in this rumination on our corporatized, media-driven world.

We returned to the use of media in live performance because of the persuasiveness of Gretchen's belief that they could coexist onstage, enhancing rather than neutralizing each other. In the 1970s, primitive technology and a lack of visual familiarity with the vocabulary of the new media on both our and the audience's part had prevented us from finding satisfactory solutions to the questions posed by the combination of live performance and media. Through Gretchen's encouragement and the success of Section 3 of *Freedom of Information*, we were once again open to the possibilities.

In *Still/Here* (1994), I set out to make a work about the commonality of human experience as represented by the inescapable fact of our mortality. I had enjoyed the community aspect of *Last Supper at Uncle Tom's Cabin*, a work that integrated 30 or more community members into each of the performances, which were held in 35 cities around the world. But having so many community people in the work had been a logistical nightmare. In *Still/Here*, I wanted the benefit of the testimony of people outside the dance world informing the content of the work, but I did not want them to be on stage. The medium of video offered a poetic way of introducing these personalities and their stories into the fabric of the piece. As part of my research for *Still/Here*'s creation, I held 14 workshops with people facing or having faced life-threatening illnesses. These "Survival Workshops Moving and Talking About Life and Death" were videotaped by Gretchen Bender.

During the performances, the individuals from the survival workshops were introduced in ghostly, gray-blue portraits, like spirits from another world. Gretchen wanted to suggest that we were communing across the unknown, while making this cool, electronic medium at once human and mysterious.

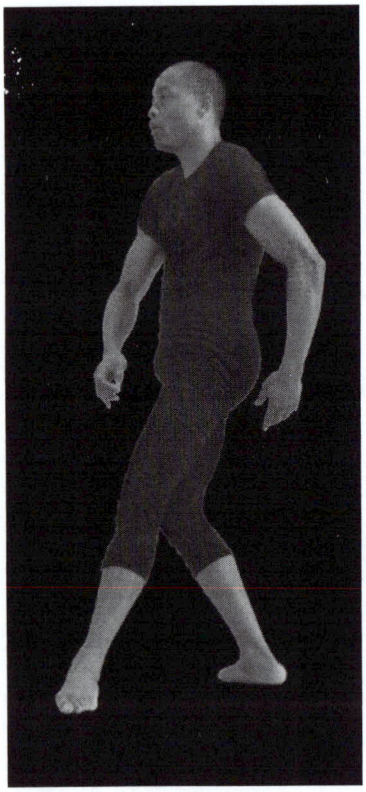

Bill T. Jones improvising during the production of *Ghostcatching*.

Motion capture markers attached to Jones's body and optically recorded and converted to digital 3D files.

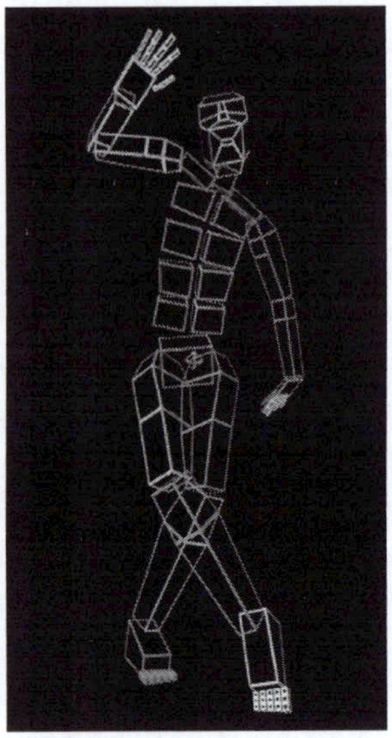

Motion capture data applied to kinematic model of the body.

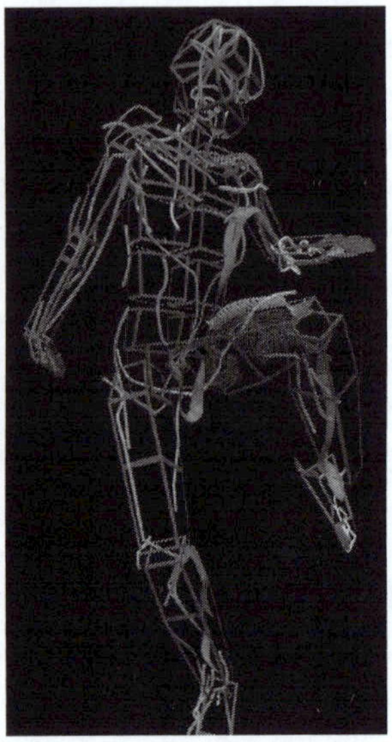

"Hand drawn" lines by Shelley Eshkar, modeled as mathematical curves.

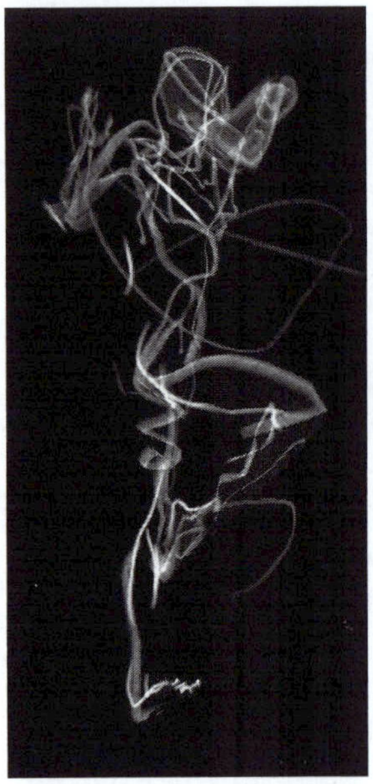

Sampled charcoal strokes applied and rendered as final drawn body.

Still from the film *Ghostcatching* (1999) by Bill T. Jones, Paul Kaiser, and Shelley Eshkar.

Series of images demonstrating the evolution of *Ghostcatching* (1999) by Bill T. Jones, Paul Kaiser, and Shelley Eshkar. Courtesy of Paul Kaiser, Bill T. Jones, and Shelley Eshkar (1999).

In 1998, Paul Kaiser and Shelley Eshkar of Riverbed Media came to me and asked if I'd participate in creating a Web site for the Keith Haring Foundation. I became excited as they described their original idea, which was to re-envision and enliven Kwong Chi Tseng's 1984 photos of me being body-painted by Keith. I thought that would be a fitting tribute to Keith, and would complete something that was suggested by the frieze-like cut-out constructions he'd made of these seven poses. In his choices of the gestures and their cinematic arrangement, Keith was already suggesting that they were a dance. Paul and Shelley promised that, through the use of digital technology, these still images could truly come alive. The idea was to motion-capture my naked body moving improvisationally, in and out of the seven iconographic poses, and then to reconstitute Keith's original drawings over my moving virtual body.

However, the rich virtual possibilities that my movement, as interpreted through motion-capture technology, offered Paul and Shelley overshadowed the original Keith Haring Web site idea and provided the framework for the creation of *Ghostcatching*, an 8-minute-long virtual dance installation commissioned by the Cooper Union. We began making what was to be called a virtual motion alphabet: a catalogue of isolations, undulations, shudders, and various other personal movement strategies that I employ in my dancing. We even discussed building software based on choreographic rules and parameters predetermined by me, capable of combining and recombining this motion alphabet. Our concept promised dances choreographed by a computer using my personal movement. This has not happened so far.

DVD 13

Ghostcatching was expensive and time-consuming to make. It was included in my solo program "The Breathing Show," along with a film by the poetic filmmaker Abraham Ravett. Abraham, the son of Czech Holocaust survivors, had sent me some very moving films he'd made over the past 20 years, some of which dealt with history, biography, and the holocaust. One was of his father, and it reminded me of the avant-garde films that had been so important to us in the 1970s. I thought that low-tech, grainy film would be a lovely contrast and counterpoint to *Ghostcatching*. Both films solved a problem for the solo performer: how to take a recess from the stage without breaking the flow of the evening. I wanted something visual that still referred to the performer in some way. Abraham decided to make his portrait of me by photographing my new garden and objects from my intimate environment. Though divergent in almost every way, both films enjoy a similar distinction: they succeed as visual portraits without their subject ever being seen.

I remain committed to live performance as my primary means of expression. However, I am also open to the possibilities of the new technology. *Ghostcatching*, with its process of extracting personal movement from the choreographer-as-prime mover and freeing this movement from the personality and temperament of the choreographer-as-performer, represents an unlikely parallel to the traditional notion of the choreographic innovator developing a personal style of movement, codifying it, and projecting the results onto a community of dancers. In both cases, this mysterious and difficult-to-define phenomenon called dance leaves its source and takes on an identity, a destiny independent of its creator. I hold to dance because it is decidedly concrete in the face of a world in which ever more experiences are facsimiles, but there is no small irony in the exciting prospect of this most natural of human phenomena—the dance—being transformed through the medium of technology into a poetic parallel virtual incarnation.

CHAPTER 18

Frequently Pondered Questions

Paul Kaiser

DVD 13
Ghostcatching (1999) 7 min 3 sec
Excerpt 2 min 34 sec

Production Note: "In these excerpts from *Ghostcatching*, fragments of Bill T. Jones's motion capture dancing have been resequenced and applied to a kinematic model rendered in a style of gesture drawing."—P. K.

The virtual dance collaborations I've been involved with have triggered unexpectedly intense interest not only in the dance and computer fields, but also in the popular press.[1] People have the sense that the intersection of art and technology is now particularly important, especially when their point of overlap is the body. As a result, I've been invited to a lot of conferences, where my goal has been to wave off any mystification that might obscure the work. If there is going to be any mystery here, let it be in the art itself, not in its technical realization or in vague theoretical formulations taking off from it.

The most interesting moments at those conferences come when questions are posed. Usually they're raised by members of the audience, though sometimes they occur to me when I'm on my own afterwards, in my hotel room or on an airplane. Here are some I keep thinking about.

WHY THE INTEREST IN ABSTRACTING MOTION FROM THE BODY?

It's true that motion-capture is a process of subtraction, of taking away. The infrared cameras have eyes only for the reflective markers worn by the performing bodies, and not for the bodies themselves. Right away we lose all vision of muscle and flesh, and with that all sense of effort as well, since we can no longer make out the actual struggle and sweat of the performing body. The face also vanishes, and with it the expressions that signal intention and feeling. Thoroughly stripped away are the dancers' stage presences: their physical beauty and charisma. What good is this?

One way to answer that question is by posing others. Is there beauty in motion seen all on its own, without seeing the body that created it? Do the virtuoso performers on stage distract us from a more ineffable beauty that we sense only vaguely when watching them? Can we force it into focus by squinting, as it were—peering through some new lenses that technology has just given us?

But this talk about seeing motion without the body is misleading. Granted, motion-capture recording produces mere data sets, collections of numbers—but software immediately converts these into visible form, into something that makes sense to our eyes. At the very least, we translate the captured motion into white dots corresponding to the markers placed on the body. As soon as those dots start moving, we sense the body implied by them, a curiously palpable form in the black void of the screen.

Most often, the motion-capture data sets are then translated into a solid 3D simulation of the body. In the program we use, Character Studio, this body is called a "biped" (which inspired the Merce Cunningham dance title). Most conventional animators model the bipeds into ever more realistic figures, simulating flesh and muscle and even face. The more realistic the appearance, however, the more artificial the feeling. The digital double falls well short of the real thing, making us most aware of the technology's inadequacy.

When I first started working in 3D, therefore, I asked myself: Why photographic realism? Isn't it true that drawing lets you see and feel more? Doesn't what you leave out of a picture show as much as what you put in? My aim in my work with Shelley Eshkar was to make a hand-drawn body—an expressive figure that you could see through like an X-ray, an animated frame that fully revealed the motions mapped onto it.

Where we sought complete realism was in the motions themselves. After all, as Cunningham wanted to know, who's interested in a head that can spin around three times? (Answer: Hollywood.) Eshkar and I kept abstracting our figures further—into dots, sticks, curves, poles—but we took care not to distort the underlying motions: no hundred-foot leaps, no impossible pivots.

We insisted that the motion be true, but you can question that, too. True in what way? Motion capture is accurate, perhaps, but when a performer's motion is captured, doesn't it suddenly occupy a radically different kind of time? Isn't it now close to timeless, the very opposite of real performance, whose essence is that it's "water running through the hands," as Cunningham says? And haven't we also made it "spaceless," since we can now put it down virtually anywhere? (I admit to feeling that the dematerialization of the stage space in *Biped* was our biggest accomplishment there.)

"Is that me?" Bill T. Jones wanted to know on first seeing his motion-capture dots on the screen. Good question: Who is the figure that's moving, once the motion is disembodied? All of *Ghostcatching* spun out of that enigma, as we multiplied Jones's identity through a series of spawns, one figure begetting the next. DVD 13 By contrast, Cunningham cheerfully ignored the issue. In our first collaboration, *Hand-drawn Spaces*, he let his chance operations combine the movements of Jeannie Steele and Jared Phillips, obliterating any differences in body size, sex, and self.

In every dance conference, a few hands are raised with questions about notation. I think it's clear that motion-capture, combined with video, will soon replace paper-based notation schemes like Laban and Benesh, which few can read anyway. But what are the criteria for good notation? Cunningham says that it must be visual: dancers learn by looking. I wonder whether it shouldn't also be creative. That is, can't dance notation be as powerful as music notation, which not only lets a musician play, but also lets a composer compose?

Notation brings us back to the question of identity. I remember ballet master Suki Schorer's reaction to a trial motion-capture we made of Balanchine's *Harlequinade*.[2] "It's actually useful," she said, "that you can't make out the individual body, only the motion. Students will start concentrating on mastering the movement itself, not on imitating the star."

WHAT DO CHOREOGRAPHY AND COMPUTER SCIENCE HAVE TO TELL EACH OTHER?

When I ask filmmaking students at liberal arts universities what they know of Alan Turing and Joseph von Neumann, I usually get puzzled looks. And I get blank stares when I mention John Cage and Merce Cunningham in computerdom.

How curious that at midcentury we had Cage/Cunningham in the arts and Turing/von Neumann in mathematics addressing many of the same questions. To my knowledge, there was no crossover between them, but many of their preoccupations—random access, chance, emergent structure—are amazingly similar. One of my students, trying to illuminate this overlap, unearthed a wonderful quote from Turing:

> An interesting variant on the idea of a digital computer is a 'digital computer with a random element'. These have instructions involving throwing a die or some equivalent electronic process . . . Sometimes such a machine is described as having free will.[3]

This relates to a question I'm frequently asked about Cunningham's legendary use of chance operations. What exactly does he do, and why? I can only report on what I saw during our *Hand-drawn Spaces* collaboration, after we'd motion-captured 71 phrases of movement. To put them together into choreographed sequences, he simply rolled his dice. He trusted that chance would find things that would never have entered his mind otherwise.

John Cage started using chance operations to get beyond the self, to transcend his personal predilections and habits. Questioning the effectiveness of this practice, I came across a remark by his mentor, Marcel Duchamp:

> Your chance is not the same as mine, is it? If I make a throw of the dice, it will never be the same as your throw. And so an act like throwing dice is a marvelous expression of your subconscious.[4]

On its face, this statement is nonsense. Are dice influenced by the person rolling them? No. Yet doesn't Duchamp aptly describe his own work here, and also Cage and Cunningham's? No matter how random their constructions, aren't the resulting works inescapably personal? To reduce this to absurdity, has Merce Cunningham ever rolled the dice and had George Balanchine or Cab Calloway or a whirling dervish emerge in a dance instead of himself? Is such self-transcendence even conceivable by these methods?

Perhaps not. But let's look back at Turing for a moment. In the same way that Cage/Cunningham think chance will give their artworks greater autonomy, Turing wonders whether chance can endow his computer with free will. Can Turing succeed where Cage and Cunningham fall short?

What's missing from Cage and Cunningham (and from many who followed)[5] is complex contingency, which comes only by building networks of IF/THEN relationships. For chance to be powerful, its effects must ripple down through many possible branches. This means that it's not pure chance but, rather, weighted probability that deserves our attention. In reality, isn't it rarely the case that multiple outcomes are equally likely?

To be more specific, in *Hand-drawn Spaces*, we saw that when Cunningham needed to find a dance phrase to follow another, he rolled his dice and accepted that choice. This worked because he'd created all 71 phrases to go with one another, and because the Character Studio software generated logical transitions between any two phrases seamlessly.

One of Character Studio's creators, Michael Girard, now imagines doing all of this cybernetically. He asks: What if one had, say, 71,000 movements to choose from rather than 71? (You may object that increasing the number of phrases also increases the number of possible interconnections by several orders of magnitude, but that's what computers are for.) In the database of movements, each phrase is classified according to its speed, rhythm, style, and other features, after which one can start to apply some rules—that is, to choreograph.

In a recent e-mail, Girard imagined several scenarios. What if one computed a piece such that dancers could perform ever-faster motions in an increasingly tight space? Or divided a company into three groups and experimented with rules like this:

> Blue group follows Green spatially and Red rhythmically
> while Red follows Blue spatially and Green rhythmically.

Choreographers routinely explore such rules and patterns as well, of course—and perhaps more subtly—but not across such a potentially vast range of phrases and permutations and conditions. "The ocean of possibilities here," Girard wrote, "is so deep it's hard to fathom."

This system is not unlike the Big Blue supercomputer that finally outplayed Gary Kasparov. However, while chess is a closed system (albeit incalculably large) with a fixed number of pieces and rules, choreography is open: you can add as many new dancers and movements as you like. Still, the brute-force searches of chess and motion-capture databases do resemble each other in that both exceed human capability.

There is another man/machine contest that's even more to the point here—the Turing Test of artificial intelligence, for which we can now imagine a dance variant. Could our hypothetical system choreograph a dance such that no one could tell whether it was the product of human or artificial intelligence? And if it passed this test—or even if it did not pass—would it not then constitute the autonomous work that Cage and Cunningham aspired to as well?

Real autonomy is an attribute of living things, which is where von Neumann comes in. First, to inquire whether artificial life forms ("automata") could evolve mathematically, he asked whether one could devise an algorithm for self-reproduction—in his view, the true test of life. He invented a marvelous playing field to run such tests, an infinite two-dimensional grid in which logical games called "cellular automata" could play themselves out. The most famous of such trials was John Conway's game *Life*, a revelation to nearly everyone who has encountered it, including me. From three simple rules governing the life and death of abstract "cells" on the grid can come self-organizing and self-reproducing systems, often of extraordinary complexity.[6]

I can almost hear some of you objecting, "Isn't this becoming too one-sided, favoring computer science over art?" The truth is that: however fascinating such artificial life experiments are, so far (for the ones I've seen, at least) they don't resonate emotionally. Having spent a lot of time playing with such systems, I reluctantly concluded long ago that they don't qualify even as unwitting, unintended works of art. One's engagement with them is simply too shallow an experience.

Walking on the swarming sidewalks of a city like New York, have you ever had the feeling—this is a personality test—that you were: (a) an unconscious performer in a complex but unacknowledged dance, or (b) a cell in a von Neumann-like self-organizing system? Either sensation could have come from your simultaneous recollection of having looked down earlier, from a high office or apartment building, at the transitory patterns formed by the pedestrians below, who couldn't help but remind you of ants. Down on the street, however, you can forget about overall patterns for a moment and concentrate instead on the singular, shifting, unrepeatable beauty of each "ordinary movement" as it unfolds before you. This is to look at the street with dance eyes, I suppose—though long before I'd acquired such a thing, I was finding the same beauty with film eyes, shooting a Manhattan intersection in Super-8 for my film *Colourblind etc* (1977). How extraordinary is the negotiation of traffic, crosswalks, and crowds by each and every pedestrian, whether a six-year-old skipping toward the WALK sign or a businessman leaning into the onrush of cars, trucks, and buses to hail a cab.

Twenty-four years later, I am again addressing the complexity of the street, but this time looking down at it from a bird's-eye view—"looking," that is, with a computer rather than a viewfinder. It's difficult to talk about a work in progress, for who knows exactly how it will turn out? But the piece, called *Pedestrian*, is another collaboration with my old partners in crime, Susan Amkraut, Eshkar, and Girard. Our plan is to replace street lamps in the city with high-powered projectors beaming looped sequences of crowd simulations directly on the sidewalk below. The intelligence of the software that Amkraut and Girard have developed is opening the door to an entirely new way of working, which is less like constructing a work than growing it.

To be more specific, imagine that you can set a simulated crowd in motion, instructing its dozens of members to move toward a point on the other side of the screen. Each crowd member draws on its own repertoire of motion-captured movements—walks, turns, stutter-steps, runs, pauses—to negotiate this task, so that you have young and old, men and women, all moving in their own characteristic fashions and all nearly touching each other but never colliding. Now create a second crowd, give it yet another range of movements, set it on a course diagonal to the first . . . and watch as the computer performs a myriad of calculations to produce an emergent pattern from their intersection, one that you could never have quite predicted.

WILL VIRTUAL DANCE REPLACE OR DIMINISH REAL DANCE?

No, I don't think so. The more we embellish dance with technology, the more we'll start longing to see the real thing again—real dancers in real time and real space, with no distractions. But it's also true that we can never turn back the clock. So isn't it just as likely we'll be seeing these unadorned dances with new eyes, new ideas, and new questions?

NOTES

1. Over the past five years, I've collaborated with choreographers Merce Cunningham, William Forsythe, and Bill T. Jones, with computer scientists Susan Amkraut and Michael Girard, and with fellow digital artist Shelley Eshkar. Interested readers can find descriptions, stills, clips, conversations, essays, and links about these works on my Web site www.riverbed.com.

2. This motion-capture session was part of a longer exploration of dance preservation, which was initiated and funded by the Estate Project for Artists with AIDS (see chap. 19 in this volume).

3. Alan Turing, *Mechanical Intelligence* (edited by D. Ince; Amsterdam: Elsevier Science Publishers, 1992), 138.

4. Calvin Tomkin, *Duchamp: A Biography* (New York: Henry Holt, 1996), 132.

5. With the exception of William Forsythe, many of whose pieces at the Frankfurt Ballet derive from sophisticated dance algorithms. See my conversation with him online at http://www.riverbed.com/duoframe/duoideas.htm

6. A good starting point to a vast and vastly interesting subject is *The Recursive Universe: Cosmic Complexity and the Limits of Scientific Knowledge* by William Poundstone (New York: Morrow, 1985). Excellent freeware for running cellular automata is easily found online. My favorite is Life32 by Johan Bontes, which (at this writing, February 2001) may be found at http://psoup.math.wisc.edu/Life32.html.

Part IV

Recasting the Dance

CHAPTER 19

AIDS and the Videotape Fetish: The Estate Project for Artists with AIDS

David Gere

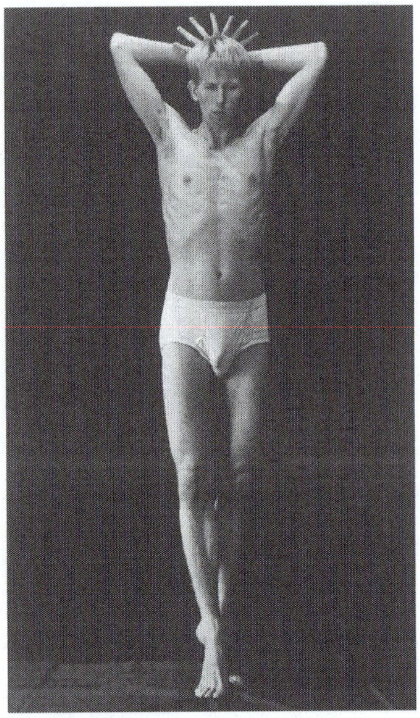

Tracy Rhoades in *Requiem* (1989). © G. Raven Traucht. Contact: tranceorpheus@hotmail.com

I keep a videotape on my shelf that I have never viewed but that I can scarcely imagine parting with. Being in Betacam format, this tape is smaller than all the others on my shelf by an inch or two. It stands metaphorically alone, diminutive in stature, mysterious in contents. I do not own a Betacam playback system, nor does anyone I know. Judging from its peeling label, the tape contains moving images of my friend Joah Lowe, who died of AIDS in 1988. I am aware that I should give this tape to an archive where it would be preserved. Seasonal temperature changes are no doubt rendering the tape brittle, and long years without being rewound may be causing my friend's image to leak and shadow. In fact, I am certain I must give this tape to a library one day, but in the meantime I keep it on my shelf, because it contains the remains of someone I once loved. I keep it because it is a fetish.

The term "fetish" has a somewhat different meaning in this context than it does for, say, Sigmund Freud. Leather, whips, fur, rubber clothing, uniform attire—this is the stuff of Freudian fetishism, updated for the end-of-the-twentieth-century fetish ball. But in the meaning I intend—a variation on one proposed by Michael Moon, a prominent Walt Whitman scholar—a fetish is a "memorial rag," a piece of clothing, a lock of hair, or a photograph, that stands in as an erotic replacement for a lost love object.[1] That, I am suggesting, is the sort of fetish the videotape on my shelf represents. It stands for someone who is irrevocably gone, to whom I can no longer speak. The remnants of the erotic object—its "rags" or, in a reference to battle trauma, its "bandages"—are preserved not as transcendent ideals; they are held as fetishes, as emblems of love. In the production of gay culture in the time of AIDS, it is of such rags that meaning is made. Such rags are kept on a shelf and, on rare occasion, slipped into the VCR.

I am not alone in keeping a videotape on my shelf as a fetish of lost love. Over a period of two years, I have conducted a survey for the Estate Project for Artists with AIDS, under the aegis of the New York-based Alliance for the Arts. The survey is designed to find out as much as possible concerning the documentation of concert dances made in the AIDS era, some specifically concerned with AIDS and some made by choreographers who were (or are) themselves struggling with HIV and AIDS. In pursuing this project, I have frequently found myself on the phone with a surviving lover, friend, sister, brother, or mother of a choreographer who has died. Time and time again, as I ask the whereabouts of the documentation of the choreographic work, I am told that the materials are contained in boxes in the basement, or out in the garage, or under the bed, or (ironically) in a closet. When I ask for the details, wanting to know exactly what is in those boxes, the emotionally exhausted voice on the other end of the line creaks palpably, like a squeaky hinge. Oh, I don't know what's in the boxes exactly; it would really take it out of me to have to look at those tapes again; can I get back to you on that? And I know in a moment that if I say "Yes, it will be okay to get back to me," I will never hear from this person again, because the death will have to be faced anew if the box is opened. At the same time, if I suggest that this surviving person might want to leave the box of videotapes, photographs, and personal papers intact and simply give it to an archive, the answer comes back sharp and clear: No, I want to keep these things, even if I never look at them. And I can only say I understand, because I too keep an unplayable videotape on my shelf, and I have for over ten years.

Fortunately, in working on the Estate Project survey, not to mention the research for a forthcoming book on dance and AIDS, I have found a small collection of survivors who are willing to show me the fetishes they hold in boxes under their beds, and as a result I have witnessed some extraordinary footage. One of the most compelling videos is a simple documentary of *Requiem*, a dance by San Francisco choreographer Tracy Rhoades, who died in 1993 at the age of 31. It was sent to me by Rhoades's friend and former manager, Joe Tuohy, who described it as one of an assortment of documentary videos in a box in the closet, and it looked it. The label on the outside indicated that the tape contained works by Bournonville, Petipa, and Alvin Ailey. When I fed the tape into my VCR, it did indeed begin with a few seconds of Bournonvillean sunniness. But suddenly the fantasy world of ballet was lost in a whiteout of fuzz and, when the image returned, it had been replaced by Rhoades standing in a pool of light at center stage. The music of the "Pie Jesu" from Fauré's *Requiem* became audible and Rhoades, a handsome, willowy figure, began a series of ecclesiastical gestures that evoked hovering halos, the elegant hand of Michelangelo's forgiving God, and Christ on the cross. Rhoades's body—lifted in a stationary bourrée—seemed to float on air. At the beginning of the piece, Rhoades had announced this as a requiem for his late boyfriend, Jim, who had died of AIDS. Now it serves as his requiem too.

Tim Wengerd, a leading dancer with the Martha Graham Dance Company in the 1970s, moved back home to Albuquerque, New Mexico, in the early 1980s to strike out on his own as an independent choreographer. He traveled to Mexico, California, and Paris, where he served as assistant director of the Paris Opera Ballet's modern dance offshoot, all the while making solos of his own. Through the list of survivors in his *New York Times* obituary published at the time of his death in 1989, my assistant, Jill Nunes, was able to track down his family in Albuquerque. When, subsequently, I was able to speak directly with Wengerd's mother, Florence Mather Wengerd, I realized I had stumbled onto a near-complete trove of his works—a hidden library of family fetishes.

Florence Wengerd explained that she kept Tim's photographs in drawers and boxes at home, that oral history audiotapes were stacked on the shelf in one room, and that nearly 30 VHS videotapes of her son's performances and choreography were neatly organized on shelves in her home. When I asked if I could see some of his work, she immediately suggested that I should see "Free," the family's shorthand for Tim's most resonant work, *The Free among the Dead,* a dance from the mid-1980s specifically on the subject of AIDS. A week after our conversation, an original videotape arrived in the mail—with a request that it be returned, of course. Even those who can part with their fetishes need them back.

I pop the tape into my machine and am immediately haunted by Wengerd's presence. The choreography, not surprisingly, is derived from the Graham aesthetic. In opening and closing sections, Wengerd uses a Zeus-like mask and black robe to dramatic effect, his bare hands expressing rage and fear and exhaustion. His expressionistic movements echo the fierceness of Diamanda Galas's music. Every emotion is tuned to a high pitch. In between, however, in the sections in which Wengerd strips down to a white unitard or just a dance belt, I am struck by the fact that his beautiful body, so in control, so intelligent, so round and full, lives now only as a shadowy image on video. When Wengerd swings his leg in a broad arc, the white appendage burns a blurry mark on the screen that endures, shimmering. The videotape is a fetish, and the images it contains are our dancing ghosts.

In 1980, John Bernd and Tim Miller inaugurated a series of dance-based performances titled *Live Boys*, a multimedia chronicle of their evolving gay relationship. In the April 1981 installment of the piece, performed at Hallwalls in Buffalo, New York, Bernd offered what must at the time have seemed a distantly metaphoric narrative: "When I met Tim, I had all these things wrong with my skin," Bernd intones in a monotone, kneeling at center stage while shrugging his shirtsleeves up lanky forearms. "About a week before I met him, I had a fungus on my skin, I had psoriasis where the fungus was, I had psoriasis on my scalp, I got poison ivy, and I was very depressed. . . . I had to walk around with bandages on my wrists. And I looked like I had tried to kill myself."

When Tim Miller unearthed the video documentation for *Live Boys* to view it again after nearly 20 years, he was taken aback by Bernd's prescient monologue, a monologue that, in retrospect, sharply foreshadows the AIDS epidemic. As we now know, a 1981 outbreak of Kaposi's sarcoma lesions and other aberrations of the skin among gay men provided the first indication that something was amiss; three months after the performance of *Live Boys*, a brief report in the July 3, 1981, edition of the *New York Times* marked the moment. A year later, in July 1982, the Centers for Disease Control declared the beginning of the AIDS epidemic and, in that same year, Bernd confronted his AIDS diagnosis, and his breakup with Miller, in *Surviving Love and Death*, arguably the first performance to address the epidemic in the first person. In 1988, at the peak of the epidemic, John Bernd died of AIDS-related complications. He was 35.

Given the intertwined histories leading from *Live Boys* to the announcement of the AIDS epidemic to *Surviving Love and Death* to the expansion in the number of AIDS deaths nationwide to Bernd's own death, the monologue in *Live Boys* takes on a significance far beyond what Bernd and Miller could have intended. These cultural productions are virtually fused with the arc of the disease. Nonetheless, the documentation of Bernd's work, specifically *Live Boys*, remains slim and under-accessed, most of it remaining uncatalogued at the Harvard Theater Collection. Indeed, were it not for the videotape Miller has kept all these years, along with Miller's memories of the piece and some sketchy descriptions in journalistic reviews, Bernd's monologue might have been completely lost to us. Without this record of *Live Boys* and Bernd's contributions to it, historians might not have known what this artist was experiencing at the time and, as a result, could only have inadequately and incompletely assessed the ways in which choreographers in the United States have been affected by HIV/AIDS. And how, without this documentation, could we fully understand what choreographers were doing to help shift the public's responses to the disease?

The Estate Project survey—to be published in a flexible, ever-changing format on the Internet, with video clips as the technology will allow—is meant to chronicle choreography in the AIDS era, focusing on activity in two cities, New York and Los Angeles. In addition to the tabulations and lists associated with any survey, however, this compendium is also an attempt to render visible the disappearing traces of an era—to unearth the remainders, the remains, the fetishes, of this particularly fraught chapter in American dance. In the late 1980s, AIDS activist and cultural commentator Paula Treichler reminded us that AIDS is an epidemic of signification—of pregnant and unwanted meanings—as well as an epidemic of virus.[2] When it comes to AIDS, Treichler explained, meanings attach themselves to people and phenomena in ways that follow no internal or scientific logic, and they proliferate. Thus, for no logical reason, the fearsome aspects of AIDS, including its apparent lethal qualities and its ability to open the body to attack from multiple fronts, attached themselves indiscriminately to gay men. Then these associations proliferated until dance itself became metaphorically infected with the disease. This survey, then, is built on the assertion that dance has served as a key site for the performance of memorialization, for grieving, for activism, and for social change, and that to know these dances and the artists who made them is to know the cultural history of the United States in the time of AIDS. The videos on our shelves and under our beds, if we can ever part with them, may make that new cultural history possible. The Estate Project dance survey can be found online at www.artistswithaids.org.

NOTES

1. Michael Moon, "Memorial Rags." In *Professions of Desire: Lesbian and Gay Studies in Literature,* eds. George E. Haggerty and Bonnie Zimmerman (New York: Modern Language Association of America, 1995), 233–40.

2. Paula Treichler, "AIDS, Homophobia, and Biomedical Discourse: An Epidemic of Signification." In *AIDS: Cultural Analysis/Cultural Activism*, ed. Douglas Crimp (Cambridge, Mass.: MIT Press, 1987), 31–70.

CHAPTER 20

Archiving Dance on Video: The First Generation

Dennis Diamond

Written by Nelli Heinonen from an interview with Dennis Diamond in New York on May 27, 2000.

I have been a dance fanatic since I was three years old. I went to New York's High School of Performing Arts, graduated in modern dance in 1967, and entered New York University's new School of the Arts dance program. In 1970, I walked into a cable TV studio, where they gave me a job. I taught myself about videotape and I already knew a lot about dance, for I'd been dancing my whole life. In 1975, I started a cable TV show called *Dance, New York Style*, a half-hour program designed to tell people what was going on in dance in the city. We'd have an interview with a choreographer, an excerpt of the piece, and a calendar at the end listing all the current dance concerts.

Later in 1975, a National Endowment for the Arts meeting at the Lincoln Center library discussed the impact of death on the performing arts. Choreographer James Waring had died; his protégé talked about his works being lost and dependent for their survival on people who could remember them. David White of Dance Theater Workshop (DTW) and I proposed to start a system of archiving dance for future generations. This was only a spit in a bucket, but monumental at the same time, because it was a concerted effort to record dance works. The project videotaped the entire performance with one camera located in the last row of the theater. This single-camera "adjusted wide shot" established for the downtown dance community a standard system for videotaping dance performances. It was not all the other things we could have done with it, such as talking to the choreographer, dancers, or musicians, or videotaping the concert from every possible angle. It was a single camera in the theater during a performance.

Prior to DTW's archival project, Jerry Robbins had set up a fund at Lincoln Center for archiving dance at the New York City Ballet. Emile Ardolino and Gordnikov Kompkin started documenting dances on film. You could only do it on film; video recording was not available at that time. Emile was a film editor and Gordnikov was a filmmaker, and they came up with this double system: one camera would be close on the pas de deux, and another camera would be wide, and they superimposed one on top of the other in the screen. In that way they

Dennis Diamond, 2001. Photo by Charles Steiner.

DVD 14
The World of Alwin Nikolais (1995)
Excerpt 2 min

Production Note: "I never start a production by asking 'how much money do you have?' I always start by asking 'what do you want to do?' That's where you have to start. We can take whatever camera we are using and hold it upside down, put it under water, shoot from another room, anything. Whatever the project may be I am always breaking the rules and developing with new innovations . . . But I am not interested in cutting edge equipment; I'm interested in the cutting edge of ideas. The people I collaborate with don't call me up and say, 'what kind of equipment do you have?' They say 'what are your ideas?'"—Dennis Diamond

had an archival recording of a lot of the Balanchine work for the Lincoln Center Library. The problem was that they didn't put music with a lot of the film because they didn't have the rights to the music.

The most revolutionary technical thing that happened in the video field was the emergence of portable recording equipment and the development of "low light" cameras, leading to the "one-man" video crew. By using half-inch reel-to-reel black-and-white video equipment, one person could function as director, camera person, technical engineer, and audio engineer. Recording could take place during a public performance with theatrical lighting. People ask why we didn't start videotaping before that. We couldn't because film, which was all that was available, required tons of light, the reels were too short, and you needed a big crew. (There was no color video of such portability until 1980.)

A 1975 Rudy Perez dance performance was the first to be recorded by the archival project. That season we recorded between 12 and 14 concerts by companies DTW was producing. In the very beginning, video archiving was carried out in a special session with work lights. The dancers wore costumes and did the dance full out, straight through, to the music, on an afternoon before their concert. Later, the advanced technology allowed us to record live performances.

As the camera person, director, audio engineer, lighting designer, and equipment schlepper, I wanted to keep the entire stage picture on the screen. Thus, I went with a wide shot. The entire width of the stage was totally in focus, with all the entrances and exits. If the work included a solo or duet, I might come in a little closer, but there was not a lot of zooming in and out. We always shot from the same angle—dead center at the back of the 99-seat house—as low as possible; we placed the camera about four to four and a half feet off the ground.

This systematic single-camera recording of dance performances was termed *archiving*. We came up with the word because we were looking to record the performance as it was done on a particular date. Using one camera in this situation, we were just recording what was going on. The style was pretty consistent; we were not trying to make a personal statement about it. We wanted people to become oblivious to the camera. Archival recording almost instantaneously became shorthand for what we were up to. David White and I believed we were providing a service to the choreographer and the company. We were just experimenting and trying to save the material. The dance companies got copies of the video for their own use. The original was sent to the Lincoln Center Library. From early on, this was to be an archival recording, to be kept in a repository.

I was working on a new frontier, learning as I went, adapting to new technologies. Archiving blossomed at DTW, and before I knew it I had created a legacy of dance recordings. I was trying to capture once-in-a-lifetime events in an ephemeral art form. We did not have experiences from which to develop the questions we now ask on a regular basis: How permanent is a videotape? How permanent is the equipment? How should it be stored? It is interesting that you can now write a grant and maybe get $25,000 to preserve archival material. In the beginning, we had 25 cents, but if we'd had $25,000 we might have made the recordings better and easier to save in the first place.

As the archival project got established, we recorded 40 performances every year, 26 presented by DTW and 14 others. We recorded at no charge to the dance company. We got our funding mostly from the NEA and New York State Council on the Arts, until the guidelines changed. As more people began to see archiving as a necessity, foundations responded that it should be put into each organization's general budget, not funded as a separate project. Thus, DTW had to move archiving into its general production budget, and eventually funding dried up. In 1989, I did the archival recordings gratis, hoping the funding would return, and then we closed the project. I had done it for about 15 years. I felt that it was important for the dance community to have these records.

A main focus of this archival project, and of the other video projects that I've done, is opening the door of video technology to choreographers. All my projects have been collaborations with choreographers and dancers. I offer my knowledge about video, they know their choreography, and together we can do something none of us could have done by ourselves. Instead of me starting at ground zero for choreography and them starting at ground zero for video, we

THE RULES

My philosophy about videotaping and working with choreographers and dancers is that there are no rules. Whether you work with a video person or a film person, the intention is to capture movement to play back.

You always find video or film people who have rules. "Oh, you don't put the camera here," or "Never put the camera above or underneath," or "Don't cross the 180° line," whatever that might mean. I worked with choreographer David Gordon, probably the second dance collaboration I initiated. David was sitting at the back of Dance Theater Workshop while I was archiving a concert. I said, "I understand you just worked on a dance film." David said, "You know, everybody has these stringent rules about recording." I said, "When you want to work without rules, give me a call—although I do have one rule: Don't drop the camera!"—D. D.

start at number 10. I look at it as a free flow of ideas. They make suggestions about the camera work and I ask them to make minor changes to the choreography. Thus, we each cross over to the other person's field without feeling threatened.

In 1994, I started collaborating on what I call Video Walls—video as dance installation art. I wondered how many different screens one could watch at one time and still have everything make sense. My first Video Walls collaboration was a record of Mikhail Baryshnikov rehearsing with Eliot Feld. I used five monitors simultaneously playing the video material. I showed Baryshnikov in four slightly different variations of the dance on four monitors; on the middle monitor was Eliot teaching Baryshnikov the movement. When Eliot saw it, he said "You have Baryshnikov up there four times and I can only get him once on stage!"

Later, I made Video Walls for pieces by Danny Buraczeski, Elizabeth Streb, the José Limón Dance Company, Alwin Nikolais, and David Grenke. DVD **14** They have been installed at the American Dance Festival, Jacob's Pillow, a couple of universities, and the Dance on Camera Showcase, a festival I started with Deirdre Towers of the Dance Films Association.

Finally, in the year 2000, I created *Dance/Video/News* to increase television exposure for dance companies. Our job is to videotape a section of the concert—up to three minutes—and edit it and give it to television stations by opening night in hopes that they will review it and/or use it in their news programs as background for the weather report. The first season was not as successful on television as we hoped because the New York area is so large and the stations are concerned with mass audiences, which makes it difficult for them to program dance. However, we broke new ground and developed relationships with three Web sites: www.danceinsider.com, www.dancemagazine.com and www.NYToday.com (a service of the *New York Times*). We convert the edited video to QuickTime and give it to the sites to run with reviews. The next thing would be to give it to the dance company for their own Web site.

Dance/Video/News gives the dance companies copies of their tapes to use as they will for promotion and booking. The video clips have been specially edited to make the movement sexy for television. Here we are not archivists, nor are we reverential to the choreography. We are serving the dance company by getting them exposure on television and the Internet. We very much live in an MTV society, getting our information quickly and visually, and I want to bring concert dance into this realm.

Why am I doing this? I have loved dance my whole life. I am a specialist in this particular area; I can blindfold myself and shoot dance very fast. The question is, how do we get more exposure for dance? Dance is the stepchild—at best—of the arts in getting exposure in mass media, unless you are doing *The Nutcracker* at Christmastime.

Whenever I have started to do something with dance and video, I have been, if not the first, then one of the first, opening a door that tons of people have come running through. In 1975, nobody was archiving dance. Now cameras are set up in the backs of theaters across the country. By collaborating as a video designer with a variety of choreographers, I broke new ground and helped make such partnerships commonplace.

I help dance companies, but I also learn from them. I don't want to come across as if I have been doing this for the field and it owes me something. In my years of working in dance and video, I have had a great time.

STANDARDIZING THE SHOOT

A member of the New York State Council for the Arts once told me I had changed the way funding people look at dance on video. By approaching each dance recording session with the same visual perspective, I had created a standard format for videotaping dance. This in turn gave the viewer of these tapes the same video parameters. I used a single video camera set up in the back of the theater with the lens opened to catch all the dance movement on stage. If there was a group of dancers, the video shot was wide. If there was a solo, the camera zoomed in to that dance figure. No part of the dancer's body was cut off. The viewer could look at a variety of dance performances, knowing that the shooting was done the same way. This is the equivalent of watching a dance competition with the performers doing the *Swan Lake* pas de deux. The judges can concentrate on the dancers' performance because the choreography, music, costumes, and lighting are the same. My guidelines for videotaping allowed the viewer to focus on the dancing and not be distracted by video "tricks" that could alter the way the dance is seen. This became the industry standard for archiving a dance performance.—D. D.

TRAINING TELEVISION DIRECTORS

In 1975, I applied for funding from the National Endowment for the Arts for my cable television program *Dance, New York Style*. Merrill Brockway was on the panel and said to me later, "I hated your program!" On another level, he thought it was fantastic, because nobody was giving dance weekly television exposure and he wanted to help improve my directing skills. Merrill invited me to participate in the American Dance Festival television workshop, designed for directors working at television stations to learn about dance, in hopes that when a concert dance company was touring America, these directors would broadcast the art form. For me, that workshop was like attending a master's program in television/dance. We worked with Brockway, Gordnikov Kompkin, and Kirk Browning, who taught their philosophy about televising dance. The uniqueness of the experience was that I was in a dance-and-television community. I became Brockway's assistant on the *Dance In America* series, and the coordinator of the ADF television workshop.

The television workshop worked to break down the television/dance barrier. When dancers came to a television studio, people would say, "Dancers, do your stuff and get out!" The dancers were always left out of the recording process. In the workshop, directors, choreographers, and dancers were equal participants. The dancers learned that the director needed to plan the camera angles. The directors learned that dancers needed to warm up their bodies in order to perform. The choreographers learned that spacing a dance for the stage was different than for television. The directors learned to show the choreographer, on the television screen, what they could do, and to ask for his or her opinion. The choreographer would say, "Oh, I can change that movement to adjust to the TV screen." Each became exposed to the other's process of creating.—D. D.

CHAPTER 21

Capturing Dances from the Past

Bonnie Oda Homsey

There is no substitute for being sequestered, as I was, in a rehearsal studio while masters like Anthony Tudor, Martha Graham, or José Limón coached and unveiled the details, secrets, and stories behind their choreography. To have them alter existing movement to suit my temperament and physicality was a dream come true! These were unforgettable moments when my destiny, as a link between the masters and the next generation, manifested itself.

The oral tradition of passing on dances is fundamental to our art form. But what happens when the choreographer has died, and the work is being resuscitated? What happens when only limited documentation of that work exists? What happens when it is discovered that, over time, several versions of the dance were created and documented by the choreographer?

Modern dance is a relatively young art form in relation to other performing arts. Only within the last century have we suffered the loss of pioneering innovators, some of whom left little documentation of their creative landmarks. In the mid-1990s, the need to safeguard the cultural legacy of dance came to the community's attention. Studies like "Images of Dance" by the National Endowment for the Arts and the Andrew W. Mellon Foundation in 1991 concluded that documentation and preservation must become priorities because the existing preservation systems had left our dance history at risk.

The personal impact of losing visionary mentors and talented colleagues to age, AIDS, and other illnesses cemented my desire to preserve the creative zeniths of a fiercely rebellious art form. The complex issues involved in restoring or reconstructing choreography in danger of being lost demand exhaustive research from multiple sources. Establishing a strong relationship with performing arts libraries is critical. Madeleine Nichols and her staff at the New York Public Library's Dance Division are invaluable to our projects. Labanotation and other forms of dance notation provide a valuable "script" to retrieve dances. At this writing, the Dance Notation Bureau has accumulated approximately 650 dance scores in its library. Of the 40 reconstruction projects that the American Repertory Dance Company (ARDC) has accomplished, four dances relied on notation as a primary tool, supplemented with film, video, and/or coaching by former dancers.

DVD 15
***Hexentanz* by Mary Wigman**
(1929) 5 min
Excerpt 1 min

Production Note: A film recording four short dances by Mary Wigman was discovered in Berlin by Ebbe Neergaard, a Danish film historian. He then donated it to the Danish Film Museum in 1975, now DFI/Film Archive.

DVD 16
***Hexentanz* as reconstructed by Bonnie Oda Homsey**
(1996) 6 min
Excerpt 2 min

Production Note: Hexentanz was a single camera shoot preserving the stark spatial pathways of Wigman's choreography and differentiating the unseen forces that her "creature" reacts to.

American Repertory Dance Co., Bonnie Oda Homsey in Mary Wigman's *Hexentanz*. Oda Homsey writes, "the expression of modern dance often emerges from physical idiosyncrasies and distinctive aesthetics of the artist. Studying film and video are valuable tools enabling choreography from the past to be performed anew." Photo by Taek.

In modern dance, where movement vocabulary often emerges from the physical idiosyncrasies and distinctive aesthetics of the choreographer, there is great value in accessing film and video to study repeatedly the elements of the dance, including the nuances of choreographic style, compositional structure, and development of movement dynamics or expression. The importance of film and video as source material within my reconstruction process cannot be overstated. For ARDC's dancers, many of whom worked directly with the pioneering innovators, watching film or video reconnects them to memories that deepen the current experience of restoring choreography.

Although preserving the breadth of the modern dance legacy is my purpose, I regret that ARDC's early reconstruction projects were not fully documented. One of these projects involved Pearl Primus's 1993 reconstruction of her 1943 *Strange Fruit*, on dancer Michele Simmons. Pearl choreographed the solo as a protest against lynchings in the South, and also as a passionate statement that such inhuman acts must never occur again. During one rehearsal, she turned to me and asked me to call her "Mna" Pearl, which, she explained, was an Efik African dialect term for "mother who did not birth you." Mna Pearl passed away several months following our rehearsals. At that time, we did not have funding for a videographer or audio recording device, so her rich anecdotes and contextual background, which contributed potent specificity to each gesture and movement, went unrecorded. I cannot share my mental images of her upper body thrown back, her blazing eyes, or the way she slapped her thigh as she talked about how dance was her "medicine," her "fist against the sickening ignorance of prejudice."

My tenure with the Martha Graham Dance Company (1973–1978, 1980) was marked by the constant schlepping of film and projector up to Graham's third floor studio. Film was a vital resource, which, in combination with former dancers and accompanist's notes on music scores, enabled us to reconstruct older repertory such as *Letter to the World*, *Deaths and Entrances*, and *Primitive Mysteries*. Personally, I relied on black-and-white company films to learn movement in preparation for coaching sessions with Martha. Martha chose not to have her dances notated, but when finances permitted, she would have them filmed, in some instances with different casts doing the same work. Her restless dissatisfaction with older works inevitably led to amended choreography tailored to the strengths of her current dancers. The existence of multiple films of the same work raises the question of which version is the "authentic" choreography for restaging purposes. During my time with her, this issue arose for dances such as *El Penitente*, *Appalachian Spring*, and *Clytemnestra*. Fortunately, Martha was involved in rehearsals and directed choices. She preferred wide-angle-shot films for in-house documentation.

Exposure to various reconstruction situations helped me to formulate my current methodology. At The Juilliard School, exhaustive research was not required because I benefited from coaching by the choreographers themselves. In contrast, while I was directing projects with ARDC, reconstructing dances at risk of being lost was complicated by variables such as limited documentation and resources, and the input of former dancers who imparted stylistic information but lacked personal knowledge of the particular works we wanted to restore.

The two-year ARDC project to restore Mary Wigman's *Hexentanz*, or "Witch Dance," used film as a primary tool. The great challenge of rebuilding this solo, recognized by many as her artistic apex, became evident when research revealed the existence of multiple versions of *Hexentanz* over a 20-year span. The 1914 solo was danced in silence at her debut concert. Following personal turmoil, the 1926 version was drastically altered with a mask, a long robe, and a percussion score. The 1934 version was a group dance within a larger work, *Frauentänze* or "Women's Dances."

It is amusing to note that, although a student of Rudolph von Laban (the inventor of Labanotation), Wigman never documented any version of the dance. Later in our process, Emma Lewis Thomas, a former Wigman dancer and assistant who helped direct my project, located and translated a book by a German dance critic, Rudolph Bach, containing a complete description of Wigman's 1926 version. The following translation by Thomas illustrates the difficulty of transcribing words into movement:

> The space is filled with hard white light . . . in the middle crouches the figure; facing front . . . closed within itself. A gate formed by the fingers covers the face . . . the backs of the hands turn toward the face. Then the gate opens like a curtain. Then suddenly the left arm draws back with a jerk as the right arm shoots upwards, the hand like a claw in the air with quick jerks of the head. Left hand/claw stabs with slight increase in tempo.[1]

What saved this project for me was a film of a performance from the 1920s containing one and one-half minutes of Wigman dancing *Hexentanz*. Incredibly, this footage of a short seated section is the only remaining visual record of the solo. My training did not include German-influenced modern dance technique, but the film permitted repeated scrutiny of Wigman's physicality, compositional preferences, rhythmic themes, and patterns, and of the dramatic nuances that illuminated the "demonic nature" of her creature.[2]

Film and video continue to be essential resources in my artistic continuum. Experience has given me a deep appreciation of these tools in my reconstruction efforts, by visually preserving the aesthetic evolution of the modern dance legacy, facilitating accessible resources, and intimately connecting future generations of dancers and viewers to the passionate and vibrant personalities of the art form.

NOTES

1. Rudolph Bach, *Das Mary Wigman Werk* (Dresden, 1933).
2. This excerpt can be seen in *Mary Wigman, 1886–1973: When Fire Dances Between the Two Poles*, directed by Allegra Fuller Snyder (Dance Horizons Video, 1982).

CHAPTER 22

Two Worlds of Balanchine: The George Balanchine Foundation Video Archives

Nancy Reynolds

There is no more urgent priority at the moment than the documentation of Balanchine's teaching and philosophy by those who worked directly with him.

–Arlene Croce (1995)

Coaching is such a personal form of communication; what I admire about the Foundation's Video Archives is that it is a "people" activity—one generation sharing its artistry with the next.

–Madeleine Nichols, curator, Dance Division, New York Public Library for the Performing Arts (1999)

What would we give to hear about Mozart from the premiere cast of *Figaro*? To discover an unknown draft of a Beethoven symphony? Or, more to our point, to get inside the head of one of the undisputed geniuses of twentieth-century ballet? Such thoughts and dreams inspired the George Balanchine Foundation Video Archives, initiated in 1995.

To begin, a word about the Foundation itself. The George Balanchine Foundation, established in 1983, is *not* identical with the George Balanchine Trust. The Trust, which might be considered the "commercial" arm, licenses the ballets for performance and arranges for them to be staged by a small stable of approved ballet masters, while the Foundation pursues educational projects. (Put another way, the Trust makes money; the Foundation spends money.) Among the Foundation's current projects are a nine-part video series on Balanchine technique and teaching philosophy called "The Balanchine Essays"; a lecture series by Nancy Goldner; a large-scale research effort, "Popular Balanchine," aimed at documenting Balanchine's commercial work and, if possible, reconstructing some Broadway choreography; an interactive multimedia tool to bring movement and text together to literally "quote" dance; and the Video Archives.

The Video Archive program, which I conceived and have directed from the start, is about process, documentation, and preservation. It is a two-pronged effort, one part relatively straightforward (yet in its own way exotic) and the other more visionary. The former, called the Archive of Lost Choreography, is

Maria Tallchief coaching *Scotch Symphony* with Nancy Reynolds (right). The George Balanchine Foundation. Photo by Brian Rushton.

DVD 17
Balanchine Interpreter Todd Bolender coaching (1997)
Excerpt 1 min 37 sec

DVD 18
Balanchine Interpreter Maria Tallchief coaching (1997)
Excerpt 3 min 52 sec

Production Note: "These are single camera shoots with a rehearsal atmosphere (little extra lighting, practice clothes and street makeup). The coaches have a body microphone and there is also a boom (shotgun) microphone and a piano microphone. These tapes are mostly about process: correction and repetition are expected events."
—Nancy Reynolds

dedicated to the retrieval of Balanchine choreography no longer performed and in danger of disappearing permanently. The aim is not necessarily to rescue entire works; fragments will do to start with, for one fragment may lead to another. On camera, retired Balanchine dancers with long memories recover and teach the lost choreography to dancers of today. Similarly, for the second prong of the project, the Interpreters Archive, the originators of famous Balanchine roles coach today's dancers in those roles, as Balanchine coached them. The goal in both instances (in addition to the obvious one of preserving the choreography) is to gain new insight into Balanchine's work—and perhaps to shed light on his creative process—through a close analysis of a specific ballet by those on whom the work was created, or with whom he worked closely to prepare a role. [*A complete list of videos shot to date can be found at the end of this chapter.*]

The basic process of "analysis" occurs as the Balanchine veterans teach and coach the choreography on camera to younger dancers over the course of several hours. The Foundation seeks to capture the body language of Balanchine dancers young and old, with the idea that this will convey far more information than purely verbal discourse. We also find that dancers, who are sometimes inhibited about expressing ideas about dance in words, lose themselves in the teaching and learning process, and in doing so, they impart not only the choreography itself but also the nuances of interpretation and phrasing, including the motivations behind the steps, in a way that would not happen in face-to-face interviews. Repetition and correction are an integral part of the taping sessions, and the young dancers are encouraged to speak up and ask questions. The atmosphere is that of a rehearsal, with practice clothes and street makeup the order of the day.

It is most definitely not a performance. We hire rehearsal pianists, so we can stop and start as often as needed, and we do the tapings in ballet studios rather than on impersonal television sound stages. (Using studios, however, means that we have to cope with everything from black clouds to brilliant sun, and certain urban intrusions such as drilling in the streets or fire alarms.) We tell the coaches not to worry about later versions or variant interpretations; what we seek are the coaches' own interpretations of the roles in light of what Balanchine said to them—what they think Balanchine wanted. The format is quite flexible and can be organized to suit the coach. Some have preferred to work with junior dancers to whom the roles must be taught from scratch, on the theory that this shows process best; others have selected dancers who are familiar with the roles, in the belief that seasoned dancers can more readily absorb and demonstrate the coach's corrections and the finer points of execution.

The teaching sessions are supplemented with a few minutes of interviews, generally focusing on the choreographic material presented or bringing up relevant points about the choreography not mentioned during the coaching. Although some anecdotal material about working with the master generally emerges, the work itself is the center of attention. This ratio of brief talk to hours of movement seems especially appropriate for Balanchine, a man of few words so far as his choreography was concerned, who spoke far more profoundly through the dance itself.

The first philosophical hurdle to overcome regarding these videos is to recognize that there is no single, "authentic" Balanchine. Balanchine was different for everyone. The Foundation is most emphatically not attempting to establish the "correct" Balanchine, nor to tell artistic directors how Balanchine should be performed. Our aim is to record without comment the many faces of Balanchine as seen through his many interpreters.

The second question to be grappled with is whether Balanchine would have wanted this. After all, he made revisions to his own ballets, without doubt in most cases preferring later versions. Various interpreters attracted his attention at one time or another and later fell out of favor. Should we memorialize discarded versions of his choreography, with dancers, no matter how illustrious, who may have been replaced by others as his inspiration? The answer is that Balanchine is a part of history. He—and his entire creative output—now belong to us all. They are ours to love, to treasure—and to scrutinize.

With my long background as a dancer and Balanchine-watcher, dreaming up new projects has been the easy part. There is such a wealth of material and so many brilliant and passionate coaches. It has been exciting beyond words to orchestrate Maria Tallchief on *Firebird*, Patricia Wilde on *Square Dance*, Todd
DVD 17 Bolender on *The Four Temperaments*, Alicia Alonso on *Theme and Variations*, Melissa Hayden on *Stars and Stripes*, Marie-Jeanne on *Concerto Barocco*, and Allegra Kent on *La Sonnambula*, and to think of a future involving, with luck, the ideas and memories of Suzanne Farrell, Jacques d'Amboise, Arthur Mitchell, and many others.

The nightmare comes with the scheduling. It is unpleasantly surprising how many studios are unsuitable for video sessions; they are too small, or too susceptible to traffic noise; they have endless walls full of windows, making light control impossible; or they are available for only a few hours at a time. (At a minimum, with the load-in of equipment taking several hours, a videotaping session requires a full sunrise-to-sunset day, and usually two or more.) And here is a real shaker: some studios don't allow toe shoes! Finally, unbelievable but true, despite the huge number of well-trained dancers around, most are either dancing to the limit in company seasons and rehearsals, relaxing on leotardless layoffs, or traveling around the world on gigs. Dancers, like studios, don't seem to have many full days to spare.

From the beginning, it was clear that the Balanchine archival tapes could provide an important record and resource. Thus, it seemed essential to use equipment and materials offering the utmost in durability, the best picture resolution, and superior sound. We consulted with many specialists, including Alan F. Lewis of the National Archives in Washington, D.C., who told us the only foolproof method of preservation was to shoot the proceedings with black-and-white film. (It would withstand World War III, he said.) This being impractical, we settled on broadcast-quality equipment of the caliber used by television networks. As for camera work, although we are, in a sense, documenting without comment, we have rejected the impassive and stationary wide-shot, which we feel diminishes the impact of the coach and makes for visual uniformity. We tell our cameramen to take risks, to go in for the occasional close-up, and sometimes to follow the dancers. With the average shoot yielding 10 or 12 hours of raw footage, which we edit down to fit a 120-minute VHS cassette, it has almost always been possible to find what we need, even if the cameraman missed something the first time around because he was looking elsewhere. Of course, in the final edited version, the integrity of the choreography is never sacrificed for "artistic" camera work.

We usually employ three-person crews to handle lighting, sound, mixing, and videography. Most often we have used a single Betacam camera, mounted on a dolly for mobility and equipped with a zoom lens with a wide-angle adapter. In special instances—such as for Alicia Alonso, who was unable to get up from her chair to approach the dancers—two cameras have been used. Low lighting is preferred because it is easier for the dancers over a long period of time and also reinforces the informal nature of the proceedings. There are usually three sources of sound: a wireless microphone on the coach, a standing mic on the piano, and a boom mic to capture any comments from the dancers, as well as the ambient sound in the room. A still photographer has been present at every shoot, an invaluable addition considering the difficulty of extracting decent still images from tape.

The series started off in high gear in 1995, when Alicia Markova, then 84, agreed to re-create the solo and parts of the pas de deux from *Le Chant du Rossignol*, created by Balanchine for her in 1925, when she was 14. Dame Alicia bears a remarkable resemblance to the queen of England (and is treated like royalty in the press), but despite her regal bearing, she proved approachable and warm. The most gossamer of all Giselles, she was still feather-light as she demonstrated, with a born teacher's eternal patience, the three-minute solo over a period of seven hours to Iohna Loots, a young graduate of the Royal Ballet School. "It's a lovely little step from Mr. B—but it's a devil!" she told Iohna of one particular toe-twister. "I know it's difficult—he gave me the most dizzy-making variation." Summing up the magic in the London studio, Barbara Newman marveled, "Directed by Markova's explicit memories, the past had turned from conjecture to possibility, and then risen to its feet and danced again."[1]

Another early ally was Maria Tallchief, for whom Balanchine created more than 20 roles. To date, she has analyzed about 13 of them for the Foundation's cameras, and we hope there will be more. Known for the brilliance and attack of her technique, Tallchief, perhaps surprisingly, paid special attention to the upper body and port de bras and used a lovely verbal image from Balanchine: DVD 18

"Look over the balustrade, into the lake," she advised Wendy Whelan, encouraging her to look over and beyond the bent arm in front of her achieve a poetic look as the Sugar Plum Fairy. "Eyes one foot above the wrist—*always*" in first arabesque and its variants, she told all the women, and somehow this head position was appropriate to every role she demonstrated, from *Scotch Symphony* to *Pas de Dix* to *Four Temperaments* to *Sylvia*. She talked about the influences of Martha Graham and Fred Astaire on Mr. B. Under her guidance, Judith Fugate remade herself completely to look more windswept in the *Scotch Symphony* pas de deux, a brilliant demonstration by an experienced artist of processing new insights on the spot. Joan Acocella praised "Tallchief's insistence on variety, surprise, dynamism: all those principles that made Balanchine's dances seem so alive, so worth looking at, and which sent you home feeling as though you had a million dollars in the bank."[2] Larry Kaplan called the sessions "electrifying."

Patricia Wilde, recorded in Pittsburgh, spoke of expressing "the song within you." Before seeing her coach the pas de deux from *Raymonda Variations*, I had not realized that the ballerina is off her center the entire time. When properly executed with a rock-solid partner, this produces a silky, flowing effect and is a great example of Balanchine's masterly craftsmanship and imagination, even in ballets that are a notch below his top level. Todd Bolender compared his feeling about the "Phlegmatic" variation in *The Four Temperaments*–that "fascinating riddle of a role"—to the characters in Beckett's *Waiting for Godot*, always searching for that indefinable something. He told a tantalizing story of Balanchine's once *almost* dancing the part, when Bolender had the flu and no understudy. Since Balanchine, as usual, had said little to him, Bolender thought it would be fascinating to see what he himself brought to it. But, although feverish, Bolender managed to get himself to the theater and go on, and Balanchine never danced the role. Marie-Jeanne brought intriguing glimpses of early-1940s Balanchine style, with her low, contained arms, subdued arabesques, and all in all, a less expansive approach. But though perhaps less expansive, it was bracing in an altogether different way: what she evoked was the flight of a hummingbird—something light, direct, swift, and very much on top of the musical beat. Franklin dancing five female solos from the 1946 *Raymonda* was, quite simply, a wonder to behold. And in answer to Doris Hering's question as to why *Theme and Variations* should be preserved, Alonso, who had just coached the ballet with the phenomenal technicians Paloma Herrera and Angel Corella, replied: "Because it is a masterpiece. The future has a right to see it."

After the thrill of the taping sessions, working so closely with legends of the dance, comes the crucial, sometimes solitary task of video editing. From the beginning, we decided it would be irresponsible merely to dump hours of raw footage into a library. Almost no one could face plowing through it all, and dancers might be embarrassed by one thing or another. Although we edit with as light a hand as possible, there seems no point in preserving choreography incorrectly executed, and we like the dancers to look their best. Thus, we cannot truly claim (as I did at the beginning of this chapter) to present the material entirely without comment. The first stages of editing, which require staring at a video monitor for hours and playing passages over and over while scribbling notes, develop visual memory, but for a words-on-paper person like myself, it has been hard not to be able to put two or more "pages" side by side, to compare, to contrast, and to avoid duplication. I must confess that fast-forwarding and reversing countless times in search of that special moment is one of the more tedious aspects of the game. Throughout, I have leaned mercilessly on—and learned end-

Melissa Hayden coaching George Balanchine's *Episodes* with members of Pacific Northwest Ballet. The George Balanchine Foundation. Photo by Brian Rushton.

lessly from—my colleague Virginia Brooks, professor of film production at Brooklyn College, who has collaborated with me on the editing of all our videos. For the editing process itself, I cannot do better than to quote her:

> Even as each recording session of the coaching (or retrieving) of Balanchine dances presents different challenges, the editing plans have evolved in a very efficient way. The process actually begins during the shooting, as notes are made about the content of each tape, where the tape changes occur, and any other information that will make editing easier. The next step is to have copies made of the camera originals. We mostly record on Betacam, and the Beta tapes are transferred to VHS with visible time code for us to use as work tapes. The VHS tapes are required for editing so the originals may be preserved for making the final masters.
>
> With two sets of work tapes, Nancy and I log all the material, making notes identified with the time code and planning where the segments will start and end. This "paper edit" I then transform into a cuts-only rough assembly, still on VHS. We review this version and if there are enough changes needed, another assembly is made. Most of our sessions are single-camera shoots, so our editing choices are limited, but it is still necessary to cut out redundancy, false starts, the occasional bad camera move, mistakes in execution, and other footage that would not add to the audience's understanding of the coaching experience or that falsely represents the choreography. When we are satisfied with the assembly, we move to the AVID offline stage. Here the original tapes are digitized (at low resolution to save memory) so we can take advantage of the computer-controlled nonlinear editing that the AVID software makes possible. Now we see the rough cuts of our assembly made "frame-accurate" and add dissolves to smooth transitions between close angles from the same camera position. We also add still photographs and credits so we can determine the final length of the program. And we manipulate the sound from the different microphones. From all

Frederic Franklin recreating a solo from the "white" pas de deux from George Balanchine's *Mozartiana* (1945) with Julie Kent of American Ballet Theatre. The George Balanchine Foundation. Photo by Brian Rushton.

this, the computer generates an EDL (edit decision list) that includes every video and audio event we have chosen. At the end of the AVID session, that edit is transferred back to analog form on VHS tape for review. If this version is satisfactory, we schedule the online session that will use the EDL to conform the original tapes with the full resolution to produce the master tape. We can also have more control over the sound levels at this stage. Originally we mastered on Betacam, but in 1997, when the technology had stabilized and because of its longer length, we switched to Digital Beta. After we approve the master, a protection copy (or "clone") is produced as well.

Celebrated at a splendid party, the George Balanchine Video Archives were inaugurated with the donation of the first seven master tapes to the Dance Division of the New York Public Library for the Performing Arts in 1997. A donation of seven additional tapes was made in 1999.The closing of the circle—sending the videos out into the world—has come with the distribution, for a nominal fee, of VHS copies of the tapes to research libraries, which we handle in cooperation with the Dance Heritage Coalition. Wonderful and valuable as the material is, we feel it is of limited value if those interested have to come to New York to see it. The George Balanchine Library Distribution Program, we believe, is a pioneering attempt to make "unique" material available in more than one venue. The institutions receiving the tapes must agree not to copy or to circulate the material in their care nor to make any commercial use of it. By 2001, the tapes had been requested and received by 43 libraries worldwide, from as near as downtown New York City to as far away as New Zealand. It is particularly heartwarming that the most recent recipient is the State Library for Music and Theatre in St. Petersburg, the city where Balanchine was born, where Stravinsky and Diaghilev lived, and where Tchaikovsky died. (For more on Balanchine, see Chapter 4.)

NOTES

1. "Dancing in Real Time," *Dance International*. Spring 1995.
2. "The Hand of Fate," *The Village Voice*. August 15, 1995.

THE GEORGE BALANCHINE FOUNDATION VIDEO ARCHIVES

Choreography by George Balanchine

✦ *indicates master tape in the New York Public Library for the Performing Arts*

ARCHIVE OF LOST CHOREOGRAPHY

DAME ALICIA MARKOVA recreating excerpts from *Le Chant du Rossignol* ✦

[Nightingale variation; excerpts from pas de deux of Nightingale and Death]

Music: Igor Stravinsky
Dancer: Iohna Loots [Royal Ballet School]
Advisors: Millicent Hodson, Kenneth Archer
Taped: January 30–February 3, 1995, London; 116 minutes

FREDERIC FRANKLIN recreating a male solo from *Raymonda* (1946) ✦

Music: Alexander Glazunov
Dancer: Nikolaj Hübbe [New York City Ballet]
Interviewer: Nancy Reynolds
Taped: May 19, 1997, New York City; 55 minutes

FREDERIC FRANKLIN recreating excerpts from *Mozartiana* (1945), with SONJA TYVEN and ROBERT LINDGREN

Music: Peter Ilich Tschaikovsky
Dancers: Lilyan Vigo [Southern Ballet Theatre], James Fayette [New York City Ballet], students from North Carolina School of the Arts
Interviewer: Nancy Reynolds
Taped: September 9–24, 1996, Winston-Salem, North Carolina; 68 minutes

FREDERIC FRANKLIN recreating two pas de deux from *Le Baiser de la Fée* (1940), with MARIA TALLCHIEF and VIDA BROWN [2 tapes] ✦

Music: Igor Stravinsky
Dancers: Nichol Hlinka, Nikolaj Hübbe, Lourdes Lopez [New York City Ballet]
Interviewer: Jack Anderson
Taped: October 21 and November 18, 1996, January 29, 1997, New York City; 80 minutes; 101 minutes

FREDERIC FRANKLIN recreating female solos from *Raymonda* (1946), with later Balanchine variations to the same music from *Pas de Dix, Raymonda Variations,* and *Cortège Hongrois*

Music: Alexander Glazunov
Dancers: Peter Boal, corps members of New York City Ballet
Interviewer: Mindy Aloff
Taped: September 13–14, 1998, New York City; 90 minutes

FREDERIC FRANKLIN recreating two pas de deux and **STANLEY ZOMPAKOS recreating the Gigue from *Mozartiana* (1945)**

Music: Peter Ilich Tschaikovsky
Dancers: Julie Kent [American Ballet Theater], Nikolaj Hübbe [New York City Ballet], Christopher Barksdale [Kansas City Ballet]
Interviewer: Nancy Reynolds
Taped: January 24, 2000, New York City, and May 5, 2000, Kansas City

TODD BOLENDER re-creating *Renard*

Music: Igor Stravinsky
Dancers: Christopher Barksdale, Andrew Carr, Sean Duus, Denise Small [Kansas City Ballet]
Interviewer: Nancy Reynolds
Taped: May 4–5, 2000, Kansas City

INTERPRETERS ARCHIVE

MARIA TALLCHIEF coaching excerpts from *Firebird* and *Orpheus* [Firebird *Berceuse*; Eurydice's solo] ✦

Music: Igor Stravinsky
Dancer: Helène Alexopoulos [New York City Ballet]
Interviewers: Arlene Croce, Nancy Reynolds
Taped: June 27, 1995, New York City; 82 minutes

MARIA TALLCHIEF coaching ballerina variation, 1st movement, from *Symphony in C* ✦

Music: Georges Bizet
Dancer: Jennie Somogyi [New York City Ballet]
Interviewers: Arlene Croce, Nancy Reynolds
Taped: June 28, 1995, New York City; 77 minutes

MARIA TALLCHIEF coaching excerpts from *Pas de Dix* [ballerina variation; excerpt from finale] ✦

Music: Alexander Glazunov
Dancer: Jennie Somogyi [New York City Ballet]

Interviewers: Arlene Croce, Nancy Reynolds
Taped: June 28, 1995, New York City; 86 minutes

MARIA TALLCHIEF coaching excerpts from George Balanchine's *The Nutcracker* [Sugar Plum Fairy variation (partial); pas de deux] ✦
Music: Peter Ilyitch Tschaikovsky
Dancers: Jennie Somogyi, Wendy Whelan, Damian Woetzel [New York City Ballet]
Interviewers: Arlene Croce, Francis Mason, Nancy Reynolds
Taped: June 28, 1995, and April 15, 1996, New York City; 110 minutes

MARIA TALLCHIEF coaching the pas de deux from *Scotch Symphony* ✦ DVD 18
Music: Felix Mendelssohn
Dancers: Judith Fugate, Peter Boal [New York City Ballet]
Interviewers: Francis Mason, Nancy Reynolds
Taped: April 14–15, 1996, New York City; 109 minutes

MARIA TALLCHIEF coaching "Sanguinic" variation from *The Four Temperaments* and *Sylvia: Pas de Deux* [ballerina solo] ✦
Music: Paul Hindemith, Léo Delibes
Dancers: Wendy Whelan, Damian Woetzel, Judith Fugate [New York City Ballet]
Interviewers: Francis Mason, Nancy Reynolds
Taped: April 14–15, 1996, New York City; 112 minutes

PATRICIA WILDE coaching excerpts from *Raymonda Variations* [2 ballerina variations; pas de deux] ✦
Music: Alexander Glazunov
Dancers: Laura Desiree, Blythe Turner, Stanko Milov [Pittsburgh Ballet Theatre]
Interviewer: Nancy Goldner
Taped: May 23–24, 1996, Pittsburgh; 120 minutes

PATRICIA WILDE coaching excerpts from *Square Dance* [pas de deux from 1st movement; excerpts from "girls' dance"; finale] ✦
Music: Antonio Vivaldi, Arcangelo Corelli
Dancers: Laura Desiree, Alexander Nagiba [Pittsburgh Ballet Theatre]
Interviewer: Nancy Goldner
Taped: May 24, 1996, Pittsburgh; 70 minutes

MARIE-JEANNE coaching *Concerto Barocco*, with JOHN TARAS, SUKI SCHORER, and MERRILL ASHLEY ✦
Music: Johann Sebastian Bach
Dancers: Students from School of American Ballet
Interviewers: Stephanie Jordan, Nancy Reynolds
Taped: June 16–17, 1996, New York City; 116 minutes

MARIA TALLCHIEF coaching excerpts from *Apollo, Firebird,* and *Swan Lake,* with PAUL MEJÍA [2 tapes]
Music: Igor Stravinsky, Peter Ilyitch Tschaikovsky
Dancers: Maria Terezia Balogh, Maria Thomas, Todd Edson, Michael Clark [Fort Worth Dallas Ballet]
Interviewer: Nancy Goldner
Taped: May 31–June 1, 1997, Fort Worth, Texas; 101 minutes; 107 minutes

ALICIA ALONSO coaching excerpts from *Theme and Variations* ✦
Music: Peter Il'ich Tschaikovsky
Dancers: Paloma Herrera, Angel Corella [American Ballet Theatre]
Interviewer: Doris Hering
Taped: January 29–30, 1998, New York City; 86 minutes

TODD BOLENDER coaching "Phlegmatic" variation from *The Four Temperaments* DVD **17**

Music: Paul Hindemith
Dancers: Albert Evans [New York City Ballet], with Christopher Barksdale [Kansas City Ballet]
Interviewer: Robert Greskovic
Taped: September 15, 1997, New York City; 113 minutes

MARIA TALLCHIEF coaching excerpts from *Pas de Dix* and *Allegro Brillante*
MARJORIE TALLCHIEF coaching a variation from *Pas de Trois* (Minkus)

Music: Alexander Glazunov, Peter Il'ich Tschaikovsky, Léon Minkus
Dancers: Iliana Lopez, Franklin Gamero, Deanna Seay, Mikhail Nikitine, Melanie Atkins [Miami City Ballet]
Interviewer: Jordan Levin
Taped: January 18–19, 1999, Miami Beach, Florida

ALLEGRA KENT coaching excerpts from *Bugaku* and *La Sonnambula*

Music: Toshiro Mayuzumi, Vittorio Rieti (after Bellini)
Dancers: Janie Taylor, Albert Evans, Peter Boal [New York City Ballet]
Interviewer: Robert Gottlieb
Taped: October 17–18, 1999

MELISSA HAYDEN coaching excerpts from *Stars and Stripes* and ***Donizetti Variations***

Music: John Philip Sousa (arr. Hershy Kay), Gaetano Donizetti
Dancers: Gillian Murphy [American Ballet Theater], Charles Askegard, Peter Boal [New York City Ballet]
Interviewer: Nancy Reynolds
Taped: November 16–17 and 22–23, 1999, New York City

MELISSA HAYDEN coaching excerpts from *Episodes* and ***Agon***

Music: Anton Webern, Igor Stravinsky
Dancers: Lisa Apple, Jeff Stanton, Louise Nadeau, Oleg Gorboulev, Christophe Maraval [Pacific Northwest Ballet]
Interviewer: Francia Russell
Taped: April 1–2, 2000

KAREN VON AROLDINGEN coaching excerpts from *Davidsbündertänze*

Music: Robert Schumann
Dancers: Charles Askegard, Jenifer Ringer [New York City Ballet]
Interviewer: Anna Kisselgoff
Taped: October 29–30, 2000, New York City

ROSELLA HIGHTOWER and MARINA EGLEVSKY coaching *Pas de Trois* (Minkus)

Music: Léon Minkus
Dancers: Eugénie Andrin, Yuka Omori [École Supérieure de Danse de Cannes], Peter Lewton [formerly Les Ballets de Monte-Carlo]
Interviewer: Nancy Reynolds
Taped: November 4–5, 2000, Cannes, France

CHAPTER 23

The Etudes Project: Using Video to Create a Canon for Contemporary Dance Educators

Carolyn Adams

As a dancer, I had the good fortune to spend 17 years performing the work of a master dance maker, Paul Taylor. I had the privilege of participating in the creation of new works, and the opportunity, over the years, to inherit roles that were created for dancers with technical and performance skills different from mine. This provided me with wonderful challenges. The best part was that I had time to grow, to rehearse and perform these rich and substantive works over a period of years, to rediscover them at different points in my development. All this took place in the decades before dancers routinely began to learn choreography from video; the transmission of information was an intensely personal experience.

When I stopped performing, some 18 years ago, and began to teach full-time, I realized something my sister, Julie Strandberg, had been aware of from her perspective as director of dance at Brown University and artistic director of a regional dance company: the importance of ongoing exposure to great repertory in the artistic development of every dancer and dance educator. The lack of access to fine repertory gnawed at us for a number of years in the 1980s, during a period when the dance field began to articulate concerns about dance preservation, kindergarten-through-university arts education, and audience development. It occurred to us that dance is probably the only field seeking to educate the next generation, to reach broad constituencies, and to perpetuate its legacy without providing the public with ongoing access to dance repertory and materials.

The valuing of an art form has everything to do with its accessibility. Imagine what it would be like if a music lover could only hear Beethoven's *Fifth Symphony* once or twice in a lifetime, and could never buy a recording. Imagine that an acting student would have to become a playwright in order to perform. Imagine gathering a group of music students at Tanglewood for a master class with James Levine, and discovering they were ignorant of his background and repertory, or had arrived with no knowledge of the works to be investigated. For too long, the dance field has described this kind of hit-and-run scenario as a "master class." If you don't know about great art you can't care about it, and if you don't care about it you won't value or seek to preserve it and pass it on. In order to have dance preservation, it's essential to have dance education and

From left, Carolyn Adams and Julie Strandberg photographed together in 1987. Personal Collection.

ongoing accessible knowledge. The widespread availability of video technology in dance departments, and video's growing involvement in the creative process of choreographers, could facilitate students' direct access to a working master in the studio.

Late in the 1980s, Julie and I thought of commissioning "Repertory Etudes," short solo or small group pieces that dancers could learn, teach, and perform forever, without royalty fees, so that they could revisit the works over time, hone technical skills, explore nuance and style, and measure artistic growth. Repertory Etudes would provide dancers with kinesthetic insight into a single work by a choreographer, or specific stylistic elements that could be found in various works within a choreographer's repertoire.

Then, in 1992, Donald McKayle and I were adjudicating the dance portion of Arts Week (the scholarship program of the National Foundation for Advancement in the Arts) in Miami, Florida. While the ballet dancers were able to perform familiar classical variations, the contemporary dancers proved to be at a disadvantage because often the works they performed were either choreographically weak or lacking in substance and rigor. McKayle offered to create the first Repertory Etude, based on his 1959 masterwork *Rainbow 'Round My Shoulder.* **DVD 19**

So we were in business, supported by funds from the American Dance Legacy Institute, the New York State Summer Institutes, the Harlem Dance Foundation, and private contributions; later, the National Endowment for the Arts began contributing as well. We began in Saratoga, exploring with middle and high school students what an Etude might be; these sessions were video-

DVD 19
Rainbow Etude
(1996) 42 min 40 sec
Excerpt 2 min

Production Note: Two cameras were used for the documentary *Images and Reflexions: Celebration of a Masterpiece*. This 50-minute tape includes the entire piece *Rainbow 'Round my Shoulder* performed by the original cast (1959) and recent interviews with cast members.

The Repertory Etudes Project (Carolyn Adams and Julie Adams Strandberg, directors) currently offers Etudes based on works by Anna Sokolow, David Parsons, Danny Grossman, and Daniel Nagrin, with plans to produce one on José Limón. The project will commission three to five Etudes each year (subject to funding), in an ongoing series to be called "The Repertory Etudes Collection—An Evolving Canon." For further information about the project, contact the American Dance Legacy Institute, Brown University, P.O. Box 1897, Providence, RI 02912, www.adli.org.

taped. McKayle actually choreographed his Etude on his students at the University of California at Irvine, and refined it that summer at the American Dance Festival; then he came back to Saratoga the following year, after we had taught it to a group of some of the same students, and coached it. At all these sites, tape rolled; there are clips from most of these situations in the resulting instructional video. We keep updating and revising it in response to questions from the field.

The Repertory Etudes Collection, which now encompasses Etudes based on five choreographers' work, includes instructional videotapes of the Etudes being taught and (when possible) coached by the choreographer—step by step, phrase by phrase, image by image. The tapes also include the Etudes in performance by both male and female dancers, with varying body types, technical levels, and ages. Supplementary materials include video footage of other works by the choreographers, interviews with the choreographers, and oral histories with dancers who have performed the works.

The Etudes are made available as a package that sells for $75 plus $10 for shipping and handling, and the artists controlling the choreography, as well as the dancers, are reaping broader exposure and employment opportunities from the circulation of these tapes. To date, more than three thousand dancers and teachers have learned and performed McKayle's *Rainbow Etude*. These dancers are beginning to bump into one other in dance studios and at festivals and conventions around the country. McKayle is frequently invited to coach the Etude and now has the opportunity to teach a true master class.

We hope that the Repertory Etudes Project will raise the expectations of touring artists, master teachers, and students alike as more and more people become familiar with the same works. The concept of common kinesthetic knowledge will become a reality, opening channels of communication for discussion and analysis of our great dances and igniting curiosity about the choreographers and their other pieces.

At the outset, we pondered the pitfalls and quality-control issues raised by this kind of unlimited access to great works. It was critical that each Etude be designed with the idea that dancers of varying abilities and exposure would have a point of entry, or a handle to grab. Since all of the choreographers, to date, are also educators, we were able to ask them to think of their 4- to 6-minute Etude as a learning tool that would introduce the students to some signature aspect of one of their full works, exposing them to specific dynamics, designs, or gestural motifs. In the case of the *Rainbow Etude*, for example, Donald McKayle chose to focus on rhythm. In correcting students, he frequently gives them leeway with some of the movements, but he is very precise about the syncopation. In this regard, he often encounters students with very advanced technique who struggle to capture the rhythm, while students with less technique master the rhythm and find subtleties in the movement that elude more technically skilled dancers.

CHAPTER 24

The Rainbow Etude

Donald McKayle

DVD 19
Rainbow Etude
(1996) 42 min 40 sec
Excerpt 2 min

Production Note: Two cameras were used for the documentary *Images and Reflexions: Celebration of a Masterpiece*. This 50-minute tape includes the entire piece *Rainbow 'Round my Shoulder* performed by the original cast (1959) and recent interviews with cast members.

Donald McKayle and Carmen De Lavallade studio photograph, 1963. Photo by Normand Maxon, from the personal collection of Donald McKayle.

Along with Carolyn Adams and Julie Strandberg, I initiated the program that became the Etude Project of the American Dance Legacy Institute. The heart of the project was to make works of master modern dance choreographers in available for study, performance, and scholarly examination by dance students, teachers, and practitioners. The model we developed has the following phases: the composition of a short dance Etude by the choreographer, based on an established masterwork; the scoring of that work in Labanotation as it was being created; the documentation of the composition sessions, rehearsals, and discussion sessions with dancers, colleagues, and viewers on video; and the dissemination of questionnaires to the field on historical perspectives, background information about the choreographer, and the impact of the original work, to be formulated into CD-ROM. These diverse elements were conceived as a multimedia volume on the Etude and the choreographer.

As the creator of the first Etude, I wanted to make as full and detailed a volume as possible, one that would serve as the paradigm against which to measure and develop subsequent entries. The Etude was created from thematic ideas and movement material from *Rainbow 'Round My Shoulder*; it was built as a solo for male or female dancer. The musical score for the Etude utilized two chain gang songs not included in the original work, which were arranged for a cappella male chorus.

Donald McKayle's ***Rainbow 'Round my Shoulder*** **(1961). From left: William Louther, Tommy Johnson, Donald McKayle, Claude Thompson, Morton Winston, Charles Neal, and Don Martin. Courtesy of the John Lindquist collection, The Harvard Theatre Collection, The Houghton Library, and the Archives of Jacob's Pillow. Photo by John Lindquist.**

The *Rainbow Etude* became such a popular work across the country that I developed it into the *Rainbow Suite* for an ensemble. I frequently get responses from students and teachers through the Dance Legacy Institute's Internet chat room, and I respond personally to their questions. The students are challenged by the work and want to know why and how I made this piece. The depth of their involvement is remarkable. Teachers are excited about the possibility of reconstructing an excerpt of a masterpiece with the help of the video, and motivated by their students' responses to this learning method. All in all, the *Rainbow Etude* has realized the goals the Etude Project set out to accomplish.

The *Rainbow Etude* packet can be accessed through the American Dance Legacy Institute at Brown University. It contains the Labanotation score, an audiocassette of the music, a videocassette of the etude in performance and in rehearsal with me directing several groups of dancers through the process, and costume renderings by Bernard Johnson. Most teachers and their students are not notation-literate, so the videocassette is the main learning tool. For those who are skilled in reading and reconstructing from Labanotation, the score is an accurate and complete presentation of the work, unencumbered by the idiosyncrasies of individual performance. The video offers an invaluable series of coaching sessions that fully delineate the movement style and dynamics, the approach to performance, and the context of idea behind the movement. When the CD-ROM is available, the packet will indeed be complete.

CHAPTER 25

Alan Lomax and Choreometrics

John Bishop

Contemplating the career of ethnomusicologist Alan Lomax makes you think of Walt Whitman's declaration "I am large, I contain multitudes." A pioneer in field recording of traditional music and one of the founders of the Library of Congress Folk Music Archive, Lomax often characterized his mission as bringing the best recording technology to the world's traditional singers and musicians, so that their art could take its rightful place as an equal beside the best classical and commercial music. His exquisite taste and a flair for eliciting great performances led to recordings of intense vitality, many of which are now available on more than 100 CDs issued by Rounder Records. His important collections include secular and sacred music of the American South, the Caribbean, Italy, Spain, and the British Isles. While living in England in the 1950s, he compiled album series of world music for the BBC and Columbia Records. Feeling that performance style was deeply embedded in culture, he worked with Victor Grauer and Roswell Rudd (musicologists), Conrad Arensberg, Edwin Erickson, Barbara Ayres, and Monika Vizedom (anthropologists), and Norman Berkowitz (computer programmer and statistician) to develop Cantometrics—"a method for systematically and holistically describing the general features of accompanied or unaccompanied song. With the cantometric system the listener can evaluate a song performance in ways that supplement the conventional measures of melody, rhythm, and harmony."[1]

Using multivariate factor analysis, a statistical method that became possible only with the emergence of computers, they found that elements of performance style were consistent within cultures, and that clusters of these style elements correlated with elements of productivity and social organization. Raymond Birdwhistell suggested, "Humans move and belong to movement communities just as they speak and belong to speech communities." Birdwhistell thought that examining world dance might unlock additional structural elements and correlations underlying the relationship between social organization and expressive culture. This required a systematic sample of dance representing geographic and culture areas, and also subsistence strategies. Lomax teamed up with movement specialists Irmgard Bartenieff and Forrestine Paulay to examine film of the world's dance forms with the objective of "recording and noting regularities and contrasts in movement patterns sufficiently frequent and gross to produce units universally applicable in cross-cultural studies."

The Choreometrics group endeared itself to the documentary film community by their unreserved valuation of data imbedded in footage. They wrote: "We regard the vast, endlessly provocative, prejudice-laden, existing sea of documentary footage as the richest and most unequivocal storehouse of information about humanity. We do not agonize over its limitations or those of the persons who shot or edited it. We come to it with an observational approach like that used by the ordinary person in everyday life, which enables him to differentiate constantly between different classes of visual experience and to behave appropriately in relation to these varieties of experience."

Their first attempts at description and codification were based on Labanotation and the idea of effort-shape. While this yielded rich data, its specificity obscured the larger patterns. They could not see the forest for the trees. They took a figurative step back and considered effort shape on a larger scale. "Choreometrics ignores the problem of the unit; it is not concerned with a step-by-step, phrase-by-phrase result so that the dance can be reproduced in its entirety from a written score. It reaches out to another level, to the level of identification where signals, constantly flowing in the kinesic stream, characterize all present in terms of age, sex, occupation, and most especially, cultural affiliation."

The Choreometrics team worked against a tradition that considered the most important meaning of a dance or piece of music as the text itself, the nuances brought to the text by each performer, and the culture bearers' interpretations. They considered dance "first as a representation and reinforcement of cultural pattern and only secondarily as an expression of individual emotion. Neither the expressive function of dance nor the emotional outlet it gives each dancer, whether modern choreographer or folk dancer, is denied. What we have seen in scores of films, however, leads inexorably to the conclusion that many aspects of movement, once thought to be idiosyncratic, vary by culture type rather than from person to person."

The Choreometrics project team produced four things. They assembled a major collection of dance film for cross-cultural comparison. They developed a method of observation and description for characterizing performance at a level removed from the specificity of the text. Their statistical analysis uncovered a set of correlations between patterns of subsistence and social organization and those of performance style. Finally, Alan Lomax interpreted some of the correlations from the perspective of a highly knowledgeable person steeped in the sensibilities of the mid-twentieth century. Four films came out of the project: *Dance and Human History*, which maps the world on two Choreometric scales, trace form and single/multi-unit truck; *Step Style* and *Palm Play*, which interpret the scales that measure the use of the feet and hands; and *The Longest Trail*, which traces similarities in movement style from Siberia through North and South America.

Collecting the film samples, analyzing the footage, running the computer programs, and evaluating the correlations represents a monumental effort in an anthropological tradition that valued comparative analysis and accepted generalization. Unfortunately, Lomax's work came to fruition as the field was undergoing a sea change and becoming suspicious of cross-cultural comparisons and simplification of expressive culture. At the same time, anthropology divided into quantitative and interpretive factions. The quantitativist practitioners, who might have been expected to admire Lomax's precise observations and rigorous analysis, were horrified at his expansive interpretations and extrapolated results. The interpretivists distrusted any system that reduced the magic of art to patterns that revealed themselves though computer analysis. Ironically, the filmed and videotaped sample of ethnographic dance grew exponentially in the last three decades of the twentieth century, making it possible to test the underlying assumptions of the system and answer the many questions about art and culture that it raises.

NOTE

1. Alan Lomax, Irmgard Bartenieff, and Forrestine Paulay, "Dance Style and Culture" in *Folk Song Style and Culture*, ed. by Alan Lomax (Washington, D.C.: American Association for the Advancement of Science, Publication no. 88, 1968). All quotations in the present chapter are from this work.

CHAPTER 26

Dance Division of the Performing Arts Library at Lincoln Center: A Day in the Life

Madeleine Nichols

Madeleine Nichols, 2001. Photo by Charles Steiner.

Eyes light up with excitement often during the course of a summer day at Lincoln Center's Performing Arts Library. Young dancers, new to New York City, discover many dance styles unknown to them back home. Between auditions for jobs, they feast on our resources, available free of charge and including films and videotapes, audiotapes, clipping files, performance programs, photographs, set and costume designs, posters, books, journals, manuscripts, and memorabilia.

A college student taking a dance history course finds the 1930s *Dance Observer* magazine reviews that Doris Humphrey read after the premieres of her choreographic works; the excitement that passes to the young reader is palpable. A world-famous choreographer locates the score of music he wants for a new dance piece. A television producer finds photographs needed for a documentary. His assistant selects moving-image footage needed for the broadcast. Through old photographs, performance programs, and oral interviews, a reporter preparing human-interest stories learns some of the history of dancers who are now victims of Alzheimer's disease or a kidnapping.

Screening tapes and thumbing through reviews, a presenter from far away gets a good impression of dance troupes he's thinking of inviting to perform in his theater next season. A prima ballerina studies every film, videotape, and photograph of her predecessors as she prepares for a classical role. Several summer-session students sit in a tight group with one of their mothers, intensely watching old films of their teacher's performance. A Broadway choreographer and his star dancer execute a step as they see it on videotape, just before the start of a rehearsal a few blocks away.

A notator patiently reexamines videotapes and music scores during the final review of a Labanotation score. The dance critic for an urban newspaper has just seen Nijinsky's diary and handled it under the supervision of a conservator. A granddaughter has tears in her eyes after discovering photographs of her grandmother's renowned dance teacher, taken when the grandmother was a student in Poland at the outset of her career with the Ballets Russes. Several professors from important university dance departments are researching new books. When they work here in the same day or week, the intensity is breathtaking to those who know major resources are being created. To a casual viewer, the Dance Division just looks like a reading room with unusually serious readers and writers.

Young people from Korea come with clear anticipation, eager to read the latest Korean dance magazine. No one on the staff understands Korean, but the library catalog listing on the Internet, as each new issue of the magazine arrives monthly, attracts the young visitors. A Russian Fulbright scholar, in the United States for the first time, absorbs every bit of information about a famous Russian choreographer who emigrated to America; the scholar is researching the first biography of Balanchine to be written and published in his native country.

Behind the walls of the public reading room, staff members respond to telephone and e-mail inquiries. They retrieve from the library shelves the old performance programs and photographs that dance companies need as they prepare promotional materials for their new seasons. They check facts for dance-specific details, at the request of the *Los Angeles Times*, the *Boston Globe,* and the *New York Times.*

On a typical day, the Dance Division sees the hopes and aspirations of every facet of the dance community. Multiple telephones start to ring by 9:30 in the morning and continue until 5:30 in the afternoon, punctuated by the sound of the fax machine with its incoming requests from around the world and responses going out again; the silent e-mail queries are opened, relayed, and answered. By 3 p.m., staff members begin to look glassy-eyed from the sheer number of transactions. They might serve on the reading room dance reference desk for an hour or two, engaging in longer conversations with on-site patrons who get eye contact and smiles as they examine materials, receive personal assistance with computer searches, or get suggestions about videotapes, photographs, and other materials.

The Dance Division of the New York Public Library, a unique repository for the documents of dance past and present, is the largest and most comprehensive archive in the world devoted to dance and the dancer. Its scope includes ballet, traditional, modern, and social dancing, as well as ice-skating and gymnastics. More than a library, it functions partly as a museum, partly as a film and videotape production center, and partly as a consulting service to the professional dance community. Exhibitions and public programs are the front line to the general public. Founded in 1944 as a separate unit in the Research Libraries of the New York Public Library (NYPL), the Dance Division now has users all over the world. It serves as a base for choreographers, dancers, critics, historians, journalists, publicists, filmmakers, graphic artists, students, and the general public. They come to the reading room in New York City, or by way of the Internet through the on-line catalog.

The collection is built from and by the dance field. Contributions from dancers and companies of the best videotapes, books, and promotional materials have created a resource that dancers know other dancers need. It provides a safe place to compare and contrast performing styles. Here you can examine the work of the successful writers who describe dance in books, in poetry, in daily newspapers, in scholarly journals, and in broadcast journalism. Films and videotapes show a vast array of examples of international communication—expressions in dance form about basic human emotions, dramas, tensions, and events—which do not require knowledge of a particular written language. The visual work of photographers over the past hundred years contains examples of myriad ways to capture that most fascinating subject, the human body. As world populations migrate to the United States, their specific dances and artists become a valuable means of sharing cultures and cultural traditions. The library materials demonstrate the ways this is being done, through items that are donated and used by the home-country generation and succeeding generations in the new geographic territory.

It is immensely valuable to have dance documents under the care of librarians specifically trained in and devoted to dance. They are professionally on the alert for what exists, what is needed, and ways to make it most accessible. Cooperative cataloging at a national level ensures that the vocabulary of dance is available within the larger memory of institutions such as libraries and museums. Our holdings broaden dance beyond a specific performance by specific dancers, taking resources to a different, longer-lasting level, as important for the general public as for the dance practitioner.

Acquisitions at NYPL are broad in scope, representing multiple countries, styles, and even current fads. To represent all that is best in dance, in all its manifestations, in whatever form of document, builds a solid foundation for study and contemplation by future generations. By linking electronically with other national libraries and specialized centers around the world, the Dance Division assures that access to materials is almost limitless. (A recent example of such a partnership is between the NYPL Performing Arts Library and the new Performing Arts Library in Singapore.) At the moment, the Internet catalog contains descriptive listings and detailed finding aids, with a few full-text or full-image items. As years pass, the balance will change, so that ultimately the resources in text and image will be accessible from anywhere, through the Internet. Now, during the transition era, visitors still must strategize about what can be obtained locally and what entails a trip to a specific repository to examine an original artifact.

Recognizing that film and videotape are deeply meaningful to the dance field, the Dance Division creates documents to augment what already exists. Jerome Robbins donated a portion of his royalties from *Fiddler on the Roof* for the purpose of commissioning filmmakers and videographers to record dance for the library, in order to build a study center of moving images. These serve as material for the choreographer to copyright a theatrical dance work; for the repertory company to study, refresh, and restage a dance work; for the presenter or funding agency to review to obtain a sense of the quality of performance; and for the documentary or educational producer to incorporate into new productions. Over 1,300 films and videotapes of dances have been produced by the Dance Division for study and preservation purposes, in cooperation with choreographers, dance companies, craft unions, and other artists involved. A corollary program at the library is the oral history archive, which creates needed interviews as historical records where information about dance will otherwise be undocumented.

Sadly, videotape is not a "preservation medium." Motion picture film, which can last beyond a hundred years, appears to be the best choice for saving moving images for future generations, but the high cost of film makes it not feasible for the vast number of dances that need to be documented. Libraries, as institutions dedicated to preservation, are key players for dance because they can bring preservation solutions to fruition. That role will be a serious one for the Dance Division, which has more than 15,000 films and 36,400 videotapes, many unique and unpublished. They include the works of some of the twentieth century's best-known dance artists, including, for example, George Balanchine, Martha Graham, Merce Cunningham, and Jerome Robbins. The Dance Division's interest in preserving the work of these figures cannot be overestimated. To marshal the financial underpinning and technical solutions to this preservation challenge in a way that will benefit the entire field of dance internationally, as well as the holdings at NYPL, is at the top of the agenda.

Today, the excellence of dancing—whether formal in a theater or a ceremony or casual in a social setting—mandates documentation. More and better moving-image documents must be created. They are the grist for the inevitable search to compare and contrast styles, artists, and companies. Films and videos join other kinds of documents, such as photographs, manuscripts, oral histories, performance and souvenir programs, posters, reviews, books, notation scores, engravings, and set and costume designs, to do justice to the art form. Together, these tools help both professionals and the public to compare the past and the present, to learn from the past as they go forward to the future. While the Dance Division has for decades produced high quality film and videotapes of important contemporary dancing that would otherwise have gone without an adequate record, more needs to be done. If videotape and even digital versions become the norm in the ordinary course of dancing, then the skills in making those documents need to be high. And the resulting tapes or electronic files need to be preserved. If ever there were a wake-up call about the importance of creating and preserving documents of dance, the high volume of use of library dance materials is it. Efforts are needed now to maintain this support and inspiration for new generations of videographers, choreographers, and dancers.

DANCE DIVISION OF THE NEW YORK PUBLIC LIBRARY

Founded in 1944 as the Dance Collection, the Dance Division of the New York Public Library is the largest and most comprehensive archive in the world devoted to the documentation of dance. Chronicling the art of dance in all its manifestations—ballet, ethnic, modern, social, and folk—the Collection is much more than a library in the usual sense of the word. It is part museum, part film production center, and part consulting service to the professional dance community. It preserves the history of dance by gathering diverse written, visual, and aural resources, and it works to ensure the art form's continuity through an active documentation program. While the Collection contains more than 30,600 reference books about dance, these account for only 3 percent of its vast holdings. Other resources available for study free of charge include:

- More than 10,000 films and videotapes, ranging from the earliest Edison reels to the latest television broadcasts; from world dances to ballets of Balanchine; from Broadway musicals to dance therapy and notation.
- Audiotapes: taped interviews and published memoirs
- Clipping files: articles from hundreds of American and foreign newspapers.
- Iconography: prints, original designs, posters, and photographs.
- Manuscripts and Memorabilia

http://www.nypl.org/research/lpa/dan/dan.html

Part V
Seeding the Field

CHAPTER 27

Dancing *Matters*

Rhoda Grauer

DVD 20
***Dancing*, Episode 4: "Dance at Court"** (1993) 56 min
Excerpt 6 min 26 sec

Dancing was more of an obsession than an idea.

I've always loved dance. I loved doing it. I loved seeing it. Dance is in my earliest memories from block parties and tap dance classes to television and the movies. At the age of ten, I was kicked out of dance school for talking in class. I shifted my professional aspirations from dance to theater, where you were expected to talk.

In 1973, I had the good fortune to work with Jerome Robbins and to become friends with Twyla Tharp. I reconnected with dance. A year later, I became the executive director of Twyla's company. It was a remarkable period of her career and a very exciting time for American dance.

Twyla introduced me to film and video—both as tools for documentation and as power tools for reaching millions of people. Twyla videotaped everything: rehearsals and performances. She and the dancers pored over the recordings. She altered and refined steps; dancers analyzed the quality and attack of their movement. Choreography grew, and performances became richer and fuller. It became clear to me that if dance artists were willing to learn how to record and read the media, video could become instrumental in advancing the art form.

A small revolution was engulfing the dance world. Dance was being shown on—and, in some cases, actually made for—television as never before. My first experience was as associate producer of *Making Television Dance: A Videotape by Twyla Tharp,* produced by the WNET/Television Lab. The TV Lab operated on the uncommon conviction of its executive director, David Loxton, that artists should have artistic control over their work and have the freedom to experiment. Twyla did just that. *Making Television Dance* follows Twyla and her dancers over a period of a year. It captures the making of a dance, private rehearsals with Twyla and Mikhail Baryshnikov in one of their earliest collaborations, conceptual conversations between Twyla and television director Don Mischer about the challenges of putting dance on television, and behind-the-scenes glimpses at the process of producing a television program. By observing Twyla's struggle to transform the basic tenets of live dance (movement through time and space) into the physical and financial realities of television ("television is about the rectangle"—a flat screen with no depth of field and manipulatable time —"and the dollar,"[11] it's expensive and offers little leeway for error), audiences got a insider's view of both choreography and television being made. Aired in New York in 1977, *Making Television Dance* is a benchmark for dance and television, both for its innovative approach to making dance for television and for its exposure of process.

In 1976, PBS launched *Dance in America*. Twyla's *Sue's Leg* was the first dance to be recorded.[2] I went from working on a free-wheeling year-long, low-budget, experimental project to the big time: full studio, big crew, multi-camera production for national television. In one airing, more people saw Twyla's work than could see it in a lifetime of live performances.

Working with Twyla, I learned that not everyone loved dance the way I did. I realized dance was not supported, reviewed, or approached with the same respect that music, theater, literature, and the visual arts attracted. Twyla said dance was an underdog in our country because it was seen as a frill, an entertainment, not as a serious reflection of or contributor to our society. It just wasn't sufficiently understood to be respected fully.

I felt television could improve that situation! *Dance in America* helped get dance seen; *Making Television Dance* helped audiences understand what they were seeing. The two together had a lot to offer dance.

A WIDER WORLD

In the late 1970s, I was recruited by National Endowment for its Arts to be director of its Dance Program. New links were forged in the chain of events that led to *Dancing*.

I attended a meeting of CORD (Conference on Research in Dance) in Hawaii. The subject was "Dances of the Pacific": Okinawa, China, Korea, Indonesia, India, Japan, the Philippines, and the Pacific Islands. What I experienced in performance and learned in lectures captivated me. Artists and scholars talked about the purposes of dance, not just movement techniques or choreographic originality. They knew *why* dances were done, not just *how* they were done. My stay in Hawaii ignited in me an intellectual interest as powerful as my visceral love for dance.

Shortly after I returned, dance writer Arlene Croce asked me to help a group of scholars, led by Selma Jeanne Cohen, find out why their application to the National Endowment for the Humanities for a dance encyclopedia had been rejected twice. I called my sister agency for clarification. The reply was: "Ms. Grauer, dance is not a subject for humanistic exploration, and therefore not eligible for NEH funding. Dance is a performance form and should be supported by the Arts Endowment, by your program!"

I asked if NEH had ever funded encyclopedias on music or theater. "Yes we have, and we would again." I was indignant, furious! This person was telling me that all these dancers and dances that I loved were less than music, less than theater. Twyla's words rang in my ears: "For Americans dance is only an entertainment."

"Aha," I replied, feeling like a detective who had trapped a witness into a confession. "The very fact that you don't know that the historical, cultural, and aesthetic complexities of dance are every bit as fundamental to the humanities as music or theater, proves the need for this publication!" The Dance Encyclopedia was funded.

My fascination with the power of television to share information, and the clear need for information on dance, came together. I wanted to work with dance and television. In 1981, Mikhail Baryshnikov, newly appointed artistic director of American Ballet Theatre (ABT), asked me to join the company to start a media department![3] Cable television was coming into its own; dance promised to be a significant part of cable programming. ABT's board wanted a person on staff devoted to guaranteeing the company's place in the new media landscape.[4] Thanks to executive director Herman Krawitz, an experienced television producer, I learned the legal and financial ins and outs of getting programs made. He introduced me to everything from budgeting, union negotiations, and contracts to co-production, finance, and distribution. In the next three years, we made four programs for American Ballet Theatre: two documentaries, *Birth of a Ballet* and *Where Dreams Debut*; and two performance specials, *Don Quixote* and *An Evening with American Ballet Theatre*. In addition, we made two more for Twyla, *The Catherine Wheel* and *Baryshnikov by Tharp*.[5]

By 1984, I had seven productions under my belt, and Jac Venza, executive producer of *Great Performances* and *Dance in America*, invited me to join the Performance Programs division of WNET, the New York Public Broadcasting System station. The next three years were devoted to working with Jac on the two series, tracking the international arts television markets, forging co-productions with foreign broadcasters, and raising production funds, as well as producing more dance programs including *Gregory Hines: Tap Dance in America* (Savion Glover's first television appearance), *Choreography by Jerome Robbins,* and David Gordon's *Made in USA* with Mikhail Baryshnikov and Valda Setterfield.

All this time, public television was expanding its programming of highly informative, entertaining multi-part documentary series on serious subjects. I was in the right place, and it was the right time to do a major documentary series on dance. Television could show viewers all over the country—and the world—that dance was much more than simple entertainment; it had meaning, it had importance. *Dancing* was launched.

PUTTING IT ALL TOGETHER

My first instinct was to make *Dancing* all about American dance: social, theatrical, spiritual, ritual. I soon realized that, aside from the dance traditions of Native Americans, just about everything we called "American" had come from or been shaped by dances from somewhere else. Ballet came from Europe. Asian dance, martial arts, and meditation practices powerfully influenced the early modern dance artists. American social dances from the Lindy Hop to rock-and-roll crazes evolved out of mixtures of African and European music and dance. Even the all-American square dance had its origins in French and English country dances. So, a series on American dance could include just about anything and everything, from everywhere. There was no established syllabus or scholarly study on world dance to follow or adapt. I couldn't do a "history" of dance because there were no moving images of dancing before the late nineteenth century, when film was invented. I didn't know where to begin.

I called a friend in Boston, a seasoned producer of multi-part series. "How do I get my head around the content of this thing?" I asked him. "It's hard to find a single scholar for a global series like this . . . the Carl Sagan of dance?"

"Forget it," was his reply. "That's your job. That's what a producer does. You have to become an expert yourself. You cannot rely on one source, or even many scholars. You have to read everything you can find, see every program on dance ever made. You have to know the subject as well as your 'authorities.' Start your research."

The series could easily embrace dances from anywhere in the world. The year was 1986, long before the World Wide Web and the enormous search capability of the Internet. How could I begin to find information on world dance? Even the Dance Collection of the New York Public Library—certainly the most thorough collection of dance literature, films and video in the country, if not the world—had limited resources on dance outside the United States and Europe.

I then turned to friends who had been gathering scholarly articles on dance from all corners of the globe for a planned encyclopedia of dance.[6] This project proved an invaluable resource with rich bibliographies, and it led me to most of the 20-odd scholars who collaborated on *Dancing*.

I devoted every spare minute of my life for the next three years[7] to researching the content of and raising the money for *Dancing*. I read everything I could get my hands on; I met with scholars, watched dance films, went to performances, talked to dancers, attended conferences, and hung out at the Dance Collection. Seeing Western theatrical dance forms was relatively easy; I could go to performances or look at videotapes in the library. Non-theatrical Western dance and traditions from Africa, Asia, and South America were hard to find, though. How could I research and write about dances I couldn't see? I came across a *New York Times* article about an Ashante chief in Brooklyn and his court and court dances. I began to explore the neighborhoods of New York and found a Yoruba community, a Baroque dance community, small ballet schools, swing dance clubs, folk dance groups, an Egyptian community. Little by little, I found almost everything I wanted to see. All the while, I pursued international co-producers,[8] and submitted applications to the NEA, the NEH, the Ford, Rockefeller, Japan, and Readers' Digest foundations, and many more.

By May of 1990 the programs were formulated, funding secured and a team of outstanding filmmakers[9] had been hired.

Now came issues of shooting style and storytelling. The idea for *Dancing* took shape long before "political correctness" became doctrine, but I had made some basic decisions about how our story should be told. I decided that everyone speaking for the dance of a particular culture would be a member of that culture. And who knew dance better than dancers? Many people thought of dancers as mute or inarticulate; I knew that wasn't true and felt the subtleties and meanings of dance would emerge more powerfully and emotionally from them. Ideally, our interviews would be with dancers who were also scholars.

Then we grappled with filming. I knew that compelling, well-told stories and actual locations were crucial to *Dancing*. I had decided to put the production of the series into the hands of seasoned documentary filmmakers, not dance performance directors. This created new challenges. Shooting dance is often about long shots revealing the dancer's full body. Documentary is often about capturing emotion in close-up. The filmmakers and I spent hours arguing the relative value of long shots versus close-ups. We struck a balance. They could shoot close-ups as long as they also shot full-body. In editing, I could fight for the shot I felt was best for the dance.

Issues of music had to be resolved. I did not want "composed" music; I wanted all sounds to come from the locations, all the music to come from the dances being explored. In shooting dance for a documentary, we used short clips of dances that might go on for hours. We tried a number of ways to make

Dancing is an eight-hour documentary about dance in world culture. Filmed on five continents, the series includes dance traditions of 18 different cultures. *Dancing* has aired globally and been adopted for use in college and university courses on world dance and culture. *Dancing* was conceived, developed, and executive produced by Rhoda Grauer.

the dance and music fit seamlessly together. Some would prove to work better than others.

For almost every location, my research team and I had identified local scholars and facilitators. With story lines, lists of scholars, and local contacts in hand, the filmmakers went off to start their own research and prepare their shoots. I soon received a call from one of the teams: "Rhoda, your materials are great. But my papers seem to be missing contacts for the Imperial Household in Tokyo. How do I get access to shoot Bugaku?"

My blood ran cold. I had slammed into the reality of production. This was no longer theory. How would we get the right to enter the Japanese Imperial Household and film? I had no idea if we could actually get permissions to shoot there—or anywhere else, for that matter. The Ashanti Festival in Ghana called for by the script takes place every 20 to 30 years. I had no idea when the next one would be. We needed a shoot in Egypt, and Desert Storm had just broken out, making Americans *persona non grata* in Egypt. Reverend Moon booked the Kirov Theatre for a full month at exactly the time we were scheduled to film *The Sleeping Beauty*.

One by one, though, things fell into place. Our researcher in Ghana reported that the Ashanti celebration was being held the following February. I remembered a friend who had grown up in Japan, and our entrée to the Royal Household was secured. The Kirov shoot was rescheduled. The Egypt shoot was relocated to Morocco. Every location and every dance in the original plan were confirmed.

The cameras rolled. In Nigeria, the director was nearly trampled by a group of switch-swinging participants in a Sango ritual. In the rushes, we see the director struggling to get the crowds to make way for his camera. The team in the Cook Islands had a great shoot but missed their plane out; with only two flights a week leaving the island, they got a forced vacation in the midst of a tight production schedule. Our cameraman in India fell off a ladder and broke one camera and one ankle, but got the footage needed.

DVD 20 In the Court of Yogyakarta, we obtained permission to film the Bedoyo, a sacred dance performed in honor of the Goddess of the South Seas to ensure rain and good crops. Though the rainy season was long over, as the dancers entered the dance *pendopo* (open pavilion), there was a sudden explosion of thunder and the skies opened.

There had not been a cloud in the sky. The rain was so loud and the lightning so bright that we had to stop the shoot. As is often the case in the tropics, the downpour lasted just a few minutes before the sun came out. Musicians retook their places, the sound and cameraman signaled their readiness, and the dancers began again. The skies burst, thunder rolled. We stopped.

After the third downpour, the local interpreter tapped me on the shoulder. "Miss Grauer, it is a well-known fact that the Goddess of the South Seas is very jealous of her Bedoyo. This is not the first time unseasonable rain has stopped it from being recorded."

"What? Is she serious, I thought?" She certainly looked serious. "You mean we just may not be able to record this dance?"

"That's right. You are welcome to keep trying, but it is possible you will not be able to do so."

I cringed. The Bedoyo was a fundamental part of our Humanities grant. I didn't have permission to omit it, or time or budget to research another option. Disaster!

A few minutes went by, and the interpreter appeared with a small group of traditionally clad women from the court. As the rain fell, they conducted a small ceremony in the center of the courtyard facing the dance pavilion: incense, holy water, some flowers, and a quiet chant. "That might help," our interpreter whispered.

The rain tapered off and the sun emerged, drying the puddles surrounding the dance pavilion. I sat transfixed. "I think you can start now," she suggested. We filmed the dance twice, and then did a number of interviews. The skies were still clear as we went to dinner.

As production and postproduction progressed over the next two years, I was exposed to more and more of the powers of dance. I became convinced that *Dancing* was destined to be, and I just happened to be the vehicle it chose to get itself made. In the spring of 1993, seven years after I got the idea, *Dancing* aired internationally.[10] I was free to move on to something else.

NOTES

1. Twyla Tharp in *Making Television Dance.*

2. *Sue's Leg: Remembering the 30s,* director, Merrill Brockway; producer: Emile Ardolino; associate producer, Judy Kinberg; executive producer, Jac Venza.

3. ABT and the Metropolitan Opera were the only American performing arts organizations to have a media department.

4. Most of those early channels no longer exist, and those that do, do not produce or program dance.

5. *Baryshnikov by Tharp* for *Dance in America*, and *The Catherine Wheel* for the BBC and *Dance in America.*

6. Cohen, Selma Jeanne, ed. *International Encyclopedia of Dance* (New York: Oxford University Press, 1998).

7. During the development and funding of *Dancing* I was still working as associate director of Performance Program, and production executive of *Great Performances* and *Dance in America.*

8. The BBC and RM Arts, two of the leading partners in cultural programming, bought into the production.

9. Muffie Meyer and Ellen Hovde of Middlemarch Films, Mark Obenhaus of Obenhaus Films, Inc., Geoff Dunlop and Jane Alexander of Screenlife Productions and Orlando Bagwell of Roja Productions.

10. For print documentation, see Gerald Jonas, *Dancing: The Pleasure, Power, and Art of Movement* (New York: H. Abrams in association with Thirteen/WNET 1992).

CHAPTER 28

A New Place for Dancing

Bob Lockyer

DVD 21
Boy (1995) 4 min 30 sec
Full work

DVD 22
Touched (1994) 14 min
Excerpt 3 min 11 sec

DVD 23
Hands (1995) 4 min 31 sec
Excerpt 2 min 28 sec

DVD 24
Le P'tit Bal (1994) 3 min 48 sec
Full Work

DVD 25
Enter Achilles (1996) 48 min
Excerpt 3 min 22 sec

I am a very lucky person. All my working life has been spent in network television at the British Broadcasting Corporation, working in production, most of it in dance, with choreographers and dancers. At the start, 30-odd years ago, we were mostly making TV versions of stage works, but recently we have also commissioned original made-for-the-screen dance works for BBC TWO in the UK. The shift to commissioning outside production companies to make programs came about for two primary reasons: a government decree that 25 percent of all broadcast programs should be made by production companies outside the Corporation; and the development of lightweight, simple video technology that did not need teams of engineers to keep it going. Until that equipment became available, only large companies like the major networks could afford such teams. (The BBC is a public broadcaster that has six channels at the time I am writing. Two are terrestrial: BBC ONE and TWO. The rest are digital channels. All are supported by an annual license fee paid by all owners of television receivers in the UK, even those who don't watch the BBC. The BBC does not screen advertising.)

When we talk about dance for the small screen, do we make a distinction between TV versions and made-for-the-screen dance works? What the camera does to dance is the same. The language of film and video making is the same. What is different is how that language is used.

An existing stage work is set, as if in stone; it is unchangeable. It is often linked to a copyrighted music score that can't be cut. If the choreographer is dead, the estate will rarely allow cuts or major changes. If you are working as a director in partnership with the choreographer, then changes might be possible. I was lucky in working with Lloyd Newson on our two DV8 films, *Strange Fish* and *Enter Achilles*. Newson understood that to make the screen versions work, major cuts would be necessary—in both cases, 90-minute-plus stage works came down to the television hour. But such radical cutting was possible musically because the pieces did not have through-composed scores, and reworking by the composers was possible for both films.

DVD 25

Usually, however, such major changes are almost impossible because of constraints of time and budget. If you are broadcasting or recording a dance

Behind the scenes of *Le P'tit Bal* (1994) by Philippe Decouflé. Photo by Malik Nahassia. DVD 24

work from a theater, in front of a paying audience, once the curtain has gone up the race has started, and it will not end until the final curtain falls.

Take the same work out of the theater and arrange to shoot it in a studio, and you can place the camera almost anywhere. You hope you can make a better version. It is not always so, mainly because stage time and screen time are different. They pass at different speeds. As audience members, we watch differently at the theater than at home or in the cinema. The former is active, the latter passive. Perhaps that's why people eat all the time in the cinema.

Watching a dance performance in the theater, each member of the audience experiences a different work. Next time you go to a dance performance, in the interval discuss with others what you have just seen. You will often discover that you could have been at different performances. Each of you will have selected different things to watch. Whether they know it or not, the choreographer and his lighting designer use lighting to get us all to look at the same thing, but there is no guarantee that they will succeed. The follow spot at the ballet ensures that the light is on the star; at contemporary dance performances, complicated lighting plots direct the audience's attention to the right place on stage. In some ways, the lighting plot is similar to the director's shooting script. Often when we come to record stage works, we change the lighting plot, because the cut to a different shot is the same as a major lighting change. Both direct the audience to a new action.

Screen a dance film in the cinema or at home, and each member of the audience will see the same thing: the set of images chosen by the director. It is the director's version of the dance work. Working with Glen Tetley several years ago,

Philippe Decouflé and Annie Lacour in *Le P'tit Bal* (1994) by Philippe Decouflé. Photo by Malik Nahassia. DVD 24

I heard him say, "You are the choreographer now, Bob. You select the images that the audience sees."

For the past few years, the BBC (with me as executive producer) and the Arts Council of England (with Rodney Wilson as their executive producer) have co-commissioned several series of "Dance for the Camera"—short, made-for-the-camera dance pieces. One, with Dutch Broadcasts NPS, resulted in several films by Dutch choreographers working with British directors.

Unlike other television programs, there is open entry for this series. We advertise nationally for choreographer/director teams who want to make dance films. The choreographers must have a professional record, having received funding from our regional and/or national arts councils; the directors must have worked in broadcast television. From 150 applications a year, Rodney Wilson and I weed out those that do not meet the criteria.

With the application form, each team submits a one-page outline of their idea. These are looked at by the selection panel, and a short list made. The lucky ones are then given £2000 to spend on developing their projects. Several months later, they present their ideas to the same panel, and if we like the developed idea and they agree to the budget—£50,000 per project—they get to make the video or film.

Some challenging projects have resulted, often evoking the question "Is it dance?" Before each new series was commissioned, the BBC/Arts Council held workshops, seminars and discussions, hoping that, as a result, new teams would be formed and choreographers and directors would be challenged to think anew about dance and the camera.

"The role of dance editor/director allows me to experience the vicarious thrill of being a choreographer without having to take the responsibility for devising the steps," says Ross MacGibbon, a former Royal Ballet dancer and now a video director/editor who specializes in network dance and opera productions. Rosemary Lee, choreographer of site-specific works and several *Dance for the Camera* projects, remarks, "The 'real choreography' takes place in the edit DVD 25 suite." "I am willing to lose vast sequences of choreography if it aids the overarching rhythm of the film," says Lloyd Newson, DV8 choreographer. Kim Bradstrup, Arc Dance Company choreographer, agrees: "We are making a film first and foremost . . . we might use movement, we might use dance, we might make a film without words, but it's the language of film we are using."

When selecting a project to go forward to production in the *Dance for the Camera* series, I'm looking, in very simple terms, for something that will work on the screen—a dance work that uses the film/video vocabulary, not one that could be seen on the stage. A choreographer making a dance piece for live performance picks a designer, music, and dancers and then gets on with it. It is still a cottage industry. Film and video making is not. In the case of *Dance for the Camera*, there is our selection process—written application, interview, project development, final selection, budgetary approval and, up to nine months later, the signed and sealed commission. But it does not stop there. Rodney Wilson and I, the two executive producers, visit the shoot on location or in the studio, comment on rushes, and, most important, view the rough cuts. That is, we see the dance work in the early stages of post-production. We watch the rough cut, make comments, discuss what we think works and what doesn't, and then agree on changes with the director and choreographer. These can be very radical—switching the order of the film, cutting whole sections and extending others. Film and video are organic; they can take off in directions you never thought of when planning and choreographing the work. That makes it important for the director to include cutaways and close-ups in the shooting scripts—often more than they think they will need. It's important to remember that the screen is a narrative form; it tells stories, and the stories can change in the edit. This has been made easier with nonlinear edit systems, with which things can be reordered; the sense and rhythm can be changed, and the dance improved.

This process can be unnerving. I can feel the sense of dread in the cutting room as we, the producers, arrive for the first viewing. I've been through it and remember it all too well. But it is, or should be, a very positive time—extra minds looking at something to see if the original intentions work. We want the projects to succeed as much as the choreographers and directors do, and we are coming to help and advise. We are new eyes seeing the project for the first time. We are removed from the problems every film or video has in the edit stages. We all want the best and will work to make it happen. All we have to remember is that our role is to make the filmmaker's film as good as it can be, not to make it as *we* would have made it.

This is a process that should be used more in the making of stage works. All too often, the choreographer and the dance work could be helped with creative criticism and comment well before the first night, when the professional critics have their say.

As I have said, the whole process of watching is different. On film you can

Boy (1995) by Peter Anderson and Rosemary Lee. Courtesy of MJW Productions. Photo by Margaret Williams. DVD 21

show details you couldn't see on stage. You can also intercut from character to character to get reactions and tell stories. The film, television, and even the computer monitor are used to pass on information—narrative. Film and video tell stories. It's very hard to make non-narrative material work on the screen, even when it's by Cunningham or Balanchine. What you miss, sitting at home, is the story to help you, and also that sense of shared experience you get sitting in the theater. How that can be relived in the video is the most difficult problem a choreographer and director face as they make dance video that is pure dancing.

Dance made for the camera has given choreographers another place to dance. The sprung floor can now give way to a beach, a bar, a school hall, or even a field. The choreographed moves of eyebrows and fingers can be as important as pirouettes and grandes jetées, or even more important. On camera, every movement must be made to tell. With editing and the grammar of film, entrances and exits disappear; with a cut, you can be anywhere.

Characters—people—matter on the screen because in close-up you can read what is happening behind the eyes. That is what makes great screen actors: the face does not grimace, but we can read their thoughts in their eyes. When working with the camera, that sort of expression has to be considered by choreographers and directors who are new to this art. If the dancers are not sure what they are meant to be thinking at any time in a sequence, it will show on the screen.

There are gains, but also some losses. The physical, "animal" excitement of live performance—that sense of fear, the "will they do it" of live performance—is almost impossible to re-create on the screen, whatever the size. It has to be replaced by a concentration on what we can see on the screen, which is all the choreographer and filmmaker have.

This lack of physical excitement has led many "dance for the camera" projects to be narratives. They tell stories through movement and do not use dancers at full stretch as in stage dance. Is that why so few ballet choreographers, using the classical ballet steps, have taken up the challenge of these projects?

But storytelling is what the screen does well, whether the screen is in your living room or in the cinema. The accompanying DVD contains BBC-produced dance works, complete or excerpted; what follows are my thoughts on the programs and things to look out for. They were all made for network television by the BBC and the Arts Council of England and so far we have commissioned over forty such projects. One of the latest has a cast of more than 30,000, not dancers but birds. This video, *Birds*, directed and edited by David Hinton using wildlife footage of birds from all over the world, won the Grand Prix at the 2000 Dance Screen in Monaco. It also caused a bit of a fuss, as many said you can't have a dance film without dancers. I think you can.

Boy has a single performer, chosen by choreographer Rosemary Lee after months of auditions. Does the chosen boy have the right sense of magic and commitment? To me, he is reenacting the games I played, years ago, as a child. The film brings back happy memories for me, but what does a woman feel? Look at the use of the long shots, the foreground objects in the frame. What role do they play? Do they make you feel you are sharing his discovery? Look at the position of the horizon in the frame and the camera placement. Listen to the sound track. DVD 21

Touched, devised by choreographer Wendy Houstoun and director David Hinton, is an attempt to break the rule "We must see the whole body—it's a dance film." In this film, you don't. All you have is a crowded bar with people who are playing out a series of interactions. This film has a remarkable sound track; watch this section with the sound turned down, and then again with it turned up. I think you will discover how much the sound tracks add to the pictures. As the location changes, so does the sound perspective; listen as it changes with the different locations and with almost every cut. This sound track adds other layers to the story created by Hinton and Houston in the cutting room. Does the fact that it was shot in black and white add to that as well? DVD 22

Hands was choreographed by Jonathan Burrows, who told me after the event that he wanted to create a director-proof work. With a single shot and two hands perhaps he has, but the director also added something: the tracking shot to find the performer, then his performance space, his lap covered with a apron. Does seeing his face, even for a few seconds, humanize this film? Does the texture on the set and on the apron add something as well? Would it have felt the same if the back wall had been stainless steel? DVD 23

After looking at these and other examples on the DVD, you will understand that everything in the frame matters. What you put into the frame matters as much as what is already there. Always search the frame for the thing that is out of place, because it might fight what you are trying to say. This could be a piece of paper on the floor; when the dance is put together, it might jump about the frame as you make each cut. It can destroy the weeks you have spent planning and shooting the project. You may find that the audience is watching the paper and not the dance. The accompanying DVD provides an important and unique research tool. Watch these excerpts again and again; switch the sound down and watch and see what differences the sound track makes. What is on the sound track? Music? Effects? Can you hear the feet?

If you want to try and make your own dance for the camera, get a video camera. Put it to your eye and watch the world go by. Only then can you start

Tom Evans in *Boy* (1995) by Peter Anderson and Rosemary Lee. Courtesy of MJW Productions. Photo by Margaret Williams.

"Working on dance for the camera enables me to direct the eye much more specifically than I can in live work. I can draw the viewer right up close and establish an intimacy between viewer and performer in a more complex way. As in all my work with performers of any age, I work from the inside out and try to find a way of embodying their personality and quality in the work. Tom is boy but boy illustrates boyhood and masculinity in a more universal sense."
—Rosemary Lee, Director of Boy

to see what the lens does to movement. Also remember that you can move about, and that the lens does not have to stay at the same distance from the ground all the time. Put the camera on the ground or point it out a window. Those simple things change the point of view on the world and make for better videos. My best wishes if you try it for yourself.

CHAPTER 29

Europeans Filming New Narrative Dance

Kelly Hargraves

DVD 25
Enter Achilles (1996) 48 min
Excerpt 3 min 22 sec

Choreography is an art of improvisation. A choreographer takes an idea into the studio—maybe a piece of music or text or just a vague concept—and starts moving through space. Popular filmmaking, traditionally, is an art of preconceived ideas. Usually a filmmaker has a script or a storyboard before he or she shoots the first scene. With the advent of video, this structure has become more flexible, but the tenets of popular film are still based in the world of theater and literature. There is a structure—character development, script, dramatic arc in the action, and *mise-en-scène*. Generally there is a conflict that the main character must resolve by the end of the film.

Contemporary dance, by contrast, has evolved apart from these tenets, with postmodern choreographers focusing on elements other than character, story, or classic narrative form. In the 1980s and 1990s, however, dance began a return to narrative as a way to instill content and meaning, and choreographers again made dances with reference to a classical story structure. Dance films, too, began to exhibit more traditional story elements, yet they still mostly avoided dialogue, relying instead on the potency of gesture and movement to tell a tale.

Telling a story with images rather than words is dance's forte, but sometimes a piece's setting remains an abstraction on stage. With the notable exceptions of choreographers like Meredith Monk, who has had audiences travel between locations, and Pina Bausch, who has built tremendous stage sets that include trees, dirt, water, and other natural elements, most contemporary dance has existed on a barren stage with minimal scenography and props. One of the most exciting things to distinguish dance film from its stage counterpart is that cinema allows our imaginations to travel to actual locations—to view princesses in their castles, soldiers in their fields, and drinkers in their pubs.

European dance and film collaborators are currently the strongest proponents of new narrative dance films, in which stories and characters inhabit real places. European dance has evolved into a hybrid of dance and theater, sharing the same general principles as classical film. When these choreographers and filmmakers work together, they inherently share a common language. They are able to relate all aspects of the film—both what is in front of the camera (*mise-en-scène*, setting, narrative) and what is behind the camera (editing, lighting,

Enter Achilles (1996) by choreographer Lloyd Newson and director Clara Van Gool. Photo by Peter Jay.

shot choices) and all aspects of the choreography to portray a story or an event through resonant movement.

This clarity of narrative purpose has helped European filmmakers like Switzerland's Pascal Magnin and Holland's Clara Von Gool develop some of the strongest examples of dance film today. Trained at film school and veterans of feature film production, both directors have collaborated with some of Europe's best choreographers. Their films have been shown at the most prestigious dance film festivals around the world, including the Grand Prix du Video Danse in France, the IMZ Dance Screen in Germany, and the Dance on Camera Festival in New York, where they have won the top prizes.

ENTER THINKING: LLOYD NEWSON AND CLARA VON GOOL'S *ENTER ACHILLES*

DVD 25

Clara Von Gool's film adaptation of DV8's *Enter Achilles* is one of the most acclaimed dance films of the 1990s. As a filmmaker, Von Gool has always been interested in telling stories without words and has thus pursued working with choreographers. She has collaborated with Angelica Oi and Jamie Watton and has choreographed films of her own, yet her collaboration with Lloyd Newson on *Enter Achilles* remains her most outstanding work. Von Gool has distinguished herself as a filmmaker by her craftsmanship. Using conventional camera work without special effects or filmic illusion, she creates a strong sense of narrative by focusing on what the camera sees. Deft editing, strong musicality, and a range of camera angles give her films a sense of realism that contemporary stage dance often lacks.

Von Gool uses the camera's ability to enhance the world surrounding the dance—the colors, textures, and sounds—to heighten the dance's story and the dynamics of its movement. This allows her to not interfere with the dance itself, keeping segments whole with little editing. For *Enter Achilles*, Von Gool and Newson set the piece where Newson first had the impulse to make it, in a British pub with its gleaming wood bar, beer taps, pool table, and beer glasses.

Lloyd Newson approaches dance-making like a film director. He prepares a script, which sets up a scenario and characters, before beginning rehearsals. He then casts his performers based specifically on the needs of the script. Perhaps most important, he writes these characters and scenarios with a clear intention. Newson is a psychologically driven choreographer whose work relates directly to the sociocultural context in which he lives. He aims for clarity of intent and content, and emotional as well as physical vigor.

The stage production of *Enter Achilles* (1995) developed out of a series of workshops in Glasgow, but its initial impetus came from a night in a pub after a day in the studio. Newson, who is always observing the action of the world around him, noticed that all his companions were drinking pints of beer. He suggested they bring the glasses into the studio the next day. This small task allowed him to explore an entire world of gesture and innuendo that questioned masculinity and how men communicate physically and verbally.

Because Newson created such a clear sketch, Von Gool knew who the characters were and why they were together in the space. We are introduced to a group of eight men having a social evening in a pub, but we are also given more details about certain members of this group. There is the seductive Superman complete with cape, the mysterious lecher, and the lonely barkeep.

Tensions are high as these virile young men flirt with and threaten one other. Conflicts arise as their motivations—fear, jealousy, and rage—begin to counteract each other. An ingenious choreography ensues, with the dancers jumping over each other or tumbling across the barroom floor, beer glasses still in hand. Von Gool enhances the stunning choreography while exploring the personalities of these men, following their intense actions with a detached eye and then zooming in to show us their more vulnerable intentions. Her camera moves in a sinuous line along with the evolving action of the choreography. Through the intimacy of film, she further heightens the already strong psychology of DV8's provocative dance.

PASCAL MAGNIN AND THE FIELDS OF DANCE FILM

Pascal Magnin has made a trilogy of dance films that offer some of the most dynamic interaction between choreography, story and real settings seen in dance film today. His *Contrecoup* (Backlash, 1997) is an adaptation of a stage piece choreographed by Guilherme Bothelho, which explores the thorny theme of domestic violence. *Contrecoup* is distinguished by its ability to tell this story cinematically while retaining characteristics of the stage production. Magnin defines two distinct worlds—the stage world and the street world—by using different locations as well as employing different film stocks and camera techniques (such as flashbacks and slow-motion shots) and varied lighting and color palettes. Close-ups capture the emotion of dancing couples as they struggle to communicate, while choreographed sections shot in the city streets add a Scorsese-like intensity and sense of reality. When Magnin begins to incorporate shots of the actual stage set, it is both a surprise and a relief to watch such aggressive dance with the distancing effect of a theatrical setting.

Enter Achilles (1996) by choreographer Lloyd Newson and director Clara Van Gool. Photo by Peter Jay.

Magnin uses complex editing and short shots to intensify the drama and tension of each scene. This allows him to move us through the parallel stories and to interweave the stage and street worlds. Near the end of the film, when the two worlds converge, the lighting begins to blend and the shots are further shortened so that the dance phrases are pieced together, regardless of their location.

Contrecoup is a good example of a dance film made in a classical narrative form that still expresses the abstraction and emotive qualities of choreography. Like a classic narrative film, *Contrecoup* is built around clearly defined characters and a story based on conflict resolution. Following a classic narrative form, the choreographer and director have made all actions spring from the desires and conflicts within and between the characters. Although *Contrecoup* contains stylized and dynamic movement patterns, each dance sequence results from psychological causes.

This study of relationships centers on the domestic strife of one couple, while simultaneously presenting the stories of three single people over the course of one night in a charged urban environment. The actions and interactions of these five are presented as parallel events, with brief encounters and interactions that link the disparate characters. We see the main characters—the couple—and witness different stages of a volatile, aggressive relationship with many physical and verbal disputes. In this classic cause-effect narrative, the couple struggles to get along.

In his earlier film *Reines d'un jour* (1996), Magnin leaves theatrical spaces behind and takes his urbane young dancers to interact with the residents of a traditional Swiss mountain village. The rugged, aged faces and bodies of the villagers contrast with the youthful exuberance of the six dancers in modern street clothes in an astonishingly beautiful juxtaposition, and an eloquent statement on the passing of time and generations.

The strength of *Reines d'un jour* is that Magnin directly relates the choreography to the story's natural surroundings. The film opens with a close-up of bodies hitting the dirt as they roll down a hillside. As the dance continues its descent to the village, subtle stories develop: one woman cradles a man's head in her hands; a woman gives an affectionate kiss to a man sleeping in the grass. Indigenous creatures become part of the choreography when bulls run through the field with their bells ringing and begin head-butting. Soon the dancers emulate the creatures as the three men and women begin pushing their heads into each other.

This eloquent mix of lush scenography, acute choreography, and vague characters creates a seemingly non-narrative series of images, but it is actually derived from a classic story structure. The moral of this story is revealed only near the end of the film, when an extremely aged woman tells of three young girls forbidden to dance who defy their elders and suddenly disappear. It is a morality tale taken from the ancients of this village and now transferred through the lives of these young dancers. (The first film of the triligy, *Pas Perdus* [Lost Steps], made in 1994, was a more conventional piece, choreographed by Noemi Lapzeson.)

By placing dances in dynamic locations and honing them with a narrative structure, films like *Enter Achilles*, *Reines d'un jour*, and *Contrecoup* bring a heightened context and sense of reality to choreography. These dance films have taken the strengths of cinematic storytelling and combined it with the visceral, emotional hooks of dance movement. Bodies in motion, rhythmic editing, and composition are the elements of this new hybrid art form where dance and film aesthetics merge and choreography tells the tale.

CHAPTER 30

Northern Exposures: Canadian Dance Film and Video

Philip Szporer

DVD 26
Pas de deux (1968) 13 min 22 sec
Excerpt 1 min 30 sec

DVD 27
Lodela (1996) 27 min
Excerpt 1 min 30 sec

DVD 28
Le Dortoir (1990) 53 min
Excerpt 3 min 7 sec

DVD 29
Falling Down Stairs (1995) 55 min
Excerpt 55 sec

DVD 30
the village trilogy (1995) 22 min 38 sec
Excerpt 3 min 7 sec

DVD 31
Risible Chick (1993) 5 min 34 sec
Excerpt 1 min 54 sec

"I think the term "movies" is such a much more wonderful term than the term "film." Because movies mean that they move. That's the essential quality."
—Norman McLaren[1]

Dance on film or video can be a transcendental experience. It can take you to the land of the gods, to another place, to another emotion—or just induce an out-of-body experience. Motion and emotion in Canadian dance/film may be defined by our northern exposure and the call of our wild, especially if the cliché that Canadian art is informed in some measure by our physical geography is true.[2]

More than 20 years have passed since a new generation of dynamic, intriguing choreographers and dancers (primarily from Quebec), including Edouard Lock, Jean-Pierre Perreault, Ginette Laurin, Paul-André Fortier, Margie Gillis and Marie Chouinard, shook the public's perceptions of what dance could express. Their "no holds barred" experimentation, taking dance beyond a narrative line and outside the realm of ballet or traditional dance, flourished throughout Canada. Over a few short years, these artists also began moving off the stage and into film and video.

In the early 1980s, many Canadian videographers came to the medium from painting, sculpture, and even writing. In this milieu, Bernar Hébert, François Girard, and others began exploring and forging a dance film/video language distinctly their own. Their styles, skills, and technical know-how—in collaboration with choreographers—brought dance culture alive on the screen.

Much earlier, the Montreal-based National Film Board of Canada (NFB), founded in 1939, emerged as one of the country's most important social and critical creative institutions. Federally funded, the NFB, which has French and English units, has trained and nurtured generations of filmmakers. One of its pioneers, Canadian animator Norman McLaren, began his filmmaking career in 1934 and came to Canada in 1941 at the request of John Grierson, the NFB's commissioner, under whom McLaren had worked at the film unit of the British Post Office.

While a student at the Glasgow School of Fine Arts, the Scottish-born McLaren had access to a film projector but not a camera. This inspired him to

DVD 26
Pas de deux
Production Note: "I was spellbound when I first saw *Pas de deux*. Norman McLaren, the legendary film animator and wizard of the optical printer, had just opened up a whole new world of perspectives for the representation of movement on screen. Ever since, his visionary approach has been a constant source of inspiration."—*Philippe Baylaucq*

DVD 27
Lodela
Production Note: "José Navas, Chi Long and myself spent two years experimenting with a new visual language. With the help of miniature video technology placed on the body, our objective was to free dance from the constraints of the proscenium stage, to bring to it all the possibilities of the language of cinema, including a wonderful form of weightlessness."–*Philippe Baylaucq, Director of* Lodela

DVD 28
Le Doroir
Production Note: "*Le Dortoir* is a conceptual piece on memories, dreams and the survival of illusions. Translating Gilles Maheu's intense stage work onto the screen was a welcomed challenge for me. As a director, working on an adaptation can be a delicate and impulsive process but entering the worls of Maheu's work was botha pleasure and an inspiration."—*François Girard, Director*

DVD 30
the village trilogy
Production Note: "Shooting in B&W outdoors was as much a budgetary decision as it was an artistic one. Of course what I sometimes forget is that it can snow in Toronto even in April. On the four-day shoot we had snow, rain and bright sunshine. What saved us from disaster was a clear storyboard and shotlist. In other words, prep 'til you drop, then you'll be able to face any challenge."–*Laura Taler, Director*

DVD 31
Risible Chick
Production Note: "*Risible Chick* was recorded on Hi-8 video, Super-8 black & white and colour film, and 16mm reversal film to parallel the urban freneticism of the movement. It's a raucous, in-your-face dance attack with equally unruly filmic approach. The production elements were begged, borrowed or stolen and it was edited at the local artist video co-op. I think the whole thing probably cost about 800 bucks all-in, which proves that whether your message is beauty or revolution, it is possible to send it out into the world on its own steam."
—*Nick de Pencier, Director*

Norman McLaren drawing a musical soundtrack in the late 1940s. © National Film Board of Canada. All Rights Reserved. Photographer unknown.

Multi-image photograph of Norman McLaren. Photo by Julius Szelei, 1965. © National Film Board of Canada. All Rights Reserved.

draw directly onto celluloid, scratching the emulsion to make the film stock transparent. Thus began a lifelong interest in creating new images mixed with sound. McLaren took his cues from the works of the German experimental filmmakers and the Russian avant-garde in both the graphic realm and in theater; he picked up where they left off and developed his art as technologies were undergoing major changes. His is one of the most cohesive and personal bodies of work to emerge from Western animated cinema in the twentieth century. Not surprisingly, his films appeal to the senses regardless of the subject matter.[3]

McLaren's work is defined by his probings into the language of motion. In *Blinkety Blank* (1954), for instance, he left some frames black, exploring in this manner the after-image that remains on the retina although no image remains on film.[4]

DVD 26

Many critics call *Pas de deux* (1967)—a visual poem of form and movement—McLaren's masterpiece. Margaret Mercier and Vincent Warren, dressed in simple white costumes, dance a slow pas de deux on a black shooting stage, their bodies silhouetted and contrasted by rear lighting. As they move across the space (in choreography by Ludmilla Chiriaeff), a series of multiple exposures extends, leaving delayed traces of images—almost ghostly imprints on the screen—frozen in position for us to contemplate. McLaren employed, in a precomputer age, a technique called chronophotography, in which the movements of the two dancers are staggered and overlaid by the optical printer to produce this stroboscopic effect.[5]

Ballet Adagio (1971) has less technical wizardry, but McLaren's idea was to stimulate our appreciation of classical ballet and allow us to observe the techniques and mechanics of adagio movements. He had David and Anna Marie Holmes, in flesh-colored leotards, photographed in slow motion. Slowing down the bodies allows the viewer to observe not only the beautiful and luscious movement, but also the details, the muscles, and the concentration demanded by formal dance. McLaren's genius shows you something that isn't obvious.

DVD 27

Following in the tradition of McLaren's landmark stylistic filmmaking is Philippe Baylaucq's *Lodela* (1996), another NFB production. When Baylaucq started *Lodela*, he began to see the parallels with McLaren.[6] Both authors' works are inspired marriages of dance and film, were shot in 35mm and in black and white, feature two dancers, and contain no words.

Chi Long, José Navas from *Lodela*, directed by Philippe Baylaucq (1996). © National Film Board of Canada. Photo by Bertrand Carriere.

McLaren's classic, revolutionary multiple image work with the optical printer—with step-printing to deconstruct the dancers' movements and to present dance on film—explored movement and space in astonishing new ways. Baylaucq's access to electronic media and his curiosity about the potential of technologies to push the boundaries of artistic language prompted him to explore what could be done with miniature cameras and innovative digital imaging.

In *Lodela*, the viewer follows an allegory from two points of view: objective and subjective. The "objective" perspective presents the dance "from the outside" as traditionally seen by an audience. The novel "subjective" eye, represented by miniature cameras attached to various points on the bodies of the dancers (José Navas, also the choreographer, and Chi Long), captures movement "from the inside" as experienced by the dancers, as close as possible to what the dancers themselves see when they move through space.[7] (This footage represents about one-third of the material retained in the final cut.)[8] Interaction with the "subjective" camera brings about an entirely new relationship to gravity and the rectangular limits associated with the traditionally horizontal dance surface. In *Lodela*, the source of gravity is light. The bodies of the dancers are attracted to it; they move in space on horizontal, vertical, and diagonal planes.

Baylaucq drew inspiration for his story line primarily from *The Tibetan Book of the Dead*, a sacred book that proposes a version of the transmigration of the soul from death to a new life. The title *Lodela* is inspired by *l'au-delà*, the French term for the hereafter. In the film, a man dies and his soul travels in an afterworld composed of darkness and light, a site between death and rebirth. The resulting film and video composition is both painterly and sculptural, creating poignant meanings and moods. Canadian-born Baylaucq, who studied sculpture and film at Hornsey and St. Martin's Schools of Art in London and was raised among painters, says that he was fascinated to tell a story in simple geometric forms, pushing the inherent poetics of the image. "A round circular disc placed in the black frame of the camera in itself creates an emotion in an abstract basis," says Baylaucq.[9]

What drew Baylaucq instinctively to McLaren was his idea that the film frame is to be treated like a canvas. The sum total of all these moving "canvases" was a greater canvas, in much the same way that Eisenstein would have argued that each of his frames contributes, through the phenomenon of montage, to a greater idea.

Bernar Hébert is another film and video maker who conveys the intimacy of the dance performance, with a perspective on the body impossible for the viewer in the traditional hall to experience. Hébert, who founded the Montreal-based production company Agent Orange (with Michel Ouellette) in the early 1980s (it later spun into Cine Qua Non), cites the work of Maya Deren as stimulating his interest in video and dance, particularly her study of the interaction between dance and cinematographic language.[10]

La La La Human Sex Duo No. 1 (1987), Hébert's original adaptation of choreography by Édouard Lock, won him acclaim and numerous awards and was broadcast internationally. The avant-garde film, audacious visually and technically, shows its Surrealist influences in an imaginary journey through the ruins of a castle lost beneath the sea, to explore a couple's (Louise Lecavalier and Marc Béland) passionate, violent, and sensual relationship.

Hébert's stated challenge is to take something artistic and make it accessible to all tastes: "I always thought the daring of *La La La Human Steps* lent itself to the surreal and the unconscious, but I wanted to do a film that would not

Chi Long, José Navas from *Lodela* (1996), directed by Philippe Baylaucq. The subjective point of view in the film was shot with a miniature video camera attached to a variety of points on the dancers' bodies. This footage represents about a third of the material retained in the final cut. Photo by Bertrand Carriere.

only attract dance fans but all movie fans."[11] For the 50-minute *Velasquez's Little Museum* (1994), the filmmaker, again working with Lock, took eight choreographic sections from La La La's *Infante: C'est Destroy*, uniting the brute force of the company's dancing, dreamy imagery à la Deren, and the seventeenth-century Baroque painter's dramatic palette.

François Girard, perhaps better known for his feature films *Thirty-Two Short Films about Glenn Gould*, and *The Red Violin*, started his career as a video artist working experimentally with short dramas, architectural films, and dance films and videos, notably an innovative adaptation for television of the Quebec imag-
DVD 28 istic theater company Carbone 14's stage production of *Le Dortoir* (1991), combining dance, music, and a whirling camera.

Dance preoccupations carry through in Girard's dramatic work, which explains his concern for visuals and storytelling in the movement, the music, the facial expressions, and the gestures, as well as in the words of the script, to convey his viewpoint. In *Thirty-Two Short Films* (1993), for instance, his distinctive camera work is both very cinematic and very movement-based; there is a 360° tracking shot, and one of the film's most evocative sections, "Gould Meets McLaren," features animated spheres dancing to Gould's music.

Former dancer, choreographer, and actor Laura Taler is another dance filmmaker who understands that camera space is a versatile site for dance and respects the qualities of that space. In 1995, she made her directorial debut with
DVD 30 *the village trilogy*, a 24-minute, 16mm filmdance, which evokes nostalgia and a search for home and roots, using black-and-white photography and expressionistic lighting and framing.

The need to use simple gestures, as developed in *Pas de deux*, surfaces in Taler's work too. In her stage work, she says, her choreography was always more about gesture and facial expression than about large choreographed movement per se: "It wasn't very dance-y dance. On film I felt I could exaggerate and accentuate those gestures and facial expressions in a way that I couldn't on stage."[12]

That's evident in *the village trilogy*, where she uses close-ups to make the obvious more apparent, and dance as a silent film language.

Taler explains that what attracts her is a piece that "creates its own separate world and takes you on this journey . . . not just people doing jumps and turns and nice movement. It doesn't matter what the movement is, what matters is creating a different space for you to dream in." In other words, she's not just showing us what the dance is, but enabling us to experience how it feels.

Like Baylaucq, Taler works long-term on her projects, knows her shots thoroughly, and produces images that are very clear and cinematic. "Usually it takes me two years in the design stage and another year and a half to do the shooting and the editing," says Taler. Because it's such a long process, most people making dance films in Canada are doing shorter things—five to seven minutes—and doing them on the cheap. "Not that (other filmmakers) don't put as much thought into it, but it's not as big of a curve. It's just, 'Fast, go, let's make a film.' That's not the way I work. I work slowly and methodically. I really like to take my time. You have to have a lot of patience and perseverance. I have to be able to live with my ideas over time."

Heartland (1997), a documentary on choreographer Bill Coleman, emerged after Taler first saw his stage piece of the same name in 1992 and fell in love with it. "I thought this would look really good on camera, a really cinematic feeling. Then one day I had the guts to go backstage and say to Bill, 'Hey, I'd love to make a film of *Heartland*,' and then a few weeks later, he dropped a huge box at my doorstep. It became a documentary just because," she says matter-of-factly.

In fact, making half-hour dance films and videos in Canada has proved notoriously difficult to do successfully because of the complicated funding relationships that must be established and the meager returns to be earned from such productions. Apart from the films made by Baylaucq, Taler, and the big guns at Rhombus Media, North America's leading producer of films and television programs on the performing arts (*Thirty-Two Short Films about Glenn Gould*, DVD 29
September Songs: The Music of Kurt Weill, *Falling Down Stairs*), and Cine Qua Non (*La Nuit de Déluge*), few longer-form programs have been produced in recent years. But Bravo!, the Toronto-based specialty broadcaster of arts and cultural programming, plays a high-profile role in assisting artists and filmmakers from across Canada through its Bravo!FACT fund, subsidizing Canadian arts videos under 12 minutes long. Fifty percent of the production costs, up to $25,000 Canadian, is provided.[20]

Rhombus Media of Toronto, formed in 1979, is renowned as one of the world's most important producers of performing arts programs. Rhombus productions have received international recognition, including consecutive International Emmy Awards for *September Songs: The Music Of Kurt Weill*, *Le Dortoir*, *Pictures on Edge*, and *Concerto*, and an Academy Award nomination for *Making Overture*. Rhombus is also responsible for such critically acclaimed movies as *The Red Violin*, *Thirty-Two Short Films about Glenn Gould*, and the six-part television series *Yo-Yo Ma: Inspired by Bach* (including *Falling Down Stairs*, chronicling the intense year-long collaboration between the musician and choreographer Mark Morris). The visual excellence and popular success of Rhombus's output, which amounts to almost a hundred films over 20 years, and the way the company supports emerging film production and directing talent, have given it an important niche in the arts community.[14]

During the 1990s, Nick de Pencier, a Toronto-based independent, made about one dance film a year. His short films are, he says, born out of necessity.

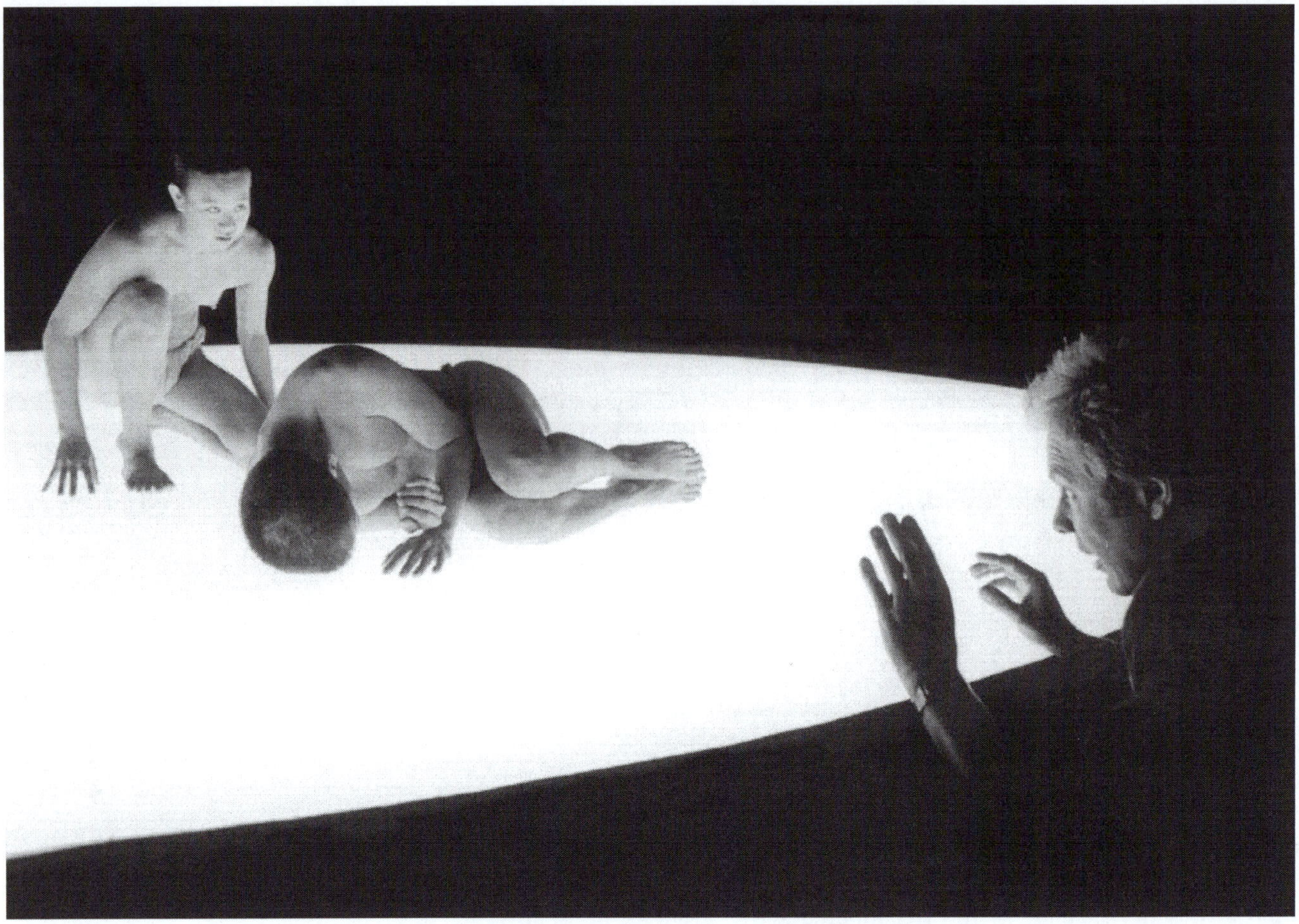

Chi Long, José Navas with director Philippe Baylaucq, *Lodela* (1996). © National Film Board of Canada. All Rights Reserved. Photo by Bertrand Carriere.

DVD 31

He admits that funding—or the lack of it—dictates the length of his films, which are all self-financed or made in tandem with Bravo!FACT or arts councils. He chooses to work with choreographer friends, unknowns, or people who are avant-garde, on the fringe, who "come under the radar screen" and therefore can't justify his receiving a big check from a broadcaster. Forced to work with minuscule budgets, he makes "quick and dirty" projects like *Risible Chick*, an edgy piece filmed on the streets of Toronto that feels very brash and in-your-face. He's adept at using whatever film stocks he can get his hands on (giving his films a collage look), and he edits at the local artists' co-op. De Pencier says he couldn't sustain an ongoing project: "I'm not wired that way. It's more interesting for me to take a shorter idea and get it done."[15]

Canadians *are* getting things done, particularly at the interface between human movement and virtual dancers. Montreal-based Softimage, the industry's leading developer of high-end software for all areas of visual productions, including tools for 3D and 2D animation, is posing the question: "Is dance only what the human body can do, or is dance what we make the human body do?" The allied Daniel Langlois Foundation, meanwhile, funds contemporary artistic practices that use digital technologies to express aesthetic and critical forms of discourse, and it encourages interdisciplinary research.

Friends in Montreal have described their country as resembling "one of the small floors on the Tower of Babel—but one where people are actually listening to one another." Perhaps now, in this period of global proliferation, our filmmakers are ready to be heard and seen beyond our borders.

NATIONAL FILM BOARD OF CANADA (NFB)

Created in 1939, the National Film Board of Canada (NFB) is a public agency that produces and distributes films and other audiovisual works which reflect Canada to Canadians and serves as the "voice" of Canada to the rest of the world. The NFB initially produced propaganda films to support Canada's war effort. Its founder and the first Government Film Commissioner, John Grierson, wanted to make the NFB the "eyes of Canada" and to ensure that it would "through a national use of cinema, see Canada and see it whole: its people and its purpose."

Around the same time, Norman McLaren was recruited to organize animation at the NFB and soon established its reputation as a world leader in the art of animation (see main text). The NFB produces films and other audiovisual works that reflect the social and cultural life of the country.

The NFB not only has a strong presence in Canada, but since its very beginnings it has been internationally recognized for the quality of its film production, for its point of view documentaries, and for its creative auteur animation. Over more than 60 years, the NFB has produced more than 9,000 titles, for which it has received more than 4,000 international awards, including nine Academy Awards, and an honorary Oscar "in recognition of its dedicated commitment to originate artistic, creative and technological activity and excellence in every area of filmmaking."

As a center of filmmaking and video technology, the NFB can pride itself on some of the most remarkable technical breakthroughs in film production. Its collection includes a vast selection of documentaries, children's films, animation, and dramatic features, covering a wide variety of subjects such as arts, science, social studies, women's issues, the economy, sports, and recreation.

www.nfb.ca

NOTES

1. Don McWilliams, "Talking to a Great Film Artist," *McGill Reporter* (April 28, 1969), 3–5.

2. Toronto independent dance film/videomaker Nick de Pencier makes a case for our sense of place and Canada's tilt on the globe: "About all of my films—even if they're in an urban setting—have dancers interacting with real landscapes in a tactile or textural way. Dancers on hockey rinks, dancers smashing into brick walls—a more literal Canadian Shield!—or in stylized modified wilderness settings."

3. William Jordan, "Norman McLaren: His Career and Techniques," *Quarterly of Film, Radio, and Television* (1953), 1.

4. McWilliams, 3.

5. Louis Giannetti, *Understanding Movies* (Englewood Cliffs, N. J.: Prentice-Hall, 1972), 398.

6. Gilles Péloquin, *Dance and Cinema* (Toronto: National Film Board of Canada, 1997).

7. Baylaucq worked with a small camera for the first time in 1990, on a project called *Beating the Raccoon*. "The tools that I came across were designed for other things, i.e., an observation camera for undercover police work," he recalls. The camera used for *Lodela* was originally purchased by Hydro-Quebec to inspect the inner structure of the cement pipes of the hydroelectric utility's large dams in northern Quebec.

8. I worked as dance consultant on *Lodela*.

9. Interview with Baylaucq.

10. Daniel Carrière, "Bernard Hébert: us la fascination du serrealism," *Le Devoir* (December 17, 1981).

11. Bill Brownstein, "Filmmaker Blends Dance, Renaissance To Make Magic," *The Gazette* (December 9, 1994), D26.

12. Interview with Taler.

13. Since 1995, based on figures posted on a recent web site, 195 shorts featuring the works of poets, sculptors, painters, architects, writers, animators, choreographers and dancers received $2.7 million CDN in juried grants.

14. Interview with Taler.

15. Interview with de Pencier.

CHAPTER 31

NHK: A Model for Performing Arts in the Media

Leonard C. Pronko

As part of its New Year's programming for January 3, 1993, Japan Broadcasting Corporation (NHK: Nihon Hoso Kyokai) telecast portions of the lengthy classic *Yoshitsune sembonzakura (Yoshitsune and the Thousand Cherry Trees),* including the travel-dance scene (*michiyuki*) known as "The Journey with the Drum" (*Hatsune no tabi*).This stunning dance piece is an example of the extraordinary offerings that Japan Broadcasting Corporation has been telecasting for the past 30 or 40 years.

Cultural programs like this one, broadcast throughout Japan, have played an important role in disseminating an understanding and appreciation of Japanese classical performing arts. A second strong media influence has been the films and television serials in which young kabuki actors perform from time to time. Fans captivated by the more familiar realistic performances have eagerly followed their favorites into the kabuki theater, where they gradually become converts to the classical form. Film and television in Japan have contributed significantly to the popularization of classical performing arts, and most notably of kabuki.

Beginning its regular television broadcasting in 1953, NHK recognized its educational mission early on and very quickly began broadcasting educational programs in the Tokyo area. By 1960, the company had initiated color television and was developing cultural specials. By the 1970s, NHK was offering nationwide weekly broadcasts of performing arts, including opera, classical music, kabuki, noh, and nihonbuyo (kabuki dance). Today, at least once a week and often more frequently, viewers all over Japan can see the greatest performers in the country in roles that they have perfected over the years. At special seasons like New Year's, NHK telecasts many hours of classical theater, interspersed with commentary and interviews. In 1992 it produced a series of programs in which one was able to see major scenes from the great classic *Yoshitsune.* Bunraku puppet performances were followed by the kabuki versions of the same scenes, and views of the historical places where the scenes take place. Throughout some 15 hours or so, fans could view most of the masterpiece and compare the original puppet version with the popular kabuki. The weekly program *Gei no Hyakusen* (Infinite Variety of Art), generally broadcast either in the late afternoon or after

The actor Seki Sanjuro strikes the opening pose of Tadanobu's narrative in *Yoshitsyne and the Thousand Cherry Trees*. Nineteenth-century woodcut by Kunisada.

8 p.m., usually includes critical introductions, and often discussions in some detail by well-known scholars, which help to place the performance in context.

Unlike the expensive specials produced spectacularly—but infrequently—in the West, NHK's programs (except for the occasional specials) are simple presentations with the emphasis on the art of the performer and the meaning of the performance. There are two types of productions: live and studio. The former are full-scale productions, while the latter are usually simply produced, but they are often as impressive as the more flamboyant live performances, since they regularly feature the greatest artists, sometimes "Living National Treasures," who bring to their performances a lifetime of learning and depth. Most frequently dance pieces are performed in the studio, since they require less stage machinery, but there is always a *hanamichi* runway, although it lacks the length and atmosphere created by a runway surrounded by living spectators. The dances may be segments from full-length kabuki plays, but more often they are single dance pieces that have been part of the kabuki repertoire for centuries. Live performances are filmed in one or another of the many noh theaters in Tokyo or some other city, while kabuki is often filmed at the Kabukiza or the National Theater in Tokyo, or at the Minamiza in Kyoto. Kabuki theaters generally have a glass booth at the rear of the main floor from which films can be made without disturbing the audience, but for a full-fledged performance—judging from the films—NHK uses at least three cameras, with close-ups at appropriate moments.

A special on the popular kabuki actor Ichikawa Ennosuke showed him performing on stage, making up backstage, under the stage running from stage to the back of the house in his dazzling quick-changes, on the train, in a restaurant, and in a small provincial theater learning an old, almost forgotten kabuki piece from a country actor.

There is infinite variety, one can see—just as the title of the television series suggests—in the NHK's performing arts broadcasts. The camera work, by skilled cameramen who clearly know the pieces they are filming, is remarkable for its clarity, simplicity, and ability to focus on the most important point of each moment. There is no gimmickry, no "clever" angles, no tricky lighting that would not be found in the stage performance itself—nothing to detract from the artists themselves. In some instances, the audience is given a backstage view unavailable to the theater spectator. We are allowed to see some of Ennosuke's quick-change techniques backstage, or how an elevator rising or a roof overturning looks from backstage. This may demystify some of the performance, but it also gives the viewer an appreciation of the technical complexity of kabuki that is not available to the usual spectator in the theater.

The piece that I have chosen as representative of the NHK broadcasts is the first scene of Act IV of the five-act play *Yoshitsune sembonzakura,* originally written for the puppet theater in 1747 and adapted to the kabuki stage in 1748. *Yoshitsune and the Thousand Cherry Trees* (which exists in a beautiful English translation by Stanleigh H. Jones, Columbia University Press, 1993) is the story of the shogun's brother, Yoshitsune, famous warrior and courtier, who must flee from his brother, who has become jealous of his popularity. The play is long and complex and contains many stories and several important threads. The plot that concerns this scene, however, follows Yoshitsune's mistress, Shizuka, as she is separated from her lover, then travels through the mountains of Yoshino to find him at last. Before they part, Yoshitsune gives Shizuka a precious heirloom noh drum named Hatsune ("the first sound"). He asks his vassal Tadanobu to accompany Shizuka and take care of her. What Yoshitsune does not know is that Tadanobu is ill and at his mother's home in the country, and a fox named Genkuro has taken his place because he wishes to be near the heirloom drum, which, it turns out, is made from the skins of his parents. In the travel-dance scene called "Michiyuki: The Journey with the Drum," Shizuka travels through the dazzling cherry blossoms of Yoshino Mountain, accompanied by the presumed Tadanobu.

A *michiyuki* or travel-dance scene is a standard scene in many kabuki plays, invariably featuring dance, with no, or very little, dialogue. Although the kabuki actor is essentially a dancer, in many scenes and entire plays he might strike the untrained observer as essentially an actor moving in a highly stylized way. But in the *michiyuki*, he is unmistakably a dancer.

The two actors featured in this film are among the most popular in kabuki today. Shizuka is performed by Bando Tamasaburo (b. 1950), one of the brightest stars of kabuki, who astonished with his maturity and skill even when he was only twenty. He has performed frequently in the West; Béjart has created pieces for him, and he appears frequently in films, television, and Western plays, for example, portraying Lady Macbeth, Desdemona, and the Lady of the Camellias.

Tadanobu is performed by Ichikawa Ennosuke (b. 1939), perhaps the greatest crowd-pleaser in kabuki with his quick-change and acrobatic techniques. But Ennosuke is also an outstanding dancer and, as one might expect of a quick-change artist, he performs both male and female roles. One of the fascinating aspects of the role of Tadanobu is his hidden fox nature, which he reveals only subtly at the beginning of the scene and at the end, when we see him lift his foot and point it, or lean forward with his hands in a paw-like pose. The role of Tadanobu virtually belongs to Ennosuke today, particularly the scene following this one, in which he plays the false and the real Tadanobu and reverts to his true fox identity with dazzling athleticism. One of the fascinating aspects of the role of Tadanobu is his hidden fox nature, which he reveals subtly from time to time, lifting his foot and pointing it (only animals point their feet in kabuki), or leaning forward with his hands in a paw-like pose, or hopping about.

The camera work here is skillful and unobtrusive, using long shots when there are several dancers moving, and closing in to catch more detail when one of the performers is dancing alone. The close-ups vary from full body to upper body and occasionally only the head. One is able to see in some detail small moves and subtle facial expressions that are often lost to audience members in the large kabuki theaters, and in this sense the camera enhances our appreciation of the performer's skill. In this particular film, we see most of the piece from straight on, but there are cameras in the right and left back corners of the theater, and another appears to be focused straight onto the *hanamichi*, so that we see the actors from the front when they perform on the runway. The camera work in these presentations invariably reveals a deep familiarity with the theatrical forms and the minute details of each performance, and an understanding of camera placement and shooting skills that comes only with long experience.

Programs like this one reflect NHK's commitment to the arts. Since it is a national television station, they reflect as well the attitudes of an enlightened government that supports the arts generously, including national theaters for noh, kabuki, and bunraku. Japanese television viewers pay a monthly fee, much as people in the U.S. do for cable television, but the offerings are much richer than U.S. cable television offers and would appear to contribute significantly to the growing young audiences at classical theater in Japan.

As an educational tool for those of us who teach Japanese theater in the West, such videos, although sometimes difficult to come by, are invaluable.[1] They offer our students a view of theater utterly unlike our own—one in which performance aspects, like dance, are every bit as important as the text, and sometimes more important. For directors preparing presentations of Japanese theater, they are a godsend, and for the few who are engaged in choreography inspired by Japanese forms they are indispensable.

Viewers of PBS Television in the U.S. who consider themselves fortunate to see four or five opera telecasts a year, as many or fewer *Dance in America* (or dance *anywhere*) programs, and who are startled to discover that theatrical "masterpiece" is a term applied to fare like *Upstairs Downstairs* rather than *Hamlet* or *Tartuffe*, must look enviously at the rich feast offered weekly to the Japanese viewer, which contrasts so starkly with our own famine. Might we not consider the sophisticated programming of NHK as a model and a goal?

NOTE

1. The most readily available Japanese theater videos are those loaned by the Japanese consulates in several cities in the U.S. Occasionally one is able to tape a program from PBS in this country, but by far the richest source is NHK—if one is fortunate enough to have a friend with a VCR in Japan.

CHAPTER 32

Taking Tools into My Own Hands: An Argentine Choreographer Finds Her Way to Film

Silvina Szperling

When I was five, my mother put me into a dance class because she thought I was too quiet. Why was I so quiet? I was watching TV. So dance and media entered my life by opposite paths, but I very much enjoyed both. At my dance class, which had a completely improvisational form, I took pleasure in feeling and expressing, playing with the movement of my body and giving it a personal structure. Whole new worlds opened in each class, thanks to my teacher, the great British-Argentine Patricia Stokoe, and her marvelous pianist (much more than an accompanist), Carlos Gianni.

Watching TV, meanwhile, I adopted a passive attitude similar to being nursed, a feeding sensation that might appear alienated to watchers but that let me go beyond the walls of my family home. Who could resist the seduction of Zorro or the Lone Ranger in a family composed mostly of women (three daughters and an ever-present mother), with a workaholic father who came home when the kids were already in bed?

In my teenage years—the early 1970s—on Argentine TV (strictly black and white until 1978) they broadcast many locally produced films on Saturday afternoons. The political climate was hot on the streets: in 1973, President Perón returned for a third term, while different wings in his party fought for the real power; in 1975, Daddy Perón died; and in 1976, a military dictatorship took over the government in the process "disappearing" 30,000 souls.

Meanwhile, on TV I enjoyed black-and-white Argentine musicals made by the dozens during the golden age of local cinema (1940–1950), like the ones by the comedians Cinco Grandes del Buen Humor ("The Good Humor Fab Five") and the excellent Nini Marshall. Many of these movies included either ballroom dancing or parodies of famous ballet pieces, like the incredible one by the Fab Five in which Jorge Luz and Pato Carret play Anna Pavlova en pointe and Vaslav Nijinsky in *L'après-midi d'un faune*. Those hilarious sketches revealed how familiar the public was with the original ballet choreographies, something that is no longer true.

Beautiful Nini Marshall wrote and acted in all her films for four decades, playing women of diverse social origins. Her best performance as a dancer was when her most popular character, Catita the innocent maid, danced her own version of *The Dying Swan*, drinking water from a fountain, blowing bubbles, and suf-

Temblor (1994) by Silvina Szperling. Photo by Guillermo Fernandez.

DVD 32
sistersister (1999) 7 min 50 sec
Excerpt 1 min

Production Note: "*sistersister* is a restaging of one scene from the stage piece *Ryoanji, the center of the dizziness*, commissioned from choreographer Susana Szperling by the Teatro Colon's Experimental Center (CETC), and premiered in October, 1999. It was shot with two cameras (a Betacam SP and a mini DV) with additional footage by a Pro DV Cam. In the editing room she played with repetitions and ellipsis, to enhance the crescendo that the scene carries. Liking too much the original lighting by Alberto Morelli and Felix Monti, she didn't correct the color difference between the two cameras in post-production, keeping the contrast between the two visions, that can also be the visions of the two women, the two dancers, the two sisters/authors (director Silvina and choreographer Susana)."—Silvina Szperling

fering a joyful agony. Inserted shots of a theater audience laughing made watchers aware of the representation inside the representation, an old cinema device.

It took me many years to go back to these beloved images. My friends Graciela Taquini and Rodrigo Alonso, both researchers in audiovisual and mixed-media fields, reconnected me with them while investigating dance and Argentine cinema for the Fifth Buenos Aires International Video-dance Festival's catalogue in 1999. They taught me that the first Argentine sound movie (c. 1934) was also the first one to put dance on a big screen. Its title was *Tango!*, and it had nothing to do with Saura's. The scenery was a Buenos Aires *barrio*. The men and women dancing on the screen were sharing a social event, integrating themselves through their bodies with immigrants from Europe and other Latin American countries.

In a country with such massive immigration, nonverbal languages, like visual and kinetic ones, are strong tools for communicating. In this case, the body itself becomes a medium, and the camera a second medium for sharing social matters that are hot at a certain historical moment.

Dance and audiovisual media came together in my life during my school days. Susana Tambutti inspired me in her dance history class, showing videos she compiled from diverse sources. A musical by Fred Astaire and Ginger Rogers, the reconstruction of Nijinsky's original version of *The Rite of Spring*, Pina Bausch and her own *Rite*, *The Green Table* by Kurt Jooss, and many others bathed my eyes and ears. Those intimate moments when the lights went down may have developed my sense of choreographic composition more than my practical choreography classes did. What I didn't suspect then was how much those sessions, in which Tambutti fiddled with the VCR, the TV set, and the wires until the image and sound came out properly, would ultimately influence my artistic development as a video-maker.

After graduation, I tried to apply my choreographic ideas to site-specific experimentation with sculptors, open urban landscapes, and unconventional performance spaces. Different scenarios triggered my creativity more than a pure kinetic idea. Interaction with an everyday place or a casual pedestrian woke me up and pushed me forward.

When I inherited some money from my father, I didn't hesitate: I wanted a video camera. I found looking through the viewfinder completely irresistible.

That camera was the first object in my family unit that belonged only to me (in fact, I think it still is). The little 8mm Sony Handi-cam became an obsession. The family went on vacation? I spent hours on my own shooting flowers. Or rocks. Or clouds. The world was resignified by that viewfinder. I discovered unknown layers of reality as I pointed at different aspects of it. An eye, a cheek, a brick in a wall, the top of a wave in the sea. A star. A leaf.

Was I too quiet then? Not at all. Holding the camera, I became very energetic. For some reason, the *chi* emerged from the center of my body, and my interaction with the real world changed. Passivity turned into activity. Far from a confrontation, a sublimated action took place in which I simply dialogued with the external world. I didn't have to make myself noticeable. Even further, I didn't have to know my own intentions before interacting with the external world. The unconscious could just derive fluidly.

When, in 1993, I saw a flyer announcing a videodance workshop for choreographers, I was hooked. Filmmaker Jorge Coscia, the teacher, believed it was easier for a choreographer to learn the cinematic language than for a filmmaker to learn dance. He had made some dance feature films, like *Cipayos* (1989, following the model of *West Side Story*), but he also knew films and videos in which the dance wasn't at the service of a movie script. The cinematic terms he opened to us (*close-up*, *wide shot*, *pan*, etc.) sounded familiar to me. The environment of the class, a room at the National Library with wide windows from which we could see a lot of the city, inspired many students' works. One of those students was Margarita Bali, who had already had a very fruitful experience choreographing for the film *El exilio de Gardel* (1986). She and her partner Tambutti had been asked by director Fernando Pino Solanas to set many scenes for the film with their company, Nucleodanza. "You should have told me that you wanted to shoot this sequence from above," complained Margarita to Pino when she realized that her choreography looked quite different through the lens of the camera. Nevertheless, the team must have come to some understanding, since they won an award for choreography at the Venice Film Festival the next year.

In that 1993 workshop, the aim was to give dance and cinema/video the same level of importance in a piece. "Videodance is an integration of two languages; one cannot live without the other," said Coscia. Some students were fascinated just watching British or French works; some of us went further. When the time came for the actual shooting, certain images came to mind: isolated parts of nude bodies. I wanted the audience to be very close to the feminine bodies. The eye of each spectator would be on one wrinkle. The women would not be perfect. I wanted old, young, fat, thin. But who would appear naked on screen? Which dancer would show herself nude in front of a video crew? I shyly started to ask friends. Everybody wanted to be in it.

Were they excited to see themselves on a screen? Were they attracted by the video world? Getting camera people was even easier. A friend from the workshop, video professional Guillermo Fernández, spent three hours sitting on a beam next to the ceiling, shooting the dancers from above. We knew he was in a trance. That piece became *Temblor*. "This is the first Argentine videodance," said Coscia.

One year later, the University of Buenos Aires wanted to screen the results of that workshop. Apart from mine, there were pieces by Melanie Alfie, Paula de Luque, and Bali. The house was full. What was all that interest about? How could an art form have its base in a group of four artists?

That year I got a videodance apprenticeship at the American Dance Festival. My teacher/boss was Douglas Rosenberg. Thanks to Stephanie and Charles

Reinhart and to my guardian angel, Joseph Fedrowitz, that hot summer in North Carolina was a turning point for me. The pains in my back went away, though I carried a Beta deck, tripods, microphones and other stuff, while the other apprentices took butoh classes and went home right after the performances. I ate almost nothing but rice and muffins but my strength grew, perhaps from the North Carolina sun, or the dance classes by Irène Hultman, Steve Paxton, and Danny Lepkoff. Perhaps the energy radiated from people I got to shoot at rehearsal or class: Eiko and Koma, Bill T. Jones, Trisha Brown.

The other source of excitement and relief that summer was my sister Susana. She had been living in New York City for four years before we met at ADF, where we shared a room for the first time in 25 years. We decided to make a videodance together. It ultimately became a diary of the trip. The trigger for *Bilingual Duetto* was a poem by Susana, beginning, "It is anything revealed in the unexpected moment." We planned, shot, edited, and screened the video in six weeks. It had its premiere at the videodance class's showing in Duke's cafeteria. All the students' videos were shown. With the last one, the character on the screen (Susana) entered the room live, by the same door that was on the screen at that moment. The whole development of double identity started then.

Other images and sounds on *Bilingual Duetto* include the faces of all the international choreographers in residence at ADF, reciting Susana's poem in their own languages at the same time, Polish, English, Romanian, Persian; two heads emerging and diving in a pool saying the same line—*constant whisper, constant whisper*—in Spanish and Japanese; clouds; the Brooklyn Bridge; a newspaper; a page full of the writing of a child (my daughter). American actress Sara Jo Berman, live, recited the poem in English while Susana invaded the audience space, dancing on the tables and seats. The two of them sat at a table pouring water that simultaneously appeared on the screen. "Are you taking drugs, Silvina?" asked boss/mentor Rosenberg when he saw a rough cut before the performance. I didn't need them.

Two things I was certain about: I could not develop my abilities in this new field on my own, and it was as expensive to send a person abroad to upgrade as to bring a foreign visitor, a master, able to stimulate potential Argentine videodance artists to think in terms of dance for the camera and, at the same time, to give them the technical knowledge to fulfill their ideas. Before going back home, I told Doug: "I'll bring you to Argentina next year. I'll make a videodance festival in Buenos Aires." "Sure, Silvina," he answered.

With a taste for pioneering that I must have inherited from my Jewish ancestors, I plunged into the project with all my heart and soul. I convinced the director of the University of Buenos Aires's Cultural Center to hold an international videodance festival. Lopérfido said: "O.K., let's go. Here you have a fax machine, some helpers, and a brand new three-tube projector." It was enough to start up.

The houses have been full many times since then. Audiences were attracted by the newness of the art form and the variety of viewpoints represented at the festival. Local choreographers not only enjoyed watching beautiful works and making contact with foreign artists such as Li-Chiao Ping, Doug Rosenberg, Elliot Caplan, Núria Font (the Spanish director of Canal Dansa), and the British multimedia group Dudendance Theatre, but also took the tools into their own hands. Margarita Bali has developed a splendid career as a videodance maker, from her first pieces *Paula en suspenso* (Paula in Suspense) and *Dos en la cornisa* (Two at the Cornice) to her more recent *Agua* (Water) and *Arena* (Sand).

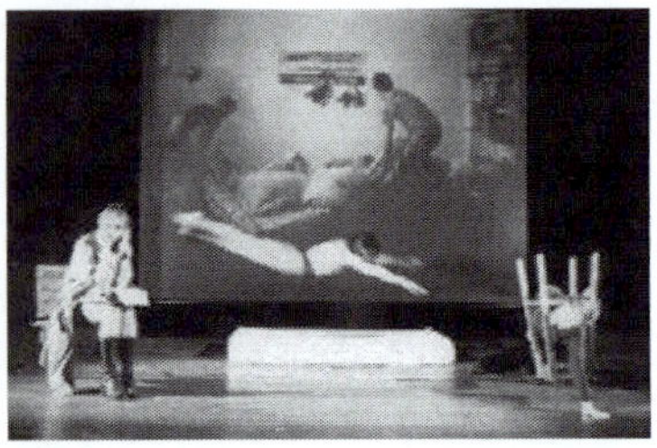

***La incomodidad de los cuerpos* (1996) by SZ Danza. Photo by Andrea Lopez.**

Many works came from the provinces, turning the festival into a medium for exchange with artists unknown in the capital. This meant that Buenos Aires's people got to see a wide range of choreographer-videomaker teams from cities like Córdoba or Santa Fe, or small villages like El Sausalito. There the group UP-PA, integrated by *wichi* aborigines, has been working since the second festival (1996) in video and multimedia (*Kathines Taiñi/Jungle dancers, Tsinay Kam/Women from Beyond*).

The melding of video images and live dance captivated and stimulated many companies at a moment when the dance scene was really depressed. Many artists started collaborations that enriched the panorama of local contemporary dance, among them Ernesto Calermo and Andrea López (UP-PA), María José Goldín, and Pablo Barboza with Silvina Cafici. Bali stands on her own, and recently received a Guggenheim Fellowship to create her *Naufragio in vitro*.

My sister Susana came back to Argentina, where we founded SZ Danza. The company mostly experiments with and showcases multimedia pieces, though Susana also choreographs "regular" dances. *Las hijas de Rosita* (Rosita's

DVD 32

Daughters, 1995), *La incomodidad de los cuerpos* (The Discomfort of Bodies), *El paseo inclinado* (The Inclined Path) (1996), and *Croquet en el living* (*Croquet in the Living Room*, 1997) are the results of our collaboration. Issues of family relationships, migration, and the human condition are the ones we most often approach. We are currently "cooking" a piece about the myth of Icarus; I have found in this joint project the mutual confidence, artistic admiration, and tension necessary to create. Laughter and tears are useful and unavoidable tools whenever they show up. Our last videodance was called *sistersister* (1999).

Television erupted into my life, or vice versa. A weekly TV show, *Videodanza,* was broadcast nationally on Argentina Televisora Color (Argentine PBS) over three months in early 2000. After some political changes, the station's director called, wanting access to our "good material"—and my services—for free. The policy of President De la Rúa and his Secretary of Culture, Darío Lopérfido, makes me think about the word *good* in that context. Will audiences remain interested? As long as the people in power offer them quality, it looks like they will. A pilot called *Danza TV* traveled the TV station's corridors, and they expressed interest. Will their interest turn into an investment? Commercial producer Gabriel Hochbaum has already made one, for the pilot, a good sign.

The problem here, as always, is money. What can an artist do with ideas without financial support? Not much. Friends and relatives may get tired of supporting an activity that is supposed to be funded by the government. As for big corporations, Argentina doesn't yet have a law that attracts business people with tax deductions.

Taking advantage of the trips that I was kindly invited to make, I am diving into other new technologies. My mind keeps on traveling through time and space. I may get to the fourth dimension.

CHAPTER 33

The Musical Formula: Song and Dance in Popular Indian Cinema

Lakshmi Srinivas

India produces 800 to 1,000 feature films a year, roughly twice the number made by Hollywood. The films reach audiences all across the country, transcending differences of regional culture, rural versus urban lifestyles, and educational background as well as divisions of caste, class, and language.[1] Movie-going is a popular pastime and outing for families. It is estimated that 75 million movie tickets are sold every week in India, a likely undercount since theaters in rural areas and "tent" cinema rarely keep records and often don't even issue tickets. Films are exported abroad and are watched by expatriate Indians in the west as well as by non-Indian audiences in the Middle East, Eastern Europe, Asia including Japan, and parts of Africa.

All feature films made for the mass market are formula films. Categories such as comedy, drama, romance, action, and so on are blurred in the Indian context as each film attempts to offer something for everyone. If any genre is identifiable, it is the musical, since all films have the requisite song-and-dance interludes. Both filmmakers and audiences expect the feature film to be a quantified product: typically, a three-and-a-half-hour film is required to have six to eight song-and-dance interludes. There seems to be no notion of too much of a good thing; in 1994, a film that included 14 such song sequences was a huge hit and remained in theaters for over a year.

Film music is the popular music of India and saturates public space. It is played over loudspeakers at festivals and weddings and in stores and restaurants. Audiences consume film music separately when they listen to radio or buy cassettes and CDs. Since the music is released before the film and music videos from the film are aired on television—also prior to the film's release in theaters—viewers often decide whether to go to a movie based on its music and dances. The music is an eclectic mix of classical and folk from different regions in India, as well as Western-style pop. Current trends are a strong influence—in the 1970s, disco featured strongly, followed by Michael Jackson's albums, and more recently Latin pop has contributed to the mix. Even the Macarena, at its height of popularity, found its way into scenes.

The importance of music to the film is seen in audio rights, accounting for as much as 30 percent of the cost of a film, and sometimes even 50 percent, according to *India Today* (Jan. 31, 2000), and in films becoming box office hits based solely on their soundtrack or on one or two picturized songs. Audiences' appreciation of music and dance can at times play havoc with screenings as viewers demand that the film be rewound and the favorite dance sequence shown repeatedly, while they sing along or even dance in the theater.

Song and dance, filmed as music videos, operate as a pragmatic narrative device. Music and dance are used to depict emotions such as love, joy, regret, and longing. They are means to say what is typically not conveyed in mundane speech in the Indian context: characters in love will break into song. Musical interludes also facilitate the expression of magic and otherworldly happenings, or they depict alternate realities such as dreams, memories, and fears. Fantastic things happen in these operatic sequences as gods and ancestors communicate with characters, the present merges with the past in the characters' lives, and the hero and heroine are transported across time and space in flashback and "flash-forward" sequences.

Song and dance sequences frequently are a means to incorporate travelogue and exotica. They often display a tenuous link to the story. A scene in present-day India suddenly shifts to a fantasy dance set in Mauritius, Sun City, South Africa, a desert in the southwestern United States, or Niagara Falls. Audiences are suddenly presented with kangaroos and a dance extravaganza outside the Sydney Opera House in a film (*Hindustani*) set firmly in Madras. Consequently, a sequence that lasts a few minutes of screen time can take several months to film, and may consume a major portion of the film's budget. For one song, producers of the film *Jeans* flew its stars to all Seven Wonders of the World, and the film was promoted as "the most expensive Indian movie ever made."

Musical interludes are spectacles with lavish sets and costuming. Outfits run the gamut from the mythological to the ultra-hip. Heroines dressed seductively as *apsaras*[2] in midriff-baring silk and jewelry frolic on Swiss hillsides. In the next frame they prance around in leather boots and miniskirts against the Grand Canyon. Props for scenes in James Bond style include Porsches, Ferraris and helicopters. Perhaps the best way to describe the films and their dances is to highlight the aesthetic of excess that defines them. According to *India Today* (1998), popular films in the late 1990s featured a mega-hit song called the "item number," for which a star might be invited to make a guest appearance in the film. In one such extravaganza, "a choreographer lined up 100 dancers and 150 camels for a song sequence." For the film *Barood*, a song sequence cost 46 lakh rupees (1 lakh=100,000)[3] and featured a space-age volcano city-cum-stadium with five split levels, inbuilt lighting, a seating capacity of 8,000, and 30-foot-tall dinosaurs." For the film *Vinashak*, "dancers cavort atop a 40-foot-high 'crystal' dome made of acrylic and mirrors to give a futuristic effect." Another description of a song interlude emphasizes the lavish spectacle reminiscent of Hollywood in the 1930s: "Six hundred people laboured for 20 days to create this quintessential Bollywood chimera. A Roman coliseum, a Harappan structure, Spanish pillars and a Grecian pool with half-clad Rubenesque ladies painted on the walls are sprawled across two kilometers at Mumbai's film city." With its direct presentational style, multiplicity of genres, and focus on spectacle, travelogue, and display, Indian cinema is closer to turn-of-the-century cinema and its aesthetic of astonishment, which Tom Gunning[4] has termed the "Cinema of Attractions."

The dances incorporate a variety of styles and traditions. Some are simply poses adopted to set off the costumes and scenery; others are based on more traditional dance styles such as *bharata natyam* and *kathak*. Dances in films today employ a more eclectic format, combining the traditional and the modern with unexpected results: characters in mini-skirts adopt the eye, hand, and neck movements of *bharata natyam*.

Various categories of song sequence are identifiable, the most common being the love song featuring the hero and heroine set against an ever-changing backdrop that moves with apparent randomness across landscapes and continents. Another category of dance features the hero and his buddy. In the film *Yes, Boss*, the hero and his best friend dance atop a piano placed on a moving delivery truck. The hero is dressed in a tuxedo with red cummerbund, and his friend is in a tight white suit. They twist to the catchy music as Bombay city passes by. Over the course of the song, the hero encounters Disney characters resembling Donald Duck and Mickey Mouse, to the delight of children in the audience, and a gang of youths on the street with whom he does some Michael Jackson-inspired dance steps. Dances are therefore collages that, like vaudeville, follow the principle of variety, rather than being continuous and coherent.

Dances serve as vehicles for showcasing a star's talents. Earlier actresses who had formal training in classical dance were sought after. Hema Malini, who reigned as Bombay cinema's Dream Girl through the 1970s and early 1980s, was known for her proficiency in *bharata natyam*. Rekha, who achieved superstar status, was also praised for her talent as a dancer. Audiences expect both male and female stars to be good dancers and critically evaluate a star's dancing ability in the film. A male star's prowess is exhibited in the dances, as the moves are often physically demanding. In the film *Chachi 420*, the hero, dressed as a middle-aged woman (the film was inspired by *Mrs. Doubtfire*), takes on hoodlums in the vegetable market. The ensuing fight is choreographed as a comedy-dance complete with karate kicks, leaps, punches and *bharata natyam* moves, since the star was trained in *bharata natyam*. In *Duplicate*, the hero, working as a chef in a fancy hotel, is given the task of preparing a banquet. The entire preparation of the feast is transformed into an elaborate and comedic "kitchen dance." The cutting of vegetables and actual cooking of the food are dance moves, characterized by exaggeration and slapstick. The ensemble includes waitresses in French maid outfits.

Indian films have no "love scenes" or sex scenes as Hollywood movies do, and until recently kissing on the screen was forbidden. The films have had to work skillfully around censorship and societal taboos, with music and dance becoming resources for such depictions. The erotic dance may or may not overlap with the love song between the hero and heroine. Erotic dances usually feature either the heroine or the "other woman." In *Chandini*, the actress Sridevi, dressed as an Apsara in white chiffon draped seductively around the hips and baring the midriff, frolics in the moonlight. In the story, her dance is a fantasy of the hero.

Water is another resource. Often the introduction of a "rain scene" in the film is a sign that an erotic rain-dance will follow. In older films, the vamp was often a dancer and the gangster's moll. The vamp's dance is a high-energy affair with lots of hip movements and pelvic thrusts. Certain actresses were known for their skill in performing such dances, and their names on theater marquees advertised this dance number to enthusiastic audiences. Erotic dances frequently capture media attention. In the film *Khalnayak*, the song "Chholi ke Peechey" (Under the Blouse) and its accompanying dance set off a media storm for its suggestive lyrics and moves. When attacked, the songwriters defended themselves by saying that what was "under the blouse" was the heart.

Over the years, Indian cinema has changed, but the format of the musical has remained. The musical is usually associated with Hollywood, but India has its indigenous "musical" genre rooted in its oral tradition and in folk theater. Religious epics such as the *Ramayana* and *Krishna Lila* are in verse form and are enacted as dance-dramas. While outsiders to the culture of popular Indian cinema may find the musicals, with their sudden shifts of scene, incongruous and difficult to follow, habitués prefer this multidimensional format. Perhaps this is what has made the films competitive. In contrast to the British, Canadian, and French film industries, which have given way to the popularity of Hollywood films, Indian film continues to enthrall its viewers.[5]

NOTES

1. Sixteen major languages are recognized by the Indian government and each has several dialects.

2. *Apsaras* in Hindu mythology are celestial nymphs and are usually depicted outdoors in forest glades. At times they are known to get involved in the lives of humans, providing magic and creating confusion.

3. Providing the exchange rate for the rupee in dollar terms would be misleading here as one would also have to have other economic data such as the buying power of the rupee at the time, the budget of the films, salaries of stars, economic data on audiences and so on which information is not available.

4. Tom Gunning, "The cinema of attractions," In *Early Cinema: Space, Frame, Narrative*, ed. by Thomas Elsaesser (British Film Institute Publishing 1990).

5. There is evidence that Indian cinema is influencing Hollywood-style filmmaking—the director of *Moulin Rouge* acknowledged the influence of Bombay cinema on the film. Films such as *American Beauty* and *Nurse Betty* include fantasy sequences patterned on Indian cinema.

CHAPTER 34

Fast Forward

Deirdre Towers

Dance video festivals around the world find young artists tapping into a collective energy that in all its swirling confusion is creating a new language. The language of dance on film and video does not yet have a tidy set of grammatical rules or rulemongers, but clearly it has the potential to capture and express what neither live dance nor traditional film can. As a blossoming form of communication, it is a force causing both partners—the dancer and the filmmaker—to appreciate dance video as an offspring with all the growing pains of a brilliant but awkward adolescent. Where is the collaboration going? What is the future for this art?

In 2001, the 29th annual Dance On Camera Festival selected a handful of gems from 150 entrants from 13 countries. Among them was an arresting 20-minute video, *ARC*, choreographed and performed by Douglas Wright. A marvelous dancer known to audiences in the United States from his stint as a member of the Paul Taylor Dance Company, Wright finds video a godsend. "I have few ways to let the world know what I'm doing here, far away in New Zealand. Making a film is like sending a message in a bottle." His choice of metaphor is telling. Associating video with an archaic form of transmission—a bottle cast adrift on the sea—Wright hints that he had low expectations formaking much of an impact with his video, but he also suggests why his video is so personal. He designed it to be viewed by strangers with whom he hopes to connect.

Ultimately, what video brings to this vital performing art is intimacy. Collaborating filmmakers and choreographers who seize the opportunity not only to shout but also to whisper their inner thoughts, to imply by gesture as well as tantalize with magnificently bold movements, seem to be on the right track.

Clearly, a spirit of independence and innovation is charging the makers of dance on camera. With their annual rhythm, festivals develop standards of excellence by way of example, and inspire producers to underwrite projects. Festivals also provide an overview of the field, demonstrating what broadcasters are funding and what choreographers are producing on their own. Independently made dance videos predominate. With the new technology

Deirdre Towers, 2001. Photo by Charles Steiner.

allowing artists to record at very little expense, the future of dance video lies in self-sufficient, self-produced products.

Dancers work with multi-layered narrative, surreal, and abstract structures, so their "moving pictures" do not resemble the realism of today's cinema. Many dance films and videos—for example, the work of Eiko and Koma—build from neither dance nor film traditions but from poetry. Even the most abstract dance, set in nature as many videos are, suggests neoRomanticism. Nature becomes a metaphor for the emotions expressed by the dance, with specific landscapes chosen to clarify the state of mind implied by the choreography. These videos reverse the point of view of the dream ballet sequences characteristic of Hollywood and Broadway musicals of the 1940s: rather than dancing in a dream, the dancer invites the viewer to dream.

Dreaming—the need to do it, to share it, to invoke it—seems a big motivating factor behind many experimental dance videos. For some, perhaps live dance seems too real, too distant, whereas dance on a large screen with the intimacy of a zoom frees the viewer. "You should dream more, Mr. Wormold," a doctor tells Graham Greene's central character in his 1958 novel *Our Man in Havana*, "The reality in this century is not to be faced." Subliminal advice that we all have lived by, to one degree or another. Maybe in 2050 a well-meaning friend will recommend a weekend free of dreams, virtual reality toys, and holographic nightclubs: "What you need, young man, is to dance more, barefoot in the grass!"

Until then, dancers, if not actually signing up to work in the dream factories of Hollywood, are making their own visions free of the constraints of broadcasters and the box office. Dancers are adapting to a techno-crazy life by choosing collaborators—composers, designers, filmmakers, or computer programmers—whom they can trust. As more collaborators understand one another's art, their products will reflect that bond.

Documenting dance will soon become the equivalent of pliés, a warm-up for the eyes and mind to be followed by a series of design and choreographic exercises specifically geared for the gravity-free universe of the screen. Conventions in dance, from ballet to hip-hop, will be reconsidered. The standard pas de deux could become a pas de quatre, with the cameraman and editor as magicians lifting the ballerina to greater heights. Contact improvisation could expand in the filmed context with a lacing of three "takes": one the visual record of the physical encounter, and then two for tracking the stream-of-consciousness reactions of each dancer. As standard crowd-pleasing tricks get turned on their heads, these media will invigorate an ageless art.

By the middle of the twenty-first century, dancers will naturally shift between thinking of themselves in two versus three dimensions. They'll be essentially bilingual, fluent in the languages of the stage and the screen. The boundaries between art disciplines will fade in tomorrow's global village, as artists of every kind mingle to express their experience of time and space. Questions of foreground and background, of planes, volume, and dynamics, effort and shape, will be practical ones for all artists. Video choreographers will "paint" with bodies, shaping and conditioning the performance space with both a surface design and depth of field. Their collaborating composers and directors will knowingly find analogies for their methods, an example already set by Belgian composer/director Thierry de Mey working with choreographer Anne Teresa de Keersmaker.

Video has gained a solid place in the museum world and the hospitality industry. This trend may be an offshoot of the drive to make every public place an amusement park. Within a decade, we may enter a gallery filled with screens connected to interactive buttons that set period figures dancing or Cubist cones spinning. Recalling Gaudí and Dali with their love of melting solids, perhaps we'll see dancers stretching and shrinking around corners, sinking into the floor, disappearing down holes. A passing viewer could play a video on wall-size monitors, pausing it to study a particular frame. Architects will commission choreographers to create dance videos to enhance ceilings much as painting did in Renaissance Italy. Wise choreographers will form alliances with artists, architects, and engineers, so that the vibrancy of dance is everywhere.

With time, arts professionals of this century will no longer fear "selling out." They'll learn how to maintain their integrity by using the medium, rather than being used. Dancers can play the same subliminal games played by corporate marketers, but with the goal of straightfoward beauty and excitement. Imagine a commercial for a dance company: a sleek car hugs the road—slogan "Velocity" (cut); an expensive watch—slogan "Precision" (cut); a field of long waving grasses—slogan "Grace" (cut); construction workers pumping iron—"True Grit" (cut); final image of leaping gazelles—slogan: "Dance." Why not thread the airwaves with fantasies of dance as skillfully manipulated as the ubiquitous images of other consumer products?

With the need to project not only to the rafters of an opera house but also in camera close-ups, dancers will learn to monitor their dynamics; they will ripen as actors; their range of expression will broaden. Drama will be a new requirement in dance schools as the demands for versatility increase. The evolution of dancer/actors and choreographer/directors will prompt more dance in television programming. The new century ushered in a return of dance theater—a return to storytelling—but also an appreciation for chaos and madcap movement. The brilliant choreography of the German dancer Sasha Walz, in the video adaptation of her 1998 stage work *Allee der Kosmonauten*, plays right into the tradition of the television situation comedy blended with the heartburn of soap opera and the bleakness of David Lynch's *Twin Peaks*. This piece might instigate a rage for choreographed soap operas. The Hispanic *telenovelas* are already so stylized that their producers might be open to approaches by choreographer/directors. The Comedy Channel and Cartoon Channel are other possibilities. Computer-generated choreography by such artists as Michael Cole could be integrated in computer games that introduce dance to children.

And don't forget the ubiquitous Internet. Dance artists are producing choreography specifically for Web sites; they could create serials, giving their fans a reason to keep coming back to the sites. With short clips on the sites, fledgling choreographers will have a risk-free environment to present themselves. Service organizations could seize the opportunity to create Web magazines, employing both established and neophyte choreographers to create episodes for programs, from the bizarre to the wicked and innovative.

But hold on! Will television and the Internet still grip society 50 years on? Other innovations may wipe television off the map. Neuroscientists, likely to be this century's pioneers, may teach us so much about our personal wiring and mapping, emotional scarring, and healing that our needs for entertainment and diversion may be redefined. Scientific institutions may commission choreographers to explain challenging concepts in ways simple enough to engage a child.

As cinematic dream machines for dance and art flourish, proper facilities in which to shoot dance will be created. Just as a theater has wings, trapdoors, revolving platforms, and sets to capture a sense of perspective, the studio of the future will have rooms high enough to shoot from overhead and deep enough for cameramen to crawl under glass floors. Glass ceilings, digitally controlled walls to imply any environment, and cameras set in the walls could be remotely controlled by dancers with the push of a button. Using the techniques of motion capture in a computer environment, dancers could create their own set designs drawn from the trajectory of their movement. The studio will have the capacity to contain all the elements: a pool with underwater cameras, a fireproof studio, tons of earth, and a gravity-free chamber.

By the year 2050, when choreographers jetpack to their studios, they'll arrive with their warm-up complete, having stretched in midair along the way. The wall-size mirror—which doubles as an archivist and a computer secretary—will greet them with a screensaver of yesterday's best aerial variation. As the dancers straggle in, the choreographer could walk through a heat-sensitive hallway programmed to search for a sound or music that is directly "in tune" with that day's/that moment's/that particular artist's sensibility.

Envision a choreographer reviewing her laptop notes: "Check video thesaurus for another leap to replace the one in time-code 01:06:20:04." "Tell Samantha she must look into her gene pool to see what can be eliminated to erase her fears about re-entering the gravity field. She is breaking the rhythm of the group in the cloud scene." "Find someone whose legs serve as complement to Samantha's torso. We'll just have to substitute her from the waist down."

All of that, thank heaven, is a long way off. Dancers will continue to find ways to adapt or sneak off to a safe haven. Dance has a purity and a reason for being that cannot be touched. As long as we get a kick out of kicking, and a rush of endorphins, we will dance, with or without that camera standing by. But as long as the camera is available, we can share the magic.

Part VI
Taking Directions

CHAPTER 35

Watching Dance with a Remote in Your Hand

Matthew Diamond

In 1990, I first directed a television program that consisted solely of dance material. That program, "Speaking in Tongues," choreographed by Paul Taylor for the *Dance In America* series on PBS, was the beginning of a stream of work that I have been privileged to do. As I reinterpret dance for the screen, I have come across a set of issues that arise again and again. Addressing these issues forms the core of the way I direct dance for the screen.

UNDERSTANDING DANCE

Having more than a rudimentary understanding of the ways choreographers communicate is crucial. Directors in any form must become familiar with the "rules" of their medium. Beyond the obvious understanding all directors have

Paul Taylor (right) in rehearsal with dancer in *Dancemaker* (1998). Courtesy of The Four Oaks Foundation, Inc.

Paul Taylor (left) coaches two dancers in *Dancemaker* (1998). Courtesy of The Four Oaks Foundation, Inc.

DVD 33
Dancemaker (1998) 98 min
Excerpt 6 min 27 sec

"*Dancemaker* was filmed in 16 mm both multi-camera (for some performances) and single camera. The crew traveled to India with the dance company and was able to capture the creation of a new dance by Paul Taylor."—Jerry Kupfer, Producer

of spoken language, there are refined crafts that go along with every genre. Drama directors are assumed to communicate with actors about emotion, conflict, and creating a tone of reality. Comedy directors must know how and when to get a laugh. Action directors have familiarity with car chases, guns, and explosives, and so on. An underlying knowledge of the tools that choreographers use is a critical entryway for the director of dance film. Reading music, being musical (a completely different talent), discerning body language, and responding to rhythm, space, shape, tone, and texture are important skills. Awareness of varying styles of dance and choreography is a must. Last, the ability to understand and retell a story is critical.

UNDERSTANDING MOVIES

A director or producer must possess a point of view about the audience's experience and the medium he or she is working in. In every theater there is a commitment to staying through the end of a work. That defines the time commitment the audience is making. There are differing expectations, though, for live events and film events. In a live event, one expects immediacy. There is both the risk of catastrophe and the hope for an incredible, once-in-a-lifetime performance. In a film, though, one is aware that each viewing is substantially the same, varying only in the nature of the venue, the audience, or the quality of the print. So what does one get from a film? Accessibility and perfection. A movie audience demands perfection (or at least as close as one can get on the day of filming). There is no forgiveness for missed pirouettes, wobbly balances, or torn costumes. The film audience also insists on accessibility. The placement of the cameras must be ideal at every possible moment. A movie demands powerful camera choices because excellent visuals are the only substitute for risk.

UNDERSTANDING TV

At home, where most people watch television, there is zero commitment to hang around for an entire program. Our society has even coined a term for what people do—*channel surfing*—but that term doesn't take into account the kind of distractions life provides for TV viewers. Everything from getting the beer out of the fridge to disposing of it afterward conspires to take viewers away from our efforts. Beyond that, there is the frame of the TV itself. It is more or less square, it sits far across the room from us, and it is usually small (I don't own a big-screen TV). And despite being somewhat hypnotic, TV does not demand much of our attention. That forces the creators of television to raise the stakes for viewers until they can't bear to take their eyes off the work.

So, there's the TV, sitting in everyone's home, willing to be turned on and filled with images. And there is life, attempting to take our attention away. The generous mistress of accessibility has a bitchy and demanding flip side. Since dance lacks the particulars of the spoken tongue to ensnare the audience in plot twists and character specificity, we must continually enhance the visuals.

SERVING THE CHOREOGRAPHY

Here we get to the crucial questions. What is intended? Is the choreographer telling a story? Creating a particular tonality? Three-dimensionalizing the music? Bombarding us with images? Creating specific characters, suggested prototypes or just bodies in space? What is the point of view? What are the underlying demands of the music, the movement vocabulary, the other design elements? Each and every answer helps to define the style of shooting. There is a vast number of choices one can make to reinterpret a work for the screen. If the choreography is unsettling, will we want the screen horizon to be reskewed? If the rhythm of the dance is choppy, should the editing be disjointed? If tranquility is intended, do we eliminate cuts altogether, or opt for dissolves over cuts? The task of reinterpretation requires a commitment to the original material utilizing the crafts of the new medium. One would never expect a novel translated to the screen to be a transliteration. One wouldn't want to tune into the Indy 500 if the program used only the overhead shot from a Goodyear blimp. Making choices in the service of the idea—that's what is crucial.

UNDERSTANDING THE DIFFERING DEMANDS OF DIFFERENT GENRES

Drama demands a close-up. Dance demands a full-figure shot. Okay, but now what do we do for the second shot? And how do we get there? First, consider geography. Where are we? On stage? In a club? On a prairie? In a prison cell?

Next, what does the music demand? That will frequently tell us how to edit, because rhythm is everything. Last and most important, what does the choreographer want us to experience? George Balanchine's work cries out to be connected to the music. Music videos rely on a combination of shock and novelty (not to mention sensuality and lots of close-ups of the singer in a surreal environment). When Savion Glover taps, we want to see a close-up of his feet. As different parties require different menus, so similar subject matters, told in differing manners, require differing treatments. Here are some of the ones I have dealt with:.

Multi-camera shoots of live performances

Nine or ten cameras are strewn around the theater with a one-time-only opportunity to capture a dance as it is being seen onstage. There are world-class performers and a paying audience of a few thousand who don't really care about a director's problems. The challenge is to make the best television program out of a compromised live situation and never interfere with the paying customers. I try to set my cameras in a combination of a semicircle and a wedge. We surround the stage from every side, without peering off into the wings. We aim a preponderance of cameras up the center alley, because most often that is where the choreographer was sitting when he laid out the work. Then it's really simple. (Not easy but simple.) Take the shot that best serves what the choreographer wanted the eye to see: patterns—take a wide shot; a hand gesture—take a close-up; a port de bras—use a waist shot. In a series of moments from a story ballet, cut to the crucial element of the story moment after moment. Last, reapproximate the tempo of the dance so that there is a subliminal sense of immediacy, even as our intellect tells us there is none.

Multi-camera shoots of studio reinterpretations

Every once in a while (for me, three times in ten years), directors get to reconceive an existing work for the screen. Each time I've done it, there has been an opportunity to utilize all the strengths of the screen to communicate the choreographer's original intentions.

The Wrecker's Ball (choreographed by Paul Taylor) is a compilation of three dances Taylor had created independently of one another. The only connection between the three was that they used popular music of three successive decades. *Company B* uses the music of the Andrews Sisters, *Funny Papers* uses novelty songs of the 1950s, and *Field of Grass* uses music by Randy Newman. Producer Judy Kinberg and I had a powerful desire to expand upon our earlier work with Taylor in *Speaking in Tongues*. That program had used a three-dimensional set by Santo Loquasto which referred back to the much simpler backdrop of the theatrical production of the dance. Now, in *Wrecker's Ball*, we decided to shoot on location, and to shoot in 360° fashion. Moreover, each dance required a different setting. Taylor, Loquasto, and I arrived at the idea of a single building that had been a USO canteen in the 1940s, then a crummy movie theater in the 1950s, and then a hippie crash pad in the early 1960s. We bracketed the entire concept by suggesting it was the last day of that building's existence, hence the title *Wrecker's Ball*.

We also decided to continually move the "proscenium" of the dance, thereby reorienting the audience and maximizing the extraordinary set Loquasto created. With some minor modifications in the choreography, we found a small auditorium and set to work. Each segment of each dance had ideas that amplified the original concept. The haunting soldiers of *Company B* were often shot as reflections in glass behind a real woman. In *Funny Papers*, we used the dancers as customers in a movie theater watching themselves as performers on, and behind, the movie screen. The climax of *Field of Grass* was originally a raucous near-riot among the dancers. In the one-time-only situation of a TV shoot, we literally put that riot in a rainstorm. These were attempts to stay faithful to the original ideas of the dances, but to utilize the tools of the screen.

The complications of staging a multi-camera shoot in a 360° setting were daunting. Most interesting, though, was the discovery that when one is faithful to real ideas, like Taylor's, there is always a way to re-create them with newly imposed limitations and opportunities.

Documentaries

Moving beyond the question of shooting dances led me to one very rewarding experience: the opportunity to tell the many stories behind the dances, in the DVD 33

Matthew Diamond. Photo by Glenda F. Hydler.

feature documentary *Dancemaker.* The question in that film, as in every documentary, is which story to tell. Documentaries are by no means reality. They are the weaving of recorded events to tell a story that reflects reality.

When the planning for *Dancemaker* began, I had several ideas in mind. The first was to explore the inner workings of an American modern dance company. It struck me that over the years an interesting phenomenon had taken place. Artists had been forced to construct businesses to showcase their work, and those businesses were expected to turn enough income to allow for the creation of more work. That seemed very American and small-business-like. Beyond that, there was a reliance on a single creative genius to come up with the impetus for a small community. That central imagination would propel careers, incomes, spin-off life choices, marriages, and a significant economic microcosm. From those two ideas emerged a wealth of human interchange, and stories galore.

It was critical that the story be about a creator as remarkable as Paul Taylor, because when all is said and done, if the dances don't work, nothing and nobody works. Three streams emerged. The first was life in the dances proper—concepts, creation, rehearsal, preparation, and performance. The second was the business framework—managerial staff, labor issues, fundraising. Last was the life that all this created—muscle pain and glamorous receptions.

Each of the 23 days we shot encompassed some of each of the above. Morning interviews flowed into afternoon rehearsal and ended with evening performances. It was massive planning (flights to India, permission to shoot in wings) dotted with incredible luck (no mirrors in the studio to hamper our shooting, no music going off in mid-performance).

With over a hundred hours of film in the can, it became a job of collation. If a dancer mentioned an anecdote from the 1960s, we wanted an illustrative clip from the archives. If a sponsor referred to the ticket situation, we needed shots of a sold-out house. If a critic talked about a specific dance, we needed to see those steps. Then it was all storytelling—in simple terms, a beginning, a middle, and an end. Surrounded by a fine production team, I tried to tell the story of Paul Taylor and Company. If one dissects the movie, one finds that it hangs on a series of questions, as all movies do. In *Dancemaker*'s main "plot," we wonder if the new dance will be created, and whether it will be any good. In the "subplots," we wonder if the musicians' problem will be solved, if the tour to India will be successful, and how the big New York season will come out.

MOST IMPORTANT: UNDERSTANDING WHO IT'S FOR

The audience, the audience, the audience. Trusting your audience, knowing your audience, and understanding their assumptions is crucial. On MTV there is one set of expectations, on PBS there is another, on Nickelodeon there is yet another. This is not to say that all the tools one learns cannot be applied in many situations. However, it is critical to acknowledge that just as certain individuals listen a particular way, audiences will watch with their own set of collective understandings. That's the trick: choosing how to shoot so the audience will want to watch.

A CODA

Shooting dance is not so much hard as it is insanely delicate. Wrong angle, wrong shot, wrong edit, and the whole thing falls apart. Of course, I started my career as a modern dancer, and I think nothing is as hard as earning a living in bare feet.

CHAPTER 36

Editing Dancemaker: *Interview with Pam Wise, Editor, A. C. E.*

Joshua W. Binder

According to film editor Pam Wise, "editing is storytelling." An accomplished editor in features and television, she won the A. C. E. Eddie Award for Best Edited Documentary of 1998 for her work on *Dancemaker*. "Editing dance," she says, "is storytelling as well." Wise does make the distinction that "there is editing dance for the archives where you have to see everything, which is not filmmaking, and there is editing dance for a film like *Dancemaker*." She prefers to edit this type of film because "it's not just a recording of a dance, and therefore it doesn't have to be all wide shots." It lets her utilize her storytelling skills, and "attempt to interpret the dance for the viewer."

DVD 33
Dancemaker (1998) 98 min
Excerpt 6 min 27 sec

Production Note: "*Dancemaker* was filmed in 16 mm both multi camera (for some performances) and single camera. The crew traveled to India with the dance company and was able to capture the creation of a new dance by Paul Taylor."—Jerry Kupfer, Producer

Wise learned storytelling technique early in her career, editing cinema verité with legendary documentary filmmakers Ricky Leacock, Charlotte Zwerin, D. A. Pennebaker, and the Maysles brothers. "Cinema verité is very challenging because there is no script." The responsibility of telling the story—that is, making the film—usually falls to the editor. "You are given all this footage and you have to make a story out of it." It is not uncommon in documentary work for the editor to be given 150 hours of film to work with, "so you have to create and attempt to maintain a story line, which you will continue to shift as you shape the film, until the film is finished." Wise capitalizes on her experience when editing: "Years and years of scanning documentary footage have enabled me to spot the best moments quickly, and weave them into a story."

Editor Pam Wise (right), A.C.E., with director Matthew Diamond at the 1999 Eddie Award ceremonies. Ms. Wise won the A.C.E Eddie Award for Best Edited Documentary for the film *Dancemaker*. Photo by Jon Koslowsky.

"In *Dancemaker*, I chose moments, movements, and dance phrases when I attempted to summarize a dance by Paul Taylor. It was a frightening responsibility, as I am not very knowledgeable of dance, but the director, Matthew Diamond, narrowed the dance footage considerably in advance and explained the dances as he understood them. And I, after working with the dances, saw patterns in Mr. Taylor's work that helped me to choose shots. For example, I began to see that many of his dances involve an 'outsider.' So with *Esplanade*, where the audience may not be focused on the girl sitting stage left reaching toward the group, I was able to start the scene with her singled out, and follow her as she wove through the group. No doubt many of my choices were incorrect as well, but Mr. Taylor has graciously never complained.

"I cut instinctually, but I do think you have to have a sense of rhythm to be an editor, period, even in [more traditional] storytelling." Wise's editing allows the energy of the choreography to come through in the film. She describes how she accomplished this in the opening sequence of *Dancemaker.* "There are a lot of music cuts in there. It was shot with one camera, from the wings, during the performance, and one camera, from the front, during dress rehearsal, and then I intercut them. We wanted the best dance moments, but they didn't necessarily cut musically—and I couldn't stay on one shot for another ten seconds just to cut more smoothly. So there are a lot of music edits, and a few cheats. You'll notice I cut from Andrew panting in the wings to him onstage from the other side, but no one's ever said anything about it. You sacrifice truth for drama and close-up movement to make the film better. But let me make it clear that you can't muck around with the larger truth. You just tell little white lies to make the larger truth clearer and more dramatic and more 'filmic.' Got it? I mean, you only have what you've been given to work with."

About the changes in the editing process, which is now almost entirely digital and nonlinear, Wise says, "Editing is easier on the AVID (as opposed to actually cutting film)." She doesn't believe there are any limitations when editing dance on a nonlinear system. "There really aren't, because you don't have to reconstitute shots, you can get right back to the dailies with the click of a mouse. You can 'gang' two shots: take one angle that's in your record side and another angle on the other side, 'gang' the two together and roll them together and see a nice edit." And it is so easy to replace shots. "If somebody's doing a spin, for example, and their hand goes across their face at a certain point and you want to use a different take, and that point is crucial, just line up the two takes at that point, click 'replace,' and it's done. To me the AVID is an editor's dream come true, but that's not what I said when I first heard of computer editing—which is unprintable."

Wise has some suggestions for the filmmaker working with dance. "Use handheld cameras, multi-cameras, with the cameras moving onstage with the dancers. It makes it really easy to cut because there is lots of energy. Do a wide pass so you can see the whole stage." She reminds filmmakers that what they bring to dance is "camera movement and the camera," and her implication is, don't be afraid to use them. People have told her they liked the film version of a dance she edited better than they liked the actual dance. "As an editor you do part of the viewers' job for them. They don't have to work as hard because you are showing them what to look at, and what to look for. So they don't have to think as much. Maybe that's it. Maybe it's also because, usually, I have to make the dance shorter, and as Mr. Taylor says [quoting Doris Humphrey], 'All dances are too long.' We do the final rewrite."

LIFE AFTER *DANCEMAKER*

What happens when an Oscar-nominated documentary hits a modern dance company? Ross Kramberg, Executive Director, Paul Taylor Dance Company, answers the question, posed by Elizabeth Zimmer in 2001.

Dancemaker has raised the company's public profile, prompting significant increases in donations, in attendance, and in bookings for both the Paul Taylor Dance Company and Taylor 2. The film was first screened at the Seattle International Film Festival in the summer of 1998, and played the international festival circuit. In March of 1999 it went into a domestic theatrical run and appeared in over 100 theaters across the country. (Schedules and other information about *Dancemaker* can be found at its web site dancemaker.org and at Taylor's, ptdc.org.)

The film aired nationally on PBS in January of 2000. In the wake of the national broadcast, our box office for the City Center 2000 season finished with 35 percent more tickets sold as compared to 1999. Gross income was up 27 percent over the previous year. We saw a stronger presence of a younger audience. This year we had a student rush ticket, but we also saw a significant increase across the board, in people who bought tickets to more than one performance, who signed up as part of a group, who ordered tickets through special theater subsidy programs such as the Theater Development Fund, and who bought full-price tickets. At one point just prior to the 2000 City Center opening, advance ticket sales were running 50 percent ahead of the previous year.

We debuted in New Zealand this year; they aired *Dancemaker* on television beforehand and the week of performances sold out. We're trying to have the film screened or aired wherever the company tours. It's been shown in 33 states. In Paris, there was a terrific response. It has already been subtitled in Spanish and French. To date it has been aired on television in Spain, Norway, Sweden, Cyprus, Mexico, Canada, Brazil, Singapore, and Finland, and been screened in theaters in Taiwan, Australia, Israel, Canada, Brazil, Germany, Britain, Portugal, India, New Zealand, and Hong Kong,

What was fascinating to me was the lag time between the film's release and its impact. To talk about the film is one thing; to talk about the Academy Award nomination is a whole other universe. I didn't see the dramatic increase until this past season, a year after *Dancemaker* went into theatrical release. When the nomination was announced, suddenly everybody was paying attention. The amount of press coverage of the company doubled. There were four pages of Taylor in the *New York Times* Arts & Leisure section one Sunday, much of it in the film columns. Matthew made a film that is accessible, compelling, and appealing to the general audience.

Imagine that the modern dance audience is the size of a dime, the ballet audience maybe the size of a quarter. Matthew threw a watermelon at the public. It got the date audience, people going out to eat popcorn. The general public felt, "I didn't know that, how wonderful!" It gave a face to our name. It's a modern dance event. You still have old cliché attitudes, old hesitancies about coming to see modern dance. But people came.

The run on PBS opened it to a whole new audience. And we saw the results at the box office. One of the comments we heard about the film after a screening was "I wish I could have seen more dancing. It makes me want to go see the company. I want to see what you're talking about."

CHAPTER 37

Accompanying Choreography: A Director's Journey

Merrill Brockway

Merrill Brockway and Girish Bhargava at editing console, 1998. Photo by: R. Bhargava.

The dance community encompasses those who train their bodies to move, the dancers; those who invent movement for those bodies, the choreographers; those who applaud moving bodies, the audience; and those who serve, the producers. This is one producer's memory of the exciting adventure of transferring dances created for the big stage to the small screen of a promising new medium, television.

During the Christmas holiday of 1974, Jac Venza, executive producer of PBS's *Great Performances*, invited me to his apartment. Jac and I had worked together at CBS, he as a scenic designer and I as a director. Since then, he had joined early public television as an arts producer.

Jac informed me of a new venture initiated by the National Endowment for the Arts: a two-year series to be called *Dance in America*. He explained that the project aimed to relocate dancing from background accompaniment to foreground headliner, where it could properly reveal its development as an art form. Since New York was the dance capital of America, Jac postulated that the grant would be awarded to WNET in New York. He then invited me to be the series producer.

I was flattered. I wanted to accept, but that was not a simple or easy decision. I was 52 years old: I had been with CBS for 22 years (they'd given me my 20-year reward, a Tiffany clock, and there was no indication that they wanted to dismiss me). And what Jac proposed was scheduled to last two years! The next few months were filled with agitation, turmoil, disorder, and unrest, until I made the resolve that a therapist later would call "the most important decision of your life."

In mid-July of 1975, I joined WNET/PBS, accompanied by my trusted assistant, Judy Kinberg, who was slated to be associate producer. We were greeted by Jac and Emile Ardolino, film editor and writer of the proposal. We were to be "the team."

Greetings from our three sponsors were filled with warm wishes, but they also articulated each one's expectation. The National Endowment for the Arts desired quality: excellence. The Corporation for Public Broadcasting wanted quantity: lots of programs. Exxon wanted tutus.

What a predicament! The team decided to play Scarlett O'Hara and "think about it tomorrow," turning our attention to the important task of prioritizing our components. At the top of the list we placed choreography. We learned that we were not authorized to commission new work; rather, we could select the best from the library of existing dances—ballet, modern, and others. Additionally, we pledged to seek the active collaboration of the choreographer, a new and untried idea at that time, and one considered not without risk.

Then came dancing, performed by superb companies.

Production was third on our list. We would present masterful dances and the finest dance in the most appropriate and affordable circumstances. We had already learned that dancing is the most expensive of all the arts to produce, calling for enormous spaces, sprung floors, extra lighting requirements, and even the simplest of scenic support.

Next we set the programs for the first season, 1976–77. Each program had its own logic. The Joffrey Ballet, a young, talented and popular company, would lead off. Next would come Martha Graham, the master of modern dance and a national living treasure. Then Twyla Tharp, the leading innovator of the period, followed by the Pennsylvania Ballet, an outstanding regional company. The final program would be a dance documentary, *Trailblazers of Modern Dance.* (To reproduce now the productions we taped 25 years ago would cost twice the money. In 1976 our budgets were between $300,000 and $500,000 per show.)

The nagging fact was that we were not overflowing with experience in presenting dance, especially on a continuing basis. Jac Venza, the executive producer, had long championed dance on television and had produced most of the programs during the decade before *Dance in America.* Emile Ardolino, coordinating producer, had studied ballet and had filmed dances for the archives of the Dance Collection of the New York Public Library at Lincoln Center. Judy Kinberg, associate producer, had been my production assistant at CBS; dance was a foreign language to her. I was the series producer and was scheduled to do most of the directing. For the eclectic *Camera Three,* which CBS delighted in referring to as "a stroll through the marketplace of ideas," I had directed several dance programs. I remember six half-hours that included Merce Cunningham, Twyla Tharp, and Maurice Béjart. (Two of those half-hours are as bad, as boring, and as uninformed as any television I have seen.)

I was not to be the only director for the series. There would be others as inexperienced as we were; and if I knew directors, each would have his very own ideas. As series producer I wanted each program to look as if it had been sired by the same father. I wanted each director to rein in his own personal impressions ("This is how I feel about this dance; this is what it means to me.") and think of himself as an accompanist for the ideas and intentions of the choreographer.

I have long been a systems person who likes to search through loose strands and weave the organizing principle. I started with that impulse, drew upon my experience as a performing pianist, and added to it gleanings from my work in television. This was the potting soil for "the System," which I hoped would be a series of guidelines, not necessarily rules, that would steer a director away from traps and bumpy ground and toward a smoother journey. Hopefully it would channel his individuality rather than suffocate it.

THE SYSTEM: AN APPROACH TO TELEVISING DANCE

Exploration

When considering a dance piece, ask: "How can video enhance this piece, or will some of its essentials be lost?" "How will the piece come through the geometric translation?"

Information

The Stage is rectangular:

Video is triangular: wider at a distance than it is close up.

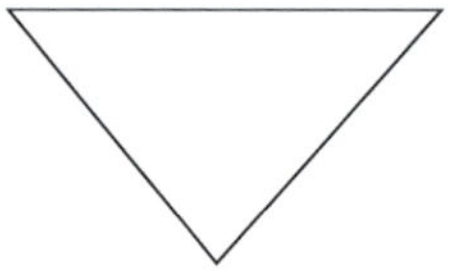

Preparation

Having chosen the piece, make a video work tape and ask "What is this piece about? Is it steps? Character? Mood? Patterns? Story telling? Use of space? Virtuosity? Spectacle? Perhaps it's a combination.

Then begin to learn the piece well enough to dance it. During this stage the director should start to script the piece with his own devised notation, complete but simple enough to be read by any assistant. The secret of this process is preparation, preparation, preparation. No "winging" (shooting spontaneously) is permitted. Conversations with the choreographer are not just invaluable but essential during this exploring stage of the process.

Next, the director should probe the shot possibilities of each of several cameras.

This system is based on the use of multiple cameras, each with its own recording machine (isolated feeds). *Dance in America* used three cameras as the model. When the director wanted six cameras, the scene was shot twice, with different camera tasks each time. That removed the clutter and expense of six cameras in the studio.

A pause for an opinion: Unless a dance was composed for a single camera, it will not be satisfactorily translated with one camera. One reason is that one camera cannot be everywhere at the same time; some significant information will be ignored. Also, the rhythm of shots is vital to a rich interpretation of the dance. (See Girish Bhargava's, chapter 41.)

Rehearsal

This is the first group get-together. In the rehearsal studio, the lines of communication must be kept open, clear, and simple among all participants, especially between the director and choreographer and the director and technicians.

First, mark the floor to simulate the space of the recording studio. That will save a lot of future confusion for cast and crew. Next, outline the rehearsal plans to the dancers and listen to their questions. The human element should be at the top of the director's mind. Dancers are the director's best friends: they should never be treated as stone-bearers for the Pyramids.

At the first rehearsal, the geometric translation from rectangle to triangle begins. This is the time for reasoned conversation between the director and choreographer, the time for minds to think together and hearts to beat together. It is also the chance for the director to try out ideas and possibilities he has been exploring.

For efficiency, break up a longer piece into sections approximately five minutes long. Determine the recording order of those sections based on the necessity of set, light, and costume changes, as well as dancer energy and psychological factors. Then rehearse in this order as often as possible so that each participant becomes familiar with the routine. When each section is set, record it on half-inch videotape for the director's final adjustments to his script.

Then the director should go home and revise his script based on this newly learned reality.

Recording

At the recording location, an awful truth must be addressed: dancers don't work on the same schedule as television crews. They are accustomed to performing in the evening from 8 p.m. on. TV crews usually work the daylight hours. For economy and efficiency (that's a euphemism for "to save money"), *Dance in America* asked the dancers to warm up, take class and be ready to rehearse and record by 11 a.m. Even then, they were not going to execute the complete dance in order, but rather a series of predetermined five-minute segments, each one to be rehearsed and then recorded. That up-and-down pattern—up for performance, down for rehearsal—was especially troublesome for the dancers. Only because of their superior training, arguably the best in the arts, could a schedule with such rigorous demands be accommodated.

The director should schedule a camera conference an hour before the dancers are scheduled to appear on the set. There, each camera person receives an individual shot sheet and views the work tape as the director explains how each one will participate. He answers any questions. Each shot sheet contains a series of tasks the camera person has been assigned. (Unlike movie-making, videodances made under "the System" are not assembled from shots that are set up but from shots selected from camera tasks.)

After all cameras have been adjusted to a common grid pattern, camera operators are reminded of the basic rules:

Frame tight, but don't cut off any appendage.
Lead the dancers, don't follow. Think of it as filming a hockey game.
Show only a teeny sliver of floor at the bottom of the picture; fill the space with headroom.
A smooth zoom, please!—no bump at beginning or end.
The tempo of the zoom comes from the tempo of the dancing.

When the recording day begins, the director soon finds out how successful his preparation has been and how well he has trained his camera operators and technical crew. The more they know, the less the dancer is drained of energy, and the better the performance will look.

At the end of the recording period, the material must be logged, and the director must study the results. There are always surprises. But, happily, they're not all bad!

Post-production

The next step is the editing. *Dance in America* was blissfully lucky; it had and still has a secret weapon, Girish Bhargava. Read his essay in this volume.

TELEVISING MARTHA: A MEMOIR

The story of Martha and me began after World War II. I had enrolled as an undergraduate at Columbia College in New York City. One day a fellow student invited me to go to a "dance program" across town. Now, why would I want to do that? In Indiana, where I grew up, you didn't watch dancing; you did it with your favorite partner. I was partial to dancing to the music of Wayne King, the Waltz King. My classmate would not be denied. He repeated, again and again, "But it's Martha Graham!" He made it sound like the name of a goddess.

We took the cross-town bus to Lexington Avenue and walked down to the 92nd Street YMHA. The program started; a small, intense woman appeared and began to seduce my attention, to speak to me with her movement. If there were other dancers, I didn't see them. This was between Martha and me. She grabbed my gut, raised it high, swung it around, and circled her body with it, then slammed it to the ground! After a long pause, she tenderly picked it up and cradled it to her breast. I would forever be her believer. She had liberated me and transported me to an unknown and magical world.

Thirty years later, in 1975, I had just been appointed series producer of PBS's new *Dance in America*. Martha was no longer dancing, but she agreed that her company would appear on our debut season. My colleague Emile Ardolino and I were sitting with Martha and her associate, Ron Protas. Before she would discuss the dances to be included, she had "requests": her broadcast time must be longer than any other program (the others were to run an hour), and only complete works would be considered (the other programs were to be excerpts of larger works). That was agreeable to me, but Emile, the always polite watchdog and our cost conscience, pointed out that this was PBS and not one of the networks, and that cost was an important factor. Martha thought barely a moment, then responded, "We must face the possibility that you don't have enough money to make this program!"

That settled, we pondered a number of dances for the program. Protas enthusiastically proposed *Clytemnestra*. Martha paused, then barked, "Do you want to kill the audience off the first year?"

Finally, the dances were agreed upon, and the program was produced with Martha's personal collaboration. "In the past," she said, "other people have tried to save me. This time I would like to save myself."

That program, "The Martha Graham Dance Company," consisted of *Diversion of Angels, Frontier, Lamentation,* and *Appalachian Spring*, plus a five-minute section of *Medea*—she broke her own "request." The broadcast revealed *Dance in America* to be a serious venture. Until then, audiences perhaps thought we were fooling around.

Two years later, Emile and I were again sitting in Martha's parlor, planning another project. Martha had been observing our programs, and she understood that audiences had seen challenging dances and that they might be ready. "I want to do *Clytemnestra*," she said. I was eager for the challenge; it was Martha's masterwork. But Martha, being Martha, had a "request." "Close-ups. Avoid the wide shot." She wanted intensity. Remember that this was deep in the 1970s. Television screens were either 9 or 12 inches. A group of dancers on a wide shot looked, as Martha observed, "like a bunch of ants." Martha and I had confronted close-ups in our first program. As she was observing Takako Asakawa's face at the end of a lift in *Diversion of Angels*, she said, "This would be a beautiful close-up." I said, "It is not a close-up; it is unformed. But if you compose a close-up, I will shoot it." She did, and I did.

Clytemnestra on stage ran one hour and 50 minutes. Martha asked if I thought that was too long for television. "A lot," I said. We talked and agreed that 1 hour and 20 minutes could properly represent the piece. I assumed she would cut scenes; she didn't. She sat on the piano bench with the composer and trimmed, as with a razor blade, 30 minutes from the score.

In the recording studio time equals money, so there is continuing pressure to push on, but not endanger the performance. The situation is disquieting. But Martha, like Balanchine, was a wonderful collaborator. In a mysterious, intuitive, subtle way—challenging me, protecting me, pulling it out of me—she guided me through the work I am most proud of.

A final haunting memory remains: Martha on the set, staring at Clytemnestra's throne, a place she would never again inhabit.—M. B.

CHAPTER 38

Portraits in Celluloid

Victoria Marks

Following my graduation from college, I headed toward New York, where I gradually became a part of a loosely knit community of dancers and choreographers and began to explore my own choreographic voice. During the 1980s and early 1990s, I led a small troupe known as the Victoria Marks Performance Company.

In 1987–88, I took a hiatus from the New York City dance scene and went to London on a Fulbright Fellowship in Choreography. There I began what has become a long-term relationship with The Place, a theater, school, and service institution for dancers and choreographers. I returned to London again in 1992 to head the choreography program at the London School of Contemporary Dance. I continued to create new pieces, and liberated from responsibility to a company and a particular group of dancers, I began to make work specifically for the individual artists I met. I began to think of myself as a "portrait artist," sensing that rather than bringing my own content to a dance, I tried to observe what was compelling about the performer(s). It was this idiosyncratic work that Margaret Williams, a filmmaker interested in dance, first encountered at one of my concerts.

DVD 34
Mothers and Daughters
(1994) 8 min 54 sec
Excerpt 1 min 49 sec

DVD 35
Outside In (1994) 14 min 3 sec
Excerpt 4 min 22 sec

When Margaret asked me to join her in making a dance for the camera in 1992, she had the mixed-ability company CandoCo in mind. Not only had I not created a dance specifically for the camera before, but I had never choreographed for disabled dancers. I was thrilled to undertake the opportunity.

In my first rehearsals with CandoCo, I set myself two immediate challenges: to understand how each dancer moved, and to understand from the dancers themselves their concerns regarding disability. I asked them to teach me, and they were very willing to do so. Each dancer had very different abilities and challenges. In our first rehearsal, I developed a movement sequence they could all accomplish with equal grace and comfort. Margaret, who videotaped every movement sequence we created, suggested after viewing the material that I rechoreograph the sequence so the choreography caused the camera to move. This "ribbon of movement" was one way the two of us worked to create a dynamic relationship between choreography and the camera. Later in the piece, I created movement sequences that made the camera circle. I loved the puzzle aspect of solving these choreographic problems.

Outside In (1994). MJW Productions and the Arts Council of England. Courtesy of the Arts Council of England. Photo by Mark Lewis.

Well into our process with CandoCo, when shooting a rehearsal, Margaret chose to frame a scene through the wheels of a chair. During our customary end-of-rehearsal session of viewing that day's work on video, we were all dismayed by the way the camera's perspective framed the dance. The dancers suggested that we stick with more "neutral" images. What crystallized for me at that moment is the fact that there are no "neutral" images. There is always a point of view, choreographically and cinematically. The sense that I could not take a "neutral" position spurred me dynamically toward the creation of a work that I hoped would shift viewers' perspectives on disability. If I had 13 minutes of a viewer's time, I'd create a piece that would irrevocably alter the viewer's perception of disability. That was the goal I set for myself.

I think of myself as something of a postmodern mutt: no single movement style or tradition feels like "home." Therefore, the choice of a movement vocabulary or style has always been a conscious one for me. For *Outside In,* I chose to work with a pseudo-tango vocabulary, liking the sense of display and the emphasis on power, allure, and partnering precisely because it might be seen as an anomaly when representing disability. As I've said, I was very conscious of the control we had, in terms of how we represented the dancers; I wanted actively to portray them as sexy, smart, and funny. It was important to undo conventional ideas about who is powerful and who deserves attention.

DVD 35

As a choreographer, I have usually attracted modest-sized audiences in theaters around the U.S. and in Europe. Realizing that one showing of *Outside In* on UK television would yield a greater audience than had ever seen my work before or might ever see it in the future awakened my perception of the opportunity I had been given. Perhaps because television audiences are more anonymous than live dance audiences, I became less concerned with how my work represented me, and more concerned with what it was doing in the public arena. I had begun to think in terms of how a dance might effect change in consciousness.

Margaret and I were charged by the BBC and the British Arts Council with the specific task of making a "dance for the camera"—creating a piece that would exist only through the camera's lens and through the editing process. Margaret and I therefore set out to undo the conventions of theatrical space and real space, and to create a magical space. Keeping to the theme of representing our mixed-ability community of dancers as individuals who are not limited in their imaginations and certainly not hampered by the environment, we decided to reveal the dancers as existing in multiple environments—inside and outdoors, underground, and in the sky. We worked to move literally through three-dimensional space, to undo the inherent flatness of film's portrayal of real space.

One of the many things I love about Margaret's directorial style is that she thinks like a painter and uses the camera as a kind of brush. She invents ingenious ways to create magic on the set, rather than relying on post-production. She enabled us to shoot a dancer floating in the sky and moving through a mirror right there in front of the camera. She had wonderful ideas about scale, perspective, and size.

All the time that we worked together, I was learning about the film medium. For example, in our initial rehearsals, Margaret quickly informed me that entrances and exits, and even some transitions, would be unnecessary. We didn't have to stay with a dancer through "real time." We could dissolve to her moments later, leaving out awkward or time-consuming physical transitions.

We began envisioning the piece as a whole in restaurants after a day's rehearsal. The choreographic development of *Outside In,* a process during which ideas and themes were formulated and made substantial through the creation of movement "scenes," resembled my process of making dances for the stage. I developed images that Margaret and I later organized into a sequence. In much the same way that I draw diagrams in my choreographic notebook to assist me in recognizing the progression within a dance, Margaret drew a storyboard to notate the sequence we envisioned.

Most difficult for me to understand were filmic ways of connecting one scene to another. As we progressed from the stage of creating material for the piece to the shoot, I learned on the fly.

Outside In was our first collaboration. We have subsequently worked together on three other films. Each project has had a distinctive character and has challenged our collaboration in new ways. *Mothers & Daughters* was initially inspired by my observations of the beautiful young dancer Anna Pons Carrera and her relationship with her mother, Marta. For that piece I conceptualized working both close-up with a single mother and daughter, and also framing a large vista of mothers and daughters seen from a great distance. This macro and micro perspective of mothers and daughters was limited by our budget and other material considerations, but it forms the primary visual concept for that piece. The film medium supported an interest I had in working with movers who were not professionally trained. It allowed us to get extremely close up to action, which let me work with small gestures, such as the sequencing of eye movements from a daughter to a mother and back again. I could also coach the

DVD 34

performers as they were being shot, and we could run a sequence several times until we got the performance we were looking for.

In my work for both the stage and film, I see myself responsible for the vision and the concept of a piece as well as for the "steps." I am very concerned with the way movement communicates ideas, and I see myself as a provocateur—a teller of stories, a shape-shifter. My perception is that the rest of the world does not see the choreographer as a thinker and conjuror as much as a step-maker. I hope that my work will join the work of other choreographers to change that perception.

In both *Outside In* and *Mothers & Daughters*, I was fascinated with the way the performers brought themes and issues to the work in ways I could not ignore. This took my "movement portraiture" further than before. There was nothing "generic" or abstract about these casts. My interest in continuing this work formed the catalyst for *Men*, my most recent film with Margaret. Here, I was interested in working with elderly men in an outdoor setting, posing the size and temporality of "nature" against older male bodies. I wanted to make a piece about power juxtaposed against mortality. We found a cast among a group of men who frequented the Senior Drop-In Center in Canmore, a mining town just outside of Banff, Alberta, Canada. (Margaret and her wonderful producing partner, Anne Beresford, orchestrated a partnership with the Banff Arts Center and the Canadian Broadcasting Corporation, as well as with our partners in the BBC and British Arts Council.)

Between *Mothers & Daughters* and *Men*, Margaret and I created a four-minute film, a solo for me called *Cover Up*. I'm not wild about this piece, and I know that part of my self-criticism must have to do with my discomfort about my own performing. However, making a four-minute piece (specified by the BBC/Arts Council) was a challenge that I don't feel we fully met. To introduce an idea, develop it, and find a conclusion in four minutes can be just as challenging as doing it in 20 minutes (or more so), but the challenges are different. In my opinion, in *Cover Up* an emphasis on visual design over content compromised the piece.

My collaborations with Margaret have had enormous impact on my life as a choreographer. Many people know my film work *only* because it is so much more widely seen than my stage work. It is also much more highly produced than my dances for stage—and, of course, Margaret's visual sense is responsible for much of that. The work on film has also encouraged me to pursue making dances for nontraditional, nonprofessional performers, and to consider not only what people do on a stage but also the histories and contexts they bring with them when they step before an audience. As much as I love the film medium, I am not a convert to it. I want to make dances for many different contexts. I have begun to think of choreography as having potential beyond its value as "art," and as something that goes beyond a cultural pastime for a privileged few. I believe in and am working on making dances that can be a catalyst for civic dialogues and community change. This lofty goal, however, does not keep me from daydreaming dances for all seasons and places, and I long for another opportunity to create work for the camera and to continue my partnership with Margaret Williams.

CHAPTER 39

Making Dance Films with Victoria Marks

Margaret Williams

> DVD 34
> **Mothers and Daughters**
> (1994) 8 min 54 sec
> Excerpt 1 min 49 sec
>
> DVD 35
> **Outside In** (1994)
> 14 min 3 sec
> Excerpt 4 min 22 sec

I had seen a performance of *Dancing to Music* by American choreographer Victoria Marks at the Institute for Contemporary Arts in London. Her choreography had a "filmic" quality which I felt would work very well on screen. I was interested to collaborate with Victoria, and I was also keen to work with the mixed-ability dance company CandoCo, so in 1993, we got together and put in an application for BBC/Arts Council of England's "Dance for the Camera" initiative to make a short dance film.

Along with about 100 other choreographers and directors, we submitted a proposal. Six teams were then chosen, given £5,000 and asked to make a pilot. The development period was an extremely productive and enjoyable time. CandoCo, Victoria, and I spent eight intensive days learning to work with one another, culminating in the production of a pilot film.

We began the week by developing a choreography that could be achieved by all of the dancers, in wheelchairs or not. Out of this developed the "portrait" sequence that opens the pilot, and from this came the key idea of a "ribbon of movement." Ideas of social dance, of partnering and pas de deux were examined and subverted in the double duet.

The pilot shows all the dancers' differing abilities and captures some of CandoCo's playful sense of humor as well as their previously unrecognized sensuality. We cannot escape (nor would we wish to) the fact that three of the featured dancers perform in wheelchairs. We, the able-bodied, are often uncomfortable looking at the disabled. We avert our eyes and shuffle past. This film invites and revels in our undivided attention. We have endeavored to confront our prejudice and embarrassment, our years of trying not to stare. We hope that we can now view dance and disability with fresh eyes.

For me the experience of working with Victoria and CandoCo was the closest I've come to drawing, something that is the basis of all my film work since art school. Even during our first meeting, there was a lot of stuff going on—tentative at first, rather like the first time the pencil hits the paper. Each day in rehearsal the "line" became more and more assured. Bits were rubbed out, changed, or strengthened. Shooting was like adding the color, and the on-line edit allowed me to make the marks even more potent and put the drawing in its finished frame.

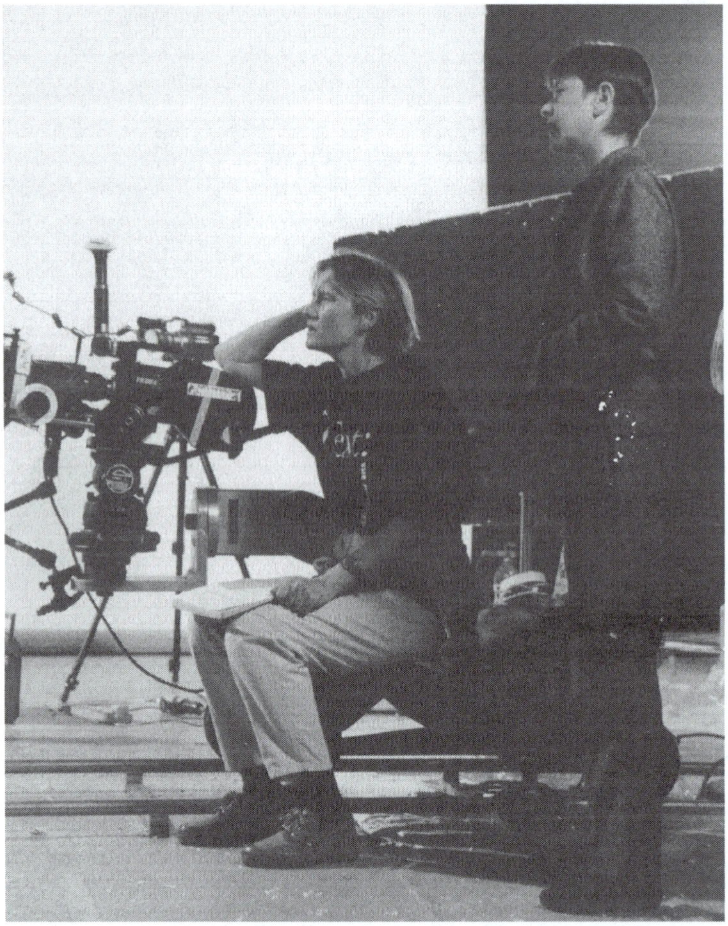

Margaret Williams (seated) and Victoria Marks. Photo by Mary Dunkin.

We submitted the pilot and were given the go-ahead to make the film *Outside In*, which was screened on BBC Television in January 1995. The pilot and *Outside In* were shot on Super 16mm film. Until that point, all my dance films had been shot on standard 16mm film.

DVD 35

I always storyboard a film. There are many advantages. I can concentrate on a particular scene; something to stare at always helps me think. I can figure out how to get from one scene to the next; I enjoy working out the transitions. The storyboard often inspires me, gives me ideas; it's a security blanket on the shoot. But most important, it lets me show everyone, particularly the choreographer and camera person, what I'm trying to achieve. I'm still amazed at how often—and not just in dance films—the structure of the finished film bears a very close resemblance to my original storyboard.

Starting from scratch on a new work, I always use a video camera in the rehearsal room. I use the camera as a notebook as we go along. If the intention is to make the piece on location, it is essential to rehearse in the space, interior or exterior. I always shoot this rehearsal material too. Working outside means dealing with the weather, and a whole other set of problems has to be faced. Victoria and I made a film called *Men*, which we shot in the Rocky Mountains of Canada in winter and summer. Initial rehearsals were indoors, but most rehearsal work was done outside, and the entire film was shot in exterior locations. The video cameras I work with currently are a Canon XL1 and a Sony VX 1000.

* * *

I strive for two things: to make a film with strong visual integrity, and not to misrepresent the choreographer's work. My preferred way of working with a choreographer is highly collaborative. I am not an awestruck dance fan; in fact, I'm a bit of an outsider. In order to make dance work on film, I have to make the film work for me; it has to stand out from all the other programmers on television. I'm more influenced by feature films than by programs on TV.

Outside In has been shown on major television networks throughout the world and is one of the BBC's most awarded music and arts films, having won the Grand Prix at Prague d'Or 1995, The National Film Board of Canada Creativity Award, the Screen Choreography Award at IMZ Dance Screen, and the Grand Prix at festivals in New York and Bulgaria.

Even with all the preparation I put into a project at the pre-production stage, I still don't know where the best place to put the camera is until it's all there in front of me: dancers and other performers, set or location, tracks, lights. The biggest challenge for me is to create an atmosphere as far removed from a stage as possible, exploring movement and space through the viewfinder rather than the proscenium arch.

With each film I make, I like to try something new. I try to achieve all special effects in the camera while on the shoot. Although I'm not averse to electronic effects, I'd prefer to try and work out how to do them in the camera on set or location. Mixes and title supers I make in the on-line edit.

When the camera comes into play, there are many limitations to deal with. The performer loses the benefits of a live performance, which are very exciting. A movement or sequence has to be repeated over and over to get it right for the camera, possibly at different ends of the day. There are inevitably a lot of demands on dancers. One of the most common is the expectation that they'll be able to repeat a phrase *now*, in a very small space, using a completely different "front."

Deciding which take to use isn't just a question of performance. All the elements come into play: lighting, focus, and the camera operating. When the camera is moving as well as the dancers, coordinating the action takes time and patience on everyone's part.

The most difficult aspect of making dance films is obtaining the financing. Once the money is in place—and there will never be enough—the practical side of filmmaking becomes more complicated. Dancers need to keep warm and to be given enough time to warm up. It's essential to have a suitable floor on which to work. The floor in dance films can be used to great effect; whether it's sand, peat, wood, rubber, glass, mud, or water, it needs to be considered. Dancers eat a lot, so we always make sure the budget can accommodate their huge appetites!

Toward the end of the 1990s in the UK, apart from the Arts Council and the BBC/ACE initiative "Dance for the Camera," there were very few opportunities to make dance films for television. However, we were able to persuade Channel 4 to make the dance series *Tights, Camera, Action*!, and over a three-year period we made two series that were broadcast on Channel 4 at 8 p.m. on Fridays. These eight half-hour "collections" of short dance films from around the world also included six new commissions. After making *Outside In*, Victoria and I were very keen to make another film together. We had been talking about relationships within the family as a starting point for a dance film. We were able to make *Mothers & Daughters* as one of the new commissions for *Tights, Camera, Action*!

For *Mothers & Daughters*, Victoria and I worked with eight mother-daughter DVD 34 pairs. Of the 16 women, only three daughters had received dance training. It was a terrific experience to use untrained performers, discover their potential, and work together to create a piece. Our main mother-daughter pair, Anna Pons Carrera and her mother Marta Carrera Plans, both come from Barcelona. Marta had never performed in any capacity before. We worked with them, trying out ideas and building a trusting relationship. Victoria and I had no previous experience to go on, except, of course, our own experience as daughters. Although much has been written about mother-and-daughter relationships, there is very little visual material (art, films, photographs) to research, so we relied heavily on instinct while making the piece.

Mothers & Daughters was filmed in the Round House in London, and we broke all the rules for making dance films. It was freezing cold; there was no electricity, so we had a generator for lights; the roof had a large skylight, which leaked, and it rained; the floor was horrible to work on. But we did it because the location was right for the piece, and no one complained.

An important aspect of my collaboration with Victoria was eating. During the rehearsals and production of *Outside In* we spent a considerable amount of time talking about ideas, testing each other's opinions. We found our creative juices started flowing in the evening, after a day rehearsing with the dancers. The best conditions for these discussions were in restaurants dotted around London, and for our film *Men*, restaurants in Los Angeles and Banff. If the restaurant had paper tablecloths, we'd make drawings for each other; otherwise, our plates had to sit upon piles of notebooks and pictures scattered across the table. We also found that red wine helped concentration and creativity.

I have no editing rules that can't be broken. I follow basic filmmaking principles like not "crossing the line," but when I'm in the cutting room I'll still try anything; I can't guarantee whether it will work until I see it. A dance on the stage has movement that has been designed to fit a certain space. Choreographers have to get people on and off the stage—they can't make them vanish. They can't "cut" from one scene to the next. One of the most liberating things for a choreographer working on film or video is that they don't have to get people on and off stage. One of the most liberating things for a filmmaker is not having to worry about the text.

A dance film is primarily concerned with movement. In silent films, movement and gesture were the driving force. If music is designed sound, then dance is designed movement. In my opinion, if you design movement, then you're choreographing, whether it's background extras in the feature film *Gladiator* or how an actor gets out of a car.

Dance is difficult to film. Money is very hard to raise. Filmmaking techniques and production management constantly have to be rethought and reinvented. These films and series would not exist without a strong collaborative relationship with key personnel. Anne Beresford has produced all the dance films Victoria and I have made together, and a lot more besides. We have learned together some of the many skills it takes to produce dance for the screen, and every time we go out filming, we're still learning something new. And we still have fun.

Mothers & Daughters was a collaboration in the truest sense of the word, and one that Victoria and I pushed further in *Cover Up* for the BBC/Arts Council third series of "Dance for the Camera," and in *Men* (1998 BBC/ACE), our most recent collaboration. We're very pleased *Men* won the Screen Choreography Award at Moving Pictures, Toronto, and the Screen Choreography prize at IMZ Dance Screen in Cologne in 1999.

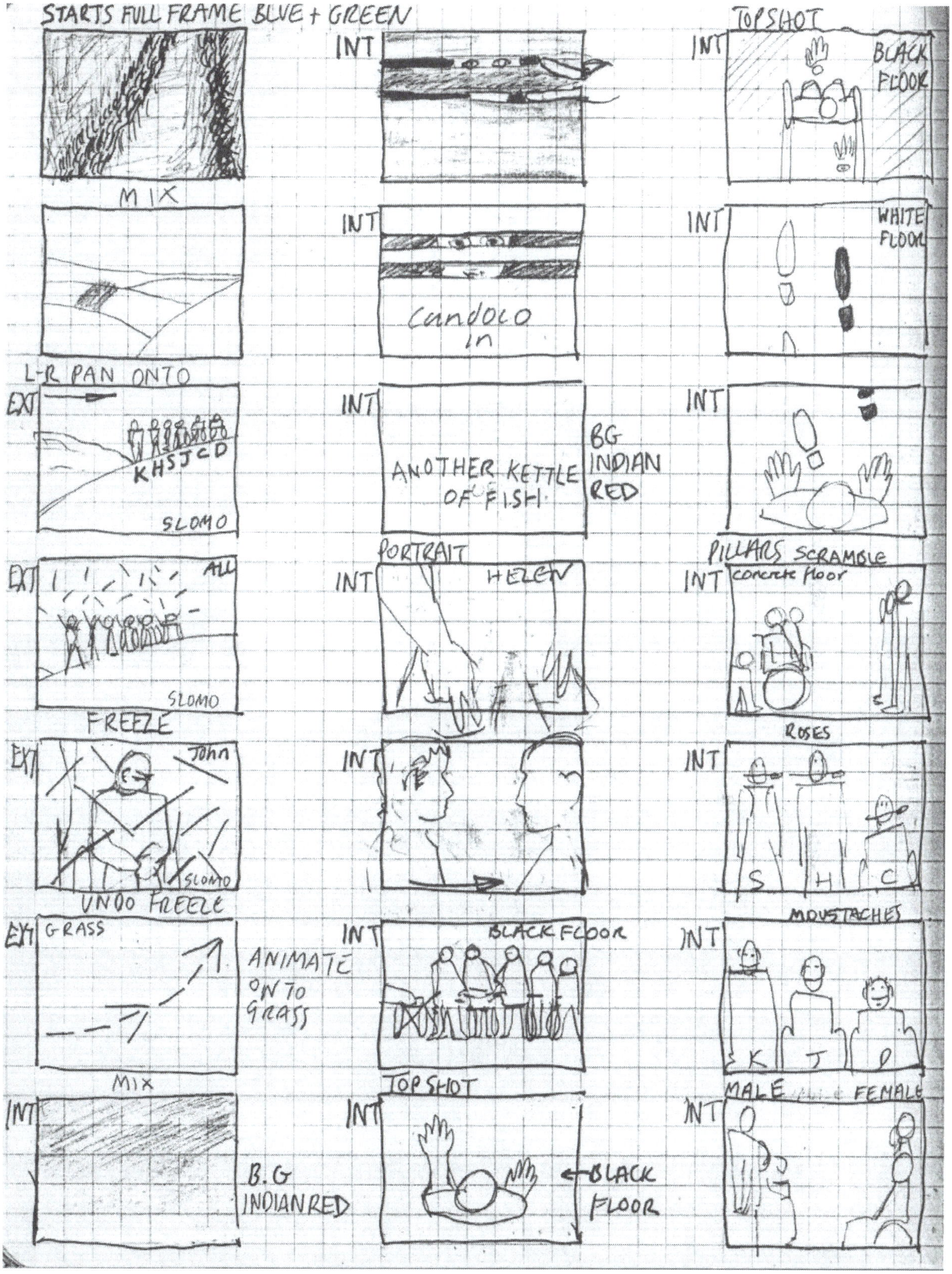

Three pages of storyboards for the film *Outside In* (1994). Storyboards by Margaret Williams. DVD 35

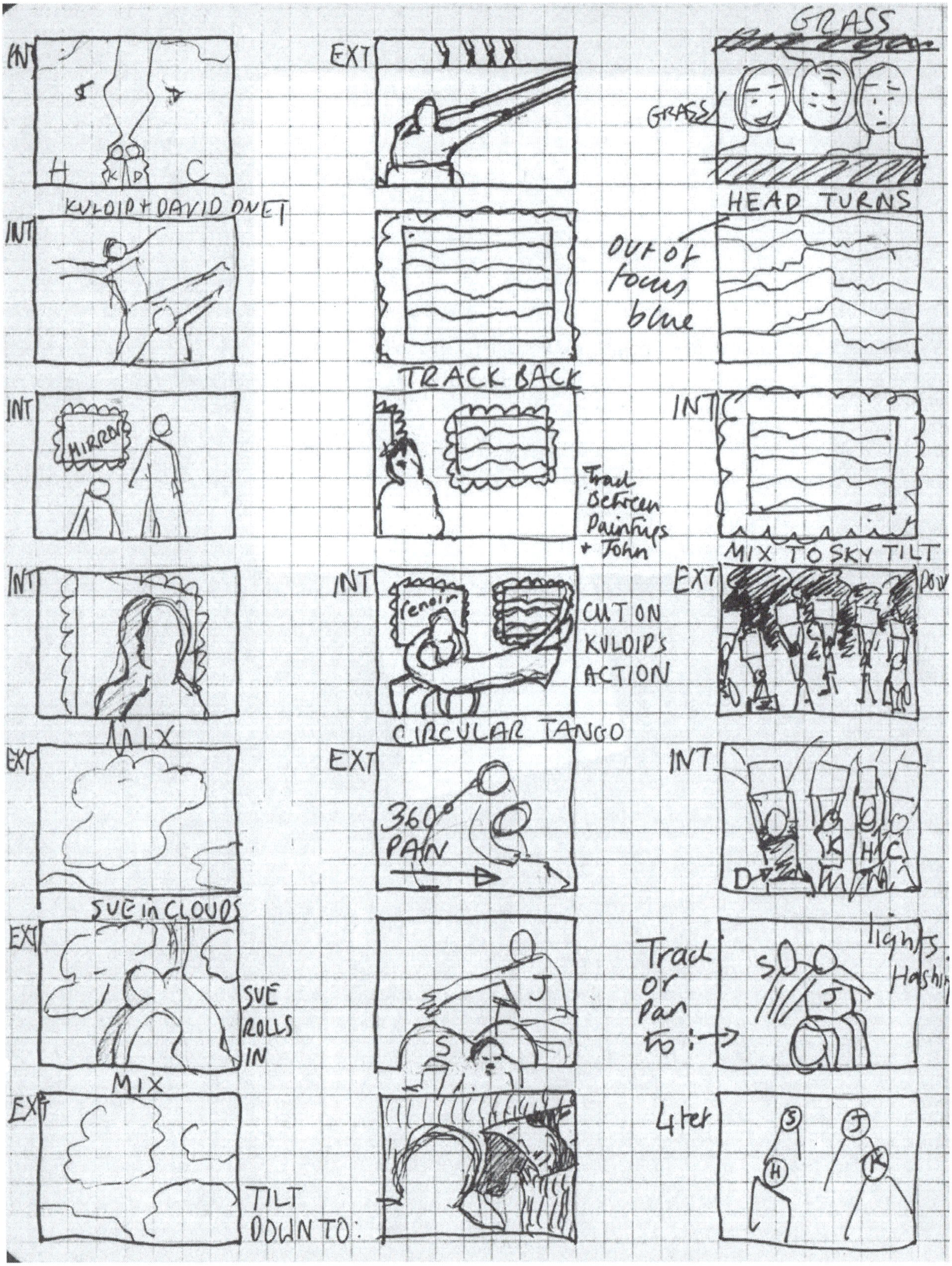
INT
H
K
D
C
EXT
GRASS
GRASS
KULDIP + DAVID DUET
INT
HEAD TURNS
OUT OF focus blue
TRACK BACK
INT
MIRROR
Track Between Paintings + John
INT
MIX TO SKY TILT DOWN
INT
INT
renoir
CUT ON KULDIP'S ACTION
EXT
MIX
CIRCULAR TANGO
EXT
EXT
360 PAN
INT
D
K
H
C
SUE in CLOUDS
EXT
SUE ROLLS IN
J
S
Track or Pan to:
lights flashing
S
J
MIX
EXT
TILT DOWN TO:
4ter
S
J
H
K

PILLARS BLACK FACES
INT
C D K
SAND BELOW
INT
WHITEFACES
INT
J S H
INT
SAND
EXT GRASS
BARE FEET
SCRAMBLE
INT
INT
SAND
EXT
TURN TO CAMERA
INT
DO TOP SHOT SCRAMBLES
INT
SAND
SUE + DAVID BACK OUT
EXT
STATUE
INT
DOUBLE OVET
SAND
INT
SUE DAVID
DICE
KULDIP
INT
MULTI COLOUR TRACKS
HELEN
CU HAND IN SAND
CIRCULAR MOVING
S C
INT
SAND
TOP SHOT TRACK WITH HELEN
TOPSHOT MARKINGS
WHO ME?
C

CHAPTER 40

Dancing with the Camera: The Dance Cinematographer

Evann E. Siebens

Rare is the cinematographer who specializes in shooting dance. Most directors of photography gain their experience in other formats, mostly narrative shorts and features, documentaries, or perhaps experimental films, before working on projects that involve dance. Why is this? Perhaps because most dance films are not large commercial projects, and good cinematographers command high salaries. Second, in spite of the explosion of dance film, most film schools and film sets where camera people learn their craft teach the art of text-driven, narrative films. Although many of the techniques and philosophies are the same, there are certain aspects to shooting dance that can be taught only in a rehearsal studio. Unfortunately, many of the choreographers and dancers who move into the film world, although versed in shooting consumer-level video, are not experienced in shooting film or high-end video, so that they are intimidated by the technology of the camera. And, as many choreographers-turned-directors have discovered, the choreography alone is not what makes the film; it is the successful transposition of the dance onto celluloid or tape that is the key to the new, augmented field of dancefilm.

This essay aims to explore some of the technical and theoretical aspects of dance film as a genre, leading to an understanding that dance cinematography, when it is fully realized, is like "dancing with a camera." First, I'd like to clarify some terms. Although filmed dance is often seen as a single genre, there are actually many subgenres within the form, including dance documentation or archival work, documentary, and dance film or dances created for film. This list could also include stage works being translated for the camera, excerpted promotional tapes used by dance companies to gain bookings, narrative shorts or feature films that include dance as a plot device, and even films in which actors spontaneously break into song and dance, otherwise known as musicals. However, I will refer to the first three forms when discussing the different aspects of shooting dance.

One of the first things I notice about the ways these terms are understood is that cinematographers with no experience in dance, when called on to film dance, often make the same stereotypical choices. Just as it is not appropriate to shoot only close-ups of feet and hands when documenting a choreographic

Left: Yannis Adoniov in *Ceci n'est pas un danse,* a film by Evann Siebens. The title references the work of René Magritte and Michel Foucault. Photo by Tomi Paasonen.

Right: Yannis Adoniov in *Ceci n'est pas un danse* by Evann Siebens. Photo by Tomi Paasonen.

work for archival purposes, so it is not essential to do a wide shot from the back of the audience when creating a dance for the camera. It is a joke in the community that shooters not versed in dance are either fascinated with feet or are busy focusing on a pretty girl who stands in the corps de ballet while the Swan Queen and Prince Albrecht are in the middle of their grand pas de deux. This is particularly true of archival documentation during a multiple camera shoot, or when shooting a documentary, in which events happen in the moment and what is being recorded is up to the person operating the camera.

First I will address the technical, then the philosophical, and finally the artistic aspects of shooting dance. Technically speaking, one of the first questions is whether to use film or video. To emphasize the difference in media, one could almost compare it to the difference between ballet and modern. Essentially, the best dancers can and will do both, but there is still considerable animosity between the two genres. I believe that the medium should be suited to the type of work. For example, shooting an archival document on film would be prohibitively expensive. Most documentaries, beyond the supremely well funded—Fred Wiseman's *Ballet* and Matthew Diamond's *Dancemaker* are two examples—are shot in some sort of video format. Yet there is a poeticism to the way film, whether 35mm, 16mm or even Super 8, looks compared to video. Most of the successful creative dance films in the 1990s have been shot on film. I believe this has less to do with the actual look of the film than with the rigor that shooting on film demands. The low cost of video can bring with it a mental laxity; one can shoot and shoot and never worry about the cost. Often this means getting ten mediocre shots instead of the one really great shot that emerges from a synchronicity between the camera and the dance.

DVD 33

The choice of camera can also have a big impact on the final look of the film. A 35mm Panavision camera is very different from a Super 16 Arriflex, which is itself very different from a Super 8 camera. Similarly, within the genre of video is a whole family of formats: Beta SP, Digital Beta, DV Cam, Mini DV, HI8, and others. Although small digital cameras are revolutionizing filmmaking, particularly in the documentary field, they will not put the film industry out of business. The more expensive the camera, the more control you have over functions such as focus, exposure, and manual zoom, and the better the images you will be able to create.

Although operating technique differs from camera to camera—and particularly between film and video—there are essential techniques common to all of them. The most obvious of these is focus. In film, one usually uses a prime lens with a fixed focal length or size (wide, normal, or telephoto). Focus is measured with a measuring tape, and the depth of field, or area that is in sharp focus, is dependent on the distance between the subject and the film plane, complicated also by the lens's focal length and f-stop. With a zoom lens, as found on most video cameras, focusing technique is different; the shot can be changed on an ongoing basis owing to the shifting focal length of the lens. This can be helpful for documentary work during which it is not expedient to stop and change lenses, but it poses its own problems when shooting dance. As a dancer moves toward the camera, the focal length between the dancer and the camera changes, meaning that the operator has to follow or rack focus. This is a very challenging camera move, and one that is usually operated by two people on a film shoot. With dance, because the subjects are so often in motion, keeping them in focus becomes one of the main challenges of the cinematographer.

Exposure is another tricky technical skill. With film, the cinematographer carefully calibrates a light meter reading for each shot, checking for different light intensities in various parts of the frame. In video, exposure is often treated more haphazardly, resulting in overexposed or underexposed figures, particularly when shooting subjects on a faraway stage with theatrical lighting. Almost every dance cinematographer has experienced a glowing, indistinguishable figure on a black stage. With video, one should expose for the hottest or brightest part of the frame, as it is easier to adjust an underexposed image than an overexposed one in post-production.

Intimately related to exposure, and often overlooked or misunderstood, is the concept of color temperature and white balance. Simply put, different kinds of light affect how the camera reads an image. With film, this is manifested in different kinds of film stock: daylight or "outdoor" film versus tungsten or "indoor" film. An outdoor shoot requires that the film be daylight balanced; an indoor shoot requires that the film be tungsten balanced. With video, however, the kind of tape remains the same regardless of the light, but the white balance must be adjusted. White balance is the difference between daylight (5400 degrees Kelvin) and tungsten (3200 degrees Kelvin) light temperatures. Problems arise when you start to mix different kinds of light. On a film shoot, windows are carefully covered with orange gels to neutralize or "balance" the daylight that spills into a location lit with tungsten lights. With video, this is often more difficult: what dance videographer hasn't been shown into a studio with large windows that allow daylight to enter, yet that is lit from above with fluorescent lights? To turn the lights off means that it's too dark, but to cover the windows is usually impossible owing to considerations of money and time. Unless you're working on a very well-financed shoot—which means that you would probably be shooting on film in the first place—a compromise must be reached. If you balance for tungsten light with daylight streaming in, it will make the whole image look slightly blue, whereas balancing for daylight with some tungsten light will create an orange effect. In my experience, the orange or "warm" tones will be better accepted by an audience than a blue, unnatural effect.

There are also special considerations for dance film that have to do with theoretical rather than technical matters. To my mind, one of the fundamental issues has to do with changing perspective from a stage focus to a film focus. This has implications for the shape of the "camera stage," the director's ability to focus the gaze of the audience as well as camera movement.

Camera space is the inverse of stage space. A proscenium stage narrows as it recedes; it is wider at the front than at the back. When we look through a lens, however, the space is narrowest at the front and widens as the subject moves farther away. This simple spatial difference has tremendous implications for choreography, particularly for the exits and entrances of dancers as seen through the camera's eye.

Another difference between stage space and film space is that the film director gets to decide where the audience lays its gaze. This is manifest in the basic differences of shot size: close-ups, medium shots, and full shots. Many people believe that dancers should be shot in a full frame, with plenty of head and foot room. For archival documentation, this is obviously the best practice since the point of the work is to capture the choreography in its entirety. However, to shoot a creative dance film in a continuous long wide shot is to miss the power of the close-up and the subtleties of choreography: a turn of the head, a movement of the hands. This freedom is what makes filming dance so exciting, though style is personal and depends on the aesthetics of the director. One dance film may feature a series of long, carefully choreographed moving shots, while another will consist of short, rapidly edited still images, creating the choreography through the editing as much as through the movement.

Camera movement is another hotly contested area that depends on style. Reacting against the roving camera and kaleidoscopic overhead shots of Busby Berkeley, Fred Astaire famously stated, "Either the camera will dance or I will." He firmly believed in the integrity of the choreography and the dancer's performance, whereas Berkeley was notorious for creating revolutionary cinematic techniques, the most famous being his signature kaleidoscopic overhead shot. Astaire and Berkeley's differences sum up one of the conundrums facing the dance filmmaker: Which will move, the dancer or the camera?

From a practical standpoint, camera movement changes whether the instrument is on a dolly, on a crane, or hand-held. Large film sets will have the means to create extensive, smooth camera moves, whereas a low-budget documentary will generally depend on a hand-held camera. There is something supremely satisfying about shooting hand-held, as it gives the operator freedom to move with the action. For me, this is the method in dance film that comes closest to "dancing with the camera." It represents a synergy between the dancer and the filmmaker that is crucial in my work. When I am familiar with the choreography of the piece I am filming, or when it is my own choreography, I am able to move with the camera along with the dancers, which produces a magical sense of kinesthetic movement. Similarly, documentary filming can be extremely similar to dance improvisation, as you must be aware of your surroundings and the action going on around you at all times, and react accordingly.

Alternately, there is the still tripod shot that has movement choreographed within the frame. One of the main principles of cinematography is to create depth in the frame, composing the various elements—whether they are moving or static—on varying planes within the frame. This is what makes a two-dimensional art form appear to be three-dimensional. When shooting dance, I often shoot diagonals in order to create the illusion of depth. Doris Humphrey said in her treatise, *The Art of Making Dances*: "Put the dancer to walking on one of those diagonals from up right to down left, and he is moving on the most powerful path on the stage."[1] Many choreographers instinctively use this diagonal, and if you are shooting a stage performance, it is extremely powerful to have the dancer travel away from and towards the camera, creating a strong sense of movement while leaving the camera in one place. Even if you are not shooting a stage, positioning dancers so that one is close to the camera and one is far away, for example, creates a sense of depth and satisfying composition.

Truffaut's cinematographer Nestor Almendros wrote the following about composition and the role of the cinematographer:

> Horizontal lines suggest repose, peace, serenity . . . Diagonal lines crossing the frame evoke action, movement, the power to overcome obstacles. Curved compositions that move circularly communicate feelings of exaltation, euphoria and joy. In the art of cinema, the director of photography's skill is measured by his capacity to keep an image clear, to "clean it," as Truffaut says, by separating each shape, be it a person or an object, in relation to a background or a set; in other words, by his ability to organize a scene visually in front of the lens and avoid confusion by emphasizing the various elements that are of interest.[2]

The background or horizon line that Almendros refers to is essential for alerting the viewer to the spatial relationship between the subject and the rest of the objects in the frame. With dance, however, there is a tendency to shoot in a space either entirely black or entirely white, which can mean that the horizon line is lost. When shooting in a neutral space, it is necessary to create a horizon line or to erect an alternate structure against which the dancer's movement can be measured. I once shot a black-and-white film in a black space and did huge dolly moves alongside the moving dancer, only to realize in the editing room that, without the horizon line, it appeared that neither the dancer nor the camera was moving at all.

The problem of the horizon line is solved when shooting on location rather than in the studio or on stage. I prefer "real" locations because they bring an essence to the dance that can never be duplicated on stage. In fact, shooting on location is one of the main reasons for putting dance on film in the first place. It also creates a sense of familiarity for audiences used to viewing films in "real" spaces, and it usually gives a narrative aspect to the film as well.

Finally, most dance films are edited to some degree, and the cinematographer must keep this in mind at all times, using techniques that I call "shooting to edit." For example, novice cinematographers tend to keep a single dancer centered in the frame at all times. Not only is this bad composition, ignoring a basic tenet that it's preferable to keep objects in the frame off center (also known as dividing the frame into thirds), but it is also the best way to get your editor to curse you. Watch how feature films are edited. Often an edit will come a moment or "beat" after a character has exited the frame, giving a sense of completion and closure to the scene, before going onto the next shot. You need to let this happen while you are shooting, letting the dancer exit the frame before moving to the next composition.

If you are trying to create continuous motion or movement, it is impossible to edit together two shots that are the same size and shot from the same angle. You will have what is called a "jump cut." This technique can be used very effectively and will be accepted by the audience if the motion is continuous, yet jump cuts are often abrasive and make the viewer question the truthfulness of the action. Again, look at feature films. A long, wide shot will be edited together with a medium shot, but because the movement is continuous, you watch it without questioning the reason for the edit. If you are shooting, you need to be aware how the film is going to be edited. If you are making a creative dance film and have control over the set, you can shoot the same movement from two different angles or with different size shots, overlapping a place where the edit can happen smoothly. If you are shooting a documentary with a video camera, however, you need to have your hand on the zoom at all times, changing the focal length of your shot constantly so that the editor can edit a "scene" together seamlessly.

In my view, dance film is a merging of the principles of dance and film, not just the shift of dance onto film. As a dancer and now a dance filmmaker, my favorite part about dance is not watching it, either on stage or on screen, not talking about it, not even filming it, but doing it. Yet when I shoot dance, I often feel the way I do when I am dancing. Essentially, I have transposed the experience of kinesthetically moving through space into dancing with my camera. I could be shooting hours of footage for a documentary, but I could still tell you the five or six shots that are magical, where I am in synch with the dancer and the movement: I often get shivers up my spine.

Shooting dance is a very visceral, creative, and non-intellectual experience. I strongly believe that dancers can make excellent cinematographers. There is a stereotype that cinematographers can only be big, burly men. Dancers, in particular women, need to buck the stereotype, get over their technology phobia, and pick up the camera. Dance film is a visual art that involves movement, strength, and physical awareness. What better field for a dancer?

NOTES

1. Doris Humphrey, *The Art of Making Dances* (New York: Grove Weidenfeld, 1959), 75.
2. Nestor Almendros, *A Man with a Camera* (London: Faber and Faber, 1980), 13.

CHAPTER 41

The Right Place at the Right Time: The Invisible Art of Editing

Girish Bhargava

Girish Bhargava. Personal collection.

Mine is truly a story of being in the right place at the right time. I was born in India. After graduating from university and working in All India Radio, at the age of 24 I found my way to Germany and work with ZDF, a German television network. Two years later, a CBS editor invited me to be a part of that network's newly emerging color television operation in the United States. It took me only a few days to buy a one-way ticket to New York. The very day I arrived, CBS went on strike.

Strapped for funds, I moved into the YMCA on 59th Street. A sympathetic CBS editor took me to Reeves Television, an independent company, where I worked until the CBS strike was settled. At CBS I worked in the news department, edited the Golf Classic, and then moved to ABC where bad luck struck again: ABC went on strike. But good luck did not desert me. Thirteen/WNET hired me to edit a major series, *The Great American Dream Machine*, which was an acclaimed success. When we finished the series in 1971, my next assignment was to edit a dance program with the celebrated choreographer Antony Tudor, centered around his dramatic *Pillar of Fire*, performed by American Ballet Theatre. Jerry Schnur was the director; this was be the first time we worked together, and the first time I edited dance.

Jerry and I encountered problems, not unexpected since very little dance had been edited on video at that time. This was the era of cumbersome two-inch reels that had to be changed often, and those reels were heavy. Also, it was a period before the invention of the AVID computerized editing system, before CMX, and even before time code (one of the most critical technical developments in video production). With multiple takes, we had no way of synchronizing each take to a prerecorded music track. We finally devised a system of combining a voice count by seconds (one to infinity) with each take. To preview an edit, we had to put several marks, in black Magic Marker, on the source tape. We finally finished, but it was exceedingly time-consuming—it took us more than four weeks. Finally Jac Venza came in and told us we'd used up our time.

That was the extent of my dance editing until, in 1975, I met Merrill Brockway, series producer of *Dance in America*, who informed me that in three weeks we would begin editing a dance project he had directed. I was apprehensive because of the difficulties of my previous dance experience. My solution was to take a vacation. The holiday was good, but the idea was not. When I returned I found myself at WNET, sitting in front of a new and completely unfamiliar editing setup, a computerized system. Merrill had done his homework and was ready to go. I took a deep breath, and we began.

I followed a simple rule: when working with a new system, don't try to learn everything it can do; rather, learn what you need to know to get each day's job done, basic things like cuts and dissolves. Everything else will come as time goes by, and you will learn the whole system. Complete each day's work without downtime. That will give you—and the person working with you—confidence. At the end of the session, I asked Merrill how the day went for him and told him I was working on a new system for the first time. He was surprised and said he never would have known had I not told him. He was pleased with the day's work, especially, he told me, "since your attention was directed to the screen rather than the computer buttons." Editing a show is like distilling a fine wine; you have to do it over and over. Once you've figured it out, you can go back to it, but you should never stop the show when you're working with a director for the first time. (A few years later, John Cage observed me at an edit session. He remarked that "the computer was invented to satisfy the needs of the Indian brain.")

I have always believed that it is more important to know *where* to edit than *how* to edit. Most editors flaunt their knowledge of editing systems. I don't care what system I use, as long as I can make the edit where it is needed.

The computer let us work much faster and more efficiently. A brief description of one of its technical features can illustrate how. Time coding a video recording is the foundation of computerized editing, enabling each video frame to be individually identified. For filmmakers, this is like edge numbers on a work print, or like addresses of houses on a street to help the post office deliver the mail. Before time code, there was no way for an editor accurately to select a video frame and identify it to the computer. The time code is an electronic signal included in a video or audio recording signal and is encoded and expressed, arbitrarily, in time (Hours: Minutes: Seconds: Frames).

As time passed, we began to use two different time codes, one for the music track and one for the visual, when we recorded and edited dance. On any particular take, the music will stay the same, and so will its time code, even though the video's time code changes, as illustrated here:

	Music TC Start Point	Video TC Start Point
Take 1	01:23:07:22	12:31:07:19
Take 2	01:23:07:22	14:29:09:12

The first frame of video of Take 1 happens at the first frame of music time code, and the same is true for Take 2. Because the music has consistently and exactly the same time code for both, the video performances can be found and compared for any point in the music through a calculation of the matching time codes. The difference between the time codes of the video of Take 1 and Take 2 is 01:57:57:23—i.e., Take 1's start point is subtracted from Take 2's to arrive at this number, called the "offset." This offset number will be the same for any video moment compared between the two takes. Using this offset, the editor can quickly direct the computer to cue up the different takes to the matching scene.

Video editing changed radically with the invention of nonlinear editing systems, such as AVID, which revolutionized the industry. Previously, linear editing required physically cutting sections of film and splicing them together to create a sequence, or electronically copying video from a source tape to an edit master tape, often incurring loss of generational quality.

In nonlinear editing, which happens on all present computer editing systems, you have instant random access to your digitized footage. Complete random access allows instantaneous cueing and retrieval of sequences, segments, shots, and frames. You can experiment and re-experiment with every edit, trimming, moving, deleting, duplicating, or modifying individual frames or entire segments of the sequence. Nonlinear editing allows significantly faster and more creative editing than traditional linear editing.

Sometimes it is necessary to match movement on a cut point. You may be off several frames, so make up the frames on the edits before or after the cut point in question. The idea is to spread the frames over a few edits, which will keep the dancers in synch with the music. (We didn't have to worry about any of this when we were editing the Martha Graham dancers; they were "on the money" on every take.)

I was most fortunate in my early career to work with a number of great choreographers: Robert Joffrey, George Balanchine, Martha Graham, Merce Cunningham, Paul Taylor, Jerome Robbins, and Twyla Tharp. My practice, if we were stuck at an edit point, was always to show the choreographer different options. We would be surprised when suddenly the choreographer would say, "That's it!" It may be difficult for a choreographer to say exactly what's on his or her mind because of unfamiliarity with video. Just keep offering alternatives, and one will be dead on.

Editing to the music is acceptable, but not when it sacrifices a dance step. Movement always rules. If you have a chance to make a clean edit and it is not musical, don't worry; once the sequence is edited, it will have its own rhythm. Many directors want to cut on the downbeat. In dance, I almost never cut on a downbeat because something is always happening on or around a downbeat—an entrance or the beginning of a step, for example. Edit just after or just before it, so the viewer can appreciate the next step cleanly; the dance is not interrupted, and the edit becomes part of the movement.

It may be necessary to make a number of edits to introduce the leading players. Sometimes that works and other times it doesn't. It feels too "cutty." My favorite opening is Martha Graham's *Appalachian Spring.* Merrill designed a crane move that would introduce all the characters without an edit. The sequence is fluid and seamless.

Earlier in my career, we asked Balanchine about the exact placement of an edit. "At the bottom of the breath," was his reply—that is, before the downbeat: 1234 X 1234, X being the space between 4 and 1. That's when the movement begins; the edit pushes it off.

On one occasion in the early 1970s, I was working with Twyla Tharp. The director had been switching to musical counts. Twyla was not pleased. Finally she said to the director, "Why don't we let Girish try it?" So I rolled the tapes from three cameras, put them in synch, and began by disregarding the music, paying attention instead to the dancers' movement. When I finished, Twyla said to the director, "This man is very sensitive to my movement." I knew I was on the right track. Another key to editing dance is to go in between the steps, so the edits are invisible.

I rarely went to the studio when a *Dance in America* program was being recorded. Both directors, Merrill and Emile Ardolino, believed in my gut instincts and said that my fresh eyes would be more valuable to them later. After the program had been recorded, the tapes viewed and logged, and the editing plan organized, the director would appear, ready to work. My first request was always the same: "All right, give me the whole scenario. What are we trying to do?" Once I heard the story, I knew I could make it all happen.

Merrill often says that the secret of dance video is editing. I agree with that—as long as the edits don't call attention to themselves, and they are not disruptive. Editing should be seamless. An edit should not be seen. My favorite memory is editing the first Martha Graham program for *Dance in America*. After we finished, Martha came to the screening of her show. I was nervous and hopeful that the editing would please her. After the screening she asked, "All right, fellows, where are the edits?" Need I say more?

From Left: Merrill Brockway, Judy Mitoma, Marlene Millar, Girish Bhargava, and Charles Dennis during the 1999 Pew Dance/Media Fellowship at UCLA. Photo by Kateri Hyung.

From Left: Morleigh Steinberg, Charles Dennis, John Bishop, Carmella Vassor, and Andy Wilson working together during the 1999 Pew Dance/Media Fellowship at UCLA. Photo by Kateri Hyung.

CHAPTER 42

Fishing for Humans: Dance and the Story of Story

Mitchell Rose

Let's look at the numbers. Last weekend, how many movie admissions were there? OK, and last weekend how many dance performance admissions were there?

And the winner is . . .

Both dance and film are available in plenty. Why, then, do people stream to the movies and stay away from dance in droves? Because film, more than dance, gives them what they want: story.

I'm often moved to tears watching a movie and entering a state of empathy with some poor schmo on the screen. I've been moved by breathtaking dance, but never to tears. I think I'm not alone. Given these two depths of experience, which night out will people choose?

In the dance world, a melding of dance and film is inevitable. Choreographers will be forced to move the mountain to increasingly home-bound audiences. There will always be a place for theater, please God, when the initiated and the curious have a hankering for seeing fallible, huffing and puffing, real bodies. But if choreographers also have a chance to speak to a vast new audience, they will.

And this is a great thing. As dance increasingly expresses itself through film and video (let me just use the word "film"—it's warmer) the art of choreography can be enhanced as it is informed by film's powerful storytelling capacity.

In his *Poetics*, Aristotle ranks the importance of these elements of drama in this hierarchy:

- Story
- Character
- Dialogue
- Idea
- Music
- Spectacle

Most dance deals with the bottom three, in reverse order, drawing primarily from the level of spectacle—to affect the eye. (Of spectacle, Aristotle comments that it just costs money. Given the budgets of most dance, this is even low-order spectacle.)

We have within us a fundamental need for story, a deep mythic desire to open our channels and receive evidence of the commonality of human experience. This quest for connection stems back to our earliest stirrings of awareness. As infants, we are wired primarily for one thing: exploration. We explore every anthill and every cabinet hinge because we are thirsty for experience. We want to know how the world works. We want to know what possibilities are out there.

And then, at night in darkened rooms, we beg to continue these explorations, now in inner worlds, hearing stories—stories that bring the universal truths of existence into our realm. Our craving for myth broadens our range of considered possibilities and readies us for life's onslaught.

That fundamental need for story never leaves us. We still are drawn to the darkened theaters where we become rapt listeners and watchers, opening our channels to that glowing rectangle and going into semi-hypnotic receptivity. We actually forget our time and place. It is a state of genuine transcendence.

This is powerful. This is core-level stuff. Film mainlines to who we are. (Plus, there are the Raisinettes, but I digress.)

Performance as observed action can be fascinating, breathtaking, and visceral, but ultimately most choreography speaks to the mind, the eye, and the body. Dance is an abstraction of primal life forces, and I would argue that abstractions, being inherently cerebral, don't reach our psyche, our mythic core, to the extent story does.

Classical story has a tripartite form. It has a beginning, a middle, and an end. Typically, there is a protagonist. The beginning: she has a world that becomes upset. The middle: she tries to overcome obstacles that prevent her from righting that imbalance. The end: she resolves the conflict and in doing so is inexorably changed.

This rings true to us because we live it every day. It is an archetypal form whose rhythm resonates deep within us. The story-shape of balance, rising action, climax, and descent is a shape that feels familiar. It feels like conversation. It feels like sex. It feels like sport. It feels like work. It feels like a day. It feels like a life. It mirrors the cosmic triptych of existence: creation, preservation, destruction.

The protagonist is on a roller-coaster as she approaches the climatic confrontation (inner or outer). The ride twists and turns, bucks and dips as it eventually climbs to the inevitable exigency in that person's life. The archetypal familiarity of the journey causes us to enter a state of empathy with the person. Even a protagonist whom we don't like or agree with, we will root for—because in doing so we root for ourselves. Transcending our own ethics and morality, we will experience the protagonist's successes and failures as if they were our own.

Thus, story invites participation. You're itching to help that poor schmo, if you could only jump up into the screen as in *The Purple Rose of Cairo*.

Let me give an example of what I think is the usefulness of narrative in dance-filmmaking by referencing one of my own humble efforts. I've made a series of dance films entitled "Modern Daydreams." Each of the episodes has a simple narrative structure that uses simple dance movement as its "bricks."

In one episode, *Deere John*, a man passing a construction site sees and falls in love with a 22-ton John Deere excavator. Together they dance a dance of discovery, fulfillment, and eventually, the loss that any diesel-based relationship must suffer. We then realize that it was all a daydream, as the man continues on his way down the street.

There could be different approaches to creating a filmed pas de deux of a man and an excavator. One, obviously, is to choreograph "interesting" (there's that word again) partnering—he gets in it; he gets on it; it lifts him up; etc. It's the movement exploration approach.

On a content level, that's basically what *Deere John* is made with. But by infusing that into a love story, it now has an emotional context that every viewer can relate to. It will resonate with everyone because we all value nothing higher than the love stories of our own lives, and we'll want to see how this guy manages his. Since everyone has made more bad choices in love partners than they would care either to admit or to remember, they'll feel a commonality of experience with the protagonist and have an investment in his travail.

In fact, I'll bet your interest in this chapter just spiked when I mentioned "bad choices in love partners," because all of a sudden there was a real relevance to your life. This is the essence of what I'm talking about in how story reaches people.

A love story of a man and a machine can, oddly, go pretty far in connecting to people, but since duets between men and machines are not common sights, there's a certain distancing that happens—it feels not of our world. This is why I chose to give the film the bookends of the man starting and ending on the street. Filmic grammar allows us to enter his dream life, where all things are possible and all things are accepted. By starting the story in reality, where everyone lives, I have an entrée into a world of limitless possibilities.

This is one of film's greatest strengths—freeing storytellers to place their stories in whatever locales they wish. There's a connection with an audience when stories can be set in a city street or an office or a bedroom—that's where we live our lives.

While story invites participation, abstract performance inherently does not; it is merely regarded. But let my position be clear: I'm pro-beauty, both of aesthetic and of concept. I think though that, when observing "beauty for beauty's sake," we are more passive watchers. There certainly is a place for that, but we should remember that people want to feel alive; people want to feel like players in the game of life.

In participating in a protagonist's quest, we feel bigger. It's perfectly valid for a choreographer to create movement for its own sake, to create dance that is beautiful and thought provoking. I tend to think, however, that the more common experience of its audience will be interest-level, not involvement-level. (How many times after a dance performance have you heard from a non-aficionado that lackluster remark, "That was very interesting"?)

As dance brushes shoulders with film, there's another aspect that I think can greatly benefit dance: purity of vision and focus of intent. I was a choreographer for a number of years but then left dance to go to film school and become a director and writer. I feel that, were I to return to choreographing, having learned something about the craft of filmic storytelling, now I'd get it right.

Most choreography is the practice of collage. Various diverse elements are assembled into a kinetic mélange. Compositional elements are introduced with loose thematic justification. As a choreographer, I was very sloppy. Too often, I presumed the audience would have magical glimpses into my thinking and would intuit my intent. I was too creatively undisciplined to lay out a logical structure whose meaning was dramatized, not indicated, engendering an earned emotional response.

Yes, I was an undisciplined choreographer, but again, I don't think I was alone. The choreographic canon, basically, is to look cool. Looking cool is cool, but cool ain't enough. It's spectacle.

Choreographers can take a valuable lesson from screenwriters. In a *good* screenplay there is a basic and simply stated premise (e.g., jealousy leads to destruction) that informs every scene. Every element of the story either supports or refutes the premise, creating a dynamic living argumentation. Every line of dialogue and every character action choice are honed to create a tightly woven tapestry.

A good screenplay is rewritten, and rewritten again and again. All fat is trimmed. Only the fittest—that which truly fits—survives. It has to be this way; too much money is at stake.

This level of discipline should be the standard in all art forms, but it should definitely be the height of the bar for dance—to have every moment be a purposeful choice, to create an unshakable structure whose content streams through a unified gestalt. If this level of care were always put into choreography, I daresay people would actually come to see it.

The allure that film enjoys is, I believe, available to some extent to theater choreographers as well as dance filmmakers, if they care to adopt a more overt use of archetypal story form. I'm not encouraging abandoning abstract and nonrepresentational dance. Nor am I encouraging, given the limitations of the specificity of dance's language, the creation of a slew of pantomimes. I'm suggesting fully considering choreographic options, and considering those box office numbers—they are graphs of people's needs.

The fact that we are able to enter into such a deep state of empathy in narrative storytelling does, I think, say something beautiful about us: that we really care about each other on a deep fundamental level. We come to the theaters . . . we even watch the videos . . . because we care.

The people entrust you with their valuable time—how far do you want to reach inside them? To reach deep, you may want to consider skewing a bit more to the narrative, for because we care, the best way to hook a human is with a human.

CHAPTER 43

Breaking the Box: Dancing the Camera with Anna Halprin

Andy Abrahams Wilson

The domains of both dance and film are bounded by walls: dance by the stage, and film by the box of the camera or screen. The adaptation of dance to film is essentially a negotiation of boundaries—often, one set replacing another. Within each discipline, however, practitioners have expressed discomfort with the constraints of these boundaries and those that would further limit experience through attempts to codify or capture that experience. Since the 1950s, Anna Halprin has reached across the divides of disciplines and communities to create dance that expresses life in a direct way as "personal and collective myth." Liberating dance from the formal and removed *box* of contemporary performance, she has brought dance back to its roots in community, ritual, and healing.

My background in visual anthropology dealt with a similar project of translating cross-cultural experience into conventional form, specifically visual form, with its own pitfalls of perspective, representation, and exploitation. Like Halprin, I was interested in media and art that reached across barriers, connecting subject to spectator to our own tangible or intangible inner and outer worlds. I met Anna in 1989, when the then 70-year-old choreographer was facilitating a workshop and community performance around the theme of living with AIDS. In graduate school at USC at the time, I was drawn to her use of dance as performance ritual and the body as vehicle for self-expression and healing. I was also coming to terms with my own dissatisfaction with the way anthropology and the "study of the other" so often removed us from our own personal experience, compelling us to express what is essentially visceral, subjective fieldwork under the guise of objectivity.

In deference to such pioneers as Victor Turner, Richard Schechner, and Barbara Myerhoff, I began to see my work as an anthropologist as a performance in itself. This had at its core a responsibility to oneself and one's community, an authentic connection between experience and expression, and a recognition that the desire to make sense out of our world was best served by joining body, mind, and spirit. While Anna Halprin was refusing to detach her art from the knowledge of the body and "real-life issues," I was looking for ways to reconcile the "science" of observation with the ineffable realms of art and embodied experience.

Anna's week-long AIDS/dance workshop, with almost 100 participants, culminated in a public performance called *Circle the Earth: Dancing with Life on the Line*. Before the performance, which took place in a school gym in Marin County, California, she spoke to the audience: "They're not here for your entertainment. They're here because they have something to say, and you're here as witnesses to support them."

In this ritual sense, where all participants—including witnesses—have a precise role, I was able to understand my own role as a filmmaker. I was a witness too, which involved respect for both the subjects and their performance, and my full participation. I was neither a detached observer nor an intruder. As a witness, intently focused, I offered a lens or mirror through which the performers could be seen and validated. When I later began to film Anna's ongoing work with HIV-positive men, this perspective helped me mitigate my concerns about being an outsider or merely a recorder of a reality beyond me. It sparked my own reflections and validation as a gay man living in the age of AIDS, and it connected me to a life rhythm of loss and healing. In doing so, it created an intimacy that broke down the barrier of the lens. Indeed, as the group accepted me as one of their own (despite my seronegative status), I understood that my feelings of being an outsider were often self-imposed—an important lesson for the interlocutor and framer of other worlds.

The success of *Circle the Earth* for both performer and witness inspired the idea of creating an ongoing performance group for people challenging AIDS. After seven months of weekly workshops, the group created a public performance called *Carry Me Home*. At one dress rehearsal, which took place on a traditional stage, Anna prepped the men and cheered them on, summing up her notions about the role of dance: "It's up to you to be so damned good, and to be so real, and to be so *with* what you're here for, and what you have to say to someone else—that we're just gonna bust this fucking box and make it alive with some kind of fucking life. I can't stand this black box!" Captured in my 1991 video *Positive Motion*, the power leapt through the performers, my camera, and, eventually, the video's viewers.

Continuing her migration from the conventional stage, Anna has returned to the earth as resource, studio, and stage for her dance and teaching work. For years she has been leading workshops along the northern California coast, and she has recently engaged in her own powerful performance work in the natural environment. She finds in nature connection, inspiration, memory, and the reflection of our own biological processes. My interest in this work, background in ritual studies, and deep connection with nature drew me as a student of—and then collaborator with—this pioneering choreographer.

In 1995, we created a video called *Embracing Earth: Dances with Nature*, in which dancers move with the rhythms and textures of the environment. With focus, intention, and a deep relationship with place, the act of climbing a tree or rolling in sand became a dance of merging or emerging. Several years later, at the age of 80, Anna shed her skin once again. With the collaboration of artist Eeo Stubblefield, she covered her nude body with mud, paint, and molasses in order to connect with nature in an unmediated way, revealing clues about living and dying and creating evocative art. This work is featured in my forthcoming video *Returning Home*.

DVD 36

"Scored" performance, a kind of structured improvisation, is the key to Anna's work, and—again, linking form and content—it is the methodology I turn to in collaborating with her. Scores, which include boundaries of time, place,

DVD 36
Returning Home (2001) 40 min
Excerpt 2 min 15 sec

Production Note: "Every performance demands a production strategy that matches it philosophically, stylistically, and methodologically. Like Halprin herself, we relied on a "structured improvisation," using one camera and no shot list. As such, the filmmaker became part of the intimacy of the dance—creating his own dance with Halprin as she would with the elements surrounding her."—A. A. W.

Filmmaker Andy Abrahams Wilson along the cliffs of the Northern California Coast, location for his film *Returning Home*. Photo courtesy of Andy A. Wilson.

resources, activities, and sometimes intention, create the container in which individual and collective creativity can emerge. If the score is not followed, the performance falters. Evaluation enables the score to be refined and meaning to be culled. Because the outcome is not predetermined in terms of either form or content, meaning is not imposed but arises simply through the score. This allows for the emergence of serendipity and revelation. In one instance, Anna was completely covered with light blue paint. She began the score by smearing on her body mud from an underground grotto, until the brown completely masked the blue. Later she was hit with meaning: she had embodied and enacted the joining of earth and sky, flesh and spirit, celebration and mourning, life and death.

In filming Anna's work, I understand myself to be part of the same process. The camera becomes my principal resource, and following movement with the open eye of the shutter my activity. A sort of meta-dance is created between my subject and me. Familiarity with place and its elements becomes paramount, just as it is for the performer. My experiential work with Anna through the years—as a dancer, not a filmmaker—has informed my film work and fostered a synchronicity of approach and philosophy. In keeping with my subject, I don't work with storyboards or scripts. Equipment and crew are kept to a bare minimum, true to the rawness, simplicity, and intimacy of her work. The process of reviewing dailies (often together) and later editing provides for refinement of filming (and performance) and the emergence of story and meaning. Why did I tilt down from the redwood treetops to reveal Anna in a crevice below ground? I didn't know any more than she about her "personal myth" of connecting sky and earth. In contrast, while Anna speaks of the celebration of the body, I see a ritual of preparation for death and burial. The filmmaker brings and leaves with his own sets of myth and meaning, as will the viewer. In the end, through archetype the collective consciousness is tapped.

In working with Anna, I usually hand-hold the camera, freeing up my own movement, emphasizing subjectivity, and allowing the energy of the dance to move me. After all, dance is the movement of energy through the medium of the body, and film is the movement of light through the medium of the lens. When the camera is in synch with the dance, and the filmer with the dancer, energy breaks through the containers of body, stage, camera, screen. We experience a transcendence, or flow, when the boundaries of subject and object, experience and consciousness, disappear. While Anna was using movement to connect inner and outer worlds, I was "dancing the camera" to create the same bridge. When intention, ability, and authenticity are aligned, focus is engaged, walls collapse, and a healing ensues. That is why we love great dance: it liberates the soul from the container of the body.

When filmmaking is most successful, the camera's presence recedes and the walls of the screen are transcended. Still, as *boxes*, the camera and viewfinder offer the unique opportunity to create tension by playing with boundaries of inside and outside, detail and breadth, time and motion, the seen and unseen. Unlike the camera's iris, the human eye cannot zoom in on detail. It takes in peripheral space. It wanders from object to object. This is part of the splendor of the eye and the "live" viewing experience, but the camera offers the unique opportunity to heighten experience through intimacy. In all my work with Anna (whose own work demands intimacy), the camera records what the observing eye may not: the clenched fist of a man with AIDS, the eyes when connection is made, the moment when two outstretched hands detach, the release of breath, the texture of mud on aged skin. Moreover, the walls of the screen or viewfinder create a palpable ten-

Anna Halprin in *Returning Home*: "My way is not to imitate the outward forms of nature, nor use nature as a backdrop, but attempt to reach into the deepest places inside myself that emphasize and empathize with its basic processes." ©1999 Eeo Stubblefield.

sion when relationships or body parts are cropped. Anathema to many dance video purists, this tactic is akin to the body or movement "isolation" for which dancers strive. Slow motion (though I've never used it with Anna) expands time and gives a breathtaking look at the body's subtle movements. Although many see it as manipulative or disrespectful of "the dance," the camera can create a choreography of its own, sweeping the viewer up in motion and emotion. When this is a result of my own intimacy with the dance or the dancer, it feels authentic, and the distancing factor of the camera is diminished.

Perhaps the "box" can be seen not merely as a construction or convention that stifles experience, but as one that also accentuates it. Despite herself, recently Anna has been performing retrospectives in theaters to sold-out crowds. In differing ways, the walls of the "black box," like those of the *camera oscura*, or of the sunlit trees or cliffs, are mirrors offering the possibility for reflection, projection, and validation: an opportunity to encapsulate incredible beauty—the human potential—and to experience connection with the awe-inspiring forces of life. Performance, as a dancer or a filmmaker, is a dialectic between experience and expression, meaning and structure, self and other. In breaking the box, we join with something beyond and perhaps greater than what we know, only to find more walls to ponder, penetrate, or perform dances around.

CHAPTER 44

The Neophyte's Tale: A Choreographer Works on Alive from Off Center

David Rousseve

In early 1990, I created a site-specific work, *Had Me Somebody But I Lost Her Very Young,* for my dance/theater company REALITY at Los Angeles's Bradbury Building. Commissioned by Elise Bernhardt, then director of the New York-based presenting organization Dancing in the Streets, the piece was part of "The Creole Series," a collection of eight full-length works that juxtaposed the true-life, early-1900s bayou stories of my Creole grandparents with my own stories from contemporary urban America. During the development process, Elise brought Joseph V. Melillo, then director of the New York International Theater Festival, to a rehearsal. After the run-through, they reiterated a comment I'd heard over and over since presenting my first evening-length piece in 1989: "Your work is wonderful, but you should consider working in film." Although I knew little about filmmaking, I intuitively agreed that the layered composition, narrative base, time-jumping framework, and intimate gestural vocabulary of my dances seemed to cry out for film. I had a secret desire to explore the medium, but in my mind there was absolutely no chance of doing so: the costs were staggering, my work was too "alternative," and my company was much too young.

Joseph and Elise personally approached *Alive from Off Center*'s Alyce Dissette to propose that we create an experimental dance film based on "The Creole Series." Frankly, I never expected Alyce to say yes. To my elation and horror, she agreed. We began to move forward on the film *Pull Your Head to the Moon—Tales of Creole Women*, with Alyce and Alive TV as executive producer, Joseph and Elise as producers, myself as writer/choreographer, and the six members of REALITY as performers. From the very beginning, Joseph and Elise wanted me to retain as much control of the actual "vision" of the film as possible. They were able to negotiate the one factor that had the largest impact on the project (and my ultimate satisfaction with it): I was permitted to select the director. (To my knowledge, for most of its other projects, Alive TV paired directors with choreographers.)

Considering the cultural content of the work, I thought the director should be African American. Further, the dramatic high point of "The Creole Series" is a horrific story of rape, murder, and revenge. I was adamant that only a woman

David Rousseve and cinematographer Ronald Gray between takes on the Brooklyn set. Photo courtesy of Ayoka Chenzira.

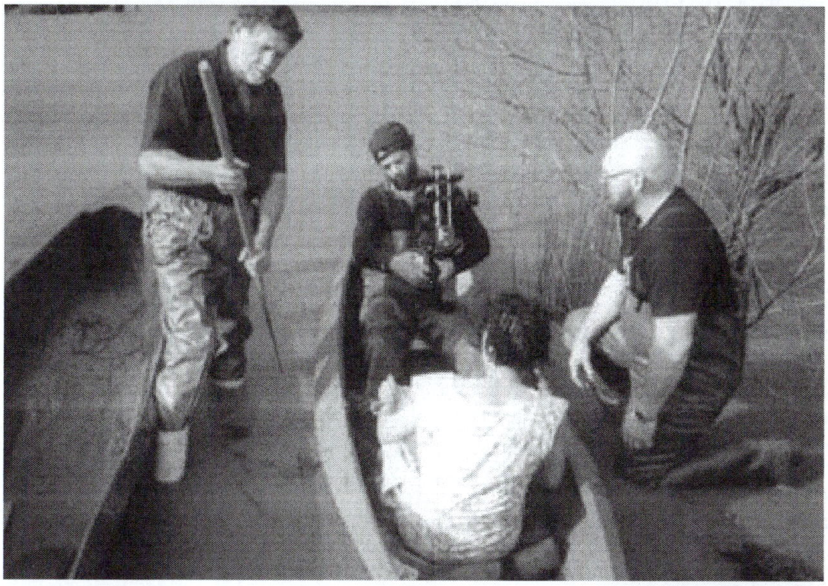

Charmaine Warren (performer), Ronald Gray (cinematographer), and Louisiana crewmembers filming on the bayou. Photo courtesy of Ayoka Chenzira.

Cast members Sondra Loring (left) and Charmaine Warren between takes in the Louisiana cornfields. Photo courtesy of Ayoka Chenzira.

could handle this material with the sensitivity it demanded. And so, oblivious to the irony of a man's feeling that a man is not sensitive enough to deal with a rape scene written by a man, I began my search for just the right African American woman to direct the project. As luck would have it, *The Village Voice* had just published a feature on African American women directors. Armed with the *Voice*'s list and terrified of calling the directors "cold," I nonetheless made those "Hello, I'm a choreographer with absolutely no film experience, but would you like to make a movie with me?" calls. Ultimately I selected Ayoka Chenzira because she had dealt so well with narrative in her prior films.

Our decision to work together made for a tight, overwhelmingly positive collaboration. Many of the nasty "Whose vision is this anyway?" conflicts I thought might emerge when a willful, wonderfully opinionated feminist director worked on a project conceived, written, choreographed, and performed by an equally willful, opinionated gay man, simply didn't happen. I allowed Ayoka into the process of writing the script (she was instrumental in adapting it), and she invited me into the editing process. She chose the shots, I chose the choreography; but everything seemed open to collaboration.

There were two other factors crucial to my having a positive "first film" experience. First, though we agreed to remain faithful to the intention of the original work, from the beginning Ayoka and I decided to use the text and choreography as source material for a film that would stand on its own, rather than document the stage work or simply film it on location. This decision radically expanded our possibilities and destroyed my expectation that the film would be literal to the original choreography.

Second, at this point in my young career, I was not overly concerned with the "composition" of the dance sections of the original mixed-media pieces. Indeed, while having no idea how to solve the problem, I was aware that the haphazard structure of the source dances was a weakness of the stage work. I used an original vocabulary, but I had no idea how to make a coherent dance out of that vocabulary. I welcomed the splicing, editing, shaping, and quick-cutting of the dance segments in *Pull*. I found the editing of a (barely) linear dance into strong, nonlinear fragments liberating. The narrative drove the film, and the dance was intended to illuminate the subtexts in powerful bursts. Lack of choreographic structure, the piece's liability on stage, became an asset in the film.

We faced several challenges in the making of the Alive TV project. We had originally asked for 30 minutes; we were given 11. Artistically, the very idea of adapting what was then four and a half hours of live material into an 11-minute film seemed daunting, and I do think there's a lack of "breath" in the final film. Of necessity, the narrative sometimes moves too quickly for full resonance. The rape scene is the devastating climax to the stage work, and we worried about how to retain its emotional power on film. We decided on a series of extreme close-ups of the dancer's face and body parts; it didn't quite work. Though the film version lacks the full impact of the stage rape scene, to this day I'm not sure how (or even if) I would suggest changing it. Something profoundly moving, that may have been intrinsic to the live emotional journey of the dancer, proved elusive on film.

Film also presented me with a much more complicated production paradigm. With my not-for-profit dance company, we raised money, created the work, and self-produced: a pretty simple paradigm. The only opinions I had to listen to were those I chose to hear. With a complicated hierarchy of executive producers, producers, and collaborators, sometimes it was hard to know to whom I had to be accountable. I also remember not understanding why approval over final cut was such an issue during negotiations, or even why it was under discussion. ("Doesn't the artist"—meaning me—"always have final say in the matter?" Oh, the innocence of youth.) Luckily, Ayoka gave me a quick lesson in the organizational structure of filmmaking. I know there was tension between Ayoka and the producers (whose background was entirely in live theater), but I was left out of the argument. Considering the requirements of filming for television, my experience was quite a positive one.

Pull also raised new issues of ownership for me. Since my live works existed only in performance, there was literally nothing to "own." Suddenly there was the idea of a "product" that could exist without the necessity of my being present to stir it up magically. Although I retained ownership of the original source material, the concept of making a film of my work that I would not ultimately own (the executive producer owned it) seemed strange to my naïve self. I had to get used to the idea that because they'd paid for the "product," they owned it. (Since the completion of the project, even though they own it, Alive TV has been wonderful about allowing us to show it just about anywhere.)

Shooting on location in the swamps of Louisiana presented its own problems. The very notion of our particular group invading the "good ole boy" world of backwoods bayou Louisiana was a challenge in itself. We arrived complete with a gay, hoop-earring-wearing choreographer; a gloriously Amazonian, dreadlocked female director; and a group of mature women performers including a diminutive Jamaican fireball who rarely held her tongue and a wonderfully tattooed lesbian activist. Breaux Bridge, Louisiana, had never seen the likes of us.

I remember eating at Mulate's restaurant, a great Cajun spot with live zydeco music and plenty of "local flava'," on our first night in town. The stares were already intense, so when very pregnant, very white Elise Bernhardt asked very paranoid, very black me to join the all-white, very "local" locals in dancing zydeco, I answered, "I'd rather not get lynched before the first day of the shoot."

I remember putting dancer Charmaine Warren into a barely floating canoe on a slime-filled, moss-hung swamp for that "gotta-have-it" shot that closes the film. As I watched her float away from the camera, I noticed that she was surrounded by a veritable herd of some bizarre animal that looked like a cross between a muskrat and an aquatic pit bull. I remember hoping that they weren't carnivorous, as Charmaine's canoe (quite authentic but quite raggedy on our "you take what you can get" budget) looked like it would sink before the shot was done. One local crewmember was endearingly hell-bent on impressing us with the local history. Just as the camera rolled and the gigantic rodents appeared, he proudly told us, one by one, that the critters might be ugly, but that the queen of England had eaten one on her last trip to the States. ("Bar-becued," I believe he said.) He was so proud of this fact that no one had the heart to say "You know, she also eats haggis—and we'd really just like to get this shot."

As the exquisite light of southern dusk arrived, Ayoka asked me to dance naked on top of a nearby hill. (Another "got-to-have-it" shot.) Unseen from the camera's viewpoint, however, on the other side of the hill, was a highway, with Southern drivers whizzing by toting Southern shotguns in their Southern pick-up trucks. As a native Southerner, I wasn't sure how receptive they'd be to seeing my naked black bottom through their windshields, no matter how magically it glowed in the just-arriving moonlight. We compromised, and I did the shot in a dance belt. I considered this my bravest career moment to date. It didn't make the movie.

Some of my most precious professional memories came from shooting *Pull*. REALITY ultimately formed a strong bond with the local crew, and one of them gave each of us the bleached vertebra of an alligator as a memento. (The tenderness of the gesture outweighed the rather large "yuk!" factor.) Of most importance, having built a career on the retelling of my grandparents' tales, to be re-creating their stories in the swamps and cotton fields of their actual milieu was a profound experience. And telling my grandparents' stories on film seemed a way to ensure that their legacy would endure. The live performances would die whenever I did. The film would go on forever.

Ironically, many of the longer-term benefits of the Alive experience had to do with theater. Unexpectedly, I changed how I compose dances. Having given so much focus to the editing, structure, and composition of the film, I began to invest more time in the formal structuring of my choreography. I began thinking of dances with a beginning, middle, and end that could be edited and shaped into a coherent whole, much like the reel of film I had seen Ayoka splicing. The layering of sound, image, and story became an even larger concern in the crafting of my theater work, after working on the meticulous layering of the expanded possibilities afforded by working in film. Finally, to this day showing the film is an invaluable part of the lecture/demonstrations I give on performance tours. It remains the most accessible and powerful way to introduce REALITY-naïve audiences to our work.

On other fronts, Alive introduced me to Ayoka Chenzira; we have continued to look for ways to translate my choreographic vocabulary to film by collaborating on two other projects. And the fact that more people saw the national broadcasts of *Pull* than have ever seen (or will ever see) my work live cannot be underestimated. Because a big part of my artistic mission is to bring my work to as wide and diverse an audience as possible, film and video represented important new possibilities.

But I suppose the most important benefit from my experience with Alive is that it allowed the impossible to become the possible. I was given the opportunity to experiment in a medium I had always wanted to explore but knew nothing about. Without Alive, I can't imagine this having happened. In the years since, my interest in the medium has grown into a desire also to choreograph from behind the camera. I was invited to the 1997 Sundance Institute's Screenwriter's Lab to pursue the idea of making a feature-length dance film out of the "Creole Series"—a project I still hope to bring to fruition someday, with myself as writer, choreographer, and director. My professional partnership with Joseph V. Melillo (now executive producer at the Brooklyn Academy of Music) has grown into the most important and long-term of my career, and in 1999 I was BAM's first "on-line artist" (www.bam.org/rousseve/index.html). This gave me the opportunity to shoot the creation of REALITY's latest work, *Love Songs*, on digital video for an interactive Web site developed in partnership with BAM's Media Lab. In 1999, I received an Irvine Fellowship in Dance, specifically to develop the skills to translate my choreographic language to film from behind the camera. Indeed, it appears quite possible that film/video may continue to play a larger and larger role for professionally. This process was begun by—and is in large part thanks to—my experience with *Alive from Off Center*.

CHAPTER 45

Seeing It Differently: Restaging The Black Dress *for* Alive from Off Center

Ellen Bromberg

In the late 1980s, I was invited to recreate a stage work for broadcast on *Alive from Off Center*. The program, entitled "Dancing on the Edge," featured three choreographers from the San Francisco Bay area: Margaret Jenkins, Joe Goode, and myself. It was a co-production of KTCA Minneapolis-St. Paul and KQED San Francisco. The producers had solicited videotapes from a number of Bay Area artists and had selected the three works they were most interested in seeing on their program. While all three of the artists' works had been created for the stage, we were told that we must reconceive them for another location. Each work had to be shortened to approximately seven minutes. In addition, and most important, we were to be paired with a director of the producers' choosing. For this project, we were to enter into an arranged marriage of sorts. For me, this marriage represented a challenging collision of cultures, gender stereotypes, and aesthetics.

The Black Dress **by Ellen Bromberg. Dancers (left to right): Lisa McCoughrean, Anne Reeb, Jean Sullivan, Wendy Diamond. Photo by Marty Sohl Photo.**

The work of mine selected by the producers was *The Black Dress*, which was inspired by the painting of the same name by Alex Katz. (In the late 1980s, I had seen Katz's retrospective at the Whitney Museum of American Art.) This larger-than-life-size painting presents multiple images of his wife, Ada, clothed in the stereotypical black dress and black pumps of the 1960s. In a painting within the painting is the partial image of a man peering from above, over the shoulders of these six identical women. Standing before this work, I had a powerful, visceral response. The tension provided by the male gazing from behind these women became a provocative metaphor for what I saw as the objectification of women in contemporary culture, particularly through the media and advertising. As a teenager and young adult, I had stopped watching television and going to feature films because I was so angered by the insulting representation of women in commercial film and media. When I saw Katz's painting, it was as if these women leaped out at me from the canvas, and I was compelled to bring them to life on stage.

When rehearsals began, I realized that I wanted the movement and form of the work to evolve from the real experiences of the dancers' lives. What became apparent was that I needed to create an environment for exploration and discovery, a safe context in which to look at the lives and experiences of the six women in this piece. As if to counteract the uniformity of the individuals in the painting, it became essential to identify the uniqueness of each of these women through her own story. Francie Glycenfer, Julie Kane, Anne Reeb, Wendy Diamond, Lisa McCoughrean, and Jean Sullivan delved into their pasts, and together we discovered the movement language that would speak through this work.

The videotape of the stage performance of the work was given to the director assigned to this project. Gino Tanasescu was a highly skilled Hollywood director with many television programs and sitcoms to his credit. In rehearsal, he brought a keen eye to the three-dimensionality now available through the eye of the camera. We rehearsed long takes of the camera, weaving through the dancers' space, allowing for a much more intimate look at the individual dancers than had previously been possible in the stage work. My first task was to begin shortening the piece. Understanding that screen time moves much more quickly than stage time, I was able to eliminate certain repetitions and thematic developments that would have seemed redundant on screen.

The difficulty arose when trying to place this dance in a real location. Who were these women? What were they going through, and what environment would support the essence of the work?

I had conceived of the work as existing in the void of psychological space. The black stage is a deep canvas, awaiting the stroke of the choreographer to imbue it with meaning and metaphor. In the stage work, designer Jose Maria Francos had created an oversized doorway, faintly visible from behind the dance, with a mysterious light seen through its small opening, as if to allude to the ever-present possibility of departure.

For the video work, we met with director Tanasescu, producer Linda Schaller, and set designer Ken Short and brainstormed to identify a suitable location. Owing to the psychological nature of the piece, it was very difficult for me to imagine a real location in which to place it. However, when Gino suggested that we place the dance in a child's dollhouse, I was taken completely by surprise. This seemed to trivialize the powerful emotions present in the work, and I found myself enraged. While it was clear that he had excellent ideas about how to approach this work as a cinematographer, it seemed to me that he didn't understand its content, or how his suggestion trivialized it. Not only this, but I perceived very little interest on his part in discussing its intent so that we

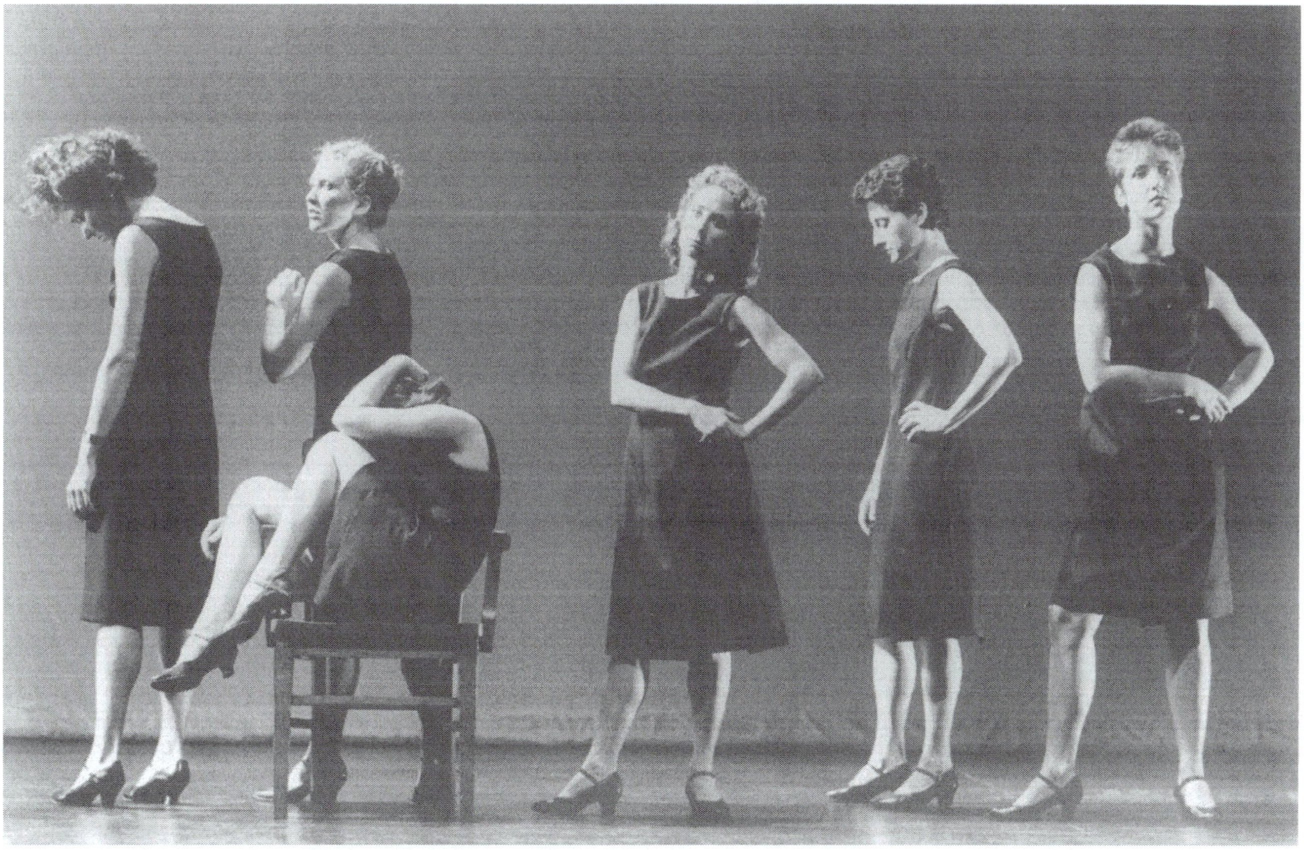

The Black Dress by Ellen Bromberg. Dancers (left to right): Julie Kane, Anne Reeb, Lisa McCoughrean (seated), Wendy Diamond, Ellen Bromberg, Jean Sullivan. Photo by Marty Sohl.

might work together as collaborators. This was disappointing to me, and our ability to communicate grew more and more strained.

Gino continued to storyboard shots, and I continued to shave time off the work without breaking its structure. This aspect of our work together was matter-of-fact and cooperative. But when we tried to have discussions about context, communication would completely break down. While Gino's professional background in Hollywood required that he read a script and make directorial decisions quickly, this approach was not helping to address deeper issues of content.

Finally, at the suggestion of the designer, we began to focus on a location that seemed appropriate. He brought in a model of the set he was envisioning, specific yet abstract enough to hold the work. It was an elegant, surreal room with large draped windows and interesting elements hanging from the walls. It alluded to a gilded cage, and the formal environment created a stark contrast to the often violent choreography.

Throughout this whole process, I was torn because, while I was encountering such difficulties, I was also tremendously honored to have this opportunity. I was a young artist who, within the field of modern dance, had always presented my work on a shoestring. Never before had I experienced so many people involved with helping to realize something of my own making.

I liked Ken's ideas and felt that we could proceed. The final blow for me came when Gino wanted to shoot a very large close-up of his eye and superimpose it behind one of the windows, as if he were voyeuristically watching the miniaturized women throughout the whole piece. This suggestion triggered a lot of anger for me; I realized that, ironically, I was directly experiencing the issues being addressed in the work itself—the objectification and dismissal of women. I met with resistance when I tried to explain why this was unacceptable, and at that point I felt that my only choice was to pull out of the program. Although I was torn about giving up this wonderful opportunity, I did not want to present a work that so blatantly contradicted my intent.

I contacted the producer to let her know my position. She very skillfully encouraged me to reconsider, saying that she would speak to the director about our difficulties. Subsequent meetings were strained, but we were able to proceed. The shoot itself was quite tense between Gino and myself as well, but in spite of this, I found the entire experience of production incredibly exciting.

With the footage shot and Gino back in Los Angeles, I began the editing process with editor Wendy Blair Slick. For me this was a great opportunity to understand editing as the second choreographic phase of translating a work to video or film. Both dance and media exist in time, and, as meaning accumulates through a succession of images, one can essentially remake the work in the editing suite. The choreographic and spatial elements become pigment on a palette with which to paint a new picture. I found this process extremely exciting and revelatory, and Wendy and I felt that we regained control of the ultimate statement of the piece.

Throughout this process, I was able to appreciate Gino's eye for capturing movement and his ability to reconceive the work for the screen's frame as opposed to the proscenium's frame. Because of his skills, Wendy and I had much to work with in the editing process. But the content and meaning of the work finally rested with us, which is where it ultimately belonged. And though Gino and I were forced into an arranged marriage of sorts, with the assistance of our producer we were able to complete the film.

Art is an artifact of the perceptions and gestures of our lives, and dance that has been preserved or reconceived on film or video allows for a more extended gesture in time. It captures the points of view of its makers and reflects the time and place from which life was seen.

I am grateful to have had the opportunity to create a work that crystallizes a point of view from the time and place in which it was made. Although the work produced and presented by *Alive from Off Center* is not the work as it was seen in the theater, it does capture something essentially true about the issues it was addressing.

Part of the beauty and poignancy of live dance performance is its ephemeral nature. Inherent in the very instant of a gesture is its loss, as if it embodies our own temporality. Though film or video can never replace the live experience, these media offer us more lasting images, thereby extending those gestures through time. The camera is a tool that magnifies and reveals the human and corporeal. Like the amplification of an acoustic instrument, it makes available certain pitches and timbres that might fall below the level of perception in a theatrical performance of dance. The increased scale of close-up shots and the limitless variety of camera angles reveal different facets of a choreographer's unique movement language, and they augment nuance in gesture and facial expression often not visible to the audience.

Choreographic structure can be redefined through the language of film and video. By utilizing a variety of editing techniques, kinesthetic communication that was once the purview of live performance can be re-presented and created anew in this hybrid form. The camera's eye has infinite potential to present, magnify, and intensify both the simplicity and complexity of human movement and its contexts, and, as such, expand a choreographer's palette of expression.

A work of art can be seen as an artifact of a process, a mark that endures as the result of a gesture. Live dance, the most ephemeral of art forms, is itself the gesture, and its enduring mark is left upon our memories. As the movements of dancer and dance are inscribed in film or video, that inscription becomes the artifact that endures over time. And by this process, as choreographers, dancers and film makers, future generations will have access to the marks we have made.—E. B.

Part VII
Frames and Interpretations

CHAPTER 46

The Camera as Choreographer in Documentary and Ethnographic Film

John Bishop

DVD 37
New England Dances (1990)
28 min 20 sec
Excerpt 3 min 56 sec

Production Note: "I made this film over several years, between 1986 and 1989, when I lived in Boston. I had made a film about virtuoso fiddlers who distilled the whole tradition into their artistry and wanted to show the complementary side, expression of the same tradition diffused through a community. It was shot in 16mm film with a traditional Aaton and Nagra."—J. B.

Many dance artists are suspicious of the camera. They expect a polite and restrained instrument that won't interfere with the "real" audience. But the camera is a great audience! It pays closer attention than anyone in a theater seat. It questions, it seeks, and it doesn't blink. Its position and movement shape and warp the universe that will be perceived on the screen. Like a choreographer, the camera defines a space, places subjects in the space, and moves them through that space. The angle of the camera emphasizes some people, movements, and expressions more than others. There are conventions of good camera work, but the results are best when the operator goes beyond skill and feels what is happening. Dance is often about the artist's expression; film and video are entirely about audience empathy, mediated by the filmmaker.

As a documentary filmmaker, I feel that "documentary" is a misnomer. To document suggests mechanical objectivity, an uncaring witness, an abjuration of the filmmaker's craft. Reality-based film, itself an art, requires acuity of observation and rigorous storytelling. Most film and television create synthetic realities out of fictions. The documentary captures actual people and events and tries to represent them in their own terms. It tries to be true. It is an exercise in epistemology, the articulate quest for what is true in a world that is largely illusion, presented in a medium of smoke and mirrors.

A good ethnographic film considers the whole culture. Even when you look at a specific activity, you set it within the social context. Since most music and dance are made within an ethnic community, an affinity group, or a professional company (and often combinations of these), the whole-culture model is particularly appropriate. Matthew Diamond's *Dancemaker*, for example, portrays the functioning of a dance company as much as it focuses on Paul Taylor and the performance of his work. The preparation, training, and community and social support of the dance company's culture make the performative moment possible. The subtext informs the film. But intention is a lot easier than action.

DVD 33

Few stresses compare to starting a documentary shoot. Conceptualizing, pitching, and planning a film are very cerebral compared to confronting your subject with a camera. Imagine Port of Spain, Trinidad, the day I arrived to shoot *Hosay Trinidad*, a film about an Islamic religious observance. Preparing to be director, camera person, and eventually editor, I'd read about the ritual, seen videotape from the previous year, and talked with my collaborators: the eminent Islamic scholar Peter Chelkowski, who brought a global historical perspective; folklorist Frank Korom, sensitive to the individual personalities and social matrix through which the event became a reality; and two experienced documentary crew members, Guha Shankar and John Terry. But Port of Spain didn't feel, smell, or sound the way I expected. There was no obvious place to start.

There *was* an obvious conclusion, a triumphant performance of drumming and parading the elaborate representations of Hussein's tomb that had been built in the preceding 40 days. The building of these *hosay* provided an obvious story arc. The film, however, had to explain the event in a larger sense— what it meant historically, religiously, and personally to the people participating. We weren't sure how to do that.

There was no apparent connection between the story my collaborators had woven and the imagery that surrounded me. Yet, in the next few days, I had to shoulder my camera and start making a film. What ensued was a marathon conversation among the crew. We were an outside eye and sensibility trying to make sense of the overall experience. A parallel conversation went on between us and consultants and friends who were inside the tradition. We visited, hung out, and drove around, the camera always at the ready, seeking the telling moments, characters, and activities that would allow us to unveil the story. Our subjects told us how it would be, what to expect, what was going right, and what was going wrong. (Sometimes they questioned us, asking our outside perspective on how their observance related to those in other parts of Islam.) As the days stretched into weeks, this inside/outside dialectic gave us a clearer idea of what we were participating in and resolved our ideas about what the film could be.

When the lab sent a report on the first footage, they said, "Looks great, but why are these people building a mosque in a garage?" That's when I knew we were on the right track; that was the question the film had to answer. Our concept crystallized one afternoon when we went to talk, on camera, with Albert

John Bishop enjoying tea with friends while shooting in Nepal. Photo by Media Generation, Naomi Bishop.

and Faroza Dookwah to clarify a few technical and historic points about the construction of the *hosay*. With tears in their eyes, they conveyed that this ritual embodied every aspect of their lives. The eloquence of their expressions, their deep feelings, conveyed more power than their words. At that moment, we realized more profoundly what we were filming, and we acquired a scene that could convey it. The form and the content merged.

My current project on Cambodian classical dance presented a different cluster of social and production challenges. My collaborators, Sam-Ang Sam and Chan Moly Sam, belong to the culture and participate in its politics. They make media productions for the dance community in both Cambodia and America, and my assignment is to be true to that tradition and add production value without crossing the grain of its aesthetic. In Phnom Penh, we filmed dances in a variety of contexts, some in full costume and some in the simpler but equally elegant practice attire. We set the dances in significant spaces: the palace pavilion, the University of Fine Arts, the National Theater where the court dance was first presented to the general public, and a temple whose stone carvings represent similar dancers from centuries before. By varying the locations, we subliminally suggested that the dance was part of Cambodia's cultural landscape. In contrast, we shot the American dancers in a studio setting, which emphasized that for Cambodian Americans, classical dance occupies a separate, nonintegral space in their lives. The tension between the dance experience in Cambodia and in the United States drives the film.

The stratification of Cambodian society made casual interviewing more problematic than in a hang-loose society like Trinidad. Rather than grabbing interviews opportunistically, we approached the elders and dance masters first and did not talk with the younger dancers until those protocols had been satisfied. The arc of Khmer speech, moreover, embodies a formality that does not yield the sound bites upon which Western documentaries are built. The film's emerging style reflects this considered, honorific approach to answering questions, in which the substance of statement cannot be separated from opening and closing. The style of the dance, and the style of the society, demanded a dif-

John Bishop on location in Nepal. Photo by Media Generation, Naomi Bishop.

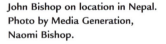

ferent approach to film and editing than I was able to use in Trinidad. Articulating those distinctions requires more sensitivity and effort than the mechanics of filmmaking.

We communicate by telling stories. Narrative is implicit in image-making. But merely seeing something doesn't allow you to transmit any of the insight, or even the facts. We remember things through the stories we tell about them. For filmmakers, narrative is critical in two areas: shooting the material, and editing the footage. If you haven't got it on film, it didn't happen, as far as the audience is concerned. And if you don't edit the raw material into a structure that can communicate, they won't get it.

Although filming is very accurate, it is not objective. It's like having a conversation, dancing a duet, or providing musical accompaniment; it is a kind of romance. What ends up on tape is what actually happened: the chemistry of the moment. The period of shooting has an arc, a start and a finish, and the experience leaves more than memories and feelings. The footage, ideally, holds many stories, many moments of insight and passion, compelling images and the capacity to evoke the sense of what happened, but few people can make sense of raw footage. Doing that requires an explicit narrative to bring out the story implicit in the coverage. The editor writes the story.

I love to shoot—it is joyous and exhilarating—but I approach editing with dread. Editing is a passion, the crowning-of-thorns, scourging-at-the-pillar, redemption-of-humankind sort of biblical Passion. As with dance, there is a measure of masochism and discipline, and the results appear effortless. Most viewers do not perceive that a film has been edited.

A well-constructed movie has an unassailable logic. The time in which the events were recorded is synthesized into the rhythm of that logic. Sound bites appear to be conversations, locations shift naturally, relevant images materialize to illustrate what is being said. Editing discovers the story in the footage and tells it in a way that will be comprehensible to a viewer.

Neither a written account nor a performance, film has its own rules of syntax, its own demands, and its own organization of concepts and impressions. It takes ideas from the written and cognitive, and physical impressions and emotions from the performative, and reprocesses them into its own kind of experience. In Judy Mitoma's *World Festival of Sacred Music* video, released in 2000 by Catchlight Films, individual filmmakers were given the unconventional credit "as seen by," acknowledging the media person's role in perceiving and reshaping the historical experience into a repeatable one.

The challenge to a television or series producer is to find forms, formats, and story structures that can be filled with varied content. The subject fits the show; the audience gets novelty within a familiar paradigm. The commercial production model, overseen by a writer/producer, distributes tasks to specialists. The independent filmmaker, particularly in the American tradition, is often a lone wolf, acting as her own producer, cinematographer, and editor. This model describes most people who make dance documentaries and ethnographic films. Their challenge is often to discover, while editing, a form that is harmonious with the content. It is bit like doing a diagramless crossword puzzle.

I began making films with my wife, who was studying animal behavior. Nonhuman primates can't explain what they are doing, so we abstracted information from what we recorded. Like most filmmakers, I believe that there is a high level of veracity in the recorded image. There is more truth in dance and interaction than in interview or demonstration. In the mid-1960s, people like

Ray Birdwhistell undertook micro-analysis of filmed human interaction to parse the invisible and unconscious parts of social communication. Alan Lomax's Choreometrics project took this inquiry to a macro level in what has been the most ambitious and extensive use of a cross-cultural film sample to date.

Lomax postulated that dance had deep cultural resonance at a different level than what the narrative of the dance purported to be or what people said about it—that significant parts of a society were encoded in the way people danced. His team developed a set of easily perceived parameters to "measure" dance on film for any culture. They looked at which body parts are used and how. They noted the synchronicity or lack of it between dancers, and the social organization of the group. They ascertained whether men and women dance at the same time, together or separately, and if they do the same things.

Lomax was looking for a language of movement that did not depend on the expertise of the dancer and was not easily altered by the cultural bias of the cameraperson. By describing dance styles as profiles of these parameters, he developed a lexicon that could compare movement across cultures. He and his associates concluded that movement style was largely consistent within a culture group, and that there were specific clusters of traits that distinguished culture areas from one another. His profiles help explain why you would never mistake an Australian aborigine dance for a sub-Saharan African one, or confuse a Polynesian dance with one of the Inuit.

Lomax profoundly affected ethnographic film. As a connoisseur of camerawork, he raged against the trivialization of cultural images, and he believed there was data in the images more important than what an entertainment-based industry made of them. In his quest for footage between 1960 and 1975, he came to know all the world's ethnographic filmmakers, the 50 or so people who created the genre. He badgered them to attend to the phrasing of speech, song, and dance, and to the spatial deployment of people; he was part of the conversation that defined the genre of ethnographic film. He charged every ethnographic filmmaker to shoot a long, full-body, full-group piece of dance, so that it could be incorporated into and refine his world sample. This didn't happen, but filmmakers acquired a new respect for music and dance and began using it as a foundation for their work. (For more on Lomax, see chapter 25)

John Marshall's 1971 *Bitter Melons*, about the Khwe San in Botswana, is a notable example. Subsequent to his contact with Choreometrics, Marshall structured this 20-minute film around *ju hoasi* songs and dancing games, taking the pace and feel from them and juxtaposing them with similar rhythms and
DVD 37 movements in vignettes of Kalahari life. When I filmed *New England Fiddles* and *New England Dances*, I was dealing with people who valued pithy statements, cyclical dances and dance music, and virtuoso solos on the fiddle and in step dancing. Even though this was culturally familiar, it took many weeks to find an editing style that worked with their music and dance and felt like they were telling the story. A film on Cambodian dance, which I am cutting now, has an entirely different envelope; the music, movement, and speech follow a different pace and arc. It requires a measure of humility to attend to what other people are doing, instead of what you could do.

Documentary and ethnographic filmmakers may seem like handmaidens to other realities, but caught in the vortex of the passing moment, they snatch what shards they can, and like the Angel of History, forever looking back while being blown forward in time, they bring a refraction of what's past into the present. They create a memory that we can examine.

CHAPTER 47

Basing a Dance Film on India's Cultural Heritage

Robert Gottlieb

In 1983, I produced and directed *Circles—Cycles Kathak Dance*, a 28-minute color film shot in New Delhi while I was a research fellow with the American Institute of Indian Studies. Kathak, a classical dance form of North India, traces its origins back more than a thousand years. It is the only Indian dance form that combines influences of both Hindu and Islamic cultures. During the eighteenth and nineteenth centuries, kathak rose to prominence by being lavishly cultivated in the royal courts of the nawabs and maharajas. The subject matter of the kathak repertoire ranges from simple themes relating to village life to sublime experiences having to do with the Hindu deities. This repertoire also includes elements of "pure dance," which is concerned with matters of rhythmic discipline. The central theme underlying the film, like so much of India's religious and cultural thinking, focuses on the concepts of circles and cycles and how these symbols are expressed in dance, as well as in music and poetry.

A departure from "pure dance" is the *abhinaya* section of the film, performed by Birju Maharaj, one of today's leading exponents of kathak. Here the emphasis is on the performer's interpretation of poetry that is being sung. According to court tradition, the dancer, in a seated position, improvises interpretations of the text to show different meanings and experiences based on a central theme of clouds, which reoccurs again and again.

Prior to this project, my research in India was concerned primarily with the study of tabla drumming. Part of this work involved photographing miniature paintings that show how tabla was performed in the previous centuries. Many of these paintings depict tabla players accompanying kathak dancers. This led me to a fuller awareness of how kathak influenced tabla practices, especially in the repertoires of the Lucknow, Delhi, and Benares players. Thus, it was not too much of a shift for me to contemplate a project on kathak. My research on tabla had brought me into contact with kathak dancers and scholars in addition to those who later participated in the filming. Prabha Marathe, head of the Kala Chhaya Dance Institute in Pune, first suggested to me the idea of producing a film, as she felt the kathak tradition had not been well documented.

In the early 1980s, filming in 16mm was widespread in India and video had not yet come into general use, so from the start I thought only of using film. I

DVD 38
Circles–Cycles Kathak Dance
(1988) 27 min 34 sec
Excerpt 3 min 50 sec

Production Note: "This production was filmed entirely in 16mm using two cameras—one for long shots, the other for close-ups. Budget restraints imposed the restriction of film/productions to a ratio of 6:1."—R. G.

Robert Gottlieb discussing set-up and lighting arrangements with cameraman Rajiv Mehotra and Satish Pande. Photo by Lois Gottlieb.

Before starting her dance, Shaswati Sen is asking for the Divine's blessing. In India, dance is regarded as an act of devotion to the gods. Photo by Lois Gottlieb.

felt confident that this would be a fitting project because I already knew many of the prominent dancers and was sure that the work would be facilitated by my prior experience with photography and the research I had done on tabla. From the beginning, I had the idea of using miniature paintings, juxtaposing them with the filmed dance poses to show how traditions were being retained. I was convinced this would contribute to the film's aesthetic appeal, as well as providing historical perspective. All the filming was done in India, using two cameras—one for long shots, the other for close-ups. An exception is the scene where Krishna's consort, Radha, looks at her image reflected in a pool. This scene, also expressing the symbolism of circles, was filmed at the residence of Kishan Rana, who at the time was the Consul General of India in San Francisco. All subsequent editing was done on Beta-Cam. From this a master one-inch videotape was made, from which a transfer to 16mm was produced.

Eva Soltes, editor and associate producer for this film, is not only a professional filmmaker but has also studied Indian dance in India. With her dedicated help, I was able to realize many of the aesthetic concepts I had envisioned. The sensitively executed narration of Zakir Hussain further contributed to the overall Indian ambience. My wife Lois, an architect, also deserves much credit. She handled all business matters, contributed some of her color slides, and helped with the editing. She kept meticulous notes and records of all timings as well as seeing to the preparation and layout of the storyboard.

The film has been aired on public television, sold to many universities, and is currently available from Documentary Educational Resources, 101 Morse Street, Watertown, MA 02472.

CHAPTER 48

About the Making of Circles–Cycles Kathak Dance

Eva Soltes

Ancient storytelling dances of India have mesmerized me since I first encountered them. I pursued this art form from an early age as a student of the legendary south Indian dancer T. Balasarawati (Bala), who had the astonishing ability to soulfully interpret ancient songs and poems by summoning characters of Hindu mythology from deep within herself. When I was presented with film of Birju Maharaj performing, I recognized some of this quality in his *abhinaya*, or storytelling—musicality, depth of expression, and playfulness—which reminded me of Bala. I knew enough to realize that very few living artists have been able to master this highly refined aspect of classical Indian dance.

DVD 38
Circles–Cycles Kathak Dance
(1988) 27 min 34 sec
Excerpt 3 min 50 sec

"This production was filmed entirely in 16mm using two cameras—one for long shots, the other for close-ups. Budget restraints imposed the restriction of film / productions to a ratio of 6:1."—Robert Gottlieb

I have faith in the ability of recorded media to transmit the essence of an art. I first encountered Bala through hearing a recording of her singing. She was several continents away, and her message reached me loud and clear. Classical Indian dance, like film, is a storytelling medium. It especially lends itself to this contemporary form because of its intimate quality and subtle use of facial expression. Intended to be experienced live by relatively small audiences, it can be successfully recorded by multiple cameras with close-ups, which make possible and even amplify the intimacy of the viewing experience.

I approach filmmaking much as I do choreographing dance. The tools available include moving and still images, music, sound, lighting, and words. I aspire to bring to the editing room a flow of movement, dramatic timing, poetry, and musicality, as I do in dance.

There are differences, though. Film is less tolerant of flaws than live performance. In film it can be more difficult to preserve the feeling of flow and spontaneity. Only the most brilliant of performances will stand the test of repeated viewing over time.

My introduction to the dance footage that was the heart of the film *Circles–Cycles Kathak Dance* came over the telephone from a good friend, a sound engineer. "I'm sending my client, Dr. Robert Gottlieb, to you because he's trying to make a film about Indian dance. I just synched the sound and the dancing doesn't look too impressive—but I hope you get a few hours of consulting out of it!"

DVD 38

Soon after, I watched the footage, which had been filmed in a studio in

India. The first few minutes of viewing gave me the impression that the dancing had a jarring quality. I soon realized that this was caused by a technical problem. Had I not spent years as a student of classical Indian dance, I might not have understood the dire necessity to move precisely with the music. I may have missed the fact that the sound and the picture began in synch but gradually drifted apart. This produced a very irritating effect: the high pitch of the ankle bells competed with the rapid footwork. (Any dancer who intends to be on the beat, and isn't, looks "off.")

Taking note of the sound synch problem, I continued to review the footage and became increasingly excited by it. Gottlieb had assembled some of India's finest dancers in the ancient North Indian classical dance tradition of kathak. He had managed to film them in 16mm with two cameras in a "black box" theatrical setting. Not only was the "pure dance" exciting, but he'd captured the subtle facial gestures of the storytelling with close-ups. The beauty of both the dancing and the filming came through.

Artists like Bala and Birju Maharaj are treasures. Film and video give us the ability to include them in the artistic legacy of our time—an honor that has, until recently, been reserved for architects, painters, sculptors, and writers, whose works exist in relatively permanent form. Even composers get repeated hearings. My passion to complete a film of this complexity was ignited.

I was fascinated by the entire array of dance performances the film presented. Four of the five dancers performed multiple solo numbers for the camera. It took repeated viewing in my studio, which I did alone late into the night, to decide whose performance moved me most deeply, over time, and should be cut into the final program.

Then came the creative, intellectual, and spiritual task of remaining true to the sacred aspect of the dance while representing it through a contemporary medium. One of my biggest challenges, which I had considered for many years previously, was how to present this complex music-theater-dance form in a way that would not interrupt its intent and flow, while at the same time making it accessible to new audiences.

My admiration for this ancient historical art—which informs us of life in the eighteenth- and nineteenth-century North Indian courts—made me attempt to conquer the technical problems. The footage largely had to be synched by eye; some was scratched in transfers or had gaps in filming. With these dance pieces, a historical context or "the story of the dance form" had to be created. Incorporating still images of miniature paintings that related to the dance was one way to demystify it. They also provided a way to cover up bad parts of the filming and a place to resynch the sound in order to continue with the dance. Split-second timing of spoken narration or placement of subtitles made a big difference in the viewer's comprehension. I always strive to make programs that are accessible and of interest to people from all levels of experience.

The key to my collaboration with Robert and Lois Gottlieb was a shared respect for Indian culture. Fortunately, Lois had a fine collection of photos she had taken of historical palaces and temples during years of living in India. These established the settings and gave authenticity to the story. Although they had never made a film before, the Gottliebs were willing to help with whatever was needed. I set a post-production schedule based on the long hours and fast pace of a BBC crew I was fresh from working with. The Gottliebs were indefatigable!

Some people think dance must be experienced live and that it cannot truly be appreciated on video or film. When it comes from the hearts and minds of artists who understand the subject matter, I believe it can. Often the most beautiful and spiritual of dance forms go largely unappreciated and unsupported because they don't present themselves commercially. I feel it is important to document the work of these great underappreciated dancers of our time, for people to partake of now and in the future. I hope that *Circles–Cycles* and other films like it will give viewers access to some of the well-guarded secrets of the creative, spiritual, and nonmaterialistic landscape of our world.

Bala was recently deceased at the time I was working on *Circles–Cycles.* She was in my thoughts throughout the making of it. Through her, I realized that with hard work it is possible to cross over culturally and develop a deep kinship with a tradition you are not born into. I dedicate my part in this film to her.

BRINGING WORLD DANCE TO THE CLASSROOM

I first saw American modern dance in the gymnasium of my high school. Every year, our gym teacher dutifully hauled out the 16mm projector to screen Martha Graham's *A Dancer's World*. Sitting on the wooden floor, I witnessed an entirely new way of thinking about dance. Coming from a working-class Los Angeles suburb, I had never been to a theater or seen a live performance, and I had never heard of Martha Graham. I remember thinking that the film was as much a mystery as it was a revelation. Little did I know that we were viewing one of the most important film documents ever made of Martha Graham, one that continues to hold my interest to this day.

Later, while an undergraduate at UCLA, I had the privilege of studying with Allegra Fuller Snyder, one of the first dance ethnologists in this country. At this time in the late 1960s, ethnographic work in dance was a fledgling field. As an accomplished filmmaker herself, Allegra understood the power of film as a research and teaching tool. For hours and hours, we pored over documents of dance from Sri Lanka, Nigeria, Japan, and a host of other cultures. I had never traveled outside California; the ethnographic films Allegra painstakingly selected launched my journey into the world of dance and the world of film/video.

—Judy Mitoma

CHAPTER 49

Ancestral Memory

Mark Eby

DVD 39
Nursed in Pele (2001) 7 min
Excerpt 3 min

Production Note: "This documentary is shot primarily on Beta SP. A two-camera shoot was used for one rehearsal sequence. Because of union regulations, we could not shoot the performance, so the narrative was constructed to climax at the "Pule" (ritual prayer) backstage before the performance."—M. E.

I have a memory. I keep it well hidden . . . tucked away in the folds of neglect that shroud the daily rituals of work and play and sex. It gnaws at the edge of my dream like a hungry shark as I swim in aqua-blue sleep—forcing me to bob abruptly to the surface like a deep-sea diver who suddenly runs out of oxygen—even though this action could force small bubbles of air into my bloodstream that will slowly make their way to my brain and end my life with a stab of concentrated pain. I open my eyes in the dark and my body is covered in sweat. This is the way memories make themselves remembered.

If I could take my memory and shed a little light on it, mold several bodies from clay and prop them in the corner, breathe life into them and teach them how to dance, I could begin to capture their movement frame by frame at 30 frames a second, and soon my memory would be made flesh. If the bodies developed a will of their own, I would interview them and call it a documentary—a memory recreated. Would I still open my eyes in the dark, covered with sweat, trying to remember—or trying to forget?

"Ancestral memory" was a term used by Pualani Kanakaole in a conversation at the UCLA National Dance/Media Leadership Conference in February of 1999. Pualani is from a leading Hawaiian family in the performance of an ancient *kahiko* style that has been passed down to successive generations in a long line of transference. She wasn't referring to a personal memory, the memories of childhood that we collect and order on a shelf in a closet reserved for that purpose. She was talking about memory that is embodied in rhythm and chant and movement and that creates a very specific response in the body of the performers and the community to which it is offered.

Many of my strongest personal memories involve the observance of embodied ancestral memory in New Guinea Highlands ceremonies. Since they are the memories of a child, many are the product of a childish curiosity or the startled fear of witnessing something for the first time. The first few years of any child's life are full of these moments—an alien being observing the strange practices of what soon becomes familiar and unremarkable.

I remember the excitement in the air as hundreds of people gathered: the ear-shattering squeals and horrified screams of huge, black, fattened pigs as

Mamalka men preparing for a *Moka* ceremony. Tuman River, Western Highlands, Papua New Guinea. Photo by Mark Eby, 1995.

they were clubbed to death, their skulls crushed by large wooden stakes; the smell of burnt pork flesh as the hair was singed off and the bloody carcasses sliced and prepared for the large earth ovens; the explosion of rocks that couldn't take the high temperature in the large bonfires that were created to heat the stones for the earth ovens; the overwhelming smoke that hung over the ceremonial ground and made you rub your eyes red.

I remember a bride price ceremony where the bride, a young girl who had been my part-time babysitter, was dressed in her finest regalia: long bird of paradise feathers, woven bark-string apron, perfumed leaves crushed into tight arm bracelets, skin oiled, and powdered. She was suddenly picked up by two of her cousins and rushed across the ceremonial grounds in a flurry of rustling feathers and leaves to her new husband's people, while they let out a piercing wail. As a child, I found the cry unexpected and startling—my babysitter did not seem happy and the wail made me tremble.

I remember courting couples at the New Year's Day fete who, again in all their regalia, painted faces, and oiled skin, would sit at the edge of the festivities in long lines, couples with their legs entwined, rubbing red-painted noses and singing songs in unison, a subtle nod of the head producing a not-so-subtle shake of their feathers in birdlike fashion.

I remember the funeral of the Ontekeleka warrior who had been killed in battle, the wailing of the women and men covered in yellow mud, yanking tufts

A dancer representing Mt. Hagen in the Mt. Hagen Cultural Show, Western Highlands Province, Papua New Guinea. Photo by Mark Eby, 1995.

of hair out of their scalps and beards as they sat massed around the coffin on a raised platform. I remember how another group of men, all brandishing spears, swept out of the coffee grove and, humming like angry hornets, circled the ceremonial grounds, stamping the earth, rushing forward and then slowing to a jog, shouting for revenge.

I remember that same tribe, years later, finally making peace with its neighbors: hundreds of warriors in their feather regalia, ceremoniously breaking their arrows in half, hundreds of men moving and singing in synchronization, performing peace on a former battlefield where they had ritualized the enforcement of environmental justice and searched to create balance in the dispute over land and the loss of life. I sat on my friend's shoulders and looked out on an ocean of feathers and men covered in black soot.

My uncle pointed to the queer little hill that pointed out of the small riverplain, like a wayward island on the edge of that ocean of feathers, and explained that it was the local Garden of Eden. "That is the origin place of the first man and woman," he said. And who was I to argue?

I have recounted these memories for a reason. It is a political act, as personal as it may appear. The reason I make films about bodies that swirl in the mist, and shuffle in the dark, and sway in long parallel lines in the midday sun—bodies that circle and step to the beat of the drum and the *ipu* and the shake of the rattle, voices that cry out in ancient song to the rhythm of the heart pumping—the reason I re-create these performances frame by frame is that they invoke a spirit rarely remembered by the world that now wraps its arms tighter and tighter around me, a world that is becoming networked and codified through the tentacles of its own digital technology. A world where bodies sit rigidly transfixed by a glowing screen, only the fingers performing a rapid tap dance on the attached keyboard, as they practice contemporary art and communication that requires no bodily contact, no presence. It encourages the proliferation of an anonymous community of rigid bodies staring at the glowing screen, all invisibly connected but strangely detached from each other.

Ancestral memories are rarely seen or heard, and their language rarely understood, in our contemporary world of transfixed bodies. It is a political act to take these performances and use digital technology to give them a voice, because it forces people to remember things they would prefer to forget, a powerful way of moving and singing and being present in community, an ancestral memory.

CHAPTER 50

When My Hair Was Brown: The Making of a Dance Documentary

Sally Sommer

Check Your Body at the Door, an hour-long documentary, focuses on some extraordinary underground club dances and dancers in New York City in the 1990s, and on the elusive, artful world of club dancing. The year 2000 marked the conclusion of eight years of filming and editing on this broadcast-quality video. One reason for making the video was to redress a gap in dance documentation: no good visual records of American social dance exist (except for Mura Dehn's classic *The Spirit Moves*). Although there may be "club dance" scenes in American feature films, I have never found any of them useful in terms of revealing what is really going on in the dancing.

Why has it taken so long to complete this film? Because the funding came in small chunks that were used up immediately for production expenses. Consequently, the production work proceeded in fits and starts. As of late 2000, I was still pursuing the last $50,000 to cover post-production online editing, clearance costs, the sound mix (and maybe even a new sound score), color corrections, research for rights permissions, and payment for video-to-film transfer so *Check Your Body* can be entered in film festivals.

I take solace from the fact that Leon Gast took 20 years to finish his Oscar-winning documentary on Mohammed Ali, *When We Were Kings*. He didn't get paid for 19 years. I will never get paid, or reimbursed for the $18,000 of my own cash I've put into the production. And I won't get an Oscar. In order to keep the project afloat, I also had to supply an office, a computer, telephones, and an assistant. Obviously, I was more driven to complete the documentary than to get paid. I'm still not bored looking at the material.

Social dance is not as easy to fund as a nice piece of modern dance or ballet choreography, which is easier to shoot and easier to edit. Television producers are reassured by a well-known dance product. Selling the unknown social dance with unknown dancers—and worse, multiracial "club" dancers who are always "drug suspects" in the eyes of the mainstream—is a formidable task, and I have not conquered it. The nature of the dancing is chaotic, not beautiful and organized, and all of that spells disaster to funders.

Although club dancing takes place in the "invisible," anonymous spaces of the underground club world, the dancing, extraordinary in its own right, has

Archie Burnett, club dancer, in *Check Your Body at the Door*. Photo by Andrew Eccles.

enormous influence on stage dance and mainstream popular dance forms around the globe. Yet its innovators remain unrecognized. The main reason for doing *Check Your Body at the Door* was to capture something of their extraordinary dancing and their imagination, and to show something about their lives.

Most of the dancers who move in this brilliant subculture are young to middle-aged African Americans, Latino Americans, and Asians. Then there's me—white-haired, white-skinned, definitely a lot older than they are. I'm frequently asked, "So how did you (old white woman) get involved in this?" The question goes directly to the heart of the matter: Do you, as the one in primary control, have the right to document this world; do you have the connections, credentials, and validity within the club world you are documenting? Aren't you just a tourist (or worse, a colonialist)?

The extreme implications of these queries reflect the questioners' mandate for cultural purism, and not coincidentally, I hear them only from academics at scholarly conferences: "If it isn't your world, your culture, don't touch it!" I don't buy it. Cultural purism doesn't exist. When the issue is raised in nonacademic settings, what people usually mean is, "Aren't you just dropping in on this world, skimming its surface, taking a few photos?" If the dancers are present when the question arises, they have an answer. Coming from them, the answer has the veracity and perspective of the Other, the Subject. As Archie Burnett, the main guide and "griot" in the film, says: "She's put in her club time. Believe me." There are multiple connotations in his reply, but he's mainly saying the club is not a monolithic culture but cosmopolitan, open to all who want to appreciate it.

In 1976, when I started writing about club dancing, my hair was brown. I still go to clubs, usually alone, between midnight and 6 a.m. (the peak times are between 2 and 4 a.m.). I set the alarm and take a nap, or wait for a dancer to phone: "Come now! It's slammin'!" No matter where, no matter what time, I've never had any problems—probably because I'm so odd that no one would mess with me. I don't fit in. I don't try. I stand out like a sore thumb. I just watch and, if asked, I'm blunt about what I'm doing and why. The years count; I've proved—with physical presence—my commitment and serious intentions. I am a familiar, if peculiar, figure in a specific club world, and those who know me clue in those who do not. Over the years I've earned the moniker "Mama," in every sense of the word.

In the film, I follow a group of about 35 deeply dedicated club dancers (a/k/a "clubheads") and go only to the underground spots where they dance. Clubs function as safe havens, and the community of dancers becomes a kind of temporary protective circle, a family that buffers and momentarily obliterates the harshness of life on the outside. Several of the participants in *Check Your Body* I have known for at least 10 years. I met Archie Burnett in 1982. These dancers are the Baryshnikovs of the social dance world. I would never have presumed to do this documentary without them, or before I "had put in my time" going to clubs.

If I had known it would take so long, I never would have started. But no first-time documentary would be started if the producers were sensible. Making a documentary is not about being sensible. It's about being obsessed. The first shoot of this film took place in 1992 at a club around 2 a.m., and the final rough-cut edit was finished in September 1999.

"Guerilla shooting" in clubs means shooting in the dark. You literally have to wait for a strobe light to hit a dancer so you (and the camera) can see something. You let the film keep running, and when you edit, you search for your "strobe light moments." It's hard to get permission to shoot in clubs because managers and owners fear you might capture a glimpse of something illegal, and they'd get busted. The dancers love the camera; in fact, there are "camera moths" perpetually placing themselves between the lens and the superb dancer you really want to shoot. It's incredibly hot; cameramen get grumpy. It's incredibly loud, and the sound guy complains. But the dancers are so committed to the project that they actually help in all these shoots by sweet-talking the managers and showing up because they know you'll be there shooting, and by stopping any potential troublemakers.

We did another kind of club shoot so we could control the lights: we rented a club and threw a party. All the dancers and all their friends came. We shot all day, fed them lunch, even scrubbed the floor so the club would be pristine for the "regular" evening crowd. We also shot in the Clark Studio Theater at Lincoln Center, against a plain white background so that form could be clearly discerned. (In a club, it's hard to see those details.) We used semi-silhouette and the solo dancer to illustrate shape and line, the graffiti quality of club dancing.

The project lurched forward, then stalled as we went through one chunk of money and waited for the next crop of applications to bear financial fruit.

In the eight years since we began, *Check Your Body at the Door* has aged, becoming a glimpse of history about a remarkable bunch of people and dance styles that existed in one decade. I'm thankful for a new wave of nostalgia about the late 1980s and 1990s, and glad the popularity of "raves" has spilled over into interest in its compeers and progenitors in underground house music and dancing. I'm thankful that *Check Your Body* can capitalize on this.

I now have a documentary different from what I had intended. Dance forms and music that were on the leading edge when we began have become, even before the film is released, styles from yesterday. At first, I was dismayed about its "historicity." The hot topic had grown cool. In truth, documenting social dance is like chasing after wild mercury spilling across a table. Dance forms are in constant flux. What is popular when you begin won't necessarily be popular when you finish—unlike a nice piece of choreographed dancing. On the other hand, our video is unique. It will have a long life; there's nothing like this slice of social-cultural history on the shelf.

Remarkably, the dancers have remained committed to the project and me because they remain committed to the dancing. The club is their institution of learning—it's rehearsal hall, classroom, and performance arena—a place to dream. Dance clubs are nurseries of invention. Club dancers are not only physically virtuosic, they make corrective social commentaries by taking the humor and fury of the decade and translating them into fast-moving improvisations, transmuting the commodities of pop culture into instant art.

A lot has transpired since we began working. One dancer is "missing in action"; we have no idea if she is alive or dead. Others went to jail, got promoted at their jobs, changed careers, had babies, or became recording stars. Clubheads who were unknown in 1993 have become well-known teachers, MTV choreographers, and dancers, the adored objects of the hordes of young Japanese groupies swarming to Manhattan, following their idols from club to club.

Filmmaking is a collaborative venture. My initial collaborator and director of photography, Michael Schwartz, died in the spring of 1994. What died with him were many of our original conceptions and goals. We'd hoped to do an hour-long broadcast-quality video, plus a digitization of the actual vocabulary of the movement. (Basically, we'd proposed to do a million-dollar project on a budget of $50,000.) An entirely new production team had to be assembled. One of the problems in assembling a new team is that new collaborators deal with the material differently. All concepts about how to shoot and how to edit the material already in the can have to be recast.

By the summer of 1995, the new team included Bobbi Tsumagari and me as co-producers, and Charlie Atlas as director. Funding received in 1992 from a pilot project, the NEA Dance Heritage Initiative, allowed us to begin shooting; it was used up by 1994. In 1996, money flowed once again. A grant from NIPAD arrived; the NEA came through again in 1997; a small private grant and donations helped to spin out funds through that year. Between 1996 and 1998, the remainder of the shooting was done at the clubs, at the dancers' jobs, on the streets, and in the studio. We edited in 1998–99 with another NEA grant received in 1998. As of this writing we have reached the last stretch. And my hair has turned white.

I don't regret the obsession. I don't regret the white hair. I do regret not getting the money together before starting. Had funding been in place, everything could have been finished in two years. Instead, I expended more time and energy scuffling for money than in making the documentary.

Fortunately, *Check Your Body at the Door* is as much about the people as about the dancing. In interviews with me, the dancers are witty, honest, beautiful, and irresistible. The viewer sees them up close when we follow them into the "outside" world, the everyday world of their lives with families and jobs (which range from subway worker to architect). Their responses to "Why dance?" are elegant. They dance for and with each other in order to hit the high plane, the "zone," to feel the exhilaration of invention, of thinking quickly on their feet, using every ounce of physical and mental agility. They dance to mourn deaths. They dance to praise God. The reasons why they dance are so fundamental to life's processes that they open up a deep truth: dance is survival.

This necessity, this truth about them and dancing, is what makes audiences fall in love—and it is what makes the video difficult to sell to anxious television producers who need to "niche" the product. Maybe this is commercial? Maybe not? Maybe this is about art? Maybe not? I say "Yes" to everything. This is the most baffling question, however: "Is it about the people or the dancing?" The next deepest truth I have learned is that you cannot separate the dancer from the dance, so *Check Your Body at the Door* attempts to be a tribute to the genius of both.

CHAPTER 51

Lines from a Filmmaker's Journal

Robert Gardner

DVD **40**
Deep Hearts (1979) 48 min 54 sec
Excerpt 4 min

These lines were written in the Niger Republic in 1978, during rare moments of respite in a struggle to film, in a sometimes brutal landscape of thorn, sand, and violent storms, inexhaustible men and women celebrating their own beauty in song and dance. The struggle resulted in the completion of a film called *Deep Hearts*, a journal containing the following brief notations, and a group of illustrative still photographs. The film, about the Borroro, who are nomadic herders, looks at a contest called *gerewol*, in which young male dancers are judged as to which of them best exemplifies Borroro ideals of beauty, grace, and manliness.

August 17/78, Birni Nkonni, 2:00 p.m. We are four in number, three *Nazaras* (Songhay for "men from Nazareth") and Gerba, our driver from Niamey. He is strong and seems an able driver. He is also, so far at least, amiable. Last night he avoided an enormous disaster by swerving at the last second around an invisible cow standing in the middle of the road enveloped by the blackest of nights.

August 18/78, Abalak. The outlook is promising. First, the rainy season has started early and continues copious; second, though the male "beauty" contests called *gerewol* have yet to begin, much buying in the markets of grain, sugar, and salt means they will soon; third, many lineages have gathered not far to the north and are making "contracts"—agreements between opposing lineages to engage each other in *gerewol*, the song and dance aspect of a larger activity called *ngaanka,* which is something like a ritual war without any killing. One lineage "attacks" or challenges another lineage, which in turn "defends." The former is guest and the latter is host. Both lineages dance, but the attacking lineage has the last night to itself until the dancing ends at dawn.

August 19/78, Abalak. Last night was cool enough to sleep until the sun rose at exactly 6 a.m. Bob Fulton, my helper here as elsewhere, is doing well considering his delicate mind/body situation. It is not that he is especially delicate but that he is tuned to such an exquisite pitch. The slightest jarring can have painful consequences.

August 20/78. I ponder a Borroro theme of some importance: the tension between a life where conduct is rigidly controlled by values, rules, and even complex taboos, and a life where it is possible to enjoy broad exemption from such

"... dancing in which aspiring 'bulls' are in contest with each other." Robert Gardner © Film Study Center, Harvard University.

constraints. A Borroro does not appear to desire power unless it is sexual mastery, nor does the society itself value or acknowledge status differences except that between the young and old. One man is basically as good as another, has the same amount of power and is as much a Borroro. Being Borroro is what is important and, above all, attaining more of what might be called "Borroroness," an attribute residing in beauty, grace, and sexual fulfillment.

August 21/78, Chikolani. It is dark in my miniature tent owing to a faulty candle that has melted before it could be lit. Insects attack from earth and sky, and I spend hours removing a multitude of burrs that are particularly fond of the insides of my pants.

I long for release from this hideous confinement in which I feel so solitary and absurd. I am hobbled hand, foot, and mind. All activity is wearisome and pointless. I say this as I listen to majestic singing accompanied by the intricate hand-clapping of the young, who are impatient to begin the songs and dances of these long-awaited days. In the background is the interminable groaning of the herds.

I think about the problems ahead, filming these Borroro who seem so smitten by modernity while still maintaining a commitment to tradition. They wear sporty sunglasses, costume jewelry, faceless wristwatches and a tawdry collection of other cast-off junk. At the same time, they are extremely conservative adherents to tribal truths and willing participants in a remarkably unenlightened social contract.

August 22/78, Chitolani. The *warsau,* gathering of the clans, seems to be dragging a bit, with people arriving and leaving in an apparently chaotic fashion. There is, I suspect, an orderliness which for now has managed to elude me completely. I am reminded of an enormous terminal in which hundreds of passengers have come with all their belongings and are waiting for the next bus. Here, though, it is not only people but also thousands of animals.

Late this afternoon some young men and women went to what is called the *daddo,* which is, I think, both a place and an idea. The place is some convenient meeting ground and the idea is of a social group composed of unmarried youth. Today it is nearby and what they are doing is dancing and singing.

August 23/78, Chitolani. The day has been extremely hot and oppressive. There was a little dancing in the morning but virtually none last night. What I have done is to make portraits with the Polaroid SX 70 of the younger male participants. But a Polaroid made is most likely a photograph lost, so intent are the subjects on possessing them. I had the idea of doing a series on the male dancers and seeing whether there was some agreement as to what set of features constituted the ideal Borroro.

August 24/78. The Wodabe (Borroro) are now hiving off in great numbers from the *warsau*. By 2 p.m. yesterday there were hardly any remaining. They drifted away all day in all directions. We will probably meet some of them again at other gatherings including the *gerewol*, which I'm told may already have

" . . . they have fielded up to thirty superb performers . . . " Robert Gardner © Film Study Center, Harvard University.

started. Its location is presently the subject of interminable discussions between lineage heads, four of whom are still in the "big house" at the north end of the *warsau* line. It is likely they are deciding matters such as which lineage is needed to support the one challenged ('attacked'). The attacked lineage is responsible for providing considerable provisioning for the attackers. Here it seems to me are echoes of Northwest Coast potlatching, where hosts and guests tried to outdo each other with displays of largesse.

6 p.m. I have wondered about survival in a place like the Sahel, where heat, dust, insects, thorns, burrs and assorted other infelicities give no quarter. My remedy is rest and quiet, even sleep. But when I lie down it becomes progressively more difficult to once again become active. The will is sapped and the mind begins to wander. I find I am hungry without knowing it, dirty without caring. The very cells seem to shrink as expectations dwindle. Even the Borroro say you have to be crazy to live in this landscape of agonies.

August 25/78, near Tadubuk. We are waiting for the lineage elder, who is our new friend and who has taken enthusiastically to instant coffee and bricks of sugar. It is he we hope will guide us to the *gerewol*, but no one seems to quite know where it is. Vague indications suggest it may be within 50 kilometers of our present position, but I sense there are other possibilities and that there is no fixed position for this occasion, in which everything depends on there being sufficient water and grazing. Our own situation in these respects looks bleaker all the time.

August 26/78, Talmazaalam (place of the *gerewol*), 11:30 a.m. During the last 24 hours I have been thinking of myself as a minor player in a vast primordial play taking place in the largest theater in the world. In fact I am but one organism in a great multitude of creatures sleeping, eating, shitting, drinking, dancing, singing, and fornicating here on the desert floor under a burning sun or cooling stars. It is a spectacular assembly, a congregation of devotees sparing nothing as they celebrate their self-regard. Last night, singing filled our cathedral of night air as I drifted between sleep and astonished waking on successive waves of polyphonic dirging.

7 p.m. I grope among thorns, scorpions, ants, beetles, and biting flies for drink, food or a place to rest. I am oppressed by the weight of my equipment and my ignorance. The Wodabe sing and dance all day and all night. It is undertaken by inexhaustible squads of young men and women who seem never to falter. All participate, remain in time impassioned, even exalted. They wear watches with hands that do not move or are not there at all; everything is suspended while this spectacle unfolds.

Gerba, the driver, is starting to crack amid what to him is simply primitive madness. He is huge, flabby, and very black. He craves the Fulani girls and is crazed by desire. They are repulsed by his attentions and flaunt their disgust. He blames us for his loss of charm and wonders what could have persuaded him to participate in such an undertaking in the first place. The bush enrages him and he quakes with anger and fear. We badly need water, sugar and tinned fruit, but especially water. The water at 'Ngall is salty, but not diluted mud as it is here at the place "where camels can wallow."

August 27/78. There is more than one dance style performed during these days. I have seen mostly what is called *rumi*, which is a circle of men maintaining a very regular beat for great lengths of time, clapping and singing as they shuffle forward and backward. I have not learned the significance of this dance but will when I can.

There is another style called *yaki*, but I have not seen it because the *rumi* is getting most of the performance time. *Gerewol*, the dancing in which aspiring "bulls" are in contest with each other, is meant to "turn" so that the attacking lineage, which has been dancing during the day looking at the sun, gives way to the defending lineage, which dances at night facing the moon.

Fulton and I were on our way to the *daddo*, the place where the *gerewol* takes place, at a moment when an extraordinary light was illuminating an astonishing scene. As the light died, the film in my camera expired and the dancing ended with young girls pointing to the "chosen" one, the "bull." Only one or two feet of film were left when I stopped, just at the moment a maiden reached outward to the "bull." DVD **40**

August 28/78, 10:30 a.m. It is midmorning and all of us, indigenes and interlopers, are recovering from a tempest that struck early last night. My pathetic tent is now perched on the lip of a small pond to which everyone comes for water or to bathe. With this storm it has grown much larger and come much closer.

Today there has been talk of sacrificing a bull. If this occurs, the *gerewol* will "turn" and the attackers will dance until dawn. It may all be over sooner than I had thought. If it is, we will leave for 'Nwagga and find the rest we need to take us through the next *gerewol* set to begin Friday.

August 29/78. This particular *gaynka*, as the whole affair is known, has begun to accelerate or maybe to collapse in on itself. There is talk of the attacking lineage not acquitting itself particularly splendidly, not enough good dancers or good dancing, too much lying around to please the elders. This phase was meant to end on Wednesday but will wind up today following some farewell ceremonies. By midday the last camel had departed, most of them in a group headed south.

Around 6 p.m. I looked at the northern horizon and watched as blackness once again filled the sky, and wondered if there would be another tempest. The answer was not long in coming. Gales were soon dismantling our living arrangements. The Sahel was convulsing and for two hours we were punished by dust, dirt, wind, and rain. In the end, I could do nothing except lie back and ponder my insignificance. I also wondered what part my own irredeemable evil might have in all this heaven-sent punishment.

August 30/78. I reel from thorn bush to thorn bush, plucking at burrs and burrowing insects. But the Wodabe seem unfazed and just keep dancing, singing, and talking as if this might be their last chance for human congress before another season of lonely wandering in the desert. They are also full of fears and anxieties that arise from the complex rules governing their conduct. Taboos, strictures, and sanctions abound and narrowly limit their choices. Personal liberty seems quite impossible under such circumstances.

August 31/78, Tamalolo, 8:30 a.m. We came here from the *gerewol* encampment yesterday afternoon. All our "defending" acquaintances were themselves leaving for their own camps to attend a gathering arranged by the government or to attend another "attack" in the northeast, closer to 'Ngall.

I am not at all sorry to have left this place of tempest and ceremony, both of which have had their high and low points. None was deficient in intensity and all have conspired to exhaust me. I had thought a week ago this would have been an appropriate warm-up for a proper *gaynka* but I am no longer so sure I want another such experience anytime soon.

September 1/78, 'Nwagga. I think of the more arresting images from the ceremonial life we have left behind, like the *gerewol* dancer's hobbled legs. I long to see something more ordinary. There seem to be many rules governing Borroro lives but maybe it's the same everywhere. They just aren't as vividly expressed as they are here. I'm struck by the ambiguity in the idea of the nomad as a prisoner of conventions.

September 2/78, Bonkar. We departed Abalak midmorning with a Tuareg guide, hoping to find the camps of the Gojanko clan off to the north between Alambaton and Bonkar. After scouring the intervening plain, we reached the camp of one of its important leaders. What greeted the eye was a dismaying confection of cultural materials, starting with Tuareg tents and ending with heaps of Western apparel and castaway merchandise. I can't remember ever seeing so squalid an assortment of material objects.

September 3/78, Chintabaradan. We have come to Chintabaradan to gather information about the Borroro of this more southern region. It is new to Patrick, our French interpreter, and this tends to deepen his already depressed mood. Each day he withdraws a little further, undertakes a little less and sleeps a little more. To all questions he now answers: "*Je ne sais pas.*"

September 4/78, Chintabaradan. It is only Patrick, Fulton, and myself in a small mud house we have found to protect us from further ravages of nature. More will be known in 48 or 72 hours of what lies in store. Meanwhile, a kingdom of flies, filth, heat, and frustration reigns triumphant.

September 5/78, Chintabaradan. I am waiting for news of Borroro activity. The Gojamkoi and Japtui are two lineages well represented hereabouts and their leaders are keeping Patrick informed, or so I'm led to believe. It seems there is some likelihood that one of these groups will "attack" and thereby set in motion a new round of *gaynkas.*

September 6/78, Chintabaradan. Nothing has been heard of *gerewols* but I mean to be patient a few more days.

September 7/78, Chintabaradan. Frustration mounts in the prolonged absence of news that might change our circumstances. I feel trapped but realize it is by choice. I look around in this forsaken outpost of nowhere and see that everyone else is trapped too and wonder what it really means to be free. It may mean no more than having the choice of imprisonments.

My thoughts are centered on the meaning of what I am trying to get from this experience. There seems to me less and less possibility of finding a transfiguring metaphor to redeem what I am finding so melancholic about Africa at this time and place. It is as though I had been deceived in some fashion when it is more likely that the deception has been my own of myself. I also question whether there is any reason ever to make a film in the manner I have made them until now.

September 8/78, Chintabaradan. We have waited all day for the Land Rover. Could Patrick have found a *gerewol*? This is one of the two likely explanations for the delay. The other is that there are mechanical problems, something that would not in the least surprise me.

September 9/78, Chintabaradan. The Land Rover and news of a relatively nearby *gerewol* arrived at about 11 a.m. This is an opportunity I feel we must seize. Our seven-day purgatory was intended to end with another chance for filmmaking and that is what seems to have happened. Although we are weaker and more dispirited than at the previous affair, Fulton agrees we should try again.

September 10/78, Assaaghay. At 4 p.m. we were ready to leave for the place where our little adopted group has decided to go. We followed them in a westerly direction, to the edge of a large pond near where I suspect the *gerewol* will be located. Many herds of cattle, sheep, and goats have converged from every quarter, indicating that word has passed to those concerned, both attackers and defenders.

September 11/78, Intautin. As late as 9 p.m. the Gojankoi attackers were at the dance ground as expected, even with the sky at its most menacing. There were eighteen dancers, which is a respectable number on the first night and especially in light of the storm that was about to descend upon us all. I went even knowing the dancing might be abbreviated since no one wants to perform in the rain.

The dancing lasted almost two hours under a three-quarter moon and in front of an immense fire. The spectators were not great in numbers but they were full of enthusiasm. At one point, an elder asked that the maidens who choose the "bull" from the ranks of those dancing be brought out so that the ceremony could be completed while everyone was dry. An old lady let him know she thought there might be a wild pig dancing, an enormous insult, and that the best thing was to keep going. Around midnight the girls came and one of them made her shy choice with a wonderful, upward swing of an arm that offhandedly indicated the "bull," chosen, I suspect, not by the young maiden herself but by the men who determine such matters.

September 12/78, Intautin. I think about being hobbled as I look at restraints everywhere around me, like the ropes tying together the forelegs of camels, and belts around dancers' legs just above the knees. I also note the rules of conduct dictating what can be said, or done, or eaten. We are all prisoners of culture one way or another.

I think too about my camera failing on the first day. I am not yet, nor do I think I will ever be, comfortable with Fulton's backup Eclair. It is not part of me the way cameras such as the Arri S I used in New Guinea or the BL I used in Ethiopia were. I continue to lurch and stumble instead of gliding quietly and smoothly in mostly vain pursuit of images.

September 13/78, Intautin. It is the fourth day in this place and I cannot help wondering why I feel so besieged. There is a great variety of discomforts and indignities assailing us from all sides but that alone cannot account for my despondency. How often is there an opportunity to witness a spectacle like *gerewol* against a backdrop of elemental nature such as there is at this moment, hundreds of miles from anywhere? Almost never, I would think. What my disquiet may demonstrate is the grip ordinary expectations have on one's wider outlook.

Last night the Japtoen lineage danced its first *gerewol* of this *gaynka*. I sat in the moonlight until it started around midnight. From time to time I wandered about to watch dancers putting on their elaborate makeup by the light of the moon or the little fires of twigs fed by the younger boys.

Despite my accumulated weariness and disappointment, I found this scene quite miraculous: men applying rouge and lipstick under an almost full moon, in preparation for a contest to decide which of them was most nearly perfect.

September 14/78, Intautin. The *gaynka* now unfolding in close proximity is growing rapidly in numbers and energy. Although the defenders seem not to have been well supported by their lineages, the attackers have been greatly helped by theirs. So many, in fact, have arrived that they have fielded up to 30 superb performers for the afternoon dances. It is clear the right decision was made to wait out those limbo-like days in Chintabaradan. It has been much

" . . . a congregation of devotees sparing nothing as they celebrate their self-regard." Robert Gardner © Film Study Center, Harvard University.

more productive here than it was up until now, partly for the reason that I know a little better how to anticipate the action. I also have some thematic notions that give this work some coherence. I even find myself thinking not just about specific forms but of an overall shape those forms might take. Maybe it is possible to make a film after all.

The idea of a "deep heart" has been intriguing me since I first heard the notion from Patrick. As far as I can tell, it is a construct of great meaning for the Borroro. It appears to make it possible for males to hide their deepest and most private feelings from each other and from public scrutiny. Apparently they live in such an exaggerated state of mutual envy and suspicion that were they to reveal their real feelings to others or others to them, there might be violent consequences. By hiding true feelings within their "deep hearts," the Borroro can at least pretend not to harbor them at all.

September 15/78, Intautin. Since midnight I have been listening to the wind and thunder which have brought a darkened sky at the start of another day of *gerewol*. The Japtoen danced despite the inclemencies and I watched at the height of their performance.

Painted and costumed dancers swayed and gyrated in front of an enormous fire sending clouds of embers and sparks across the rain-swept desert floor. The sound of the dancers' leg rattles and chorused voices was alternately swallowed and amplified by the shifting winds. It was a contest between men and the elements. It seemed that Nature might at any moment hurl us all to the furthest horizon.

In the morning I waited for the light to appear but it never did. It seemed strange to be here and not see the sun rise in its accustomed fashion. I took it as an omen that we should leave, and so we did. We were in Chintabaradan at 3 p.m. At 7 p.m. we were in Tahoua, only hours from Niamey.

We have gone and the Wodabe will be gone themselves in a matter of hours. In a better set of circumstances, we might have left in their company.

September 16/78, Tahoua and Niamey. I feel strangely incomplete and filled by a vague sadness about leaving, even though I am not sure what it is I would do were I to stay. It is over and I do not know what it is that has ended.

Part VIII
Resources

CHAPTER 52

Video Preservation

Leslie Hansen Kopp

Leslie Hansen Kopp in the office, 2001. Photo by Charles Steiner.

No other single technological invention has had as great an impact on the field of dance documentation as video. Dancers and choreographers use video for a wide range of purposes, from documenting rehearsals and performances to auditioning performers and supporting grant proposals. In the past decade, video has become the tool for recording movement. However, videotape is not an archival medium; that is, videotape is neither permanent nor a complete documentary record of a dance.

Videotapes are fragile, with a lifespan that may be only 10 to 20 years at best. Documenting dance with videotape alone would be like documenting a symphony with a phonograph or compact disc, and neglecting the score. Video recordings should always be considered a component of dance archives, along with programs, photographs, choreographic notes, set and costume designs, and other archival documents.

HOW VIDEOTAPE WORKS

Videotape is made of three basic components. First, there is the tape base itself, which is usually made of Mylar®, a polyester film. The second component is composed of bits of metallic oxide compounds, which actually record the magnetic signals. These oxide compounds are held to the tape with the third component, the binder.

Alan Lewis, an expert in audio-visual archives management, suggests that an easy way to remember the structure of videotape is to visualize crunchy peanut butter on a cracker. The cracker is the base tape; the nut chunks are the magnetic oxide, and the peanut butter itself is the binder. All three elements that make up videotape are easily damaged; the binder is perhaps the most fragile.

Several factors affect the lifespan of videotape, including tape quality, humidity and temperature, handling, storage, and the condition of playback equipment. The factors that work to destroy video—heat, tension, and friction—occur every time you play a tape. When you put a videocassette in your machine, the tape is pulled and stretched against a drum that holds the recording/playback heads, creating both friction and heat. In other words, each time a video is played, it loses some of its quality.

"Dropout," a flash of light in the video image, is actually caused by a scrape in the tape binder that has taken some of the magnetic oxide off with it. Advanced dropout will appear as "snow" in playback. A wobbly image can indicate that the magnetic bits are about to jump off. Any of these symptoms is a signal to make a new viewing copy of the videotape.

In archival terms, videotape is a machine-readable record—that is, a magnetic medium that requires a machine to translate it into recognizable images. Unlike film, a photographic medium that requires only light and magnification to "read," videotape requires playback equipment. Hold a piece of film up to the light, and you will see an image; hold a piece of videotape up to the light, and all you will see is brown plastic.

The video recorder works by taking a stream of electrical pulses from the pick-up camera and using them to "drive" an electromagnet that influences the magnetic particles on a ribbon of tape that passes by it. The process is similar to that of recording sound; however, videotape must carry much more information than audiotape. To record video, more than five million pieces of information must be stored for each second of picture and sound.

In order to accomplish such a feat, video recorders move both the tape and the recording heads. The tape moves slowly forward while the recording heads are attached to a drum that spins at a faster speed. The drum holding the video heads spins 25 to 30 times a second, and each of the two heads records one field, or half of a video picture. The heads, which are used for both recording and playback, are fixed at slightly different angles to prevent interference between the two tracks. The whole drum tilts so that the tape is scanned helically; each track slants diagonally across the tape at an angle. This process is called helical scan recording.

Besides the diagonally slanting picture signals, videotape also records sound. On ordinary VHS and Beta tapes, the sound track runs along the top edge of the tape and is recorded by a stationary head. However, Hi-Fi and 8mm video formats record sound utilizing heads mounted in the spinning drum. The higher writing speed makes possible much better sound quality.

VIDEO SYSTEMS AND FORMATS

There are three different color television standards in use internationally. The three systems differ in a number of ways, principally in the way they encode color, in the number of times the picture is replaced each second, and in tape speed.

In North America, much of Latin America, and Japan, the prevailing system is NTSC, which stands for National Television Systems Committee. Most of Europe uses a system called PAL (Phase Alternation Line). France, nations of the former Soviet Union, and some Middle Eastern countries use SECAM (Sequential Couleur à Mémoire). A tape recorded in one of the international systems cannot be played back on machines of the other systems.

With dance being recorded on virtually every format available—VHS, Beta, and 8mm; one-inch, half-inch, cassette, and reel-to-reel—format variations pose a problem. Rapid changes in the industry have rendered dozens of formats obsolete, and dance repositories are forced to become museums of technology in order to play many older videotapes.

If you purchase a new video recorder, try to keep the outdated machine. Today, it is becoming increasingly difficult to find parts for reel-to-reel and Beta machines. Even if videotape were a permanent medium, you might not find the hardware for playback in 10 years.

If you have any reel-to-reel tapes in your collection, copy them onto a more stable format now! Always keep a master videotape, and make copies for viewing. Check your tapes at least once a year for deterioration.

PRESERVATION AND STORAGE

Recordings on videotape are not permanent! Even under the best conditions, a videotape may last only a few years. Every time you play a video, the tape is exposed to heat, tension, and friction, and some of the magnetic material that holds the image wears off.

There are thousands of horror stories of performances and works "lost" because they were "preserved" only on videotape. Proper care, identification, handling, and storage of videotape will give your performances a chance to survive:

Use quality brand-name tapes; you literally get what you pay for.

Label tapes immediately after recording (they all look alike from the outside).

Always remove the erase prevention tabs on tapes that you intend to save. Some formats have a red button or switch.

Dub viewing copies from a master tape. Keep masters and copies in different places.

Copy deteriorating tapes immediately onto stable formats. View tapes at least once a year to check for deterioration.

Never touch the tape inside its cassette housing.

Avoid using freeze-frame, pause, and skip-scan features. Damage will occur at the point where the tape is stopped; skip-scan accelerates dropout.

Rewind tapes evenly before storage; uneven tension can harm the tape. Always fast-forward to the end of the tape, and then rewind. Never leave a tape stopped in the middle.

Store tapes upright, like books, not flat like pancakes (the soundtrack is located on the edge of the tape); cassette tapes should be placed with the heavy end down.

Use high-quality hard cases to safeguard tapes from physical damage. Cardboard sleeves provide little protection.

Protect videotapes from magnetic fields and vibrations; do not store them on top of or next to loudspeakers, electrical fixtures, television sets, or even videocassette players.

Keep tapes clean, cool, and dry. Optimum ranges of temperature and humidity for video storage and use are 65°-70° F and 35%-45% RH. What is important here are constant levels; wide fluctuations cause the most damage. Likewise, protect videotapes from dust and direct light.

Make sure the VCR works properly before playing a tape. Malfunctioning machines are the biggest cause of tape catastrophe.

Maintain recording and playback equipment. Depend on trained, qualified personnel for repairs.

ARRANGEMENT AND DESCRIPTION

Videotapes can be described with a relatively simple shelf list or a more complex catalog. When identifying, cataloging, and labeling videotapes, be sure to include the following elements of description:

Company, group, or individual name

Title of work or event

Length of recording

Date and place of recording

Format/System and tape speed

Color or black-and-white

Performers

Production credits

Performance, dress rehearsal, or rehearsal

Videographer

Master or dub

Also include notes concerning shoot, tape damage, subject matter, restrictions on use, etc. Create a data entry sheet for each tape in your collection, or make a log by photocopying and annotating programs.

CHAPTER 53

Whose Rights Are Right?

Madeleine Nichols

Why can't I use this film clip in my documentary? Can I screen that telecast in my classroom? Isn't this videotape my work about your dance? How can you take my dance and call it your video?

The issues underlying these questions revolve around copyright and contracts. Copyright is controlled by federal statute, grounded in Article I of the United States Constitution as well as in international treaties, GATT and WIPO being among the foremost. Contracts may run between a choreographer and a composer, a videographer and a dance company, a choreographer and a dance company, a union and a dance company, or other combinations.

When we look at a dance film, we see the result of a collaboration. Involved are a filmmaker, a choreographer, a composer, perhaps a writer, perhaps scenic and costume designers, perhaps lighting designers, supporting craftsmen for the filmmaker such as sound specialists, and of course performers, who may include the dancers, musicians, and a narrator. The contracts tied to a dance film involve the making of the film as well as the content of the film. The funding supporting the film may involve other explicit contractual obligations. Some of the contracts may pre-date the making of the film, but underlie it nonetheless. Just by looking at the film, it is not possible to know who really owns the rights.

One of the most puzzling questions is who owns the traditional dance of a specific culture. Can anyone just take it for any use merely because it is centuries old? In the dance community, the best rule is to bring respect to your every action. If you honor the work of another, then you will seek to understand the other's view about the work. Tell that person what you want to do, so there are no surprises. Most requests for permission to use a work are granted. Sometimes money must be paid.

In the best cases, there will be title credits to guide you. If you want to use the film you see, for example to teach in a classroom or to include in your documentary or telecast or gala performance, then clearing the rights for your use must be added to your tasks. If it's your film or your choreography, then you want to be certain that your credit is clearly on the film, so that your work is not used against your wishes.

The owner of the copyright has the exclusive right to display publicly, to perform publicly, to copy, to prepare derivative works, and to distribute the work by sale or loan or other manner. The "work" is an original expression in tangible form. A film, a music composition, and a dance are each a distinct "work" automatically protected by copyright in the United States. Thus, the dance film you are seeing can be carrying the protection for the film as well as separate underlying protection for the music and for the choreography.

Generally, this automatic copyright protection lasts for the lifetime of the creator plus 70 years. Cases of works for hire will depend on particular facts. Likewise, satire and situations of the limited "fair use" exception call for legal expertise.

The rights owner may license the copyright to another, making the trail of clearances more intricate or simpler, depending on the bargaining power that was at play in the making of the film. For example, the Dance Division at the New York Public Library often obtains the right to display a film and to preserve it; it owns the tangible physical object, without owning the intangible copyrights ("intellectual property").

Two resources for specifics about copyright, including the statute, forms, and answers to frequently asked questions, are the United States Copyright Office (www.lcweb.loc.gov/copyright) and the University of Texas Office of the General Counsel (www.utsystem.edu/ogc/intellectualproperty–click on copyright).

Why do the rights matter? Someone who creates a work should benefit from any financial profit the work may yield. That is the balance underpinning the copyright protection structured in the federal statute and international treaties. Dissemination and distribution of dance films are central to the health of the discipline of dance. For that economic flow to operate, the path of rights ownership needs to be made explicit by the creator, and it needs to be followed by the user.

CHAPTER 54

Resource and Preservation Guide

Leslie Hansen Kopp

FILM AND VIDEO PRESERVATION: ASSOCIATIONS, ORGANIZATIONS AND PROFESSIONAL GROUPS IN THE US AND CANADA

Professional Membership Associations

The following professional membership associations deal with film and video preservation issues.

ACA: Association of Canadian Archivists
http://aca.archives.ca/index.htm
The Association of Canadian Archivists (ACA) has a fourfold focus: providing leadership for everyone engaged in the preservation of Canada's documentary heritage; encouraging awareness of archival activities and developments and the importance of archives to modern society; advocating the interests and needs of professional archivists before government and other regulatory agencies; and communicating to further the understanding and cooperation amongst members of the Canadian archival system and other information- and culture-based professions.

ALA: American Library Association
http://www.ala.org/
The American Library Association provides leadership for the development, promotion, and improvement of library and information services and the profession of librarianship in order to enhance learning and ensure access to information for all.

AMIA: Association of Moving Image Archivists
http://www.amianet.org/index.html
The Association of Moving Image Archivists (AMIA) is a nonprofit professional association established to advance the field of moving image archiving by fostering cooperation among individuals and organizations concerned with the collection, preservation, exhibition and use of moving image materials. The specific objectives of the association are to:

- Provide a regular means of exchanging information, ideas and assistance.
- Take responsible positions on archival matters affecting moving images and related materials.
- Encourage public awareness of and interest in the preservation and use of moving images as an important educational, historical, and cultural resource.
- Promote moving image archival activities, including preservation, cataloging and documentation, and access, through such means as meetings workshops, publications, and direct assistance.
- Support the education and professional development of moving image archivists.
- Develop and promote professional standards and practices for moving image archival materials.
- Stimulate and facilitate research on archival matters affecting moving images.

CLA: Canadian Library Association
http://www.cla.ca/top/SiteMap.htm
The Canadian Library Association (CLA) is a nonprofit voluntary organization, governed by an elected Executive Council, which is advised by more than 30 interest groups and committees. The Association's five constituent divisions are: Canadian Association of College and University Libraries (CACUL), including the Community and Technical College (CTCL) section; Canadian Association of Public Libraries (CAPL), including the Canadian Association of Childrens' Librarians (CACL) section; Canadian Association of Special Libraries and Information Services (CASLIS), with chapters in Calgary, Edmonton, Manitoba, Ottawa, Toronto and Atlantic Canada; Canadian Library Trustees' Association; and Canadian School Library Association, including the School Library Administrators' (SLAS) section.

DFA: Dance Films Association, Inc.
http://www.dancefilmsassn.org
Dance Films Association, Inc. (DFA), a nonprofit, tax-exempt, membership organization, supports all these efforts by promoting excellence in dance films and video and public awareness through festivals, screenings, publications, grants, and workshops. DFA has sponsored annual Dance on Camera festivals since 1971, produced six guides to dance films and videos in circulation, and organized numerous events across the country. It remains the only service organization in the world dedicated to both the dance and film community.

FIAF: International Federation of Film Archives
http://www.cinema.ucla.edu/fiaf/default.html
The International Federation of Film Archives (FIAF) brings together institutions dedicated to rescuing films both as cultural heritage and as historical documents. Founded in Paris in 1938, FIAF is a collaborative association of the world's leading film archives whose purpose has always been to ensure the proper preservation and showing of motion pictures. Today, more than 100 archives in over 60 countries collect, restore, and exhibit films and cinema documentation spanning the entire history of film.
In addition to these primary goals, FIAF also seeks:

- to promote film culture and facilitate historical research
- to help create new archives around the world
- to foster training and expertise in film preservation
- to encourage the collection and preservation of documents and other cinema-related materials
- to develop cooperation between archives and to ensure the international availability of films and cinema documents.

FIAT/IFTA: International Federation of Television Archives
http://www.nb.no/fiat/whatis.html
The International Federation of Television Archives (FIAT/IFTA) is a nonprofit association of television archives, set up on June 13, 1977, in Rome by the BBC, RAI, ARD, and INA. The association's objectives are: to encourage cooperation among their members; to promote the compatibility of audio-visual documentation systems as well as documentation exchange; to approach to techniques and supports to preserve audiovisual material and the appraisal and diffusion of this material. At an international level, interest increases because of the research and approach FIAT/IFTA carries out to try to achieve the best preservation possible of the material and to make the different documentation systems compatible in order to reach the easiest access and the widest diffusion of the material preserved by the worldwide Television Archives.

NAB: National Association of Broadcasters
http://www.nab.org/
The National Association of Broadcasters is a full-service trade association that promotes and protects the interests of radio and television broadcasters in Washington and around the world. NAB is the broadcaster's voice before Congress, federal agencies, and the courts. They also serve a growing number of associate and international broadcaster members. NAB works to keep members out front on policy issues, technology, and management trends. The staff provides ongoing and "late breaking" broadcast news, industry research and legal expertise.

National Film Board of Canada
www.nfb.ca
Created in 1939, the National Film Board of Canada (NFB) is a public agency that produces and distributes films and other audiovisual works which reflect Canada to Canadians and the rest of the world. It is an exceptional fountain of creativity, which since its very beginnings has played a crucial role in Canadian and international filmmaking. The NFB, as the storehouse of a large part of the country's audiovisual heritage, in

the form of a collection of more than 10,000 titles, has always been and remains a cultural organization, while acting as an important catalyst of social change. It is also a center of filmmaking and video technology and can pride itself on some of the most remarkable technical breakthroughs in film production.

SAA: Society of American Archivists
http://www.archivists.org/
Founded in 1936, the Society of American Archivists (SAA) is North America's oldest and largest national archival professional association. Serving the educational and informational needs of more than 3,400 individual and institutional members, SAA provides leadership to ensure the identification, preservation, and use of records of historical value.

Technical Standards Organizations

The following organizations provide information on technical specifications for film, video, and television.

ANSI: American National Standards Institute
http://www.ansi.org/
This private, nonprofit organization serves as administrator and coordinator of the United States private-sector voluntary standardization and conformity assessment systems.

EIA: Electronic Industries Association
http://www.eia.org/
This site contains information about the U.S. electronics manufacturing industry and its trade organization, the Electronics Industries Association.

IEEE: Institute of Electrical and Electronics Engineers
http://www.ieee.org/
This is the site of the world's largest technical professional society whose objectives are to advance the theory and practice of electrical, electronics and computer engineering, and computer science. Provides news and information, links, and access to online publications.

NSSN: National Standards Systems Network
http://www.nssn.org/
This site is designed to provide users with access to a wide range of standards information from major standards developers. The site contains an integrated catalogue database of more than 100,000 standards currently in use.

SMPTE: Society of Motion Picture and Television Engineers
http://www.smpte.org/
This site contains information about SMPTE, its activities and publications. An online index to SMPTE Standards, Recommended Practices, and Engineering Guidelines is available.

Technical Membership Groups

MPEG.ORG
http://www.mpeg.org/~tristan/MPEG/MPEG-content.html
This site claims to house the most complete and up-to-date index of MPEG (Motion Picture Experts Group) resources on the Internet. Their search engine provides access to 2,000 links and references.

TIG: Telecine Internet group
http://www.alegria.com/telecinehome.html
This site provides access to research and general reference for film and video related topics. Also provides instructions for joining a listserv dedicated to information about telecines.

Copyright Issues

Canadian Copyright Law
http://www.mcgrawhill.ca/copyrightlaw
McGraw-Hill Ryerson Ltd.
Promotional site for the book *Canadian Copyright Law* by Lesley Ellen Harris. Contains excerpts from the book, reviews, FAQ's about Canadian Copyright Law and links to information about the current legislation.

US Copyright Office Home Page
http://lcweb.loc.gov/copyright/
Library of Congress

General: Copyright and Fair Use
http://fairuse.stanford.edu/
Provides online access to primary materials; current legislation, cases and issues; resources on the internet; and an overview of copyright law.

Moving Images: Copyright, Fair Use, and Other Matters
http://www.tcf.ua.edu/ScreenSite/
University of Alabama, Telecommunication and Film Department

Other Useful Preservation Information Websites

Commission on Preservation and Access: Reports
http://www.clir.org
The mission of the CPA is to encourage collaboration among libraries and allied organizations to ensure the preservation of the published and documentary record in all formats, and to provide enduring access to scholarly information. Page contains links to publications, committees and task forces and the current initiatives of the CPA. Site contains online access to CPA reports and Annual Reports (1989–1996)

NFPB: National Film Preservation Board
http://lcweb.loc.gov/film/
Library of Congress
This site contains basic information on the NFPB, the National Film Registry, National Film Preservation Foundation, and the National Film Registry tour. Links are provided, as well as information about copyright and other legal issues, and the Library of Congress film resources.

NFPB: National Film Preservation Board: Television and Videotape Study
http://lcweb.loc.gov/film/tv.html
Library of Congress
Page contains information about the Television and Videotape Study, as well as updates on the expected release of the report.

AFI: American Film Institute
http://www.afionline.org
Informative page providing some explanations for the disappearance of our moving image heritage, examples of film deterioration and restoration, a basic bibliography and other preservation links.

RLG: Research Libraries Group
http://www.rlg.org/digital/index.html
This page contains information on current digital initiatives at RLG with links to the various research and working groups' sites.

Dance Preservation Resources

American Dance Legacy Institute
www.brown.edu/Departments/Theatre_Speech_Dance/Amer._Dance_Legacy_Inst..html

Bay Area Video Coalition
www.bavc.org

Dance/USA
www.danceusa.org
There are also numerous regional and local dance service organizations. Dance/USA can provide information about these organizations.

Dance Heritage Coalition
www.danceheritage.org

Dance Librarians' Discussion Group
Mail the command: subscribe DLDG-L to listserv@listserv.INDIANA.EDU

Dance Notation Bureau
www.dancenotation.org

Preserve, Inc.
www.preserve-inc.org

Save As: Dance
www.save-as-dance.org

SELECTED DANCE LIBRARIES AND ARCHIVES IN THE UNITED STATES AND CANADA

Arizona

Cross-Cultural Dance Resources
www.ccdr.org
518 South Agassiz Street
Flagstaff, AZ 86001
(520) 774-8108

California

Ballet of the Bolshoi Theatre Archive Collection
325 South Hudson Avenue
Los Angeles, CA 90020
(213) 931-8705

Young Research Library
www.library.ucla.edu/libraries/url
University of California at Los Angeles
405 Hilgard Avenue
Los Angeles, CA 90024-1575
(310) 825-2422

Fine Arts Museums of San Francisco
www.thinker.org
Theatre and Dance Collection
M. H. deYoung Museum
Golden Gate Park
San Francisco, CA 94118
(415) 775-3600

San Francisco Performing Arts Library and Museum (SF-PALM)
www.sfpalm.org
401 Van Ness Avenue, 4th Floor
San Francisco, CA 94102
(415) 255-4800

Connecticut
Serge Lifar Collection of Ballet, Set, and Costume Designs
Wadsworth Atheneum
www.wadsworthatheneum.org
600 Main Street
Hartford, CT 06103
(203) 278-2670

District of Columbia
George Washington University
Dance Archives
Gelman Library, Special Collections
www.gwu.edu/gelman/
2130 H Street, NW
Washington, DC 20052
(202) 994-1340

Library of Congress Home Page
www.lcweb.loc.gov/rr/mopic
Motion Picture, Broadcasting, and Recorded Sound Division
James Madison Memorial Building, Room 338
Washington, DC 20540
(202) 707-5000

Library of Congress Dance: An Illustrated Guide
www.lcweb.loc.gov
Music Division
James Madison Memorial Building, Room 113
Washington, DC 20540
(202) 707-3744

Illinois
Chicago Dance Archive
Newberry Library
www.newberry.org
34 Walton Street
Chicago, IL 60610
(312) 943-9090

Stigler Dance Collection
Chicago Public Library
http://cpl.lib.uic.edu/CPL.html
78 East Washington
Chicago, IL 60602
(312) 747-4846

Massachusetts
Harvard Theatre Collection
Harvard College Library
Harvard University
http://hcl.harvard.edu/houghton/departments/htc/theatre.html
Cambridge, MA 02138
(617) 495-2445

Jacob's Pillow Dance Festival
www.jacobspillow.com
P.O. Box 287
Lee, MA 01238
(413) 637-1322

Michigan
Music and Performing Arts Department
Detroit Public Library
www.detroit.lib.mi.us
5201 Woodward Avenue
Detroit, MI 48202

Minnesota
Dance Book Collection
Saint Paul Public Library
www.stpaul.lib.mn.us
90 Fourth Street West
St. Paul, MN 55102
(612) 292-6207

New York
Merce Cunningham Dance
www.merce.org
463 West Street
New York, NY 10014
(212) 255-3130

Dance Division—New York Public Library for the Performing Arts
www.nypl.org/research/lpa/dan/dan.html
40 Lincoln Center Plaza
New York, NY 10023-7498
(212) 870-1655

Dance Notation Bureau
www.dancenotation.org
151 West 30th Street, Suite 202
New York, NY 10001
(212) 564-0985

Dance Theatre of Harlem
www.dancetheatreofharlem.org
466 West 152nd Street
New York, NY 10031
(212) 690-2800

The Juilliard School
www.juilliard.edu
Lila Acheson Wallace Library
60 Lincoln Center Plaza
New York, NY 10023
(212) 799-5000

José Limón Dance Foundation
www.limon.org
611 Broadway, 9th Floor
New York, NY 10012
(212) 777-3353

Museum of the City of New York
Theatre Collection
www.mcny.org
Fifth Avenue at 103rd Street
New York, NY 10029
(212) 534-1672

Museum of Television and Radio
www.mtr.org
25 West 52nd Street
New York, NY 10019
(212) 621-6600

National Museum of Dance
www.dancemuseum.org
South Broadway
Saratoga Springs, NY 12866
(518) 584-2225

Schomburg Center for Research in Black Culture
http://gopher.nypl.org/research/sc/scr/genref.html
515 Lenox Avenue
New York, NY 10027
(212) 491-2200

Paul Taylor Dance Company
www.ptdc.org
552 Broadway
New York, NY 10012
(212) 431-5562

North Carolina
American Dance Festival
www.americandancefestival.org
P.O. Box 6097
College Station
Durham, NC 27708-6097
(919) 684-6402

Ohio
OSU Department of Dance
www.dance.ohio-state.edu
Ohio State University
Columbus, OH 43210
(614) 292-7977

Jerome Lawrence and Robert E. Lee Theatre Research Institute
www.lib.ohio-state.edu/triweb/
Ohio State University
1430 Lincoln Tower
1800 Cannon Drive
Columbus, OH 43210-1230
(614) 292-6614

Pennsylvania
The University of the Arts
www.uarts.edu
Broad and Pine Streets
Philadelphia, PA 19102
(215) 875-1111

Texas
Theater Arts Collection Harry Ransom Humanities Research Center
Harry Ransom Humanities Research Center
www.hrc.utexas.edu
P.O. Drawer 7219
University of Texas
Austin, TX 78713-7219
(512) 471-9122

Vermont

Bennington College Dance Archives
www.bennington.edu
Bennington College
Bennington, VT 05201
(802) 442-5401

Washington

Pacific Northwest Ballet
www.pnb.org
301 Mercer Street
Seattle, WA 98109
(206) 441-9411

Wisconsin

Wisconsin Center for Theatre Research
State Historical Society of Wisconsin
www.shsw.wisc.edu
816 State Street
Madison, WI 53706
(608) 262-3266

Canada

Bibliothèque de la Danse
Ecole Supérieure de Danse de Quebec
4816 Rue Rivard
Montreal, Quebec H2J 2N6 Canada

Dance Collection Danse
www.dcd.ca
145 George Street
Toronto, Ontario M5A 2M6 Canada
(416) 365-3233

Metropolitan Toronto Reference Library
www.mtrl.toronto.on.ca
789 Yonge Street
Toronto, Ontario M4W 2G8 Canada
(416) 393-7077

National Ballet of Canada Archive and Erik Bruhn Library
www.national.ballet.ca
470 Queens Quay West
Toronto, Ontario M5C 1G9 Canada
(416) 362-1041

SELECTED BIBLIOGRAPHY

General

AMIA Newsletter. The Newsletter of the Association of Moving Image Archivists. Los Angeles: AMIA, 1988–. Published quarterly.

Boston, George, ed. *Archiving the Audio-Visual Heritage*. Third Joint Technical Symposium, proceedings. May 3–5, 1990. Canadian Museum of Civilization, Ottawa, Ontario. Published by UNESCO and the Technical Coordinating Committee [FIAF, FIAF, IASA, and ICA], 1992.

Child, Dr. Margaret S., compiler. *Directory of Information Sources on Scientific Research Related to the Preservation of Sound Recordings, Still and Moving Images and Magnetic Tape*. Washington, D.C.: The Commission on Preservation and Access, September 1993.

Harrison, Helen P., ed. *Audiovisual Archive Literature: Select Bibliography*. General Information Program and UNISIST, United Nations Educational, Scientific and Cultural Organization. Paris: UNESCO, February 1992. Composed of three parts: 1) bibliographic references arranged by subject with limited annotations; 2) an author index; and 3) a subject index. Includes sections on: "History and development of Archives"; the management of "Film Archives" and "Broadcasting Archives"; film, newsfilm, nitrate, and video "Materials"; "Preservation" and "Restoration" of moving images; "Legal Issues"; "Standards"; "Automation" in film and video cataloging; "Appraisal" of moving images; "Storage"; "Handling"; "Disaster Preparedness"; etc.

Kopp, Leslie Hansen, ed. *Dance Archives: A Practical Manual for Documenting and Preserving the Ephemeral Art*. New York: Preserve, Inc., 1995.

Film Preservation

Film Preservation 1993: A Study of the Current State of American Film Preservation. Report of the Librarian of Congress, in consultation with the National Film Preservation Board of the Library of Congress. Volume 1: Report; Volume 2: Los Angeles Hearing; Volume 3: Washington, DC Hearing; Volume 4: Submissions. Washington, DC: U.S. Government Printing Office, 1993.

Image Permanence Institute. *The IPI Storage Guide for Acetate Film*. Rochester, NY: Image Permanence Institute, Rochester Institute of Technology, 1993. Includes a booklet, graph, table, and slide wheel.

Redefining Film Preservation: A National Plan. Recommendations of the Librarian of Congress in consultation with the National Film Preservation Board. Washington, D.C.: Library of Congress, August 1994.

Videotape

Boyle, Deirdre. *Video Preservation: Securing the Future of the Past*. New York: Media Alliance, 1993.

Jimenez, Mona and Liss Platt, eds. *Magnetic Media Preservation Sourcebook*. New York: Media Alliance, 1998.

Murphy, William T., ed. *Television and Video Preservation 1997: A Report on the Current State of American Television and Video Preservation*. Washington, DC: Library of Congress, 1997.

Van Bogart, John W.C. *Magnetic Tape Storage and Handling*. Washington, DC: Commission on Preservation and Access, 1995.

Wheeler, Jim. "Videotape Storage: How to Make Your Videotapes Last for Decades . . . or Centuries." *American Cinematographer*, 64:1 (January 1983), 23–25.

Wheeler, Jim. "Long Term Storage of Video Tape." *SMPTE Journal* (June 1983), 650–654.

Cataloging

Davidson, Steven and Gregory Lukow, eds. *The Administration of Television Newsfilm and Videotape Collections: A Curatorial Manual*. Miami, FL: Louis Wolfson II Media History Center and American Film Institute National Center for Film anad Video Preservation, 1999.

National Archives and Records Administration. *Managing Audiovisual Records, Second Edition*. College Park, MD: National Archives and Records Administration, 1996.

Walch, Victoria Irons. *Standards for Archival Description: A Handbook*. Chicago: Society of American Archivists, 1993. Guide to 85 standards (and the organizations that developed them), including USMARC formats, cataloging rules, thesauri, and standards for automated systems.

White-Henson, Wendy, compiler. *Archival Moving Image Materials: A Cataloging Manual*. Washington, DC: Library of Congress, Motion Picture, Broadcasting and Recorded Sound Division, 1984.

CHAPTER 55

Filmography

Deirdre Towers

This filmography is intended for the reader new to the world of dance on camera. Breadth of approach, from documentary to dance conceived for the camera, along with examples of excellence, was the guiding principle behind this list. These titles are personal favorites drawn from recent dance video and film festivals and from *Dance On Camera: A Guide to Dance Films and Videos,* compiled over the last 30 years by Dance Films Association.

We recommend that you check with the website of Dance Films Association, www.dancefilmsassn.org for distributor information, which is constantly changing, and/or check in the dance libraries listed in the reference section.

ABRACADABRA, 1999, 38 min. (France)
Choreographer/Director: Philippe Decouflé; Producer: Francois Roussillon, Pascale Henrot for Oibo, Arte; Dancers: DCA; Distributor: NVC Arts.
"A film without logic, with no head and no beginning or end," says this French choreographer, world-renowned for his choreography for the opening of the 1992 Winter Olympics in France. "*Abracadabra* is a kind of memo pad filled with a year's worth of choreographic ideas for the cinema," says Decouflé. "The only claim to coherence is that all the ideas come from my head."

ACROBATIC DANCE OF THE SNAKE MAIDENS, 1968, 33 min. (Ivory Coast)
Director: H. Himmelheber; Distributor: Penn State University.
Small girls from the villages of Dan and Guere in western Ivory Coast in Africa perform acrobatic feats. Then they are whirled into the air by their trainer and wound around his body. This title exemplifies the enormous variety of ethnomusicology films produced by the Wissenschaftlichen Institute in Germany in the 1950s and 1960s.

ACROBATS OF GOD, 1968, 22 min. (USA)
Choreographer: Martha Graham; Director: David Wilson; Distributor: Viewfinders.
Graham's dance—adapted for television by John Butler—celebrates the trials, denial, glories and delights of being a dancer. There are 15 videos of Graham's choreography in circulation, 11 of which feature the great artist herself. Not to be missed!

ADOLESCENCE, 1966, 22 min. (France)
Director: Vladimir Forgency; Dancers: Sonia Petrovna, Madame Egorova; Distributor: Indiana University.
A young girl studies ballet with 84-year-old Madame Egorova, whose arm movements testify to her former life as a member of Serge Diaghilev's Ballets Russes. Despite the girl's diligence, she fails her first audition. This short touchingly combines photography, narrative, and a slice of ballet history.

AIR FOR THE G STRING, 1934, 7 min. (USA)
Choreographer: Doris Humphrey; Composer: J. S. Bach; Distributor: Dance Films Association, Dance Horizons.
Five women framed by two pillars perform a vintage modern dance set to the adagio from Bach's "Air for the G String." As there are 12 videos that feature Humphrey's choreography currently circulating, this is only one suggestion. DVD **16**

ALICIA ALONSO: ALICIA, 1976, 75 min. (USA)
Choreographers: Marius Petipa, Alberto Alonso; Dancers: Alicia Alonso, Azari Plesetski with the Ballet Nacional de Cuba; Director: Victor Casaus; Producer: Cuban Film Institute; Distributor: Kultur.
Featured in Dance Films Association's first competitive Dance On Camera Festival, this portrait of the famous, nearly blind Cuban ballerina includes interviews and excerpts from *Giselle, Don Quixote, Grand Pas de Quatre*, and *Swan Lake*.

ALLEE DER KOSMONAUTEN, 1998, 58 min. (Germany)
Choreographer/Director/Producer/Distributor: Sasha Waltz; Co-director: Elliot Caplan; Producer: Jochen Sandig; Composers: Lars Rudolph, Hanno Leichtmann; Dancers: Nadia Cusimano, Luc Dunberry, Juan Kruz Diaz de Garaio Esnaola, Nicola Mascia, Takako Suzuki, Laurie Young.
Shot as a cross between a sitcom and a beautiful nightmare, this portrait of a family captures the neurotic twinges reverberating both within and between family members.

ALL THAT JAZZ, 1979, 120 min. (USA)
Choreographer/Director/Writer: Bob Fosse; Dancers: Ann Reinking, Ben Vereen; Distributor: Facets Multimedia.
This landmark film exhibits both the directing and choreographic genius of Broadway's Bob Fosse. He reveals his obsessions, his creative drive, and his loves and phobias as he struggles with his weakening heart.

ALVIN AILEY: MEMORIES AND VISIONS, 1974, 54 min. (USA)
Choreographer: Alvin Ailey; Director: Stan Lathan: Dancers: Judith Jamison, Sara Yarborough, Dudley Williams; Composer: Ralph Vaughan Williams; Distributor: University of California Extension Center.
A performance documentary of Ailey's company with excerpts from many of his greatest hits: *Blues Suite, Cry, The Lark Ascending, Revelations, House of the Rising Sun*, and others with a cast of huge personalities.

ALWAYS FOR PLEASURE, 1978, 58 min. (USA)
Director: Les Blank; Distributor: Flower Films.
Documentary on the Black Indian dances and parades as part of the celebrations in Mardi Gras in New Orleans, with stops at a jazz funeral and St. Patrick's Day festivals.

AMERICAN BALLET THEATRE: A CLOSE-UP IN TIME, 1973, 90 min. (USA)
Choreographers: Antony Tudor, Agnes de Mille, Alvin Ailey, Michel Fokine, Marius Petipa, Harold Lander, Lev Ivanov, David Blair; Director; Jerome Schur; Dancers: Cynthia Gregory, Ivan Nagy, Sallie Wilson, Ted Kivitt, and the American Ballet Theatre.
The choreographers and company founder Lucia Chase discuss ABT's history and repertoire. Selections from *Pillar of Fire, Swan Lake, Les Sylphides, Rodeo, Etudes*, and *The River*.

ARENA, 1997, 9 min. (Argentina)
Producer/Choreographer/Distributor: Margarita Bali.
In this perpetual walk to nowhere, the sands alter the state of mind in a compelling short inspired by the political crisis in Argentina.

ART OF TOUCH, 1994, 30 min. (UK)
Choreographer: Siobhan Davies; Director: Ross MacGibbon; Producer: Stephany Marks for the BBC; Dance Company: Siobhan Davies Company; Composers: Matteo Fargion, Scarlatti; Distributor: BBC Worldwide.
Seven modern dancers scamper through space, scooping up air as they go in this performance documentary made for television.

ATTRAVERSO (Through), 1999, 14 min. (Italy)
Choreographer/Producer/Distributor: Enzo Procopio; Director: Gino Sgreva; Dancers: Enzo Procopio Dancers; Composer: Paolo Bragaglia.
In a place whose confines are indecipherable, between segmented spaces and inclined floors, individuals encounter each other in their search for a way out. Filters of nets separate the shadows from the bodies, the dark from the light, the inside from the out. Now and again a possible sky appears beyond the obstacles in this dance adapted for video.

BAD, 1987, 30 min. (USA)
Choreographers: Michael Jackson, Gregg Burge, Jeffrey Daniels; Director: Martin Scorsese; Composer: Michael Jackson; Producer/Distributor: CBS Records.
This half-hour promotion for Jackson's album by the same name has all the strengths of a feature film. This urban fairy tale of winning through intimidation has the bleak edge of a prizefight. Jackson's gang has updated the military goosestep so that every muscle stands at attention, ready for attack. There are no switchblades, no blood, just a cocky come-on of a dance that turns wolves–Jackson's opponents–into lambs.

LE BAL, 1980, 112 min. (Italy)
Dancers: Etienne Guichard, Francesca de Rosa; Director: Ettore Scola; Producer: Giorgio Silvagni for Almi/Warner Brothers; Distributor: Direct Cinema.
Set in a Paris dance hall spanning 1930s to 1980s, this marvelous film has everything: dance, politics, history, sex, pathos, costumes to cherish, characters to imitate, and cinematography to study.

THE BALANCHINE LIBRARY, 1981, 1995, 1996 (USA)
Choreographer: George Balanchine; Director: Merrill Brockway, Emile Ardolino; Dancers from the 1981 version: Suzanne Farrell, Jacques d'Amboise, Peter Martins, Ib Anderson, Karin von Aroldingen, Adam Luders, Sara Leland, Heather Watts; 1995–1996 versions: Darci Kistler, Nilas Martins, Kyra Nichols, Isabel Guerin, Zhanna Ayupova; Distributors: Corinth, Viewfinders, Dance Horizons, Nonesuch Records.
In addition to the library, which includes both performance and instructional videos, the Museum of Broadcasting released a fascinating book: A *Celebration of George Balanchine: The Television Work* (1984). Along with a marvelous essay by George Balanchine and another by director Emile Ardolino, it has a list of Balanchine's extensive work for television: network specials, the *Kate Smith Hour*, the *Ed Sullivan Show*, the *Bell Telephone Hour*, early 1960s specials, the PBS chronology, French Network of the Canadian Broadcasting Corporation, and cable. One could spend a lifetime studying the Balanchine works, whether on stage or screen. Enjoy!

BALLET ADAGIO, 1971, 10 min. (Canada)
Choreographer: Asaf Messerer, rearranged by David Holmes; Director: Norman McLaren; Composer: Tomaso Albinoni; Dancers: David and Anna Marie Holmes.
The entire dance is filmed in slow motion to heighten the viewer's appreciation of the skill and technique involved in classical dance and the adagio form.

BALLET MÉCANIQUE, 1924, 15 min. (France)
Director: Fernand Léger; Distributors: Museum of Modern Art, Biograph.
This classic, the only film made by the French painter, an artist of the Cubist school, plays with the idea of mechanization. An example of choreography made in the editing process, the film presents dancing wire whisks and swirling copper pots; a woman repeatedly climbs a steep flight of stairs with a heavy sack.

BEACH BIRDS FOR CAMERA, 1992, 28 min. (USA)
Choreographer/Distributor: Merce Cunningham; Director: Elliot Caplan; Composer: John Cage; Dancers: Merce Cunningham Dance Company.
Twenty-eight or more videos made by the master modern dancer are available from the Cunningham Foundation. As one of the first modern dancers to explore the use of technology, Cunningham remains a leader in the bridge between technology and dance. One of the most poignant portraits, *Merce Cunningham: A Life in Dance* was completed in 2000 as directed by Charles Atlas. Along with Balanchine, Cunningham can be an equally absorbing study in how one choreographer's work translates to video.

BELLA FIGURA, 1998, 31 min. (Holland)
Choreographer: Jiři Kylian; Director: Hans Hulscher; Dancers: Nederlands Dans Theater; Distributor: RM Associates.
A streamlined screen adaptation of the ballet choreographed in 1995, which Kylian describes as projecting "a feeling of falling down in a dream and waking up with a broken rib."

BELLY BOAT HUSTLE, 1998, 4 min. (Canada)
Choreographer: Nicole Mion; Director/Producer/Distributor: Sandra Sawatzky; Produced for Bravo!FACT.
A hilarious escapade of five synchronized fly fishermen, shot in the Canadian Rockies.

BLOOD WEDDING, 1981, 71 min. (Spain)
Choreographer: Antonio Gades; Director: Carlos Saura; Producer: Emiliano Piedra; Dancers: Cristina Hoyos, Antonio Gades; Distributor: Xenon.
The first of a flamenco trilogy based on Federico García Lorca's tragedy about a young bride who runs off with a previous lover remains a dance film classic, rarely surpassed.

BLUE ANGEL, 1988, 78 min. (USA)
Choreographer: Roland Petit; Director: Dirk Sanders; Dancers: Dominique Khalfouni, Roland Petit, Pierre Aviotte; Distributor: Kultur.
Based on Heinrich Mann's story of a cabaret dancer (that Marlene Dietrich made famous in Josef von Sternberg's film of the same title), the ballet centers around the malicious joys of toying with a man.

BOLERO AND PICTURES AT AN EXHIBITION, 1994, 66 min. (Canada/USA)
Choreographers: Lar Lubovitch, Moses Pendleton; Composers: Maurice Ravel, Modest Petrovich Mussorgsky; Distributor: Dance Horizon.
A love duet set to Ravel's music, shot overhead in an intoxicating way, and a comical, literal take on *Pictures at an Exhibition* shot in a gallery.

BOOK OF DAYS, 1988, 75 min. (USA)
Choreographer/Director/Composer: Meredith Monk; Producer: Tatge/Lasseur Productions; Distributor: The Stutz Company.
An exploration of the meaning of time, using thematic material to draw parallels between medieval and contemporary life. DVD **10**

BOY, 1995, 5 min. (England)
A film by Rosemary Lee and Peter Anderson; Producers: Anne Beresford and Margaret Williams for MJW Productions, the BBC and the Arts Council of England; Composer: Graeme Miller; Dancer: Tom Evans.
A boy moves with playful agility creating his own private world of an empty coastal landscape. DVD **21**

BREATH, 1999, 18 min. (USA)
Choreographer/Dancers/Distributors: Eiko and Koma; Director: Jerry Pantzer; Producer: Dance Collection, The New York Public Library for the Performing Arts.
Distilled from the six-week performance installation at the Whitney Museum by a company renowned for their butoh-inspired training. Director Pantzer says, "Eiko and Koma merge with a dim, primordial landscape, yielding abstract forms of body and movement. Out of their timeless dream, a new consciousness begins to evolve." For more examples of their work, see *Tentacle* (1983) and *Bone Dream* (1985) from *Arc* Videodance, *Elegy* (1984) and *Undertow* (1988) from Electronic Arts Intermix, and *Husk* (1987).

BRIDGE OF HESITATION, 1997, 5 min. (Australia)
Producer/Choreographer/Dancer/Distributor: Alan Schacher; Dancers: Ari Ehrlich, Tim Rushton; Composer: Rik Rue.
The closing caption of this wild short suggests its motivation: "Conscience-troubled men hover between action and consequence."

BRUCE, 1998, 3 min. (USA)
Choreographer/Dancer: Bruce Jackson; Producer/Distributor: Ruth Sergel.
Speaks to notions of expectation, grace, and the beauty of communicating through movement from the perspective of a wheelchair-bound dancer.

BURNT, 1998, 15 min. (Germany)
Choreographer: Vera Sander; Producer/Director/Distributor: Holger Gruss; Composers: C-Schulz & Hajsch; Dancers: Carmen Balochini, Tom Kappler, Sean Stephens.
Two men and a woman meet. Each plays a role—whether self-determined or psychically predetermined remains a mystery.

CALL ME MADAM, 1998, 40 min. (UK)
Choreographer/Dancer: Dame Ninette de Valois; Director: Ross MacGibbon; Producer: Stephany Marks for the BBC; Dancers: Birmingham Royal Ballet, Royal Ballet, Royal Ballet School; Distributor: BBC Worldwide.
To celebrate Dame Ninette de Valois's 100th birthday, friends, colleagues and former pupils, including Pamela May, Beryl Gray, Lynn Seymour, Anthony Dowell, and David Bintley, talk about the achievements of the woman known to dancers throughout the world as "Madam." This documentary features today's stars Darcey Bussell, Sarah Wildor, and Joseph Cipolla rehearsing roles from ballets created by de Valois, with archive footage of Madam teaching, rehearsing, and talking. Ninette de Valois founded the Royal Ballet School, and the company she started in 1931 grew into the Royal Ballet and Birmingham Royal Ballet.

CAMARA, 1996, 16 min. (Canada)
Choreographers: Gretchen Schiller, Deraldo Ferreira; Director/Distributor: Gretchen Schiller; Dancer: Deraldo Ferreira; Music: Grupo de Capoeira; Producer: Sara Diamond, Banff Centre for the Arts.
An experimental documentary on capoeira dancer Deraldo Ferreira. Capoeira Angola combines martial arts, gymnastics, dance, spirituality, history, song, and improvisation.

CAMERA THREE CBS (USA)
Choreographer/Dancers: Various; Distributor: Creative Arts Television.
Many of the early Camera Three programs are available for distribution. Whether you are looking for dances from Cambodia, Spain, or other exotic lands, or are in need of footage of various celebrity dancers from the 1960s, Camera Three has kept its archives in circulation.

CAN'T STOP NOW, 1998, 54 min. (Canada)
Choreographers: Jiři Kylian, Patrick Delacroix; Director/Producer: Eileen Thalenberg; Dancers: Martine van Hamel, Gary Chryst, Sabine Kupferberg, Jeanne Solan, Gerard Lemaître, and Karen Kain; Composers: J. S. Bach, P. Tchaikovsky; Producers: Gail McIntyre, Paul Cadieux; Distributors: Filmoption International, Filmmaker's Library.
This documentary captures the emotional drive and power of dancers, all over the age of 40, who make up Jĭri Kylian's Holland-based Netherlands Dance Theatre III. Breaking stereotypes of the limitation of the older dancer, this company pushes the boundaries of what dance can be.

CARMEN, 1984, 99 min. (Spain)
Choreographer: Antonio Gades; Director: Carlos Saura; Dancers: Cristina Hoyos, Laura del Sol, Antonio Gades; Composers: Paco de Lucia, Georges Bizet; Distributor: Swank.
Carmen, the original femme fatale, exercises her erotic skill both on and offstage in this flamenco play-within-a-play.

LA CHAMBRE, 1988, 11 min. (France)
Choreographer/Director/Distributor: Joelle Bouvier/Regis Obadia; Composer: Denis Lavaillant.
Obadia/Bouvier created several amazing videos in the 1980s during a golden period for video dance in France. This particular video, which was broadcast in the USA, is set in a bare room in which a woman speaks of weariness, expectation, and mounting desire.

CHANNELS/INSERTS, 1982, 32 min. (USA)
Choreographer: Merce Cunningham; Director: Charles Atlas; Composer: David Tudor; Producer: Cunningham Dance Foundation; Dancers: Merce Cunningham Dance Company.
The directors place the cast and scene in such a way as to give the sense of dual events happening concurrently. They divided the studio into 16 possible areas for dancing. Cunningham then applied the *I Ching* to determine the order in which the divisions were used. (Spain, *Dance on Camera*, 1998). **DVD 3**

CHOREA, 1996, 5 min. (USA)
Choreographer/Director/Distributor: Jodi Kaplan; Dancers: Nina Zavarin, Cait Lyddy; Music: Josef Vik.
A dance choreographed for the screen, impossible to be done on stage, shot in black and white, with an original sense of rhythm and drama.

CIRCLES—CYCLES KATHAK DANCE, 1988, 28 min. (USA)
Director/ Producer: Robert Gottlieb; Principal Dancers: Jai Kishan, Birju Maharaj, Shaswati Sen, Daksha Sheth.
Narrated by Zakir Hussain, this film explores kathak, the classical dance of Northern India. Includes stills of miniature paintings and architectural photography reflective of the dance. **DVD 38**

CONTRECOUP, 1997, 26 min. (Switzerland)
Choreographer: Guilherme Botelho;
Director/Distributor: Pascal Magnin; Composers: Andres García, Robert Grassi.
Two men and a woman battle with their inner demons in this brilliant video adaptation of a stage choreography.

CORNERED, 1998, 5 min. (Canada)
Choreographer/Dancer: Susanna Hood;
Director/Distributor: Michael Downing; Composers: Brennan Green; Produced by Bravo!FACT.
The dancer and cameraman partner each other beautifully in exercises true to the psychological and physical implications of being cornered.

COURRIER DU PACIFIQUE, 1998, 33 min. (France)
Choreographer: Serge Copardon; Director: Kamal Musale; Dancers: The Nomades Company; Composers: Jean Schwartz, Benat Achiary, M. Etchocopar; Producer: Les Films du Lotus; Distributor: 10 Francs Production.
A winner of the Grand Prix de Video Danse, this video dance is based on the emigration of the Basques and their life dependent on the sea.

COVER GIRL, 1944, 107 min. (USA)
Choreographers: Stanley Donen, Gene Kelly, Seymour Felix, Jack Cole; Director: Charles Vidor; Dancers; Rita Hayworth, Gene Kelly; Producer: Columbia; Distributor: Facets.
Besides the chance to gaze on Rita in one of her most stunning moments, this video is a must see for dance film aficionados because of the innovative duet of Gene Kelly dancing with his best partner, himself, in "Alter Ego."

CUERPO PRESENTE/EL MAR, 1998, 50 min. (Mexico)
Choreographer/Director/Dancer/Distributor: Jenet Tame; Dancers: Marina Acevedo, Mariana Guzman, Maria Sánchez; Composers: Per Nogaard, Jose Navarro, Chopin, Conlon Nancarrow.
A performance documentary of modern dance and inventive exploration of video dance.

CURTAIN OF EYES, 1998, 13 min. (USA)
Director/Distributor: Daniele Wilmouth;
Choreographer: Katsura Kan; Choreographer-Dancers: Okyon, Lee, Izuru Mori, Takechiyo Mariya; Composer: Adrian Freedman.
A striking short that combines the aesthetics of butoh with provocative close-ups and imagery.

DADANCE, 1998, 4:30 min. (UK)
Choreographers/Distributor: Hugh Wheadon, Emmie Elmaz; Directors: Robb Horsley, Hugh Wheadon; Dancers: Emmie Elmaz, Polly Benge, Charlotte Peck.
This dance film inspired by the spirit of Dada is a collage of movement and rhythm.

DANCE AND HUMAN HISTORY, 1974, 40 min. (USA)
Director: Alan Lomax; Distributor: University of California Extension Center.
Analyzing dance from a geometric perspective, anthropologist groups types of dance in terms of linear, curvilinear or spiral tendencies, and whether the dancer's torso is moved as a block or divided into units. Three variables (climate, method of food production, and sexual division of labor) determine the shapes of dance.

DANCE: ANNA SOKOLOW'S ROOMS, 1967, 30 min. (USA)
Choreographer: Anna Sokolow; Director: Dave Geisel; Dancers: Anna Sokolow, Ze'eva Cohen, Jeff Duncan, Jack Moore; Distributor: Indiana University, PennState.
Escape, Going, Desire and *Panic*, four brilliant modern dance pieces choreographed in 1954, express isolation, alienation, loneliness, and hunger of the soul.

DANCE BLACK AMERICA, 1983, 90 min. (USA)
Choreographers: Alvin Ailey, Charles Moore, Garth Fagan, Chuck Davis; Directors: D. A. Pennebaker, Chris Hegedus; Distributors: Dance Horizons, Facets.
An onstage/offstage documentary of a festival held at Brooklyn Academy of Music. Dances performed included *Fontessa and Friends, Lindy Hop, From Before, Junkie, Juba*, and *Cakewalk*. Telecast on Great Performances, PBS Channel 13, New York on Jan. 27, 1985.

DANCE CHROMATIC, 1959, 7 min. (USA)
Dancer: Nancy Fenster; Director: Ed Emshwiller; Distributor: Film-maker's Cooperative.
This fusion of dance, abstract painting, and a percussive score is hypnotic.

DANCE IN AMERICA (series, over 75 titles), 1975–Present, 60 min. each (USA)
Directors: Merrill Brockway, Thomas Grimm, Judy Kinberg, Emile Ardolino; Producers: Merrill Brockway, Jac Venza, Emile Ardolino, Judy Kinberg for Thirteen/WNET in association with a variety of European broadcasters.
Features many of the foremost dance companies in America. Four programs a year broadcast on national public television produced with the aim of preserving and sharing the best of American dance (Spain, *Dance on Camera*, 1998).

DANCE IN AMERICA: EVERYBODY DANCE NOW, 1992, 60 min. (USA)
Choreographers: Cholly Atkins, Jamale Graves, Michael Kidd; Producer: Margaret Selby
Distributor: VPI.
This breakthrough documentary erased the boundary between arts and entertainment in that the producers of *Dance In America*, known for their formal presentation of classic modern dance and ballet, recognized street performers as masters in their own right. Dancers, choreographers, and film directors share their insight into street dance, along with footage from various music videos.

DANCEMAKER, 1998, 98 min. (USA)
Choreographer: Paul Taylor; Director: Matthew Diamond; Dance Company: Paul Taylor Dance; Producer/Distributor: Four Oaks Foundation.
This documentary, nominated for an Academy Award, follows the rise of modern dancer Paul Taylor from solitary child to dancer to master choreographer. For other work by Matthew Diamond and Paul Taylor, see *Speaking in Tongues*, 1991, from Viewfinders and/or Dance Horizons.

A DANCER'S WORLD, 1957, 30 min. (USA)
Choreographer/Dancer: Martha Graham; Director Peter Glushanok; Dancers: Mary Hinkson, Bertram Ross, Yuriko Kimura; Composer: Cameron McCosh; Producer: Nathan Kroll for WGED-TV/Pittsburgh; Distributor: Kultur, Museum of Modern Art.
Preparing for the role of Jocasta in her *Night Journey*, Martha Graham shares her philosophy and her life as a dancer. Her company demonstrates their technical and psychological preparation before they rehearse.

DANCING (Series, 8 Episodes), 1993, 60 min. each
Producer: Thirteen/WNET, RM Arts and BBC Television.
This eight-part series, filmed in 18 countries from India to the former USSR, and including Brazilian to African American forms, explores dance as a form of communication and expression in a variety of cultural contexts (Spain, *Dance on Camera*, 1998). DVD **20**

DANCING INSIDE, 1998, 38 min. (UK)
Choreographers: Jane Dudley, Frank Bock; Director: Gillian Lacey; Producer/Distributor: Tony Dowmunt.
An acclaimed former member of Martha Graham's company and a teacher in England for decades, Jane Dudley is 87 and arthritic. This documentary encapsulates her reveries and her drive to keep performing with the limited movement she still has. Computer animation provides what age would otherwise disallow.

DANS I NYA DIMENSIONER (Dance In New Dimensions), 1986, 55 min. (Sweden)
Choreographer: Birgit Cullberg; Director: Mans Reutersward; Producer: Swedish Radio-TV; Dancers: Mona Elgh, Lenna Wennergren, Niklas Ek, and Cullberg Ballet; Distributor: Proprius Publishing Co.
Birgit Cullberg (1908–1999) was a pioneer, a creative, independent thinker, and an influential choreographer, acclaimed not only for her dramatic ballets, but for her imaginative experiments with videodance. Ten excerpted examples of the innovative collaboration of Cullberg and Mans Reutersward: *The Wicked Queen* (1961), *The Swain and the Six Princesses* (1963), *Eurydice Is Dead* (1969), *Red Wine in Green Glasses* (1971, awarded the Prix Italia), *Revolt* (1972), *Peer Gynt* (1977), *School for Wives* (1974), *Miss Julie* (1980), *Pulcinella and Pimpinella* (1982), *Abballet* (1984).

DEAD DREAMS OF MONOCHROME MEN, 1989, 52 min. (UK)
Choreographer: Lloyd Newson; Director: David Hinton; Dancers: DV8; Distributor: RM Associates.
A gruesome classic dance reconceived for the camera in which four men enact a sequence of developing relationships. They experience desire and fear, obsession and distrust, frenzy, and despair. Each encounter seems to carry them further toward the far extremes of desolation and loneliness.

DEEP HEARTS, 1979, 49 min. (USA)
Director: Robert Gardner; Producer: Harvard University Film Study Center.
A film about the dances of the Borroro Fulani, a nomadic tribe in the Niger Republic of Africa. Looks at a competition called *gerewol*, in which young male dancers compete in a contest of beauty, grace, and manliness. **DVD 40**

DEERE JOHN, 2000 (USA)
Director: Mitchell Rose
A filmed pas de deux between a man and an excavating machine.

DOLLY, 1998, 17 min. (USA)
Choreographer/Director/Distributor: Michael Cole; Composer: Emanuel Dimas De Melo Pimenta.
A dance created with the animation software *LifeForms* by a former member of Merce Cunningham Dance Company.

LE DORTOIR, 1990, 53 min. (Canada)
Choreographers: Danielle Tardif, Gilles Maheu; Director: François Girard; Dance Company: Carbone 14; Producer: Niv Fichman for Rhombus International, Distributor: Bullfrog Films, Rhombus Media.
The program tells the story of a man's journey back into memory and imagination to escape and finally overcome a personal crisis. Set in a convent dormitory, it is a disturbing, nostalgic chronicle of fleeting impressions told through dance, music and images that range from the erotic to the violent. **DVD 28**

DUET, 1990, 10:30 min. (USA)
Choreographer/Director/Distributor: Jody Oberfelder-Riehm.
The director, eight months pregnant, choreographed and performed a sculptural dance to the rhythm of fetal heartbeats.

DUNE DANCE, 1980, 40 min. (USA)
Director/Distributor: Carolyn Brown; Cinematographer: Jim Klosty; Dancers: Sara Rudner, Wendy Rogers, Meg Harper, Charles Atlas, Robert Clifford.
Shot on the dunes of Cape Cod in Massachusetts, the improvised romp in the sand presents a delightful contrast to a traditional ballet score.

DUST, 1998, 9 min. (UK)
Choreographer/Dancer: Miriam King; Director/Composer: Anthony Atanasio; Distributor: Lux.
The solitary journey of a stranded long-distance swimmer in a waterless world. Searching for the sea of her dreams, her struggle eventually brings rain, regeneration, and hope.

EARLY DANCE FILMS 1894–1912, 12 min. (USA)
Dancers: Cathrina Bartho, Loie Fuller, Annabelle Moore, Ella Lola Karina; Distributor: Dance Film Archive.
First dancers ever filmed. Among the shorts are *Annabelle, Nymph and the Waves, Flag Dance, Animated Picture Studio,* and *Chrissie Sheridan*.

ELLIS ISLAND, 1982, 30 min., (USA)
Choreographer/Director/Composer: Meredith Monk; Distributor: Stutz Company.
In this chilling portrait of New York City's chief entry station to the U.S., the camera sweeps past the debris of decaying buildings to rest on a group of turn-of-the-century immigrants whose predicament is relayed through dance and simple, telling gestures.

ENIGMA VARIATIONS, 1970, 33 min. (UK)
Choreographer: Frederick Ashton; Director: James Archibald; Dancers: Svetlana Beriosova, Anthony Dowell, Stanley Holden; Composer: Edward Elgar; Distributor: Dance Film Archive.
Performance record of the story ballet, full of marvelous characters.

ENTR'ACTE, 1924, 18 min. (France)
Choreographer: Jean Borlin; Director: Rene Clair; Distributor: Dance Film Archive.
This zany, Dada-inspired silent formed part of Jean Borlin's *Relache,* performed by the Ballets Suédois.

ENTER ACHILLES, 1996, 50 min. (UK)
Director: Clara Van Gool; Choreographer: Lloyd Newson; Dance Company: DV8 Physical Theatre; Music: Adrian Johnson; Producer: Bob Lockyer, BBC Music Television; Distributor: RM Associates.
Set in a pub, this Emmy Award-winning video adaptation of a stage work challenges us to consider how oppressive men have been to themselves and one another. **DVD 25**

EXIT, 1997, 10 min. (UK)
Director: Clara van Gool; Choreographer: Jamie Walton; Music: Marvin Black; Producer/Distributor: Basilisk Communications.
A dive bomber crashes into the sea and the pilot bails out, setting the tone for another disastrous descent. Underneath the city of London, mayhem reigns in a dank tunnel where distressed urbanites fight to maintain their sanity.

FALLING DOWN STAIRS, 1995, 55 min. (USA)
Choreographer: Mark Morris; Director: Barbara Willis Sweete; Musician: Yo-Yo Ma; Composer: Johann Sebastian Bach; Dance Company: Mark Morris Dance Group; Producer: Niv Fichman for Rhombus Media.
Part of the Yo-Yo Ma *Inspired by Bach* television series, the film intimately chronicles a year-long intensive collaboration between Morris and Ma. Includes a finale performance of Bach's Cello Suite #3 choreographed for the screen. DVD **29**

FANTASIA, 1940, 120 min. (USA)
Director: Ben Sharpsteen; Producer: Walt Disney; Composers: Johann Sebastian Bach, Peter Il'ich Tchaikovsky, Paul Dukas, Igor Stravinsky, Ludwig von Beethoven, Modest Petrovich Mussorgsky, Franz Schubert.
Disney's triumph of choreography within animated form, set to eight concert pieces.

FLASHDANCE, 1983, 95 min. (USA)
Choreographer: Jeffrey Hornaday; Director: Adrian Lyne; Dancers: Marine Jahan, Jennifer Beals; Producer/Distributor: Paramount.
With a dynamite dancer replacing a comely actress for the whirlwind finale, this feature manages to present dance and film as the perfect climax for this will-to-win story. Blue-collar worker by day, erotic dancer by night and lover whenever feasible, the heroine shocks and delights the jury when she auditions for the Pittsburgh Ballet.

FLYING DOWN TO RIO, 1933, 89 min. (USA)
Choreographers: Dave Gould, Fred Astaire, Hermes Pan; Director: Thornton Freeland; Dancers: Ginger Rogers, Dolores del Rio, Fred Astaire; Distributor: Facets.
Best known for the dance on a fleet of airplanes, this music also features Astaire and Roger's first dance on screen in "The Carioca."

FORBIDDEN CITY, 1989, 56 min. (USA)
Director: Arthur Dong; Dancers: Tony and Wing, Mary Mammon, Dottie Sun, Jack Mei Ling; Composer: Gary Stockdale; Distributor: CrossCurrent Media.
This documentary takes us back to the Forbidden City nightclub, the Chinese Cotton Club of the 1930s and 1940s in San Francisco. Video includes clips of Chinese American performers who appeared regularly at the club along with discussions on how their careers were thwarted by racism.

THE GEORGE BALANCHINE INTERPRETERS ARCHIVE, 1994– (USA)
Choreographer: George Balanchine; Project Director: Nancy Reynolds; Producers: The George Balanchine Foundation and Reusch Dance Video.
Since 1994, the Foundation has been compiling two vast archives; the Archive of Lost Choreography (to retrieve Balanchine work not currently in repertory) and the Interpreters Archive (to capture the creators of Balanchine roles teaching and discussing them with dancers of today). Among many others, the Interpreters Archive includes Maria Tallchief coaching New York City Ballet dancers Judith Fugate and Peter Boal in *Scotch Symphony* and Todd Bolender coaching Albert Evans in *The Four Temperaments* (George Balanchine Foundation materials). DVD **18** DVD **17**

GHOSTCATCHING, 1999, 7 min. (USA)
Choreographer/Dancer: Bill T. Jones; Image and Sound: Paul Kaiser, Shelley Eshkar; Producer: Riverbed.
An innovative virtual dance created using motion capture technology. DVD **13**

HANDS, 1995, 4.31 min. (England)
Choreography and performance by Jonathan Burrows; Director: Adam Roberts; Music Composed by: Matteo Fargion; Producers: Fiona Morris, Rodney Wilson, Bob Lockyer; Production company: a Dancelines production for BBC-TV and The Arts Council of England.
A movement exploration using only the hands. The piece begins with a pan across a room and settles on a close-up of the dancer's hands in his lap, which remains the focal point for the entire piece. DVD **23**

HANYA: PORTRAIT OF A DANCE PIONEER, 1984, 55 min. (USA)
Choreographer: Hanya Holm; Directors: Marilyn Cristofori, Nancy Mason Hauser, John Ittleson; Distributor: Dance Horizons.
Clips of performances, conversations with choreographer/teacher Hanya Holm, and interviews with Alwin Nikolais and Glen Tetley, who worked with her. Valerie Bettis dances in the Holm style outdoors in Colorado, where Holm taught for 40 years.

HE MAKES ME FEEL LIKE DANCIN', 1983, 51 min. (USA)
Choreographer: Jacques d'Amboise; Director: Emile Ardolino; Distributor: Direct Cinema.
Academy and Emmy Award-winner. Jacques d'Amboise, former New York City Ballet principal dancer, auditions children to participate in his National Dance Institute. One thousand children learn to dance and perform in an event at Madison Square Garden with guest artists Judy Collins, Kevin Kline, and others.

HEPA!, 1999, 6 min. (USA)
Animator/Distributor: Laura Margulies.
Saucy salsa created with animation mixed with live action by an artist commissioned by Robert Redford to create a "sun dance" short for Sundance Festival 2000.

HERR, 1994, 5.16 min. (Canada)
Choreographer: Joe Laughlin; Director: John Greyson; Producer: Sara Diamond for the Banff Centre for the Arts, Alberta. Dancers: Allison Hiscott, Lynn Sheppard, Tonya Livingstone, Chantal Deeble; Produced in association with Bravo!FACT.
This mocking look at male bonding as performed by women in drag is an adaptation of a 1997 show titled "Harald, Billy, Stan and Jack."

A HOLLOW PLACE, 1999, 6 min. (Canada)
Choreographer/Dancers: Christal Pite, Drew Davidson; Director: Dan Sadler; Producers: Sylvain Lavigne, Michael Harilaid; Produced in association with Bravo!FACT.
A lone dancer in an open field protects herself from flying objects until she takes shelter in a garage, only to encounter a man of dubious intentions.

HOW I WORK, 1996, 48 min.
Choreographer: William Forsythe; Director: Mike Figgis; Interviewee: William Forsythe; Producer: Sophie Gardiner.
Featuring interviews with the choreographer and footage of the Frankfurt Ballet in rehearsal.

HURTLE, 1998, 10 min. (New Zealand)
Director/Choreographer/Distributor: Shona McCullagh; Produced by Margaret Slater.
Two nuns seek a spiritual truth and relief from mortal discomfort in this zany short.

HUSK, 1987, 10 min. (USA)
Choreographer/Director/Producer: Eiko and Koma. Performed by: Eiko.
Dance for the camera piece exploring the relationship between the camera, the body, and primal mythology.
DVD 9

IL SEGRETO DI PULCINELLA, 1998, 43 min. (Switzerland)
Choreographer: Bruno Steiner; Director/Writer: Carlo Ippolito; Producer/Distributor: Beatrice Grossman, for TSI-Swiss TV; Dance Company: Movers; Composer: Igor Stravinsky.
Multiplying Pulcinellas conquer the lords of earth and then heaven in this charming video that combines primitive set design tricks with contemporary technology tricks.

IMPACT, 1990, 10 min. (USA)
Choreographer: Elizabeth Streb; Director/Distributor: Michael Schwartz.
True to its name, *Impact* brings us right into contact with a group of performances in vigorous gymnastic patterns.

IM . . . PULSE, 2000, 12 min. (Finland)
Choreographer/Dancer/Distributor: Mikko Kallinen; Director: Jori Polkki; Composer: Alan Stones; 3D Design: Pauli Hurme; 3D Animation: Uwyi Shestakov.
A stylish, surreal video of computer-generated choreography that stretches our definition of space and time.

IN APNEE, 1998, 57 min. (Belgium)
Choreographer: Wim Vandekeybus; Producer/Distributor: Khadouj Films; Director: Lut Vandekeybus; Composers: Peter Vermeersch, George Van Dam.
Documents the process and life of a dance company that inspired a whole generation of dancers.

INTOLERANCE, 1916, 163 min. (USA)
Director/Producer: D. W. Griffith; Choreographer: Ruth St. Denis, Gertrude Bambrick; Original Music by: Joseph Carl Breil, Carl Davis and D. W. Griffith
Considered one of D. W. Griffith's greatest works, this classic silent film examines intolerance in four historical eras. Includes several dance sequences, most notably in the Babylonian scenes. DVD 5

INVISIBLE WINGS, 1999, 27 min. (USA)
Choreographer: Joanna Haigood; Director: Nuria Olive-Belles; Dancers: Zaccho Dance Theatre; Composer: Linda Tillery; Producer/Distributor: Jacob's Pillow Dance Festival.
America's oldest dance festival, Jacob's Pillow, occupies an eighteenth-century farm site that also served as a stop on the Underground Railroad for runaway slaves in the Civil War era. This documentary chronicles the process of choreographing a site-specific work that evokes this heritage and features scenes from the final production.

IOWA BLIZZARD, 1973, 11 min. (USA)
Choreographer/Director/Distributor: Elaine Summers; Director: Bill Rowley.
A dance mid-snowstorm with images of the dancers multiplied, reversed, and presented in slow motion in a sweet example of split screen technique.

JAZZ DANCE, 1980, 4 min. (USA)
Dancer: Gay Delanghe; Director: Doris Chase; Composer: Jelly Roll Morton; Distributor: Museum of Modern Art.
Doris Chase explains, "I used an outline generator and controlled the time sequence with a slow-motion disc to choreograph with the dancer."

JENI LEGON: LIVING IN A GREAT BIG WAY, 1998, 49 min. (Canada)
Choreographer/Dancer: Jeni Legon; Director: Grant Greschuk; Producer: Selwyn Jacob for National Film Board of Canada; Distributor: National Film Board of Canada.
The legendary tap dancer shares her story of being a Black performer in Hollywood in the 1930s and 1940s, her views of Canada's diversity, and her passion for following her dream.

KAMMER, KAMMER, 2000, approx. 120 min. (Germany)
Choreographer/Director: William Forsythe; a piece by William Forsythe; Producer: Ballett Frankfurt; Dancers: Ballett Frankfurt; video editing design by Philip Bussman; Text by Anne Carson and Douglas A. Martin.
Digital recording documenting the multimedia stage production. DVD 12

KINETIC MOLPAI, 1935
Choreographer: Ted Shawn; Director: Jess Meeker; Featuring Ted Shawn and His Men Dancers. DVD 7

KUS PO KUSU, 1998, 51 min. (Czechoslovakia)
Producer: Czech Television; Director/Choreographer: Michael Caban; Choreographer: Simon Caban; Dance Company: Ballet Unit Cramp.
Translated as *Piece by Piece*, this video, which Philippe Decouflé said should "win a mad movie prize," presents seven moving art ideas inspired by late twentieth century music.

LA MORT DU CYGNE, 1937, 90 min. (France)
Choreographer: Serge Lifar; Directors: Jean-Benît Lévy, Jean Epstein; Dancers: Yvette Chauvire, Mia Slavenska, Janine Charrat.
This marvelous feature film centers around a student dancer who worships a rising star in the Paris Opera Ballet and considers the star's rival an invader. MGM produced an unfortunate remake, a vehicle for Margaret O'Brien called *The Unfinished Dance.*

LATCHO DROM, 1994, 104 min. (France)
Director: Tony Gatlif; Distributor: New Yorker Films.
Shot in eight countries from Afghanistan to Spain by a Gypsy director, this video brings us into the hearts of the Gypsies through amazing photography, music, and dance.

LE P'TIT BAL, 1993, 4 min. (France)
Choreographer/Director/Dancer/Distributor: Philippe Decouflé; Producer: Oïbo, Télèma Arcanal; Composers: Robert Nyel, Gaby Verlor; Dancers: Phillipe Decouflé, Pascale Houbin, Annie Lacour.
In this wonderful little piece, two lovers sitting at a table in field of long waving grasses express their emotions in gestures derived from sign language.

LIMELIGHT, 1952, 144 min. (USA)
Director/Composer: Charles Chaplin; Dancers: Andre Eglevsky, Melissa Hayden, Distributor: CBS/Fox.
The great silent comedian joins Buster Keaton in this feature centered around an attempt to rescue a ballerina from despair.

LITTLE LIEUTENANT, 1993, 6 min. (USA)
Choreographer: Sally Silvers; Directors: Sally Silvers, Henry Hills; Composer: Kurt Weill; Distributor: Filmmaker's Cooperative.
Combines news footage with a dance reflecting the Weimar era.

LITTLEST REBEL, 1935, 70 min. (USA)
Dancers: Shirley Temple, Bill Robinson; Director: David Butler; Producer: Twentieth Century Fox; Distributors: Facets.
Only one of 19 movies made by the child star, this feature is notable for her duet with the great tap dancer Bill Robinson, and for the child's determination to save her father, a Confederate soldier.

LODELA, 1996, 27 min. (Canada)
Choreographer: José Navas; Director: Philippe Baylaucq; Dancers: José Navas, Chi Long; Distributor: National Film Board of Canada.
An arresting duet inspired by the *Tibetan Book of the Dead*, shot from the perspective of the audience and that of the performer. DVD **27**

THE LONGEST TRAIL, 1984, 60 min. (USA)
Directors/Producers: Alan Lomax and Forrestine Paulay of the Choreometrics Project, Center for Social Sciences and Department of Anthropology, Columbia University.
Part of the series "Rhythms of Earth: A Global Anthology of Dance Seen in Cross-cultural Perspective," *The Longest Trail* is a dance geography of the American Indian people. It explores the Arctic background of North and South American Indian dance styles, suggesting hunting behavior and animal movement as sources for native dance. Part 1, Siberia to Guatemala. Part 2, Panama to Tierra del Fuego. (New York Public Library Database)

MAKAROVA: IN A CLASS OF HER OWN, 1985, 60 min. (UK)
Choreographer: Roland Petit; Director: Derek Bailey; Dancer: Natalia Makarova; Distributor: Dance Horizons.
The Russian ballerina takes a private class with her coach Irina Yakobsen. Makarova offers her insights on the differences between Romantic and classical technique and the Russian and Western approaches to dance.

MAKING DANCES: SEVEN POSTMODERN CHOREOGRAPHERS, 1980, 89 min. (USA)
Choreographers: Trisha Brown, Lucinda Childs, Douglas Dunn, David Gordon, Kenneth King, Meredith Monk, Sara Rudner; Director/Distributor: Michael Blackwood.
Seven artists inspired by the Martha Graham-Merce Cunningham tradition perform and talk about their art. Performances include *Accumulation with Talking Plus Water Motor* by Brown; *Dance* by Childs; *Foot Rules* by Dunn; *An Audience with the Pope, One Part of the Matter* by Gordon; *World Raid* by King; *Education of the Girlchild* and *Dolmen Music* by Monk; and *Modern Dances* by Rudner.

MARGIE GILLIS—WILD HEARTS IN STRANGE TIMES, 1996, 58 min. (Canada)
Choreographers: Margie Gillis, James Kudelka, Stephanie Ballard; Producer/Writer: Veronica Tennant for CBC Radio-Canada; Director: Joan Tosoni; Dancers: Margie Gillis, Rex Harrington, Seana McKenna, Ashley MacIsaac, Paola Styron, and the students of the National Ballet School of Canada; Composer: Leonard Cohen, J. S. Bach, Ashley MacIsaac, H. Purcell, Gustav Mahler; Distributor: CBC International Sales.
This performance biography was conceived by producer Veronica Tennant, former ballerina of the National Ballet of Canada. Joining Gillis is opera superstar Jessye Norman.

MARTHA GRAHAM DANCE COMPANY, 1976, 90 min. (USA)
Choreographer: Martha Graham; Director: Merrill Brockway for Thirteen/WNET *Dance In America*; Dancers: Peter Sparling, Elisa Monte, Peggy Lyman, Takako Asakawa, Janet Eilber; Composers: Zoltan Kodaly, Louis Horst, Aaron Copland, Samuel Barber; Distributor: Indiana University.
This award-winner has Graham introducing her *Diversion of Angels* (1948), *Lamentation* (1930), *Frontier, Adorations, Appalachian Spring* (1944), and Medea's solo (danced by Takako Asakawa) from *Cave of the Heart.*

MARY WIGMAN: FOUR SOLOS, 1929, 10 min. (Germany)
Choreographer/Dancer: Mary Wigman; Distributor: Museum of Modern Art.
The dramatic German dancer who had a powerful influence on Martha Graham performs *Seraphic Song, Pastorale, Dance of Summer,* and *Witch Dance.* DVD **15**

MAYA DEREN: EXPERIMENTAL FILMS, 1943–1959, 76 min. (USA)
Director: Maya Deren; Dancer: Talley Beatty; Distributor: Mystic Fire Video, Women Make Movies.
"Each film," wrote Maya Deren, "was built as a chamber and became a corridor, like a chain reaction." The collection of this innovative filmmaker includes *Meshes of the Afternoon, At Land, A Study in Choreography for Camera, Ritual in Transfigured Time, Meditation on Violence* and *The Very Eye of Night.* DVD **1**

THE MEN WHO DANCED: THE STORY OF TED SHAWN'S MALE DANCERS 1933–1940, 1986, 30 min. (USA)
Choreographer: Ted Shawn, Director: Ron Honsa; Distributor: Dance Horizons.
A reunion of the members of Ted Shawn's all-male troupe includes interviews, flashback stills, and performance footage. Founded in 1933, the company had a daily routine of working in the fields, dancing, and building Jacob's Pillow, a performance center in Massachusetts.

MERCE BY MERCE BY PAIK, 1978, 30 min. (USA)
Choreographer: Merce Cunningham; Directors: Nam June Paik, Shigeko Kubota, Charles Atlas; Distributor: Electronic Arts Intermix.
This dance choreographed for the camera illustrates that time and movement are reversible. Includes *Blue Studio, Merce and Marcel,* and Russell Connor's interview with Marcel Duchamp.

A MIDSUMMER NIGHT'S DREAM, 1998, 60 min. (UK)
Choreographer: George Balanchine; Director: Ross MacGibbon; Producer: Nigel Sheperd; Dancers: Pacific Northwest Ballet; Composer: Felix Mendelssohn; Distributor: BBC Worldwide.
A masterful recording in high definition of the full-length ballet performed at the Sadlers Wells Theatre in London in the spring of 1999.

MILT AND HONI, 1996, 90 min. (USA)
Choreographer: Charles Honi Coles, Brenda Bufalino; Director/Distributor: Louise Tiranoff.
This documentary captures the friendship and relationship of two legends of American jazz, bass player Milt Hinton and tap dancer Honi Coles. Using the original and archival footage that spans the last century, the documentary shows couples doing the Charleston, Honi Coles and his brother at the Cotton Club, and jazz greats Cab Calloway and Dizzy Gillespie.

THE MIME OF MARCEL MARCEAU, 1972, 23 min. (France)
Choreographer/Dancer: Marcel Marceau; Director: David Camus; Distributor: Coronet/MTI.
The French master mime plays Bip and other characters and explains the background of each gesture.

MOTHER AND CHILD, 1996, 9 min. (USA)
Choreographer/Dancer: Maureen Fleming; Director/Producer/Distributor: Jeff Bush; Composer: Henryk Gorecki.
A director and a dancer, long-time collaborators, partner each other effortlessly in this Butoh-inspired dance.

MOTHERS AND DAUGHTERS, 1994, 9 min. (UK)
Choreographer: Victoria Marks; Director: Margaret Williams; Dancers: Anna Pons Carrera, Marta Carrera, and others; Composer: Jocelyn Pook; Singer: Melanie Pappenheim; Producer: Anne Beresford and MJW Productions for Channel 4 Television.
Involving 10 actual mother-daughter pairs as performers, the piece explores mother-daughter relationships through movement and gesture. DVD **34**

MY GRANDFATHER DANCES, 1998, 10 min. (USA)
Dancer/choreographer Anna Halprin; Director/Distributor: Douglas Rosenberg.
A touching, storytelling tribute to the grandfather who inspired the San Francisco-based modern dance pioneer.

NAGRIN VIDEOTAPE LIBRARY OF DANCE, 1948–90, 16 films and videos (USA)
Choreographer/Dancer/Distributor: Daniel Nagrin.
The archive of the great loner of modern dance, master of the cool character, Daniel Nagrin.

NEW ENGLAND DANCES, 1990, 28 min. (USA)
Director/Producer: John Bishop and Media Generation.
Documentary on the revival of traditional music and dance in Maine and Massachusetts, told in the words of local callers, musicians, and dancers. (New York Public Library Database) DVD **37**

NIK AND MURRAY, 1986, 56 min. (USA)
Choreographer: Murray Louis; Director: Christian Blackwood; Distributor: Museum of Modern Art.
Alwin Nikolais and Murray Louis, collaborators for more than twenty years, share their life together on and off stage. Includes clips of their piece *School for Bird People,* performed in the streets of Aix-en-Provence.

NINE VARIATIONS ON A DANCE THEME, 1966, 13 min. (USA)
Director/Producer: Hilary Harris; Danced by: Bettie de Jong; Composer: McNeil Robinson; Distributor: Mystic Fine Video
An exploration of dance in which a simple dance theme is repeated and interpreted in a number of ways using the basic elements of motion picture craft: editing, camera angle, and camera movement. DVD **2**

NO MAPS ON MY TAPS, 1979, 58 min. (USA)
Director/Producer: George T. Nierenberg; Choreographers/Dancers: Bunny Briggs, Chuck Green, Sandman Sims; Musical Director: Lionel Hampton.
Insight into tap dancing with historical footage from the 1930s and portraits of three master hoofers, and a finale at Harlem's Smalls Paradise, hosted by Lionel Hampton and his big band. (Spain, *Dance on Camera,* 1998) DVD **8**

NURSED IN PELE, 2000, 9 min. (USA)
Choregrapher: Halau o Kekuhi; Director: Mark Eby; Performers: Halau o Kekuhi and the Kumu Hula Association of Los Angeles; Music: Halau o Kekuhi; Producer: Bluestocking Films, Catchlight Films, and the World Arts Foundation.
"Nursed in Pele" is a phrase used by Kaipo Frias to describe the dance repertoire of hula that springs from the eruptive volcano personae, Pele and Hi'iaka. This documentary short follows Nalani Kanaka'ole and Halau o Kekuhi as they join the Los Angeles Hawaiian community to perform at the Hollywood Bowl during the 1999 World Festival of Sacred Music. DVD **39**

NUSSIN, 1998, 14 min. (Netherlands)
Director/Distributor: Clara Van Gool; Dancers: Bennie Bartels, Martine Berghuijs, Claudia Codega, Dries van der Post; Composer: Vincent van Warmerdam; Producer: Egmond Film and TV in co-production with the NPS.
A tango party gets out of hand, spreading into all the rooms of an apartment until it leaks out into a bleak wintry landscape.

OMNIBUS, 1999, 26 min. (Spain)
Choreographer: Ramon Oller; Director/Distributor: Francisco Millan; Producer: Inigo Conzalez de Lara; Dancers: Nuria Moreno with Compánía Metros; Composer: Oscar Roig.
Based on a tale by Argentinean writer Julio Cortazár, this four-part dance has a winning surrealist opening in a journey by grievers on their way to a cemetery. It features the lighting and camera work of Teo Escamilla, renowned for his work on Carlos Saura's flamenco trilogy.

ONSDAG (Wednesday), 1996, 20 min. (Norway)
Director/Distributor: Kjersti Martinsen.
An unpretentious but effective documentary about eight women who have met to dance every Wednesday for 50 years.

OUTSIDE IN, 1994, 15 min. (UK)
Choreographer: Victoria Marks; Director: Margaret Williams; Dancers: CandoCo Dance Co; Composer: Steve Beresford; Producer/Distributor: Anne Beresford for MJW Productions, Arts Council.
This award-winning journey, along tracks and pathways both real and imaginary, brings discoveries of physicality, identity, and movement among disabled and non-disabled dancers. Seek from MJW or the Arts Council *Mothers and Daughters* and *Men*, created by the same team. 1994 was a winning year for the dance video series created by the Arts Council. Another favorite from this series is "Touched" choreographed by Wendy Houstoun, directed by David Hinton.
DVD **35**

PALM PLAY, 1980, 30 min.
Directors/Producer: Alan Lomax, Irmgard Bartenieff, Forrestine Paulay.
Illustrates six types of palm gestures prevalent in the dances of the Far East, Indonesia, and Europe, as an attempt to understand the nature of their respective societies. (Spain, *Dance on Camera,* 1998)

PARAFANGO, 1983–84, 29 min. (USA)
Choreographer: Karole Armitage; Director: Charles Atlas; Dancers: Michael Clark, Philippe Decouflé, Nathalie Richard, Jean Guizeroix, Karole Armitage; Distributor: The Kitchen.
A montage of rehearsals with plots and subplots revolving around the choreographer and four male partners. War rages, buildings collapse, trees fall, and a cashier whiles the day away watching television.

PAS DE DEUX, 1968, 14 min. (Canada)
Choreographer: Ludmilla Chiriaeff; Director: Norman McLaren; Dancers: Margaret Mercier, Vincent Warren; Distributor: National Film Board of Canada.
Two principals of Les Grands Ballets Canadiens, silhouetted by rear lighting and multiplied through the exposure of individual frames up to eleven times, perform a pas de deux as manipulated by the master animator. By the same animator, Norman McLaren, the 1971 *Ballet Adagio* is available from the National Film Board of Canada. DVD **26**

PEARL/PLAIN, 1998, 8 min. (USA)
Director/Dancer/Distributor: Carol Kyles Finley; Dancer: Camille Jackson; Composer: Gillian Welch.
This video poem explores the loyalty and odd formality of a friendship.

POET KALIDAS' AS SHAKUNTALA, 1998, 88 min. (USA)
Choreographer/Dancer/Distributor: Satya N. Charka; Director: Paul Zehrer; Dancers: East-West School of Dance; Composer: Shankar Shanbhoge.
A Sanskrit drama of ancient India stemming from the epic tradition of *Mahabharata.*

POINTS IN SPACE, 1986, 55 min. (USA)
Choreographer: Merce Cunningham; Director: Elliot Caplan, Merce Cunningham; Composer: John Cage; Producer: Bob Lockyer of BBC-TV and Cunningham Dance Foundation; Dance Company: Merce Cunningham Dance Company.
Rehearsals and interviews with the artists take the viewer through the complexities of bringing a dance to television. (Spain, *Dance on Camera*, 1998) DVD **4**

A PORTRAIT OF GISELLE, 1981, 98 min. (USA)
Choreographers: Jean Coralli, Jules Perrot; Director: Muriel Balash; Dancers: Alicia Alonso, Yvette Chauvire, Carla Fracci, Alicia Markova, Olga Spessivtzeva, Galina Ulanova, Natalia Makarova, Patricia McBride; Distributor: Kultur.
An Academy Award-winning documentary on the Romantic ballet, with its performance history and insights on its technical and dramatic demands. Eight of the greatest Giselles illustrate the points with footage of their performances dating from 1932. Dolin also prepares Patricia McBride for the title role.

POSITIVE MOTION, 1992, 37 min. (USA)
Choreographer: Anna Halprin; Director: Andy Wilson; Distributor: University of California Extension Center.
The men of an HIV/AIDS group in San Francisco express their feelings through dance to combat their fears and the isolation of their condition.

PULL YOUR HEAD TO THE MOON, 1992, 12 min. (USA)
Choreographer: David Roussève; Director: Ayoka Chenzira; Dancers: Aziza, Sondra Loring, Renee Redding-Jones, David Roussève, Genevieve Roussève, Julie Tolentino, Charmaine Warren; Producer: Alive-TV; Distributor: KTCA-TV.
The artists trace the experience of the choreographer's current New York life and that of his Creole grandmother growing up in Louisiana during the 1920s.

QUARRY, 1977, 80 min. (USA)
Choreographer/Composer: Meredith Monk; Director: Amrak Nowak; Distributor: Dance Film Archive.
This Obie-award winning opera in three movements: a lullaby, march, and requiem depicting a child's half comprehending vision of war and the Holocaust.

RAINBOW ETUDE, 1996, 50 min. (USA)
Choreographer: Donald McKayle; Director: Peter Etnoyer; Producers: Carolyn Adams and Julie A. Strandberg; Dancers: U.C. Irvine Students. DVD **19**

THE RED SHOES, 1948, 135 min. (UK)
Choreographer: Léonide Massine; Directors: Michael Powell, Emeric Pressburger; Dancers: Moira Shearer, Ludmilla Tcherina, Robert Helpmann, Léonide Massine; Distributor: Facets.
Classic feature film based on the Hans Christian Andersen fairytale. A young ballerina, obsessed with her art, marries a young composer equally absorbed in his. Torn between loyalties to her director and her love, the ballerina meets a tragic ending.

REINES D'UN JOUR, 1996, 25 min. (Switzerland)
Director/Distributor: Pascal Magnin; Choreographers/Dancers: Marie-Louise Nespolo, Christine Kung; Dancers: Veronique Ferrero, Roberto Molo, Mikel Aristegui, Antonio Bull; Music: Philippe Héritier; Producer: Claudine Kaehr, Television Suisse Romande.
Six tumbling bodies on mountain slopes of the Alps, caught between Heaven and Earth, among the cows and the villagers, make a tribute to the beauty of nature in this landmark dance video.

RETURN OF THE FIREBIRD, 1997, 116 min. (Russia)
Director/Dancer/Distributor: Andris Liepa; Choreographer: Michel Fokine; Staged by: Isabelle Fokine and Andris Liepa; Dancers: Nina Ananiashvili, Tatiana Beletskaya, Ilze Liepa, Gedeminas Taranda, and Victor Yeriomenko; Composers: Igor Stravinsky, Nikolai Rimsky-Korsakov; Producer: Mosfilm Studios.
A film version of Fokine's *Petrouchka*, *The Firebird*, and *Scheherazade*.

RETURNING HOME, 2001, 40 min. (USA)
Director: Andy Wilson; Choreographer/Dancer: Anna Halprin; Producer: Open Eye Pictures.
Includes an interview with Anna Halprin and beautiful documentation of one of her improvisations in nature.
DVD 36

RISIBLE CHICK, 1993, 5 min. (Canada)
Choreographer: Leslie Lindsay; Director: Nick de Pencier; Dancer: Lisa Prebianca; Music: Dave Clark, Blake Howard, Henry Moth; Producer: Mercury Films.
DVD 31

ROAD TO THE STAMPING GROUND, 1987, 58 min. (Netherlands)
Choreographer: Jiři Kylian; Director: David Muir, Hans Hulscher; Distributor: Dance Horizons.
In this biography of a ballet, Czech-born choreographer Jiri Kylian attends the annual gathering of 500 aboriginal tribes on Groote Eylandt, an island off Australia. Ten years later, footage of Kylian's rehearsals of the dance, inspired by the event, are intercut with close-ups of the aboriginal dances.

ROYAL WEDDING, 1951, 93 min. (USA)
Choreographer: Nick Castle; Director: Stanley Donen; Dancers: Fred Astaire, Jane Powell; Composer: Burton Lane; Distributors: Facets, Swank, MGM.
This Astaire classic feature about a brother and sister dance team in London must be seen for its famous trick-dance on the walls and ceiling, set to the tune of "You're All the World To Me."

SENSUAL SOLITUDE, 1998, 7 min. (France)
Producer/Distributor: Agathe Berman; Director: Nils Tavernier; Dancers: Kader Belarbi, Frédérique Bauer, Chrislaure Nollet, Anne Rebeschini, Julie Ferrier; Composer: Marc Perrone.
A sequence of five dances—solo, minuet, waltz, tango solo—on the themes of seduction, love, and fatigue.

SENZA—WITHOUT, 1998, 10 min. (Italy)
Choreographer; Simona Lisi; Director: Massimo Angelucci Comazzini; Dancer: Simona Lisi; Composer: G. Rossini.
Amusing short, shot in a restaurant, edited to fit the nuances of the music.

SEVEN BRIDES FOR SEVEN BROTHERS, 1954, 120 min. (USA)
Choreographers: Michael Kidd, Matt Mattox; Director: Stanley Donen; Dancers: Jacques d'Amboise, Marc Platt, Russ Tamblyn, Matt Mattox; Composer: Gene de Paul; Distributor: Swank, Facets.
Six rowdy Oregon farmers come to town looking for wives after their eldest brother finds a mate. A landmark dance film with choreography conceived for the screen. Dance numbers include "House-Raising Dance" and "Lonesome Polecat." Based on a story by Stephen Vincent Benet.

SINGIN' IN THE RAIN, 1952, 120 min. (USA)
Choreographer/Directors: Gene Kelly, Stanley Donen; Dancers: Gene Kelly, Debby Reynolds, Donald O'Connor, Cyd Charisse; Composer: Nacio Herb Brown; Distributor: Swank, Facets.
Classic spoof of Hollywood at the dawn of the sound era, with unforgettable dances in the rain, on tabletops, over sofas, on stairs, and on deserted sets.

SISTERSISTER, 1999, 8 min. (Argentina)
Choreographer: Susana Szperling; Director: Silvina Szperling; Producer: SZ Danza / SZPep; Dancers: Celia Brown, Fedra Fouroulis; Music: Willie Campins.
Two dancers (sisters, friends, lovers?) live their life of routine, tension, and care for each other. DVD **32**

SIX SOLOS: LI CHIAO-PING, 1998, 50 min. (USA)
Choreographers: Mark Dendy, David Dorfman, Joe Goode, Daniel Nagrin, Gus Solomons, Jr., Mel Wong; Director: Douglas Rosenberg; Dancer: Li Chiao-Ping; Distributor: Artworks.
This documentary follows the making of *The Men's Project*, an evening-length show of solos by internationally recognized choreographers.

16 MILLIMETER EARRINGS, 1979, 25 min. (USA)
Choreographer/Dancer: Meredith Monk; Director/Distributor: Robert Withers.
A recreation of a dance/theater solo first performed in 1966 by the versatile composer-dancer-filmmaker who had subsequent great success with *Ellis Island* and *Book of Days* (1988), distributed by The Stutz Company.
DVD **11**

SOLO, 1995, 8 min. (France)
Choreographer/Dancer: William Forsythe; Director: Thomas Lovell Balogh; Composer: Thom Willems; Producer: Beatrice Dupont, RD Studio Productions, France 2 and the BBC; Distributor: NVC Arts.
An elegant solo work performed by Forsythe himself. Shot in black and white. The director uses carefully chosen cuts to heighten the kinesthetic experience of the movement.

SOLSTICE, 1998, 11 min. (France)
Choreographers: H. Fattoumi/E. Lamoureux; Director: Christophe Bargues; Dancers: Hela Fattoumi, Eric Lamourex; Composer: Ch. Sechet, A. Brahem.
A duet that becomes a trio as the cameraman joins the dance.

SON IMAGE DANSE, 1998, 64 min. (Belgium)
Choreographer: Akarova;
Choreographer/Dancer/Composer: Michele Noiret; Producer/distributor: Silence Asbl, Kamalalam, Compagnie Tandem; Director: Michel Jakar.
Follows the great Belgian dancer Akarova, age 90, as she coaches a young dancer in the quiet of her apartment.

A SONG OF THE BODY, 1999, 11 min. (USA)
Choreographers: Meredith Rainey, Jeffrey Gribler, Cidney Spohn, Matthew Neenan;
Director/Distributor: J. Tobin Rothlein; Dancers: The Pennsylvania Ballet.
A photographic story about the connection of four dancer-choreographers to their work and experiences with HIV/AIDS.

SPARGIMENTO, 1999, 25 min. (Italy)
Choreographers/Distributors: Laura Balis and Cinzia Romiti; Director: Kiko Stella; Dancers: Corte Sconta, Laura Balis, Paolo Baccareni, Lisa Da Boit, Soraya Perez, Franco Reffo, Giovanni Scarella, Midori Watanabe; Composer: Nicola Sani.
Derived from a stage work twice as long, this video shows seven dancers moving as one passionate, vulnerable, and dreamy body thrown by a flood of dynamics. They took their inspiration from the form of the biblical psalm, but the voices are not sacred. The song is just a cry of emotions, sentiments and ideas flung toward nothingness.

STEP STYLE, 1980, 29 min. (USA)
Directors: Alan Lomax and Forrestine Paulay; Distributor: University of California Extension Media Center.
A cross-cultural study of leg and foot movements in dance styles throughout the world, showing them to be related to productive activities and social structure. Shows that dances emphasizing lower leg agility and the pointing of heel and toe are typical of highly stratified, socially complex cultures, where lower leg activity is crucial in establishing social distance and strata. (http.orion2.library.ucla.edu)

STICKS ON THE MOVE, 1983, 4 min. (USA)
Choreographer/Director: Pooh Kaye; Composer: John Kilgore; Distributor: Picture Start.
Single shots of people chewing on, riding on, and twirling on sticks, magically stitched together with the stop-motion animation technique.

THE STORY OF VERNON AND IRENE CASTLE, 1939, 94 min. (USA)
Choreographers: Fred Astaire, Hermes Pan; Dancers: Fred Astaire, Ginger Rogers; Director: Henry C. Potter; Producer: RKO; Distributor: Facets.
Whether you love ballroom or fashion, this is a fascinating biography of the couple, Vernon and Irene Castle, who triggered the popularity of ballroom dancing at the turn of the century. To see the couple themselves, see *Trailblazers of Modern Dance*.

STRICTLY BALLROOM, 1992, 94 min. (Australia)
Choreographer/dancers: Paul Mercurio, Antonio Vargas; Director: Baz Luhrmann; Distributor: Facets.
The story of a ballroom competition in which a rebellious contestant scandalizes traditionalists by introducing new steps of his own. This feature pokes affectionate jabs at the rituals of both flamenco and ballroom.

A STUDY IN CHOREOGRAPHY FOR CAMERA, 1945, 2 min. (USA)
Director: Maya Deren; Dancer: Talley Beatty; Distributor: Mystic Fire Video.
Deren, a pioneer in avant-garde film, explores alternative perspectives of space and time in this early experimental cinedance (silent film). DVD 1

A SUN DANCE, 1998, 6:30 min. (USA)
Choreographer/Dancer: Ali Fischer; Director/Distributor: Dikayl.
Inspired by the idea of dance and joy of light itself, this video includes scenes shot with an open aperture to cradle or warp the dancer with sunlight, intensifying their oneness.

SURE, 1995, 11 min. (Australia)
Director/Choreographer/Distributor: Tracie Mitchell; Composer: Georgina Veevers.
Captures women, their place in contemporary society, and their potential power as individuals in the face of choice.

SUZANNE FARRELL: ELUSIVE MUSE, 1996, 90 min. (USA)
Choreographer: George Balanchine; Director: Anne Belle; Distributor: Seahorse Films.
The third in a trilogy which includes *Reflections of a Dancer: Alexandra Danilova* and *Dancing for Mr. B.*, this documentary gives Farrell a chance to tell her story of her relationship with her mentor George Balanchine, founder of New York City Ballet.

TANGOS: THE EXILE OF GARDEL, 1985, 125 min. (Argentina)
Choreographer: Margarita Bali; Director: Fernando Sloanas; Distributor: The New Yorker.
Argentines bemoaning their political exile in Paris create a tragicomedy with music and dance in many locations. With black and white footage evocative of tango singer Carlos Gardel, who died in 1935.

TANTALUS, 1997, 7:30 min. (Canada)
Choreographer/Dancer: David Pressault; Director: Kevin Cottam; Producer: Erin Smith; Distributor: Sydney Netter Distribution; Composer: Gilles Goyette.
An eerie tone hums through this sculptural film based on the Greek myth.

TARI RICKSHAW, 1998, 4 min. (Canada)
Choreographer: Peter Chin; Producer/Director: Nick de Pencier; Producer: David Brady, Pipe Dream Communications; Produced/Distributed by Bravo!FACT.
A rickshaw passenger, traveling down Toronto's Yonge Street on a busy night, fidgets and gestures his way into an armchair ballet fit for viewing by Asian royalty.

TERRITORIAL CLAIMS, 1997, 20 min. (Ireland)
Director: Donal Haughey; Choreographer: Mary Nunan; Music: Tommy Hayes; Company/Distributor: Daghdha Dance Company; Producer: University of Limerick.
This screen adaptation of a staged work juxtaposes politics and emotions, highlighting two reactions to life: the straight and narrow and the gnarled and twisted.

THAT'S ENTERTAINMENT, 1974, 1976, 1993, 133 min. each (USA)
Dancers: Fred Astaire, Gene Kelly, Lisa Minnelli, Cyd Charisse, Esther Williams, and more; Directors: Jack Haley, Jr., Gene Kelly; Producer: MGM/UA; Distributors: Facets, Swank, MGM/UA.
A dazzling, comprehensive guide to film choreography involving over 100 numbers from musicals, comedies and dramas. A must for any student of musical theatre and dance film.

THREE, 1998, 16 min. (USA)
Choreographer/Dancers/Distributors: Ralph Lemon, Bebe Miller; Director: Isaac Julien;
Producer: Craig Paull; Executive Producers: Tricia Pierson, Ann Rosenthal; Actress: Cleo Sylvester
A sketch of three characters and their relationships.

THREE KNOCKS ON THE DOOR, 1998, 56 min. (Australia)
Producer/distributor: Aanya Whitehead; Director: Kevin Lucas; Choreographers: Philippe Gentry, Mary Underwood; Composer: Ian McDonald.
This documentary reveals the magic of puppeteer Philippe Gentry, who creates beauty out of disorder.

TOUCHED, 1994, 14 min. (England)
Choreographer: Wendy Houstoun; Director: David Hinton; Dancers: Frank Bock, Jordi Cortes Molina, Emma Gladstone, Jeremy James, Louise Mulvey, Liz Ranken, Caroline Reece, Malcolm Shields; Composer: Adrian Johnston; Producers: Airtight Films for BBC and the Arts Council of England.
A subtle exploration of pub culture through movement and innuendo, featuring a minimal but intricate soundscape throughout. DVD **22**

TRAILBLAZERS OF MODERN DANCE, 1977, 60 min. (USA)
Choreographers: Frederick Ashton, Ted Shawn, Ruth St. Denis, Martha Graham, Doris Humphrey, Isadora Duncan; Director: Emile Ardolino; Producers: Merrill Brockway, Judy Kinberg for Thirteen/WNET; Dancers: Annabelle Gamson, Ted Shawn, Lynn Seymour, Helen Tamiris, Ruth St. Denis, Doris Humphrey, Martha Graham, Vernon and Irene Castle, Anna Pavlova, Loie Fuller; Distributors; Indiana University, University of California Extension Center.
Reviews the evolution of American modern dance from 1900 to the early 1930s with vintage clips and dances reconstructed for television. A wonderful historical journey.

TSAR'S BOX: GALINA ULANOVA, 1997, 30 min. (Russia)
Choreographer: Marius Petipa and others; Writer/interviewer: Galina Mshanskaya; Directors: Tatyana Andreyeva, Yevgeniya Popova; Dancers: Galina Ulanova, Konstantin Sergeyev, Yuriy Kondratov, Pyotr Gusev, Vladimir Preobrazhenskiy, Andris Liepa; Producer/Distributor: Russian State Tele-Radio Company.
Shot in the Maryinsky Theater in St. Petersburg, this interview program was made two months before the great Russian ballerina died. Included among the clips of archival footage are fragments from *Swan Lake, Romeo and Juliet, Nocturne, Giselle, Fountain of Bakhchisaray, 7th Waltz,* and *The Dying Swan.*

TWYLA THARP: MAKING TELEVISION DANCE, 1977, 59 min. (USA)
Choreographer/Dancer: Twyla Tharp; Director: Don Mischer; Dancers: Twyla Tharp, Mikhail Baryshnikov and Twyla Tharp Dance Company; Distributor: University of California Extension Center.
Twyla Tharp explains the relationship between television and dance and her rationale for exercises choreographed for the camera. Features a rehearsal with Baryshnikov of *Once More Frank* and her *Country Dances* set for five dancers.

UNTITLED, 1989, 15 min. (USA)
Choreographer/Dancer: Bill T. Jones; Director: John Sanborn, Mary Perillo; Distributor: The Kitchen.
The choreographer/dancer creates a moving tribute to his longtime partner Arnie Zane with an inspired use of the medium to layer the performance with images.

URBAN CLAN, 1998, 54 min. (Australia)
Choreographer: Stephen Page; Director/Writer: Michelle Mahrer; Dancers: Russell Page and the Bangarra Dance Theatre; Composer: David Page; Producers: Aanya Whitehead & Paul Humfress for Australian Film Finance Corp, BBC, ABC, and RD Studio France.
Three Page brothers explore their Aboriginal roots and strive to understand and fuse aspects of Aboriginal and Islander life with contemporary dance movement.

THE VILLAGE TRILOGY, 1995, 24 min. (Canada)
Choreographer/Dancer/Director/Producer/Distributor: Laura Taler; Dancers: José Navas, Luc Ouellette, Donald Himes, Kim Frank, Jim Allodi, Jane Townsend, Darcey Callison; Music: Philip Strong.
Winner of the first Cinedance Award in Canada in 1995, this trilogy inspired by the displacement and destruction of World War II successfully evokes the supremacy of the spirit. The creator describes her film as "returning to the physical language of early cinema." Contact the distributor for the equally arresting dance videos *Heartland, Dances for a Small Screen*, and Dance On Camera Festival 2001's best of festival: *A Very Dangerous Pastime.* DVD **30**

WEST SIDE STORY, 1961, 155 min. (USA)
Choreographer: Jerome Robbins; Directors: Robert Wise, Jerome Robbins; Dancers: Rita Moreno, Eliot Feld, Russ Tamblyn; Composer: Leonard Bernstein; Distributor: Facets.
This landmark musical adapted for film centers around an ill-fated love match.

WHITE SOUND, 1998, 51 min. (France)
Choreographer: Mathilde Monnier; Director: Valerie Urrea; Producer: Films Penelope; Distributor: Ideal Audience.
This touching documentary film shows how a choreographer gained the trust of a young, autistic woman through dance improvisation.

WITNESSED, 1998, 5 min. (Canada)
Choreographer/Director/Distributor: Allen Kaeja; Director: Mark Adam; Kaeja d'Dancers; Composer: Edgardo Moreno.
Depicting relationships beyond the walls of the Ghetto during the Holocaust, *Witnessed*, one of a trilogy, is a story of displacement, unrelenting fear, and community support.

WORLD FESTIVAL OF SACRED MUSIC, 2000, 83 min. (USA)
Features: His Holiness the Dalai Lama, Ulali, Alchemy Handbell Ensemble, Halau O Kekuhi, World Tea Party, Meredith Monk, Drepung Loseling Monks with the Mystical Arts of Tibet World Tour, Robert Een, Percussion Artists Workshop (PAWS), Elk Whistle, Pasha Ninateen, Adaawe, The Agape International Choir, Andrae Crouch & The Valley Gospel Choir, Cantorial All-Stars, Gamelan Sekar Jaya, Jai Uttal & The Pagan Love Orchestra, Ali Jihad Racy Ensemble, Cantor Eva Robbins, and First AME Church Brookinaires Gospel Choir; Executive Producer: Judy Mitoma; Producers: Jeanette Volturno and Trey Wilkins; Distributor: Foundation for World Arts.
Sixteen film teams and multiple sound teams collaborated to capture the heartbeat of the World Festival of Sacred Music in Los Angeles in the fall of 1999.
DVD **39**

WORLD OF ALWIN NIKOLAIS, 1995
Choreographer: Alwin Nikolais; Artistic Director: Murray Louis; Director and Producer: Dennis Diamond and Video D Studios; Narrated by Murray Louis. DVD **14**

YURI SOLOVIEV: I'M TIRED OF LIVING IN MY NATIVE LAND, 1999, 52 min. (Russia)
Dancers: Irina Kolpakova, Gabriela Komleeva, Natalia Makarova, Alla Sizova, Yuri Soloviev;
Director/Producer: Galina Mshankaya;
Producer/Distributor: Russian State Tele-Radio Company.
A eulogy for Yuri Soloviev (1940–1977), a ballet dancer who committed suicide in his prime despite his enormous talent and international appreciation of his gifts. The press called him "the genius of the Russian ballet," and "flying Yuri, the Spaceman." A graduate of the Vaganova Academy, he became the leading soloist at the Kirov Ballet. Clips are drawn from the following ballets: *Festival of Flowers, Le Corsaire, Sleeping Beauty, Laurencia, La Bayadère, Creation of the World, Zephyr and Flora, Chopiniana,* and a pas de deux by Auber.

EDITORS AND CONTRIBUTORS

EDITORS

Judy Mitoma, director of the UCLA Center for Intercultural Performance, is also Professor of Dance at UCLA in the Department of World Arts and Cultures. A dance ethnologist and dancer by training, her areas of specialization are Java and Bali in Indonesia, and Japan. She served as chair of World Arts and Cultures from 1982 to 1997, establishing full departmental status for the program in 1995. She worked on the 1984 Olympic Arts Festival and served as a co-curator of the 1990 Los Angeles Festival with Peter Sellars. Independently directing several Asian Performing Arts Summer Institutes (APASI) in 1977, 1979, 1981, 1984, and 1988 she has brought many artists from Asia to the UCLA campus. In 1991, Mitoma was a Warren Weaver Fellow at the Rockefeller Foundation, conducting research in the arts of West Africa. In 1995, she established the Center for Intercultural Performance (CIP) to support research, creative experimentation, documentation, and public outreach for the UCLA campus. Under her leadership UCLA/CIP has launched three major initiatives: the Asia Pacific Performing Arts Exchange Program (APPEX), funded by The Ford Foundation; the UCLA National Dance/Media Project, funded by the Pew Charitable Trusts; and a Humanities Residency Fellowship program with the Rockefeller Foundation. Mitoma is a consultant to the New England Foundation for the Arts and the Asia Society, and is actively involved in the Los Angeles arts community. In the fall of 1999, she implemented the World Festival of Sacred Music—the Americas, 85 events throughout the city of Los Angeles as a gesture for peace and universal responsibility for the next millennium. Currently, Mitoma is compiling a Festival CD and DVD and serves as the editor-in-chief for *Envisioning Dance on Film and Video.*

Elizabeth Zimmer is a senior editor and writer at *The Village Voice* in New York City, a dance critic at the *Philadelphia Inquirer*, and a freelance contributor to many publications including the *Los Angeles Times*, the *Washington Post, Harper's Bazaar, The Perfect Vision*, and the Web site of the Public Broadcasting System. She edited *Body Against Body: The Dance and Other Collaborations of Bill T. Jones and Arnie Zane*, published by Station Hill Press in 1989, and is the co-author and editor of *Dance: A Social Study*, a dance history curriculum for language arts and social studies teachers. She has been writing about the arts since 1971 in a variety of media on both coasts of the United States and Canada, and has taught writing and dance history at universities and colleges across the continent. A graduate of Bennington College, she holds a master's degree in English from the State University of New York at Stony Brook. She has studied many forms of dance.

Dale Ann Stieber has been working in film and television production and exhibition for 20 years. Her documentary work in the arts includes the films *In Search of Kundun with Martin Scorsese* (producer), *Forever Hollywood* (line producer) for the American Cinematheque, and the three-part television special *A*

Personal Journey with Martin Scorsese through American Movies (line producer).

Nelli Heinonen is a dancer, scholar, and arts administrator and has a long-term interest in dance and media. She is based in Helsinki, Finland and currently works for the Finnish Sports Federation establishing regional networks for women around the country and promoting women's leadership in the field. Ms. Heinonen received her MA in Culture and Performance from the University of California, Los Angeles in the Department of World Arts and Cultures.

Norah Zuñiga Shaw is a choreographer, producer, dancer, and writer based in California and Costa Rica. A graduate of Hampshire College, she received her MFA in Dance from the University of California, Los Angeles in the Department of World Arts and Cultures. She has a longstanding interest in dancefilm and telematics.

CONTRIBUTORS

Carolyn Adams, a former Paul Taylor dancer, and her sister Julie A. Strandberg, executive director of the American Dance Legacy Institute, are documenting reconstructions of American dance masterpieces, including works by Donald McKayle, Sophie Maslow, Eve Gentry, Daniel Nagrin, and Mary Anthony, through the use of digital video and scanned archival materials as part of the Institute's New Dance Group Anthology Project, funded in part by the NEA. This project includes the commissioning and documenting of Repertory Etudes™, study pieces based on masterworks and accessible to dancers without royalty fees. The Etudes are documented through videotape and Labanotation. Ms. Adams is co-founder of the Harlem Dance Foundation, curator for the American Dance Legacy Institute, a member of the Juilliard School faculty, and founding artistic director of the New York State Summer School of Dance. Since retiring from the stage in 1982, she has served the dance field as board member, panelist, and dance education consultant and chaired Dance/USA's National Task Force on Dance Education.

Girish Bhargava is president and senior editor of Telstar Post, Inc., a video post-production facility located in New York City. He received his first Emmy Award in 1991 for *Adams Chronicles*, a 13-hour drama series, and a second for the CBS Television special, *The Muppets Celebrate Jim Henson*. He edited the Peabody Award-winning *Everybody Dance Now* for *Dance in America*. Other Emmy Award nominations include *Bob Fosse: Steam Heat*, *The Hard Nut*, and *Variety and Virtuosity: American Ballet Theatre Now*. In 1994, Bhargava won the Monitor Award for Best Editor for his work on George Balanchine's *The Nutcracker*. He has worked with virtually every great American contemporary choreographer including George Balanchine, Martha Graham, Jerome Robbins, Paul Taylor, Agnes de Mille, Merce Cunningham, and Twyla Tharp. He recently worked on a documentary about Jacques d'Amboise and his National Dance Institute students, a follow-up to the Oscar-winning film *He Makes Me Feel Like Dancin'*.

Larry Billman studied dance with Lou Mosconi, Lester Horton, Jack Cole, and Eugene Loring, and then began a 15-year career of film, television, stage and nightclub performances. Making the transition to writer/director of live entertainment, he began writing magazine articles about the choreographers and dancing performers who had inspired him, which led to *Film Choreographers and Dance Directors*, published by McFarland in 1997. In 1998, he founded the Academy of Dance on Film, a nonprofit research center in Hollywood which documents and honors movement makers in commercial film, television, and music video. He has lectured on dance in film at the University of California at Irvine, California State University Long Beach, San Diego State University, and other schools, colleges, and universities. A contributing writer to *The Oxford International Encyclopedia of Dance*, he is profiled in *Who's Who in Entertainment* and *Who's Who in America*.

Joshua W. Binder is the son of choreographer Sharon Kinney and filmmaker John Binder. He has been a writer and worked in film production since 1992. He graduated from UCLA with a degree in English literature, but spent the first few years after college working as a paramedic for the Los Angeles City Fire Department. He left the fire department to pursue a career in film and media. He was a staff writer and story editor on the television series *The Lazarus Man* with Robert Urich and has written several feature-length scripts. A producer on *From the Horse's Mouth, The Documentary*, a dance film Ms. Kinney directed, he also directed a black-and-white 16mm short film entitled *Pandora's Box*. As an assistant director he has worked on several independent feature films. Presently he is the writer of "The Games," a section of *Brntwd Magazine*.

John Bishop, Adjunct Assistant Professor of Culture and Performance (Videography) at UCLA, is a documentary filmmaker known primarily for his work on cultural and anthropological subjects. His films include *The Land Where the Blues Began* with Alan Lomax, *The Last Window* about Charles Connick's stained glass studio, *Rhesus Play* about social behavior of free-ranging monkeys, *New England Fiddles,* and *New England Dances*. In 1995, he produced a revision of the popular anthropology series *Faces of Culture* for Coast Telecourses. His most recent films are *Himalayan Herders* about a temple village in the mountains of Nepal, and *Hosay Trinidad* about the Islamic Muharam observance in Trinidad. He is currently editing a film on Cambodian classical dance. He has worked with the Human Studies Film Archives at the Smithsonian accessioning John Marshall's footage of the Ju'hoa Bushmen, and has shot footage in Namibia for Marshall's current production on the Ju'hoasi.

Merrill Brockway was trained as a pianist. Beginning in 1953 in Philadelphia and after 1962 in New York, he produced and directed films and videotapes for CBS/TV, notably *Camera Three*, a series CBS touted as "a stroll through the marketplace of ideas" that ranged widely in the arts. In 1975 Brockway joined PBS as series producer of *Dance in America*. He directed 15 programs, including *Martha Graham's "Clytemnestra,"* which won a Golden Hugo Award; *Choreography by Balanchine #3*, which took a Directors Guild of America Award; and *Choreography by Balanchine #4* and *Songs for A Dead Warrior,* which garnered Emmys. In 1980 Brockway joined CBS Cable as executive producer of arts programming; he directed the video of Balanchine's final ballet, *Davidsbündlertänze*. He also directed film and video biographies of Balanchine (nominated for a DGA Award), Agnes de Mille (which won an Emmy), Stella Adler, and Tennessee Williams.

Ellen Bromberg performed with the Utah Repertory Dance Theater and was most influenced by the work of Anna Sokolow and José Limón. She has received numerous awards and grants for her work, including two Choreography Fellowships from the National Endowment for the Arts and a Performing Arts Fellowship in Choreography from the Arizona Commission on the Arts. She received a Bonnie Bird North American Choreography Award and has also received two Bay Area Isadora Duncan Dance Awards: one for Outstanding Achievement in Choreography for *The Black Dress,* and another for the multimedia piece *Singing Myself a Lullaby*, created in collaboration with John Henry and Douglas Rosenberg. She has been commissioned to create new work by many companies and presenters, including the American Dance Festival, the Laban Centre, and the Institute for Studies in the Arts at ASU. Her work has been broadcast on PBS Television's *Alive from Off Center*, San Francisco's KQED-TV, and Wisconsin Public Television.

Virginia Brooks is Professor of Film and Head of Production at Brooklyn College/CUNY. Her first interest in dance was recorded in *Choreography for Toddler and Circulating Lawn Sprinkler* (c. 1936, 16mm, black-and-white, director: A. Wuppermann). Much later, she received an MFA in film directing and a PhD in Theater/Film (Columbia University). From 1978 to 1981, while coordinator of the Jerome Robbins Film Archive of the Dance Collection of the New York Public Library, she wrote her dissertation, *The Art and Craft of Filming Dance as Documentary*. Since 1995 she has been video editor for the Balanchine Foundation's Interpreters Archive and Archive of Lost Choreography. She has made films on the School of American Ballet, Charles Weidman, and Antonina Tumkovsky, and more than 100 archival records at the School of American Ballet and Riverside Dance Festival. Dr. Brooks is currently working on a film profile of Felia Doubrovska.

Lynn Dally, dancer, choreographer, and artistic director of the Jazz Tap Ensemble, is a recognized leader in the renaissance of tap dance in the U.S. and abroad. She has created more than 30 original tap choreographies and toured worldwide, performing at Carnegie Hall with Gregory Hines, Jacob's Pillow with Jimmy Slyde, New York's Joyce Theater with Harold Nicholas, Brenda Bufalino, and Savion Glover, the Smithsonian with Honi Coles, the Kennedy Center, Paris' Theatre de la Ville, and Lyon's 4th Biennale, "An American Story." Winner of numerous grants and choreographic commissions, Dally recently received the prestigious Irvine Fellowship in Dance 2000 and the Guggenheim Fellowship in Choreography 2001. Dally is featured in *JTE Live in Concert, Two Takes on Tap*, and *TapDancin'*. Based in Los Angeles, she also directs JTE's Caravan Project for gifted teen tap dancers, produces the live series Jazz Tap @ The Bakery, and is currently teaching in UCLA's Department of World Arts and Cultures.

Dennis Diamond creates video magic from Lincoln Center to Broadway, from the sawdust ring at Ringling Brothers Circus to solo performing artists. President of Video D Studios, Inc., a vehicle for dance/video collaborations, he initiated the archival project at Dance Theater Workshop. He was video designer on Broadway for Bill Irwin's *Largely, New York*, Larry Gelbart's *Mastergate*, John Leguizamo's *Spic-O-Rama*, Philip Glass's *La Belle et la Bête*, and Blue Man Group's *TUBES*. Home videos include *Basic Ballet with Finis Jhung*; *World of Alwin Nikolais*; *José Limón Technique*; and *Harry: Dance and Other Works by Senta Driver.* He is grateful to Video D's talented staff, Michael P. Hesse, Christine O'Neil, David Quinn, Thomas Kennedy, and spiritual leader Irving Ziffer. Diamond's career would not be possible without the undying support of his parents Irwin and Pearl, who believed that a broad education would lead their children to choose work bringing them happiness and success. Kisses to Queen Honey Geiger and Alexander Ziffer Diamond.

Matthew Diamond was nominated for both an Academy Award and a Director's Guild Award for his feature documentary, *Dancemaker*, about choreographer Paul Taylor. Among many honors, it was named Best Feature Film by the International Documentary Association. For PBS's *Great Performances* he has directed numerous specials including the Emmy Award winning *Le Corsaire* with American Ballet Theatre, Paul Taylor's *The Wrecker's Ball*, Garth Fagan's *Griot NY*, *The Balanchine Celebration*, Mark Morris's *The Hard Nut*, and Paul Taylor's *Speaking In Tongues*. In 1995, he won the Director's Guild Award for Outstanding Director/Musical Variety for *Some Enchanted Evening: Celebrating Oscar Hammerstein*. He also directed the television productions of Broadway's *Victor, Victoria, Crazy For You*, several "In Performance at the White House" specials, and *Piano Grand* starring Billy Joel. A recent project was the ABC TV movie *These Old Broads*, starring Shirley MacLaine, Debbie Reynolds, Joan Collins, and Elizabeth Taylor.

Alyce Dissette was executive producer of the PBS national series *Alive from Off Center/Alive TV* (1990–93). Her programs won numerous awards and citations, including a CABLE ACE Award in 1994 for her co-production with MTV News. Following her work at Alive, she pursued projects in digital media. In 1994 she administered the first international digital art competition for "WIRED" Interval Research and Voyager Co.; produced a contemporary poetry/spoken word Web site with more than 20 artists and an online poetry contest sponsored in 1995 by Hugo Boss; and co-produced a Web site for artist James Turrell. Dissette is a former producer for the David Gordon/Pick Up Co., spearheading Gordon's *United States* project. She was also executive director for ODC/San Francisco and currently serves on the company's board. She has produced new works by performance artist John Kelly and the first theatrical work by Pulitzer Prize-winning cartoonist Art Spiegelman.

Mark Eby, a documentary filmmaker and writer with a focus on the performing arts, in 1995 received a Fulbright grant in Theater Arts and conducted a video and photographic survey of regional indigenous performance traditions in Melanesia. He holds an MA in dance from the World Arts and Cultures Department at UCLA; his thesis, entitled *Dance Trembling: Memory, Metaphor, Melanesia,* includes narratives molded from the memory of a childhood that alternated between the New Guinea Highlands and northern Kentucky suburbs. He has received a UCLA National Dance Media Fellowship, a grant from the National Initiative To Preserve America's Dance, and has been involved in documentaries about the World Festival of Sacred Music, the Heritage of African Music, the Asia Pacific Performance Exchange Program, and the Pacific Arts Festival. He currently works at the Center for Digital Arts and the Center for Intercultural Performance at UCLA.

Robert Gardner's first long film, *Dead Birds,* was released in 1964. It was added to the Library of Congress National Register of classic American films in 1998. He has made other feature length nonfiction films, including *Rivers of Sand*, *The Nuer* (on which he collaborated with Hillary Harris), *Deep Hearts*, *Forest of Bliss*, and *Ika Hands.* In all his films, especially *Passenger*, he has been deeply concerned with the choreographic nature of filmmaking, which he has always found something of a dance. His most recent work includes *Roads End* about what has become of the place and the people depicted in *Dead Birds*, and a DVD about *Forest of Bliss*, containing an exchange of ideas with Stan Brakhage. His new book, *Making Forest of Bliss*, includes a DVD of the film.

Beth Genné is Associate Professor in the Dance Department, Center for World Performance and the Residential College at the University of Michigan. She has published articles in *Dance Research, Dance Chronicle,* the *London Dancing Times*, *Art Journal*, and in the books *Following in Sir Fred's Steps*, *Psychoanalytic Perspectives on Art,* and *The Fonteyn Phenomenon.* Her book The *Making of a Choreographer* concerns the early years of Dame Ninette de Valois. She has been awarded a Getty Postdoctoral Fellowship in the History of Art and the Humanities and is currently working on a book on dance in the film musicals of Minnelli, Kelly, and Donen.

David Gere is an associate professor in the Department of World Arts and Cultures at UCLA. He is a co-editor of *Looking Out: Perspectives on Dance and Criticism in a Multicultural World* (Schirmer, 1995) and is currently writing a book on dance and corporeality in the AIDS era. Gere served as co-director of the Dance Critics Association from 1992 through 1995 and was a scholar-in-residence each summer between 1996 and 2000 at Jacob's Pillow Dance Festival. In fall 1998, after completing his PhD in Dance History and Theory at the University of California, Riverside, Gere was invited to be a fellow of the University of California Humanities Research Institute as a participant in the Interdisciplinary Queer Studies Group. He has completed a survey of choreographers affected by HIV/AIDS in Los Angeles and New York, commissioned by the Estate Project for Artists with AIDS.

Robert Gottlieb pursued careers as a professional musician, teacher, and ethnomusicologist at the University of California, Riverside, and the Evergreen State College, Olympia, WA. He first went to India as a Fulbright Scholar to teach western music in Calcutta. He later did postdoctoral studies in ethnomusicology with Mantle Hood at UCLA. Following this he returned many times to India, as Research Fellow with both the Fulbright program and the American Institute of Indian Studies. His work on tabla drumming and kathak dance brought him into contact with musicians, dancers, and scholars, and the world of miniature paintings, which he photographed in connection with historical researches. He later returned to India to produce and direct the film *Circles-Cycles Kathak Dance*. The kathak project was first supported by the Dance Division of the New York Public Library for the Performing Arts, and subsequently sponsored by the Skaggs Foundation and the American Institute of Indian Studies.

Rhoda Grauer has been a producer of the performing arts—live and on television and radio—since 1971. Her media credits include *Dancing*, an eight-hour documentary series on world dance; *Gregory Hines's Tap Dance in America*, *Baryshnikov by Tharp*, and *Making Television Dance*. Awards include Emmys, a Bessie Award, the National Endowment for the Arts Chairman's Award, and the Ohio State Award. Grauer was co-founder of Yayasan Kelola, the first arts service organization in Indonesia; director of Media and Performing Arts at the Asia Society; production executive for *Great Performances* and *Dance in America*; director of media at American Ballet Theatre; director of the Dance Program at the National Endowment for the Arts; executive director of the Twyla Tharp Dance Foundation; and associate director of the Spoleto Festival of Two Worlds in Italy. She lives and works between New York and Bali, and is producing two films on traditional Indonesian elders.

Amy Greenfield has been making screen dances since the 1970s. The Museum of Modern Art in New York cites her as having "developed a new form of video dance, choreographing for the video camera and TV screen." Her award-winning films and videos have been screened at major international film/video festivals in Berlin, London, Edinburgh, Houston, Atlanta, New York, and at international film/video/dance festivals, and at museums and theaters from Toronto to Russia to Japan. The Whitney Museum of American Art recently featured her *Element* in its series of the most important avant-garde American films made by women. Her ground-breaking holographic dance sculptures are in major museum collections in the U.S. and Canada. Her first feature filmdance, *Antigone/Rites Of Passion*, starring Bertram Ross, Janet Eilber, and Greenfield, is currently available in stores on DVD and videocassette, from Winstar.

Robert Greskovic writes about dance for the *Wall Street Journal*. A freelance dance writer and critic and the author of *Ballet 101: The Complete Guide To Learning and Loving the Ballet* (Hyperion, 1988), he has been writing about dance since 1972. He is associate editor at *Ballet Review*, videos editor for *DanceView*, New York correspondent for *Dance International*, dance essayist for *Britannica Book of the Year*, and New York correspondent for *Ballett International/Tanz Aktuell*. He has taught dance history and dance aesthetics at City University of New York's Hunter College, Sarah Lawrence College, and CUNY's City College, and lectured on dance for the Metropolitan Opera Guild, at the

Carlisle Project, and at New York University. His dance reviews and feature stories have appeared in *The Village Voice*, The *Los Angeles Times*, The *New York Times*, and other newspapers. He lives in Brooklyn, New York.

Kelly Hargraves, a choreographer, dancer, and media artist from Canada, presently lives in Los Angeles. She has a BA in Communication Studies from the University of Windsor, a BFA in Contemporary Dance from Concordia University, and an MA from New York University, where her thesis focused on contemporary dance-film. From 1990 to 1992, she was a creator and performer with PoMo CoMo Artist and Scientist Collective, performing throughout Canada, the U.S., and in Europe, including a performance at the prestigious Ars Electronica Festival in Austria. She has most recently presented her solo choreography in Toronto, Montreal, and New York. Her video works have been presented in festivals and video series including the 2000 American Dance Festival, Marin County Festival of Dance, the Festival International de Nouvelle Danse du Montréal (FIND), and Il Choreografico Ellectronico in Naples, Italy. She has written for *Ballet Tanz International*, *The Dance Insider*, *Dance Online*, and *Dance Connection Magazine.*

Bonnie Oda Homsey, artistic director of American Repertory Dance Company, was a principal with the Martha Graham company. Graham created roles for her in dances featuring Rudolph Nureyev. She toured internationally and taped several *Dance In America* programs. Ms. Homsey attended the Juilliard School, where she performed works by Tudor, Sokolow, Limón, and Graham, and received her MFA from the University of California, Irvine. She has served as a panelist for the National Endowment for the Arts, California Arts Council, Dance/USA, and Dance Heritage Coalition Research Group, among others. She has worked on projects for American Film Institute's Directing Workshop for Women. Currently, she teaches at UC Irvine, is Chair of Dance for the Princess Grace Foundation, and guest editor for *Choreography and Dance*, and has launched a state-funded exemplary arts education initiative. A recipient of four Lester Horton Awards, Ms. Homsey is the mother of three daughters.

Bill T. Jones, before forming the Bill T. Jones/Arnie Zane Dance Company in 1982, choreographed and performed nationally and internationally as a soloist and duet company with his late partner, Arnie Zane. Mr. Jones created more than 50 works for his own company and received numerous commissions from various other companies. *The Breathing Show*, his evening-length solo, premiered in the fall of 1999. Mr. Jones received honorary doctorates from the Art Institute of Chicago, Bard College, the Juilliard School, and Swarthmore College. His published works include *Last Night on Earth*, a memoir (Pantheon Books, 1995), *Body Against Body: The Dance and Other Collaborations of Bill T. Jones and Arnie Zane* (Station Hill Press, 1989), and *Dance*, a children's book (Hyperion Press, 1998). He contributed to *Continuous Replay: The Photography of Arnie Zane* (MIT Press, 1999).

Paul Kaiser is an artist whose work has appeared at Lincoln Center, MASS MoCA, the Barbican Center, the Whitney Museum, and many other venues. He has received a ComputerWorld/Smithsonian Award (1991), a Guggenheim Fellowship (1996), and awards from the Foundation for Contemporary Performance Art (1998), the Congress on Research in Dance (2000), and the Bessies (2000). Kaiser's early art (1975–81) was in experimental film and voice. From 1982 to 1991, he taught students with learning disabilities, with whom he collaborated on making multimedia depictions of their own minds. He later applied this approach to *Visionary of Theater*, an interactive documentary on Robert Wilson. Recently, Kaiser created the virtual dances *Hand-drawn Spaces* (1998) and *Biped* (1999), both with Merce Cunningham and Shelley Eshkar, and *Ghostcatching* (1999), with Bill T. Jones and Eshkar. Solo abstract works include *Flicker-track + Verge* (1999–2000). Recent works include *Pedestrian* (a collaborative public art installation), and *Trace*, an installation for the Brooklyn Academy of Music.

Leslie Hansen Kopp, an archivist and musicologist, was general administrator of the George Balanchine Foundation. Previously she was founder and executive director of Preserve, Inc. She is affiliated with numerous professional associations, including the Society of American Archivists, the Dance Librarians' Discussion Group, and Dance/USA. She edited and published the award-winning book, *Dance Archives: A Practical Manual for Documenting and Preserving the Ephemeral Art*, and *Afterimages*, a quarterly journal, and has served as an archives preservation consultant to numerous organizations and individuals in the fine and lively arts. She has toured the United States presenting workshops on archives management and dance and technology. In 1989, Kopp received a Bentley Fellowship for her work in dance documentation. She was a co-author of the study *Images of American Dance: Documenting and Preserving a Cultural Heritage*, and has contributed to *Advances in Preservation and Access*, *Beyond Memory*, *Dansource News*, and the *International Dictionary of Modern Dance*.

Bob Lockyer is an executive producer in BBC Classical Music with responsibilities for all television dance programs on terrestrial and digital channels. Working with the Arts Council of England, he has produced more than 40 short dance videos especially created for the small screen, which have been seen and sold around the world; the idea has been copied in many countries. Other programs he has been responsible for include film versions of DV8's *Strange Fish* and *Enter Achilles*, and major relays of dance performances by the Royal Ballet, Birmingham Royal Ballet, and Rambert Dance Company. His major television series, *The Dancer's Body*, will air in the UK in 2002. He helped to found Dance UK, a service organization which helps dancers and dance companies around Britain, and runs the UK's Healthier Dancer Programme, chairing it for its first 10 years. He also teaches "Dance and the Camera" workshops in the UK, Europe, Canada, Australia, South Africa, and New Zealand, and has taught at UCLA. Lockyer also helps to organize IMZ's international dance film and video festival, Dance Screen.

Victoria Marks is a "portrait artist" who creates dances for the stage, for film, in community settings, and for professional dancers. Her work magnifies and develops the unique characters of the people she works with, and communicates them, through performance, to a wider audience She is currently Associate Professor in the Department of World Arts and Cultures at UCLA. She was honored with the 1997 Alpert Award for Outstanding Achievement in Choreography, and has been the recipient of grants from the National Endowment for the Arts, the New York State Council on the Arts, the New York Foundation for the Arts, and the London Arts Board, among others. She has received a Fulbright Fellowship in Choreography, and numerous awards for her dance films, including the Grand Prix in the Video Danse Festival (1996 and 1995), the Golden Antennae Award from Bulgaria, the IMZ Award for best screen choreography (twice), and the Best of Show in the Dance Films Association's Dance and the Camera Festival.

Donald McKayle has been named one of America's Irreplaceable Dance Treasures by the Dance Heritage Coalition of the Library of Congress. He has choreographed more than 50 concert dances. His masterworks—*Games*, *Rainbow 'Round My Shoulder*, *District Storyville*, *Songs of the Disinherited*—are modern dance classics performed around the world. Recent choreography includes *House of Tears*, *Danger Run*, *Death and Eros*, and *Children of the Passage*. His Broadway work won five Tony nominations, an Outer Critics Circle Award, and the NAACP Image Award. His work for film includes Disney's *Bedknobs and Broomsticks* and *The Great White Hope*. He has received the Capezio Award, the Samuel H. Scripps/American Dance Festival Award, two NEA Fellowships, the Dance/USA Honors, and an Irvine Fellowship. A master educator, he has received the Balasaraswati/Joy Ann Dewey Beinecke Endowed Chair for Distinguished Teaching, UCI's Distinguished Faculty Lectureship Award for Research, and the UCI Medal, the highest honor given by the University of California, Irvine, where he is Professor of Dance.

Meredith Monk is a composer, performer, and creator of new opera and musical theater works, films, and installations. A pioneer in what is now called "extended vocal technique" and "interdisciplinary performance," she has created more than 150 works and received numerous awards, including a MacArthur "Genius" Fellowship, two Guggenheim Fellowships, three Obies, and a Bessie for Sustained Creative Achievement. In 1968 she founded The House, a company dedicated to an interdisciplinary approach to performance. She formed Meredith Monk and Vocal Ensemble in 1978 to perform her unique musical compositions. Monk has made more than a dozen recordings, and her music has been heard in several films, including *La Nouvelle Vague* by Jean-Luc Godard and *The Big Lebowski* by Joel and Ethan Coen. A pioneer of site-specific works, she is also an accomplished filmmaker. Lincoln Center Festival 2000 honored her music with a three-concert retrospective. In October 1999, Monk performed a *Vocal Offering* for His Holiness, the Dalai Lama, as part of the World Festival of Sacred Music in Los Angeles.

Madeleine Nichols is Curator of the Dance Division, The New York Public Library for the Performing Arts at Lincoln Center, where she formerly served as head of the Jerome Robbins Archive of the Recorded Moving Image. She is also an attorney, specializing in contracts, estates, and copyright, and Adjunct Professor at New York University's School of Education. Active in professional associations in the fields of law, libraries, and dance, she is presently on the editorial board of the Society of Dance History Scholars and a member of the Atlantic Center for the Arts National Advisory Council. She is a founding member of the Dance Heritage Coalition and the American Library Association's Dance Librarian's Committee. Her continuing interests are the international protection of artists' rights and economic concerns, and the implications of media and technology in arts and education.

Eiko Otake and her partner Koma joined the Hijikata company in Tokyo in 1971. Their collaboration began as an experiment and by 1972 had developed into an exclusive partnership. They also studied with Kazuo Ohno, but determined to choreograph and perform only their own works. Between 1972 and 1976, they studied and toured in Europe. In 1976, they moved to New York, where the Japan Society sponsored their first American performance (*White Dance*). Since then, they have presented their works across North America, Europe, and Asia. For almost 20 years they have also created dance/videos as a parallel way of reaching audiences. The most recent is *Breath*, a collaboration with videographer Jerry Pantzer, based on the Whitney Museum installation of the same name. Named Guggenheim Fellows for 1984, they were also awarded one of the first "Bessies" the same year and were honored again in 1990. In 1996 they were named MacArthur Fellows.

Norton Owen is director of preservation for Jacob's Pillow Dance Festival, and a consultant to the José Limón Dance Foundation. In 2000, Dance/USA named Owen a recipient of its Ernie Award, honoring "unsung heroes who have led exemplary lives in dance." He is the author of *A Certain Place: The Jacob's Pillow Story* and is a contributing author to two recent books, *José Limón: An Unfinished Memoir* and *Jose Limón: The Artist Re-Viewed.* Mr. Owen has been the curator for major exhibitions at the National Museum of Dance (Saratoga Springs, New York) on Anna Sokolow, Paul Taylor, Merce Cunningham, Bronislava Nijinska, and Ted Shawn, and he has been co-curator of exhibits at the New York Public Library for the Performing Arts and the Harvard Theatre Collection. He is vice chairman of the Dance Heritage Coalition and serves on the boards of several other dance organizations.

Leonard C. Pronko is Professor of Theater at Pomona College, where he has directed numerous kabuki productions in English since 1965. He is the author of half a dozen books on theater, including *Avant-garde* and *Theatre East and West.* In 1970, he was the first non-Japanese to study at the kabuki training program at the National Theatre of Japan. He has studied with Fujima Kansuma, Fujima Daisuke, Fujima Kangoro, Hanayagi Chiyo, and Hanayagi Juraku. In 1972 he received a Los Angeles Drama Critics Circle Award "for bringing kabuki to the west and sharing it," and in 1986 was awarded the Order of the Sacred Treasure by the government of Japan. In 1997 he received the ATHE (Association for Theatre in Higher Education) award for Outstanding Teacher of Theater in Higher Education.

Nancy Reynolds danced with the New York City Ballet and then began a new career as an editor and author. Her publications include *Repertory in Review: Forty Years of the New York City Ballet* (De la Torre Bueno Prize, 1977), *Dance Classics* (co-authored with Susan Reimer-Torn, 1982), *The Dance Catalog*, and *Choreography by George Balanchine: A Catalogue of Works*, for which she was research director. She was also research director for *Balanchine*, a two-part documentary for PBS. She is an editor of the multivolume *International Encyclopedia of Dance* (Oxford University Press, 1998) and is writing a history of theatrical dance in the twentieth century, to be published by Yale University Press. Since becoming director of research for the George Balanchine Foundation in 1994, Ms. Reynolds has collaborated on videotape projects with Dame Alicia Markova, Maria Tallchief, Patricia Wilde, Marie-Jeanne, Frederic Franklin, Todd Bolender, Allegra Kent, and Melissa Hayden, among others.

Mitchell Rose was a New York-based choreographer specializing in comedic dance-theater from 1975 to 1990, performing in such places as the Spoleto Festivals in the U.S. and Italy, the Joyce Theater, Jacob's Pillow Dance Festival, and Central Park's Delacorte Theatre, as well as in international touring and television appearances. The *New York Times* dubbed him "the dance world's Woody Allen," which stuck and became his professional identity. Eventually he was drawn more to visual media and disbanded his company to become a Directing Fellow at the American Film Institute. Since then he has directed and written projects for film, television, and the Internet. His films have won 24 awards at film festivals. He received a 2000 NIPAD grant to create *Modern Daydreams*, a suite of four Chaplinesque dance films which airs as a web series on Hypnotic.com, Universal Studios' netcasting Web site.

David Rousseve is artistic director of the dance/theater company REALITY. Commissioned three times by the Brooklyn Academy of Music's Next Wave Festival, REALITY has performed across the United States, Europe, and South America. Roussève is the recipient of a 2000 Bessie award, a 1999 Irvine Fellowship in Dance, the 1996 Cal Arts/Alpert Award, and seven consecutive fellowships from the NEA. He has created works for the Houston Ballet, Atlanta Ballet, Ballet Hispanico, the Cleo Parker Robinson Company, and other troupes. Roussève was a screenwriting fellow in the Sundance Film Festival's 1998 Screenplay Development Lab. He is currently Associate Professor of Choreography at UCLA's Department of World Arts and Cultures.

Evann E. Siebens works as a dance cinematographer and videographer and has filmed dancers such as Bill T. Jones, Mikhail Baryshnikov, José Navas, Sara Rudner, and Viola Farber. She was recently the cinematographer for a feature film entitled *The Madness Channel*, a documentary on modern dancers entitled *From the Horse's Mouth*, and a documentary on choreographer Molissa Fenley and New York City Ballet dancer Peter Boal. She directed a documentary on hula dancers and the Hawaiian community that received support from the Pew Charitable Trust, NYSCA, and the NEA. Siebens is collaborating with choreographer Gabri Christa on a television series for the Black Filmmakers Foundation TV Lab, and has been commissioned to direct a short documentary for the Limón Foundation. Her short films *POTHEAD* and *do not call it fixity . . .* have been seen at film festivals around the world and have aired on arts networks in Canada and Europe.

Eva Soltes, dancer/choreographer and producer/director, has launched more than 1,000 performing and media arts programs internationally for television, radio, and live concert. Her broadcast credits include producer of *West Coast Story*, a program about California composers for BBC-TV; producer/director/editor of *Building A Dream*, a journey in design and construction with one of Frank Lloyd Wright's apprentices; associate producer and editor of *Circles–Cycles Kathak Dance*, an award-winning dance documentary; and co-producer of *Saxophone Diplomacy*, made on location in the former Soviet Union. As artist-in-residence at the Pompidou Center in Paris, she produced and directed a multi-image documentary about Mexican composer Conlon Nancarrow. Soltes is a performer and teacher of Bharatanatyam dance, and studied extensively with T. Balasaraswati. As a choreographer she has toured with composer Lou Harrison and collaborated with poet Gary Snyder. She is currently completing a documentary about Harrison and building her own dance/video studio in San Francisco.

Sally Sommer is Professor in the graduate program in American Studies in Dance at Florida State University. She has lectured in France, Spain, and the Netherlands. Since the mid-1970s, she has published hundreds of reviews and articles on stage dance as well as vernacular dance, which have appeared in such publications as *The Village Voice*, the *New York Times*, *Newsday*, *Dance Magazine*, and *The Drama Review*. Her articles have appeared in anthologies and she has contributed dance entries to five encyclopedias and published a book, *Ballroom* (1987). She has been a panelist for numerous national, state, and private foundations, and commented on dance and performance for National Public Radio. She has worked on television documentaries on tap dance, social dance, and the Peabody Award-winning *Everybody Dance Now*!, which examines dance in music videos. Her hour-long documentary on American popular dance, *Check Your Body at the Door*, focuses on club dancers and dancing in New York City.

Lakshmi Srinivas received her PhD from the University of California, Los Angeles, in 1999, and then taught at the departments of Sociology and World Arts and Cultures at UCLA. As a postdoctoral fellow and lecturer in sociology at Brandeis University, she taught courses on cinema and spectatorship and the family. She was Visiting Assistant Professor in Sociology at Wellesley College in 2001–2002. Her current research interest is in visual sociology, especially cinema, popular culture and its consumption, transnationalism, and globalization. She is also interested in social inequality, gender relations, and the family. Her work is interdisciplinary, bridging the fields of sociology and anthropology. Her essays have appeared in journals such as *Visual Anthropology*, *Economic and Political Weekly of India*, and *Media, Culture and Society*.

Ernestine Stodelle, a member and soloist of the Doris Humphrey Concert Group and Humphrey-Weidman Company between 1929 and 1935, was dance critic and feature writer for the *New Haven Register*, director and teacher at her own Studio of Dance in Cheshire, Connecticut, and Adjunct Associate Professor at New York University, where she has conducted a postgraduate course in Writing Dance Criticism since 1970. She has lectured and given seminars on dance history, esthetics, and criticism at numerous colleges and universities. Among her many accomplishments are the reconstructions of Doris Humphrey's *Air for the G String* and *Two Ecstatic Themes* for the José Limón Dance Company. She was married to syndicated columnist and author John Chamberlain, and is the mother of four children.

Roslyn Sulcas grew up in Cape Town, South Africa, where she danced briefly before pursuing a master's degree in literature at the University of Cape Town, and a doctorate at York University, England, and then Paris VII (Jussieu). The first Ballett Frankfurt season in Paris moved her to begin writing about dance, and she became the Paris correspondent for *Dance and Dancers*, *Dance Magazine*, *Dance International*, and *The European*, as well as writing frequently for other publications and working at the Paris Opera Ballet. In 1996, she moved to New York, where she works both as an editor and a writer. Her work has appeared in *Dance Magazine*, *Dance Now*, *Elle*, *Newsday*, the *New York Times*, *Pointe*, *The Village Voice*, and *Stagebill*. She is currently working on a book about William Forsythe.

Silvina Szperling, dancer, choreographer, video artist, curator, and reviewer, is technical director of SZ Danza. A choreographer since 1986, since 1993 she has devoted herself to video-dance, multimedia pieces, and dance documentaries. She has received grants from Cuballet, the American Dance Festival, and the National Fund for the Arts. Szperling served on the "Dance for the Camera" panel at the international dance and technology conference at Arizona State University in 1999, and also at the Dance for the Camera Symposium (University of Wisconsin at Madison, 2000). Her video pieces have been screened at festivals in Argentina and abroad. *Temblor*, her first video-dance, won the "best editing" award from Argentina's National Secretary of Culture and has been included in the National Museum of Fine Arts' video collection, as well as in the Dance Division of the New York Public Library. The founder and director of the Festival Internacional de Video-danza de Buenos Aires, an annual event since 1995, Szperling has curated Argentine and foreign video-dance selections for both local and international exhibitions. She also writes for local newspapers and magazines.

Philip Szporer, a Montreal-based freelance writer, broadcaster, filmmaker, and lecturer, is a scholar-in-residence at Jacob's Pillow and a 1999 UCLA National Dance/Media Project Fellow. He has done various broadcast projects for Canadian, British, American, and Dutch public radio and television networks. Publication credits include *HOUR* (dance writer and critic), *Ballet International*, *The Village Voice*, and *Dance Connection*. He served as dance consultant on the National Film Board of Canada's experimental dance film *Lodela*. In 1999, he co-produced/directed (with Marlene Millar and Carmella Vassor) the video documentaries *Eko and Sen Hea: A Journey Beyond: Creating Across Cultures*, about the Asia Pacific Performance Exchange; and *Universal Tea*, a video segment for a documentary on the World Festival of Sacred Music. That same team is currently producing/directing a feature-length documentary, *The Heart of Ms. Brown*. With Marlene Millar and Lynda Gaudreau, he co-directed video segments for Compagnie de Brune's *Encyclopedia: DOCUMENT 1* (1999).

Deirdre Towers has a BA from Kirkland/Hamilton College and an MA in Arts Administration from New York University. In 1980, she created Dance Films Association (DFA) as a non-profit umbrella for a cross-cultural documentary on the tango she was producing. Progressing from editor of DFA's *Dance on Camera Journal* to writing the *Guide to Dance Films and Videos*, she is currently the co-director of the Dance on Camera Festival and executive director of DFA. She has repeatedly attended the Grand Prix de Video Danse, Dance Screen, International Emmys, and American Dance Festival's video festival as a panel moderator, participant, and jury member. She spent an undergraduate semester studying in Ghana.

David Vaughan studied dance in London with Marie Rambert and Audrey de Vos, and in New York at the School of American Ballet and with Antony Tudor, Merce Cunningham, and Richard Thomas. He has danced, sung, acted, and choreographed in London, Paris, on and off Broadway, in American regional theaters, in film, television, ballet and modern dance companies, and cabaret. He is the archivist of the Cunningham Dance Foundation and the author of *Merce Cunningham: Fifty Years* (Aperture, 1997) and of *Frederick Ashton and His Ballets* (revised edition, Dance

Books, 1999), and was a member of the editorial board of the *International Encyclopedia of Dance* (Oxford University Press, 1998). At the Dancing in the Millennium Conference in Washington, DC, in July 2000, he received the 2000 CORD (Congress on Research in Dance) Award for Outstanding Leadership in Dance Research; in September 2001 he was honored with a New York Dance and Performance Award (Bessie) for Sustained Achievement.

Jac Venza is executive producer of *Great Performances* and director of cultural and arts programs, Thirteen/WNET New York. He has been a major figure in harnessing the power of television to achieve international recognition for America's finest performing artists. He began his career at CBS in 1950 working as a designer and subsequently as a director and producer. In 1964, he was one of the original producers assembled for National Educational Television (NET), the Ford Foundation project that served as the origin of public television. In 1972, Mr. Venza created a new framework for the performing arts on PBS, *Great Performances*, which has received every major television honor, including nearly 50 Emmy Awards. He created the concepts for *Theater in America* and *Dance in America*, initiating television collaboration with performers and companies throughout the country. In honor of the series' 25th anniversary season and approximately 600 programs, he was awarded the primetime Emmy's Governor's Award for Lifetime Achievement, the International Emmy Founders Award, the New York Emmy Chapter's Silver Circle Award, and the Corporation for Public Broadcasting's Ralph Lowell Award, and was honored in May 2000 with a personal Peabody Award.

Karen Washburn graduated from UCLA's Department of World Arts and Cultures with a Masters in dance and cultural studies in 2001. Her main research interest has been the relationship between dance, politics, and culture. Recent projects include a Fulbright Fellowhsip to central Java, Indonesia to research the classical dances of Yogyakarta. She currently lives in Los Angeles, where she writes, dances, and works as a movement therapist.

Margaret Williams started her own film production company in 1975 and has been working as an independent producer and director ever since. She has made multi-camera music productions for television, documentaries, and many short films, including the award-winning dance films *Outside In, Mothers and Daughters,* and *Men*, all choreographed by Victoria Marks. In 1999 she completed *13 Different Keys*, a half-hour dance film choreographed by Siobhan Davies with Deborah Bull for England's Channel 4, as well as the two-hour opera *Powder Her Face* by composer Thomas Adès, and the cinema short *Going, Going* for the BFI/C4. In 2000 she completed *Watermark*, a new choreography for the camera with Jiři Kylian and Netherlands Dance Theater 3, and *Fountain* with choreographer Miriam King for the BBC/ACE. She directed the Benjamin Britten opera *Owen Wingrave* for Channel 4 and developed her first feature film script, *Sacred Country*, with writer Rose Tremain for the Film Council.

Andy Abrahams Wilson is a San Francisco-based independent filmmaker and cinematographer. He has been honored with several awards for his work, including an Emmy nomination. With a background in film and cultural anthropology, he views the camera as an opportunity to explore his subjects both artistically and journalistically. Productions include the HBO special *Bubbeh Lee and Me* and the PBS-broadcast *Hope Is the Thing with Feathers*. A recipient of a 1999 Pew Charitable Trust Fellowship in Dance/Media, Wilson has produced several films about dance or dancers, including *Positive Motion*, *Embracing Earth*, *Casualty*, and *Finding Home*. He is in production on the documentary feature *Alfredo's Fire*, about a Sicilian writer who set himself on fire at the Vatican as a protest against the church's condemnation of homosexuality. Wilson is budget director of the film distribution cooperative New Day Films and a member of the Academy of Television Arts and Sciences.

Pam Wise, A.C.E., learned to edit cinema verité documentaries working with the masters Ricky Leacock, Charlotte Zwerin, D. A. Pennebaker, Bob Drew, John Marshall, and the Maysles brothers. She began her film career recording sound and editing the film *Isabella Stewart Gardner* with Leacock. Ms. Wise has honed her storytelling skills and music and dance editing on such films as *Horowitz Plays Mozart,* a Maysles film which premiered at the New York Film Festival, *Carnegie Hall Gets Plastered* (co-director), *A Tribute to Hank Williams,* Randa Haines's *Shut Up and Dance, Songs of the Civil War, John Lennon Live in NY,* and Trisha Brown's *Accumulation with Water Motor* (directed by Jonathan Demme). She edited music videos by Malcolm McLaren, Cyndi Lauper, Julio Iglesias, Diana Ross, Stevie Ray Vaughn, and Yoko Ono. Pam Wise has also edited features (*Meteor Man, Hits, Loon*), network and cable movies, specials, comedies, pilots, and series. She won a 1999 A.C.E. Eddie Award for Best Edited Documentary for *Dancemaker*.

SELECTED BIBLIOGRAPHY

compiled by Karen Washburn

Acocella, Joan. 1995. "The Hand of Fate." *Village Voice.*

Almendros, Nestor. 1980. *A Man with a Camera.* London: Faber and Faber.

Aloff, Mindy. 1981–1982. "Film Translation of Meredith Monk's Work." *Millenium Film Journal* 10/11.

Altman, Rick, ed. 1981. *Genre, the Musical: A Reader.* London: Routledge and Kegan Paul.

Anderson, Bert. 1970. "The Filmmaker Speaks: An Interview with Norman McLaren." *Film Library Quarterly* 3, no. 2:13–17.

Anson, Robert Sam. 2000. "Birth of an MTV Nation."

Arigon, Daniel. 1991. *Grammar of the Film Language.* Los Angeles: Silman-James Press.

"Art of Interpretive Dance Brought to Audiences through Medium of Film." 1922. *Musical America.*

Baker, Mary Susan. 1983. "Status Survey of the Mediated Instructional Materials Used for Dance in the Area of Higher Education." Ph.D. diss., University of Colorado at Boulder.

Bakstein, Karen Sue. 1996. "Dancing Images: Choreography, the Cinema, and Culture." Ph.D. diss., New York University.

Barrett, John Townsend. 1968. "A Descriptive Study of Selected Uses of Dance on Television: 1948–1958." Ph.D. diss., University of Michigan.

Becker, Nancy F. 1983. "Filming Cunningham Dance: A Conversation with Charles Atlas, Part 1." *Dance Theatre Journal* 1, no. 1.

——. 1982. "Locale: A Filmdance Created by Merce Cunningham and Charles Atlas." M.A. thesis, New York University.

Billman, Larry. 1997. *Film Choreographers and Dance Directors: An Illustrated Biographical Encyclopedia, with a History and Filmographies, 1893 through 1995.* Jefferson: McFarland.

Birringer, Johannes. 1998. *Media and Performance: Along the Border.* Baltimore: Johns Hopkins University Press.

——. 2000. *Performance on the Edge: Transformations of Culture.* London/ New Brunswick: Athlone Press.

——. "Syllabus: Environments I."

Bishop, John. 1988. *Making It in Video.* New York: McGraw-Hill.

Bopp, Mary S. 1994. *Research in Dance: A Guide to Resources.* New York: G.K. Hall.

Boston, George, ed. 1991. *Guide to the Basic Technical Equipment Required by Audio, Film, and Television Archives.* Written by the members of the Coordinating Committee for the Technical Commissions of the International Organizations for Audio, Film, and Television Archives. Sponsored by FIAF, FIAT, IASA, ICA, and UNESCO.

Boyd, Chris. 1996. Critical talks: Is Technology the Future for Dance? Paper presented at the symposium, Is technology the future for dance? *Third Green Mill Dance Project*, Melbourne, 35–38 .

Boyle, Deirdre. 1993. *Video Preservation: Securing the Future of the Past.* New York: Media Alliance.

Bozzini, Annie. 1991. "They Film as They Dance. The New Generation of Filmmakers/Choreographers in France." *Ballett International* 14, no. 1: 36–41.

Briginshaw, Valerie A. 1997. "Keep Your Great City

Paris!: The Lament of the Empress and Other Women." In *Dance in the City*, Helen Thomas, ed., 35–49. New York: St. Martin's.

Brooks, Virginia. 1991. "Apollo in Translation." *New Dance Review*: 7–10.

——. 1993. "Dance and Film: Changing Perspectives in a Changing World." *Ballett International/Tanz Aktuell* : 14–19.

——. 1995. "Dance, communication and new technology." Paper presented at symposium Dance Memory (La memòria de la dansa), Fifth International Conference of Dance Historians, Barcelona, 211–27.

——. 1989. "Restoring the Meaning in Cinematic Movement: What is Text in a Dance Film?' *IRIS* 9:69–103.

——. 1984. "Why Dance Films Do Not Look Right." *Studies in Visual Communication* 10, no. 2:44–67.

Buckland, Theresa. 1998. "Dance and Music Video: Some Preliminary Observations." In *The Routledge Dance Studies Reader*, Alexandra Carter, ed., 218–87. New York: Routledge.

Burnside, Fiona. 1994. "Moving Pictures in a Black Marble Frame: IMZ Dance Screen Festival, Lyon." *Dance Theatre Journal* 11, no. 3:14–17.

Burstow, Stephen. 1993. "Dance on Screen." Paper presented at The Green Mill Dance Project, Melbourne, 58–59.

Burton, Carolyn. 1977. "The Influence of Instructional Media on Attitudes of Modern Dance Students toward Movement." Ph.D. diss., University of Georgia.

Caplan, Elliot. 1990. "Dance as Seen From the Perspective of the Camera." *Ballett International*: 8–13.

"The Career of Norman McLaren." 1973. *Cinema Canada*, no. 9:43–49.

Carroll, Noel. 2000. "Toward a Definition of Motion Picture Dance." *Paper Presented at Dance on Camera Symposium*, University of Wisconsin, Madison.

Carter, Alexandra, ed. 1998. *The Routledge Dance Studies Reader*. New York: Routledge.

Carter, Vana Patrice. 1992. "Choreography for the Camera: An Historical, Critical, and Empirical Study." Ph.D. diss., Western Michigan University.

Chaplin, Saul. 1994. *The Golden Age of Movie Musicals and Me*. Norman: University of Oklahoma Press.

Charness, Casey. 1976. "An Abstract of Hollywood Cine-Dance: A Description of the Interrelationship of Camerawork and Choreography in Films by Stanley Donen and Gene Kelly." Ph.D. diss., New York University .

Christiansen, Rupert. 1996. "Weakness in the Heel." *Dance Theatre Journal* 13, no. 1:4–5.

Chujoy, Anatole. 1967. *The Dance Encyclopedia*. New York: Simon and Schuster.

Clark, James. 1958. "Interview with Stanley Donen." *Films and Filming*.

Clark, VeVe A., Millicent Hodson and Catrina Neiman. 1984. *The Legend of Maya Deren: A Documentary Biography and Collected Works*. New York: Anthology Film Archives/ Film Culture.

Cohen, Selma Jeanne, ed. 1967. *Dance Perspectives*. Vol. 30. New York: Dance Perspectives, Inc.

Cohn, Emma. 1987. "Mura Dehn: The Preservation of Black Jazz Dance on Film." *Sightlines*: 7–11.

Como, William. 1987. "L'oasi 'Sundance.' "*Ballettoggi (Milano)* 49:37–38.

Cook, Olive. 1963. *Movement in Two Dimensions*. London: Hutchinson.

Copeland, Roger, ed. 1983. *What Is Dance?: Readings in Theory and Criticism*. New York: Oxford University Press.

Cox, Dan. 1984. "Video Fever!" *Dance Magazine*, October.

Croce, Arlene. 1997. *Afterimages*. New York: Knopf.

——. 1972. *The Fred Astaire and Ginger Rogers Book*. New York: Outerbridge and Lazard.

Cubitt, Sean. 1993. *Videography: Video Media as Art and Culture*. New York: St. Martin's.

Cunningham, Merce. 1985. *The Dancer and the Dance: Merce Cunningham in Conversation with Jacqueline Lesschaeve*. London: Marion Boyars.

Dance on Camera Journal: A Dance Films Association Publication. 1998.

Delameter, Jerome. 1981. *Dance in the Hollywood Musical*. Ann Arbor: UMI Research.

Deren, Maya. 1967. *Dance Perspectives* 30:10–13.

——. 1965. *Film Culture*, no. 39.

——. 1983. *Film Culture*, no. 72–74.

Devereaux, Leslie and Roger Hillman, eds. 1995. *Fields of Vision: Essays in Film Studies, Visual Anthropology, and Photography*. Berkeley and Los Angeles: University of California Press.

Dixon, Mike. 1996. "Filming *Enter Achilles*." *Dance Europe* no. 2:13–15.

Dodds, Sherril. 1997. "'Televisualized' bodies and changing perspectives." *Dance Theatre Journal* 13, no. 4:44–47.

Dunning, Jennifer, Joseph McLellan and Steven Winn. 1997. *Great Performances: A Celebration*. San Francisco: Bay Books and Tapes.

Evans, Edwin. 1927. "Screen-ballet." *Dancing Times* : 330, 332.

Faller, Greg S. 1987. "The Function of Star-Image and Performance in the Hollywood Musical: Sonja Henie, Esther Williams, and Eleanor Powell." Ph.D. diss., Northwestern University.

Farley, Christopher John. 2000. "All the Right Moves," *Time*, September 11.

Feuer, Jane. 1982. *The Hollywood Musical*. Bloomington: Indiana University Press.

Frith, Andrew Goodwin and Lawrence Grossberg, eds. 1993. *Sound and Vision: The Music Video Reader*. London and New York: Routledge.

Fuller, Graham. 1994. "Gene Kelly." *Interview*, May.

Gargaro, Kenneth V. 1979. "The Work of Bob Fosse and the Choreographer-Directors in the Translation of Musicals to the Screen." Ph.D. diss., University of Pittsburgh.

Genne, Beth Eliot. 1984. "The Film Musicals of Vincente Minnelli and the Team of Gene Kelly and Stanley Donen: 1944–1958 (Volumes 1 and 2)." Ph.D. diss., University of Michigan.

Ghei, Kiren Elizebeth. 1988. "Hindi Cinema Dance from Video to Stage: A Study of Indian Immigrant Culture in Los Angeles." M.A. thesis, University of California, Los Angeles.

Giannetti, Louis. 1972. *Understanding Movies*. Englewood Cliffs, N.J.: Prentice-Hall.

Glazer, Danit. 1995. "Video and dance / Danit Glazer." M.A. thesis, Teachers College, Columbia University.

Goodwin, Andrew. 1992. *Dancing in the Distraction Factory: Music Television and Popular Culture*. Minneapolis: University of Minnesota Press.

Greenfield, Amy, ed. 1983. *Filmdance Festival: A Project of the Experimental Intermedia Foundation at the Public Theater*. New York: The Foundation.

Greskovic, Robert. 1993. "The Video Library: Revelations." *Dance View* 10, no. 3:30–33.

——. 1994. "The Video's Not the Thing." *Dance View* 12, no. 2:23–28.

Grubb, Kevin. 1988. "Basil Blasts Off." *Dance Magazine*, March.

Hahn, T. 1999. "Videodance in France." *Ballet International*: 36.

Hall, Doug and Sally Jo Fifer, eds. 1990. *Illuminating Video: An Essential Guide to Video Art*. New York: Aperture/Bay Area Video Coalition.

Harris, Hilary. 1967. *Dance Perspectives* 30:44–47.

Hartt-Fournier, Laurinda. 1993. "Bob Fosse and Dance in the Motion Picture: Beyond the Surface." M.F.A. thesis, York University (Ontario, Canada).

Hebdidge, Dick. 1988. *Hiding in the Light*. New York: Routledge.

Heilmann, Brigitte. 1999. "MTV Dances." *Ballett International/Tanz Aktuell*:40–42.

Hill, Constance Valis. 2000. *Brotherhood in Rhythm*. New York: Oxford University Press.

Hoberman, J. 1993. *42nd Street*. London: BFI Film Classics.

Humphrey, Doris. 1959. *The Art of Making Dances*. New York: Grove Weidenfeld.

Hungerford, Mary Jane. 1946. "Dancing in Commercial Motion Pictures." Ph.D. diss, Columbia University.

——. 1947. "Must Screen Dances Be Incidental?"

Hunt, Marilyn. 1996. "Merrill Brockway, a Master Filmmaker Who Trusts the Dancing." *Dance Magazine*, September:66–69.

International Encyclopedia of Dance. 1998. New York: Oxford University Press.

Johnson, Albert. 1956. "The Tenth Muse in San Francisco" (transcription of a lecture by Gene Kelly). *Sight, Sound, Summer*.

Johnson, Catherine J. and Allegra Fuller Snyder. 1999. *Securing Our Dance Heritage: Issues on the Documentation and Preservation of Dance*. Washington, D.C.: Council on Library and Information Resources.

Johnson, Robert. 1997. "Male Bonding: DV8 Dancers Question Your Manhood." *Bay Area Reporter* 27, no. 45:40–43.

Jonas, Gerald. 1992. *Dancing: The Pleasure, Power, and Art of Movement*. New York: Harry Abrams in association with Thirteen/WNET.

Jordan, Stephanie and Dave Allen, eds. 1993. *Parallel Lines: Media Representations of Dance*. London: John Libbey.

Jordan, Stephanie and Jonathan Thrift. 1995. "The Multiple Languages of Dance and Television : Art and Scholarly Practice." Paper presented at symposium Dance Memory (La memòria de la dansa), Fifth International Conference of Dance Historians, Barcelona, 229–37.

Jordan, Susan. 1996. "Being There: Parallel Lines—the Projected Image of Dance Versus the Live Encounter." Paper presented at the symposium, Is technology the future for dance? *Third Green Mill Dance Project*, Melbourne, 89–94.

Jowitt, Deborah, ed. 1997. *Meredith Monk*. Baltimore: Johns Hopkins University Press.

——. 1977. "Tricks on the Tube and in a Tent." *Village Voice*: 73.

Kaplan, E. Ann. 1987. *Rocking around the Clock: Music Television, Postmodernism, and Consumer Culture*. New York: Routledge.

Katz, Steven D. 1991. *Film Directing Shot by Shot: Visualizing from Concept to Screen*. Studio City: Michael Wiese Productions in conjunction with Focal Press.

Kelly, Gene. 1979. "Dialogue on Film." *American Film*.

Kendall, Elizabeth. 1984. *Where She Danced*. Berkeley and Los Angeles: University of California Press.

Kim, Hyon-ok. 1995. "Working with a Video To Create and Preserve a Choreography: Creating a New Language in Choreography and in Video-dance." Paper presented at symposium Dance memory (La memòria de la dansa). Fifth International Conference of Dance Historians, Barcelona, 239–43.

Knight, Arthur. 1967. *Dance Perspectives* 30:4–9.

——. 1947. "Dancing in Films." *Dance Index* 6, no. 8:180–199.

Knight, Julia, ed. 1996. *Diverse Practices: A Critical Reader on British Video Art*. Luton: University of Luton Press.

Knox, Donald. 1972. *The Magic Factory: How MGM Made "An American in Paris."* New York: Praeger.

Kopp, Leslie Hansen. 1995. *Dance Archives: A Practical Manual for Documenting and Preserving the Ephemeral Art*. New York: Preserve, Inc.

Kower, Yvonne. 1996. "Being There: Dance Film/Video History, a Perspective." Paper presented at the symposium, Is technology the future for dance? *Third Green Mill Dance Project*, Melbourne, 84–88.

Kozel, Susan. 1995. "Reshaping Space: Focusing Time." *Dance Theatre Journal* 12, no. 2: 3–7.

Leong, Russell, ed. 1991. *Moving the Image: Independent Asian Pacific American Media Arts*. Los Angeles: Visual Communications/ UCLA Asian American Studies Center.

Loizos, Peter. 1993. *Innovation in Ethnographic Film: From Innocence to Self-consciousness*. Chicago.

Lomax, Alan, ed. 1968. *Folk Song Style and Culture*. Washington, D.C.: American Association for the Advancement of Science, Publication #88.

Lorber, Richard. 1977. "Videodance." Ph.D. diss., Columbia University.

Lunenfeld, Peter, ed. 1999. *The Digital Dialectic: New Essays on New Media*. Cambridge, Mass: MIT Press.

Maletic, Vera. 1987–1988. "Videodance-Technology-Attitude Shift." *Dance Research Journal* 19, no. 2:3–6.

McLaren, Norman. 1970. "Interview on *Pas de Deux*." *Film News*.

McPherson, Katrina. 1997. "A Passion for Screen Dance." *Dance Theatre Journal* 13, no. 4:48–50.

Mitchell, Kate. 1994. "Videotaping Dance: A Comparative Project." M.A. thesis, University of California, Los Angeles.

Moon, Michael. 1995. "Memorial Rags." In *Professions of Desire: Lesbian and Gay Studies in Literature*, George El Haggerty and Bonie Zimmerman, eds., 233–40. New York: Modern Language Association.

Mueller, John E. 1985. *Astaire Dancing: The Musical Films*. New York: Knopf.

——. 1979. *Dance Film Directory: An Annotated and Evaluative Guide to Films on Ballet and Modern Dance*. Princeton, N.J.: Princeton Book Co.

——. 1974. *Films on Ballet and Modern Dance: Notes and a Directory*. New York: American Dance Guild.

——. 1975. "Pas de Deux." *Dance Magazine*.

Murphy, William T. 1997. *Television and Video Preservation 1997: A Report on the Current State of American Television and Video Preservation*. Washington, D.C.: Library of Congress.

Newbry, E. Colleen. 1987. "Media-dance: A Collaborative Contribution, Merce Cunningham with Directors Charles Atlas and Elliot Caplan." M.F.A. thesis, University of California, Irvine.

Newman, Barbara. 1995. "Dancing in Real Time." *Dance International*.

Noll, Ellen Louise. 1986. "A Study of Eugene Loring's Philosophy and Methodology in His Choreographic Work for The Hollywood Film." M.F.A. thesis, University of California, Irvine.

Penney, Phillis Annette. 1981. "Ballet and Modern Dance on Television in the Decade of the 70's." Ph.D. diss., University of North Carolina at Greensboro.

Ploebst, Helmut. 1999. "The IMC: Initiator of Dance Screen." *Ballett International/Tanz Aktuell*: 31.

Poindexter, Betty. 1963. "Ted Shawn: His Personal Life, His Professional Career, and His Contributions to the Development of Dance in the United States of America from 1891 to 1963." Ph.D. diss., Texas Woman's University.

Poundstone, William. 1985. *The Recursive Universe: Cosmic Complexity and the Limits of Scientific Knowledge*. New York: Morrow.

Pratt, George C. 1973. *Spellbound in Darkness*. Greenwich, CT: New York Graphics Society.

Redefining Film Preservation: A National Plan. Recommendations of the Librarian of Congress in Consultation with the National Film Preservation Board. 1994. Washington, D.C.: Library of Congress.

The Relationship of Film to Dance: A Report and Analysis of Problems, Needs, Possibilities, and Potentials in this Area. 1968. Washington, D.C.: Unpublished report for NEA Dance Program Office.

Renov, Michael and Erika Suderburg, eds. 1996. *Resolutions: Contemporary Video Practices.* Minneapolis: University of Minnesota Press.
Reynolds, Leslie Ann. 1982. "A Film Manual for the Filmmaker/ Dancer." M.A. thesis, University of California, Los Angeles.
Richard, Valliere T. 1982. *Norman McLaren: Manipulator of Movement: The National Film Board Years, 1947–67.* New York: Associated University Presses.
Robertson, Allen. 1995. "DV8 x 2." *Dance Now* 4, no. 4:84–85.
Rose, Brian. n.d. "Directing for Mr. B.: The Creative Collaboration between George Balanchine and Merrill Brockway." *Television Quarterly*: 60–66.
Rosenberg, Doug. 1999. "Video Space: A Site for Choreography." *Leonardo Online*. Web page available at http://www.mit.edu/ejournals/Leonardo/reviews/raw/rosvid.html.
Rosenthal, Alan. 1970. "Norman McLaren on Pas de Deux." *Journal of the University Association* 22, no. 1:11–15.
Rosiny, Claudia. 1990. "Dance as Seen from the Perspective of the Camera (Interview with Elliot Caplan, filmmaker for the Cunningham Dance Foundation)." *Ballett International* 13, no. 9:8–13.
——. 1994. "Dance Films and Video Dance: Current State of an Art Form." Dance Screen 1994. *Ballett International/ Tanz Aktuell* : 82–83.
——. 1999. "Dance for the Moving Image." *Ballett International/Tanz Aktuell*: 32–33.
——. 1990. "Film Review: Pina Bausch." *The Lament of the Empress. Ballett International* 13, no. 6/7:74.
——. 1996. "Hard Acts to Follow: Report on Dance Screen 1996." *Ballett International/Tanz Aktuell*: 30–31.
Rubin, Martin. 1993. *Showstoppers: Busby Berkeley and the Tradition of Spectacle*. New York: Columbia University Press.
Russell, Catherine. 1999. *Experimental Ethnography: The Work of Film in the Age of Video*. Durham: Duke University Press.
"September Calendar. The Museum of Modern Art Presents a Gene Kelly Dance Film Festival." 1962. *Dance Magazine*.
Shawn, Ted. 1940. *Dance We Must*. Pittsfield, MA: Eagle Printing and Binding.
——. 1959. *Thirty-three Years of American Dance*. Pittsfield, MA: Eagle Printing and Binding.
Siegel, Marcia. "Syllabus: Dance on Screen."
Silverman, Stanley. 1996. *Dancing on the Ceiling*. New York: Knopf.
Sloan, Ronna Elain. 1983. "Bob Fosse: An Analytic-Critical Study." Ph.D. diss., City University of New York.
——. 1967. "A Filmic Approach to Dance: A Theoretical Exploration." University of California, Los Angeles.
Snyder, Allegra Fuller. 1965. "Three Kinds of Dance Films: A Welcome Clarification." *Dance Magazine* 39:34–39.
Somerville, Ian. 1994. "Black and White Dance on Brown Tape." *Dance Now* 3, no. 3:87–91.
Spain, Louise ed.1998. *Dance on Camera: A Guide to Dance Films and Videos*. Lanham, MD: Scarecrow Press.
Spottiswoode, Raymond. 1962. *A Grammar of Film*. Berkeley: University of California Press.
Steinke, Gary Lee. 1979. "An Analysis of the Dance Sequences in Busby Berkeley's Films: *Forty Second Street; Footlight Parade;* and *Gold Diggers of 1935*." Ph.D. diss., University of Michigan.
——. 1999. "Dance Screen 99." *Dance Now* 8, no. 2:87–89.
Sulcas, Roslyn. 1995. "Kinetic Isometries." *Dance International.*
Takeda, Izumo. 1993. *Yoshitsune and the Thousand Cherry Trees: A Masterpiece of the Eighteenth-Century Japanese Puppet Theater*. Trans. by Stanleigh H. Jones. New York: Columbia University Press.
Tamaris, Helen. 1959. "Film and/or Notation." *Dance Observer*: 117–18.
Tannenbaum, Rob. 1999. "100 Greatest Music Videos Ever Made." *TV Guide*, December 4.
Terry, Walter. 1976. *Ted Shawn, Father of American Dance*. New York: Dial Press.
Thom, Rose Anne. 1991. "Viewpoints." *Dance Magazine,* November: 62.
Thomas, Tony and Jim Terry. 1973. *The Busby Berkeley Book*. Greenwich, CT: New York Graphic Society.
Tomkins, Calvin. 1996. *Duchamp: A Biography*. New York: Henry Holt.
Towers, Deirdre. 1984–1989. [Regular monthly articles on dance video.] *Dance Magazine.*
——. 1983–1996. "Dance On Camera News." *Dance Films Association's bimonthly publication.*
——. 1987. "Pas de Deux: Choreographers and Producers Pair Up at Sundance." *The Independent*, December:8–9.
——. 1997–present. "Dance On Camera Journal." *Dance Films Association' bimonthly publication.*
——. 1998. "Mix and Match: Recent Dance/Video Collaborations." *The Independent*, October:13–5.
Treichler, Paul. 1987. "AIDS, Homophobia, and

Biomedical Discourse: An Epidemic of Signification." In *AIDS: Cultural Analysis/Cultural Activism,* Douglas Crimp, ed., 31–70. Cambridge, MA: MIT Press.
Turing, Alan. 1992. *Mechanical Intelligence.* Edited by D. Ince. Amsterdam and New York: Elsevier Science.
Valliere, Richard T. 1982. *Manipulator of Movement: the National Film Board Years 1947–1967.* New York: Associated University Presses.
Vaughan, David. 1948–1949. "Dance in the Cinema." *Sequence* 6:6–13.
——. 1981–1982. "Locale: The Collaboration of Merce Cunningham and Charles Atlas." *Millennium Film Journal,* no. 10/11.
——. 1982. "Channels/ Inserts: Cunningham and Atlas." *Millenium Film Journal,* no. 12.
——. 1997. *Merce Cunningham: Fifty Years.* New York: Aperture.
Vernallis, Carol. 1994. "The Aesthetics of Music Video: The Relation of Music and Image." Ph.D. diss., University of California, San Diego.
Video Encyclopedia of the 20th Century: Dance Selections. 1989. Los Angeles: UCLA Office of Instructional Development.
Walker Arts Center. 1998. *Art Performs Life: Merce Cunningham/ Meredith Monk/ Bill T. Jones.* Minneapolis: Print Craft.
Warren, Charles, ed. 1996. *Beyond Document: Essays on Nonfiction Film.* Hanover: Wesleyan University Press.
Watson, Keith. 1996. *"Decodex." Dance Now* 5, no. 4:82–84.
William, Jordan. 1953. "Norman McLaren: His Career and Techniques." *Quarterly of Film, Radio, and Television.*
Winston, Brian. 1995. *Claiming the Real. The Griersonian Documentary and Its Legitimations.* London: British Film Institute Publishing.
Wollen, Peter with Vicky Allan. 1996. "Sight and Sound A–Z of Cinema." *Sight and Sound* 7, no. 9: 28–31.
Zimmer, Elizabeth. 1999. "The Lens and the Dancer: Dance on Video." *The Perfect Vision* July/August, issue 25: 59–62.

INDEX

Note: italic page number indicates picture.